The Work of Ramakrishna Mission in Meghalaya: A Study of the East Khasi Hills District

The Work of Ramakrishna Mission in Meghalaya: A Study of the East Khasi Hills District

V.S. Lalrinawma

2012

The Work of Ramakrishna Mission in Meghalaya – Published by the Rev. Dr. Ashish Amos of Indian Society for Promoting Christian Knowledge (ISPCK), Post Box 1585, 1654 Madarsa Road, Kashmere Gate, Delhi-110006.

© Author, 2012

All rights reserved. No part of this book may be reproduced or transmitted in any form or by any means, electronic, mechanical, photocopying, recording, or by any information storage and retrieval system, without the prior permission in writing from the publisher.

The views expressed in the book are those of the authors and the publisher takes no responsibility for any of the statements.

The book *"The Work of Ramakrishna Mission in Meghalaya: A Study of the East Khasi Hills District"* is based on the doctoral thesis *The Impact of the Ramakrishna Mission on the Socio-Economic and Cultural Life of the Khasis in the East Khasi Hills District of Meghalaya,* which was submitted to SHIATS University. It is published with permission.

ISBN: 978-81-8465-233-8

Laser typeset by **ISPCK,** Post Box 1585,
1654 Madarsa Road, Kashmere Gate, Delhi-110006
Tel: 23866322, 23866323
e-mail–ashish@ispck.org.in • ella@ispck.org.in
website-www.ispck.org.

Dedicated to
My Son,
Michael Lalrindika (L)

Contents

Dedication	v
Foreword	ix
Acknowledgements	xi
Chapter 1 Introduction	1-15
Chapter 2 Review of Literature	16-34
Chapter 3 A Brief Historical Review of the Origin and Development of the Ramakrishna Mission in India	35-51
Chapter 4 Socio-Cultural and Religious Life of the Khasis in the East Khasi Hills District	52-154
Chapter 5 The Work of the Ramakrishna Mission in the East Khasi Hills District	155-200
Chapter 6 Socio-Cultural and Religious Changes through the Ramakrishna Mission in the Khasi Society	201-290
Chapter 7 Conclusion	291-307
Bibliography	308-335

Foreword

Thakur Ramakrishna Paramhamsa is one of the foremost personalities of the nineteenth century of awakening and renaissance in religious and social state of affairs of Bengal. He was a Rishi in the Upanishadic tradition, though was associated with ritualistic and sectarian Shakta Hindu religious denomination. His ecumenicity, simple life-style and use of parables, stories and fables to communicate religious teachings won the simple and learned into his discipleship of distinct fellowship. It was after his Final Liberation, that a movement under the leadership of Swami Vivekananda took shape into a Mission to spread his message and teachings. In less than half a century, Ramakrishna missionaries in saffron robes could be seen all over India and beyond.

Dr. V.S. Lalrinawma has taken upon himself to trace the history and activities of Ramakrishna Mission among the Khasis, one of the indigenous inhabitants of the state of Meghalaya in north-east India. He informs us that though the Mission entered the State in 1920, and provided much needed education and health services to the Khasi people, there is hardly any work on the history and contribution of the Mission. His attempt through research, now being published under the title, *The Work of Ramakrishna Mission: A Study of the East Khasi Hills District*, is a welcome step to fill-in the gap. The book deals not only with the history, activities and teachings of the Mission but also amply throws light on the social, cultural and religious life of the Khasis. The author has taken special care in highlighting the changes that have been brought about by the British Government, Christian missionaries and the Ramakrishna Mission.

Dr. Lalrinawma has used various sources, other than the Mission's, in his investigation and did some field research to tap oral history which should be a necessary part of tracing the histories of indigenous people. Given the fact that this work is the product of a research done by a Christian, and that too a theologically trained person, the book may provide an opportunity for critical comments and serious discussions among the scholars of history, Hindu renaissance and Ramakrishna Mission. This may also encourage many more to undertake further enquiry and research on Ramakrishna Mission in the other parts of northeast India.

I appreciate Dr. Lalrinawma for his scholarly work, and sincerely hope that he will continue his interest in research and produce useful information for students and scholars. I heartily recommend the book to anyone who cares to study the missionary works of people of faith other than their own. At the same time the church is also challenged to rethink its mission activities.

Rev. Dr. Ravi Tiwari
Registrar,
Senate of Serampore College (University)

Acknowledgements

This book has emerged out of my doctoral research. The objective of this book is to provide information on the historical development, activities and teachings of the Ramakrishna Mission and the socio-cultural and religious changes it has brought about in the East Khasi Hills District of Meghalaya.

No attempt at a beginning is without indebtedness to those who have contributed to this book in different ways. I take this opportunity to express my deep sense of gratitude to Professor (Dr.) Nahar Singh, Director for Extension SHIATS University & Rev. Professor (Dr.) E. R. Tongper, in the Department of Philosophy, North Eastern Hill University, for their inspiring and systematic advices and comments during the research. I am also indebted to Professor (Dr.) Roger Gaikwad, Principal, Aizawl Theological College for his valuable suggestions and all types of help that I received from him. I am grateful to Mrs. Zomuani Gaikwad for her encouragement, prayer, support and hospitality during this research.

I am also grateful to Rev. Professor (Dr.) Ravi Tiwari, the Registrar of Senate of Serampore College (University) for having kindly written a foreword to this book. I would like to thank Rev. Professor (Dr.) O. L. Snaitang, presently teaching in Aizawl Theological College in the Department of History of Christianity, for going through the manuscripts and making some remarks. I acknowledge my thanks to the Theological Education Board of the Mizoram Presbyterian Synod for granting me permission to pursue my doctoral studies.

My sincere thanks are due to Mrs. Lalnghinglovi Sailo and Mr. R. Zakhuma, my in-laws, for supporting me in their prayers during difficult days that I passed through. Many thanks are also due to Rt. Revd. Professor (Dr.) Jagdhari Masih, Director at Sam Higginbottom Institute of Agriculture, Technology &

Sciences- Deemed University, Allahabad, for his kind help and encouragement through out my struggle for achieving the goal.

My special gratitude and appreciation also go to Mr. Sundeep Chawdhary, Assistant General Secretary (Ecumenical Relations) of Indian Society for Promoting Christian Knowledge (ISPCK), Delhi for undertaking the publication of this third book.

Last but not the least, the credit for the success of this work goes to my wife, Mrs. R. Lalzuithangi, who had been a pillar of strength especially at times when I needed encouragement. I also need to acknowledge the moral strength and support that I received from my son, George Lalfakawma.

June 30, 2010

Rev. Dr. V. S. Lalrinawma
Associate Professor
Aizawl Theological College
Durtlang, Mizoram

Chapter 1

Introduction

Meghalaya, a small hill state in the north-eastern part of India, is the abode of three matrilineal tribes. The main tribal groups are Khasis, Jaintias and Garos. There are seven districts in the Meghalaya state. Almost 86% of the population in Meghalaya consists of tribals.[1]

Etymologically the term 'Khasi' is a compound of two words, "Kha" and "Si". *Kha* means "born of" while *"Si"* refers to an ancient mother. Therefore the term "Khasi" means "born of a mother".[2] It assumes a great degree of significance when one tries to go into their social origin because apparently the name Khasi is itself indicative of their matrilineal system of reckoning descent.[3]

Khasis are one of the tribal communities of India. They hold the distinction of being one of the few remaining matrilineal tribes of the world. *Kur* (clan) is the first social entity of the Khasis, round which every social institution revolves. Religion starts within the *kur* and religion plays a predominant role not only in the social life of the people but in the political life of the people as well. The religion of the Khasis is monotheistic in character as they believe in one God.[4] They rely very much on supernatural powers for whatever happens to them, either good or bad. The cultural life of the Khasis is corporate, in consonance with other aspects of their social life.[5]

---

[1] Ramesh Chandra, *Environment Forest and Tribes*, (Udaipur: Himanshu Publications, 2000), 15-16.
[2] Hamlet Bareh, *The History and Culture of the Khasi People* (Guwahati: Spectrum Publications, 1997), 10.
[3] Nadeem Hasnain, *Tribal India* (Delhi: Palaka Prakashan, 1991), 122.
[4] Dr. S.K. Chattopadyay, *Tribal Institutions of Meghalaya,* Guwahati: Spectrum Publications, 1985, 159.
[5] Pariyaram M. Chako, "Introduction", *Matriliny in Meghalaya: Tradition and Change,* ed. (New Delhi: Regency Publications, 1998), 1.

Before the Britishers established their supremacy in the early 19th century, the region relatively remained isolated. The British annexed Khasi Hills in 1833 and the Jaintia Hills in 1835 and the isolation of the area was ended and the traditional independent structure was brought under a comprehensive central control. The traditional political system could not offer resistance to the new political powers.[6]

The Christian missionaries arrived in Khasi hills in 1841. These events opened up the region to the outside world. Some non-tribals came to work in different capacities. With the advent of Christianity and Western education, transformation in the social life became inevitable. Western education brought first by Christian missions and the Welsh Presbyterian Mission reduced the Khasi language to writing in the Roman alphabet. Western culture came as a challenge to the Khasi traditional religion and culture. The traditional economy was greatly disturbed by the introduction of monetary and market economy. The introduction of a money economy and consumer goods created new concept of wealth.[7]

The introduction and expansion of roads and other communication channels was breaking down the age-old isolation of the hill tribes. The change gathered more momentum from 1874 when Shillong became the capital of Assam. The traditional independent political structure was brought under a comprehensive central administration. With the advent of British rule, the powers and functions of the traditional institutions were taken away from them and they were put under the overall control and supervision of the District Council. The introduction of the new administrative structures and material goods had radical political, social and cultural implications. The effects of the District Council on these traditional institutions and chieftainships were tremendous.[8] Khasi tribal life was challenged

---

[6] Pariyaram M. Chacko, *Matriliny in Meghalaya: Tradition and Change*, edited, *op.cit.*, 1-2.

[7] Dr. O.L.Snaitang, *Christianity and Social Change in North East India*, (Calcutta: Vendrame Institute FIRMA KLM PRIVATE LIMITED, 1993), 46-47.

[8] G.N. Bag, *Rural Transformation in Tribal Areas*, (New Delhi: Akansha Publishing House, 2001), 5.

and influenced by the accelerated overall changes in the socio-cultural and religious life of the people from outside through the introduction of education, medical facilities, development of infrastructural and communication facilities. Development brought with it new avenues of employment, resulting in a large exodus of people from the rural to the urban areas where there were chances to earn more. Due to spread of literacy, the younger generation found white-collar jobs. There was a need to elevate the levels of living and quality of life. This mass exodus of people brought with it a change in the family and social and cultural system.

However, the response of the Khasi village groups to these challenges varied from area to area. As a result we can see rural Khasi households in certain villages living as settled agriculturalists, while others, due to education, have chosen other trades like government or private jobs, trades, cottage industries, agricultural or casual labourer. Unlike other tribals in north, west and south India and in some states in North East India, Khasi society in the East Khasi Hills District has advanced a long way in its political and economic development.

The growth of Shillong and other urban and semi-urban market centres and the presence therein of a large number of non-Khasis introduced the Khasis to other cultures. Due to education and modernisation the traditional power resting in the mother's brother came into conflict in the present situation.[9] Education played an important role in socio-cultural transformation. About 60 percent of the Khasis embraced Christianity. The integration of the area in the colonial dominion of the British resulted in a change by exposing the traditional Khasi society to modern forces. While the change was innovative in certain respects, it killed some of the traditional industries, institutions, etc.[10] Western culture is responsible for the

---

[9] Swasti Biswas, "Preservation of Tribal Culture in North East India", *Tribal Studies in North East India*, ed. by Sarthak Sengupta, (New Delhi: Mittal Publications, 2002), 21-23.

[10] H.G. Joshi, *Meghalaya: Past and Present*, (New Delhi: Mittal Publications, 2004), 210-11.

transformation of Khasi cultural life. The progress of Christianity was considered as a challenge to the traditional culture of the Khasis. Christians no longer observed their old religious beliefs and rituals. In Christian areas old usages of megalithic erections, households and community religious celebrations and festivals, funeral rites, house buildings and village ceremonies have been obliterated. This situation caused a section of the traditional Khasi intellectuals to resort to certain measures for the preservation of their religion and culture by inspiring the people that every Khasi should be proud of his/her rich heritage. This cultural awakening found its expression through a literary movement, viz. Seng Khasi Organisation.

U Jeebon Roy and U Rabon Singh played a very important role in this organisation. Jeebon Roy came into close contact with the Brahmo Samaj, which had appointed a permanent representative in the Khasi Hills and established a number of temples in Shillong and Cherra areas. Jeebon Roy also examined the Khasi religion and gained a strong insight into the Khasi and Hindu religions. He considered the traditional Khasi religion as a sister religion of the Hindus, rooted in Indian soil and having similarities in customs and beliefs. He visualised a place for the Khasis in the broader frame-work of the indigenous Indian culture. The Seng Khasi Organisation has helped the traditional Khasis to revive and preserve their traditional religion and cultural values which were fast dying out due to the lack of patronage and depreciation by modernisation and the British Government.

The Brahmo Samaj was established in 1882 at Calcutta by Raja Ram Mohan Roy and a branch of it was established by Nilmony in 1915 at Shillong at the initiative of M. Das Gupta. Shillong became the centre of Brahmo Samaj activities with the help of Rai Bahadur, Amar Chander Bhattacharjee and H. Nandi. It helped the traditional Khasis to preserve their traditional religion, social norms and culture. The Samaj opened schools to educate the Khasis.[11] The Khasis found something attractive in the Brahmo faith, especially the worship of God in the formless

---

[11] Mary Pristilla Rina Lyngdoh, *The Festivals in the History and Culture of the Khasi*, (New Delhi: Vikas Publishing House Pvt. Ltd., 1991), 177.

manner, a practice, which is closely akin to their philosophy of religion. The Brahmo Movement in the Khasi Hills played an important role in the field of social reforms and in forming the modern society. The Brahmo Samaj established several schools in the district. But due to their failure in continuing their Mission, they handed their work over to the Ramakrishna Mission.[12] The most successful among the Indian Missions in the research area is the Ramakrishna Movement.

Brief History of Ramakrishna Mission and Its Activities:

The Ramakrishna Mission was founded on 1st May, 1897 by Swami Vivekananda and was registered on May 4, 1909 under the Society Registration Act XXI of 1860 with its management vested in a governing body consisting of Trustees of the Belur Math for 1909-1910.[13] The Mission started its activities in the East Khasi Hills under the leadership of Swami Prabhananda (known as Ketaki Maharaj) from Sylhet in 1920. The Mission opened its first Primary School at Shella (East Khasi Hills District) in 1924. The activities of the Mission were gradually extended to different villages like Cherrapunji, Sohbar, Kalibari, Laitryngrew, Laitdiengsai, Nongwar, Majai, Mawmluh, Mawlong, Mawkhar, Mawsmai, Mylliem, Shella and Umwai.[14]

As a part of its programme of service, the Ramakrishna Mission paid special attention to the health and education of the Khasis by running dispensaries, mobile health units and schools. For rural tribal youth and women development, the Mission operates some training programmes. Rural development programmes of the Ramakrishna Mission aimed at desired changes in every sphere of life, i.e. social, cultural, economic, technological, political and religious.[15] In the East Khasi Hills District the Ramakrishna Mission runs 58 schools, 2 permanent

---

[12] Quoted from Ramakrishna Mission Cherrapunji Office Record.
[13] Swami Gambhirananda, *History of Ramakrishna Math and Ramakrishna Mission*, (Calcutta: Advaita Ashrama, 1983), 248-265.
[14] Prof. S.C. Dube, "The Tribal Situation in India", *Annual Magazine of Ramakrishna Mission*, (Narainpur: Ramakrishna Mission, 1989), 151-155.
[15] Swami Bhajananda, "*Rural Development Work in the Perspective of Swami Vivekananda's Social Philosophy*", *Souvenir 2000*, (Asansol: Ramakrishna Mission High School, 2002), 10-12.

dispensaries, 2 mobile dispensaries, 3 training centres, 3 libraries, 3 hostels and 2 computer training centres.[16] The aim of the Mission is to practice and spread *Sanatana Dharma* (the Eternal Religion), strengthen the traditional Khasis in their traditional faith and culture and to block the traditional Khasis from embracing Christianity.[17]

The Ramakrishna Mission gave equal importance to women's upliftment through education, vocational training and medical care in different parts of the East Khasi Hills District.[18]

Like the Christian missionaries and British Government, the Ramakrishna Mission has also brought changes in the field of education, economy, employment, living standard, health, cultural and religious life to some extent. So far no one has done research on the contributions of the Ramakrishna Mission to the socio-cultural and religious life of the Khasis through education and social service. Through this research an attempt has been made to discover the changes brought about by the Ramakrishna Mission in the socio-cultural and religious life of the Khasis in the East Khasi Hills District of Meghalaya.

Statement of the Problem: The present study is an attempt to investigate the changes brought about by the Ramakrishna Mission in the socio- cultural and religious life of the Khasis in the East Khasi Hills District of Meghalaya.

Justification and Importance of the Study

There are many studies available on the anthropology, religion, socio-economic & cultural aspects of the tribal people in India as well as outside India. However, very few studies have been done on the socio-cultural and religious life of the Khasis in Meghalaya. So far no research has been done on **the work of the Ramakrishna Mission in Meghalaya: A Study of the East Khasi**

---

[16] Swami Budhananda, *The Ramakrishna Movement*, (Calcutta: Advaita Ashrama, 1994), 138-141.

[17] n.n., *Ramakrishna Mission: Centenary Memorial Annual Report* (April 2000 - March 2001), Varansh: Ramakrishna Mission Home of Service, 2002, 5.

[18] n.n., *Report of the Ramakrishna Math and Ramakrishna Mission*, (Hawrah: Ramakrishna Math: Ramakrishna Mission, n.d.), 19.

Hills District. Through the teachings and different activities of the Ramakrishna Mission, the Khasis in the East Khasi Hills District of Meghalaya have started realising the importance of the indigenous socio-cultural and religious values, which were disappearing slowly. Therefore, it is necessary to assess the changes through the significant contribution of the Ramakrishna Mission to the development of the socio-cultural and religious life of the Khasis in the East Khasi Hills District of Meghalaya. The findings of the study will help the Government of Meghalaya and voluntary organisations in planning for the development of the socio-cultural and religious lives of the people. Above all, the Khasis themselves can be benefited from this study, as it will throw light on some aspects of socio-cultural and religious life. It will also give them a fairly good understanding of their way of living.

Objectives of the Study: This research is undertaken with the objective of studying the Ramakrishna Mission and the changes brought about by it in the study area. The specific objectives of the study are as follows:

1. To study the historical growth, teachings and activities of the Ramakrishna Mission in the East Khasi Hills District.
2. To examine the socio-cultural and religious life of the Khasi community in the East Khasi Hills District.
3. To study the changes brought about by the Ramakrishna Mission in the socio-cultural and religious life of the Khasis in the study area.

Methodology: The purpose of this study is to present briefly the research methodology. During this research, descriptive-analytical methods have been applied. The author has made use of anthropological, philosophical and sociological approaches accompanied by empirical investigation in order to find the exact results.

Anthropological approach deals with origin of the people, language, customs and social institutions. This approach studies religion as a cultural order that gives significance to human and their world.[19] It has proved most effective in investigating primal religion in particular. Anthropology embraces the total spectrum of human's social and natural behaviour. Through this method we study such religions which do not have either the scriptures, or religious organisations or a worship house.

The philosophical exposition and appraisal of religious issues still continues to be a major part or context and method for the study of religion.[20] Philosophy seeks to analyse concepts like God, salvation, creation, worship, sacrifice and eternal life. It also studies theological concepts, as well as the phenomena of religious experience and the activity of worship. Philosophy in India in one sense is the pathway to religion and in another sense the culmination of religion.[21]

The sociological approach to the study of society tries to search for the religious perception and experiences of the community. Emile Durkheim defined religion as "a unified system of beliefs and practices related to sacred things, that is to say things set apart and forbidden, beliefs and practices which unite into one single moral community."[22] Religion is a form of social cement. Religion is a means to bind together the members of a society or a social group into a moral community. Weber emphasised the dialectical relationship between religious ideas and their social environment. He also said that the impact of a new religious movement could have social, economic and religious consequences.

The study of a given society is the study of the totality of its interacting parts, or how family relations, legal forms, political structures, religious practices, artistic expressions, mores, and customs contribute to the successful functioning of social life as

---

[19] K.P. Aleaz, *Dimensions of Indian Religion: Study, Experience and Interaction*, (Calcutta: Punthi Pustak, 1995), 27-29.

[20] Christopher Augustus Bixel Tirkey, *Religion/Primal Religions*, (Delhi: ISPCK, 1998), 53.

[21] K.P. Aleaz, *Dimensions of Indian Religion: Study, Experience and Interaction*, op.cit., 24-27.

[22] L. Schneider, *Sociological Approach to Religion*, (New York: John Wiley and Sons, Inc., 1970), 11.

INTRODUCTION

a whole. The author, while applying the sociological method looks at the Khasi traditional religion as uniting the community members of the traditional Khasi religion in order to form one single moral community maintaining their identity. With a sociological perspective, the author looks at the varieties of religious experiences of the people, which have provided social unity along with cohesive identity.[23] By applying sociological method during this study, he has observed and learned the common religious and cultural practices and the social heritage of the Khasi society in the East Khasi Hills District. Since culture is inseparable, involved with human social life and activities, the study of Khasi religious identity too has a great deal to do with the rich Khasi tribal cultural components.

In the analytical method multi-stage sampling procedure has been applied. Keeping in view the purpose and objectives of the study, information and opinions were obtained through personal interviews with the help of a re-structural schedule.

Sampling Design

Multi-stage sampling procedure was adopted for the selection of samples.

1. In the first stage – The District was selected purposively.
2. In the second stage – The block was selected randomly.
3. In the third stage – The villages were selected randomly.
4. In the fourth stage – The respondents were selected randomly.

Stage First- Selection of District

There are seven districts in the state of Meghalaya. Out of seven districts, the East Khasi Hills district was selected purposively. It was selected because it has been an important District from the perspective of the activities of the Ramakrishna Mission. Moreover, the researcher was connected with this District. Good

---

[23] K.P.Aleaz, *Dimensions of Indian Religion: Study, Experience and Interaction*, op.cit., 20-21.

- **Adopted Villages:** Adopted villages are those villages where the Ramakrishna Mission has been doing its service actively.
- **Non-adopted Villages:** Non-adopted villages are those villages where the Ramakrishna Mission has not been doing any activity.

communication facility and resources are available for conducting this research.

Stage Second- Selection of Block

There are seven community development blocks in the East Khasi Hills District. In order to select a desired block, a complete list of all the blocks was obtained from the District headquarters of the East Khasi Hills District, and these blocks were arranged in ascending order according to their area under Ramakrishna Mission's service and then Shella-Bholaganj Community Development Block was selected randomly.

Stage Third- Selection of Villages

A complete list of all the villages was obtained from the Block headquarters. There are 157 villages in the Shella-Bholaganj Block. Out of 157 villages, the Ramakrishna Mission was serving actively in 70 villages. Then selective villages were stratified into two groups on the basis of adopted villages by the Ramakrishna Mission and non-adopted villages where the Ramakrishna Mission was not serving. Then a list was prepared on adopted and non-adopted villages separately and both the groups were arranged in two groups separately on the basis of their size of population. Then 5 villages from each group were selected in both the categories. The detailed description of the villages is given in table No. 1.

Table No. 1.1 Name of the selected villages from Shella-Bholaganj Block

Sl. No.	Random Number of Villages in Shella-Bholaganj Community Development Block	Name of the selected villages in Shella-Bholaganj Community Development Block
A.	Adopted villages	70 Villages
1	17	Ishamati
2	24	Laitryngew
3	47	Mawmluh
4	49	Mawsmai
5	59	Sohbar
B.	Non-adopted villages	87 Villages
1	23	Laitlyndop

INTRODUCTION

Contd., Table No. 1.1 Name of the selected
villages from Shella-Bholaganj Block

2	43	Mawrah
3	49	Phong
4	52	Rngimawsaw
5	62	Umkhabaw

Table No. 1.1 shows the list of selected sample villages. Altogether 10 villages were randomly selected from both the groups.

Stage Fourth- Selection of Households

A complete list of all the households was obtained from the village *Panchayat Pradhans* in adopted and non-adopted selected villages. These households were arranged alphabetically in ascending order in adopted and non-adopted villages.

Then 10% rural households were selected randomly from both the adopted and non-adopted villages. The detailed description of the selected rural households is shown in table No.1.2

Table No.1.2 Selection of Respondents/
Households from adopted & non-adopted villages

Sl	Name of Selected Villages	Total No. of Households Selected Villages	No. of Selected Rural Households
	Adopted Villages		
1	Ishamati	180	18
2	Sohbar	230	23
3	Mawsmai	250	25
4	Mawmluh	420	42
5	Laitryngew	480	48
6.	Total No. of Households	1560	156
	Non-Adopted Villages		
1	Rngimawsaw	132	13
2	Phong	174	18
3	Laitlyndop	232	23
4	Mawrah	302	30
5	Umkhabaw	400	40
6	Total No. of Households	1240	124

Altogether 280 households were selected randomly from both the groups.

Types of Data

The present study was based both on primary as well as secondary data.

Primary Data

The primary data was collected from the respondents with the help of specially prepared and pre-tested schedule employing the personal interview method. Each question or statement was read to the respondents and they were asked to react clearly and cordially to each of the question on the three-point scale of the following:

        A   = Agree
        UD   = Undecided
        DA   = Disagree

Secondary Data

The secondary data was collected from the District Headquarters Office, District Statistical Office and Block Headquarters, through books, periodicals, journals, magazines, internet, published materials and literature available during the course of study.

Basic Terms

This section deals with some important terms used in this study. They are discussed separately below:

1. Religion

The term 'religion' is derived from the Latin term 'religio', which is originated from 'religere' or 'religare' which means 'to treat with care' or 'to bind'. It includes all that which long lines of truth seeking thinkers and writers have thought to be characteristics of 'religion.'[24]

Leonce de Grandmaison defines religion as "the sum total of beliefs, sentiments, and practices, individual and social, which

---

[24] Christopher Augustus Bixel Tirkey, *Religion/Primal Religion*, (New Delhi: ISPCK, 1998), 17.

have for their object a power which a human being recognises as supreme, on which he depends and with which he can enter into relation."[25] Similarly E. Durkheim defines religion as "a set of beliefs, symbols and practices, which are based on the ideas of the sacred, and which unites believers into a socio-religious community."[26] These beliefs and practices form the doctrines and rituals of religion. However Joseph M. Kitagawa defines, "A living religion is not merely a system of doctrines and beliefs but a whole way of life."

The term religion connotes a system of beliefs in a Supreme Being, values, symbols and practices that give meaning to individual, groups, society and to the cosmos without making any distinction. It also provides directions for life and inter-personal-relationships.

2. Culture

The concept of culture, together with that of society, is one of the most widely used notions in sociology. The term 'culture' is derived from the Latin noun 'cultura' and the verb 'colere' with the meaning of 'tending' or 'cultivation' or 'tilling the soil'. Culture may be defined as "the belief, values, behaviour and material objects shared by a particular people."[27] For instance, E. B. Tylor defines culture as "that complex whole which includes knowledge, belief, art, morals, laws, customs, any other capabilities and habits acquired by man as a member of society." Some others may define 'culture' to include music, art, and good manners. The word 'culture' could also be defined in broader terms to include traditional manners, customs, work tools, dress, food habits, architecture, and transmitted values of unwritten laws and moral behaviours peculiar to certain ethnic groups. Thus, culture refers to the whole way of life of the members of one society. It includes dress, customary laws, family life and pattern of work and leisure pursuits. Every culture consists of the values the members of a given group hold, the norms they

---

[25] *Ibid.*, 11.
[26] *Ibid.*
[27] A.R.N. Srivastava, *What is Anthropology?* (Allahabad: K.K. Publications, 1998), 8.

follow and the material goods they create.[28] It is the sum total of the ways of doing and thinking. These are shared by the members of a society, when acted upon they produce behavior considered acceptable within that society. In other words religion is the substance of culture and culture is the form of religion. If culture is the body, religion is the soul of culture.

3. Society

Society may be defined as a total complex of human relationships in so far as they grow out of action in terms of means and relationships, intrinsic or symbolic. John H. Cuber defined society "as a group of people who have lived together long enough to become organised to consider themselves and be considered as a unit more or less distinct from other human units."

Society is a social organisation made up of a group of people who share a geographical area and culture. It may denote anything from a primitive non-literate people to a modern industrial nation-state, or from the most general reference to human kind to a relatively small-organised group of people. It is governed by a system of rules and regulations, and has a structure, which ensures the governance and smooth functioning of the life of the community. Society and culture are interdependent concepts.

4. Household/Family

The word 'family' has been taken from the Roman word, "famulus" meaning a "servant" and a Latin word "familia", meaning "household". A household/family is the first institution in the history of man and unit of human society. E.W. Burgess defines family "as a group of persons united by ties of marriage, blood or adoption, constituting a single household interacting or inter-communicating with each other in their respective social roles of husband and wife, mother and father, son and daughter, brother and sister creating and maintaining a common culture."

---

[28] Anthony Giddens, *Sociology*, (Oxford: Polity Press, 1989), 31.

5. Division of Chapters

This book is divided into seven chapters. The first chapter deals with the general introduction. Chapter two deals with literature review. Chapter three studies the brief historical review of the origin and development of the Ramakrishna Mission in India. Chapter four highlights the socio-cultural and religious life of the Khasis in the East Khasi Hills District. Chapter five highlights the work of the Ramakrishna Mission in the East Khasi Hills District. Chapter six examines the socio-cultural & religious changes brought about by the Ramakrishna Mission in the Khasi society. Chapter seven discusses the conclusion.

B A a b

Chapter 2

REVIEW OF LITERATURE

The basic conceptual framework employed in the present study on "The Ramakrishna Mission and changes in Socio-Cultural and Religious life of the rural Khasis in the East Khasi Hills District of Meghalaya," was centred around the socio-economic, cultural and religious elements in the Khasi society and the changes through the Ramakrishna Mission activities and teachings in the Khasi society. Hence, all the reviews collected for the study were organised under the above mentioned themes. Hence, review of the literature is related to the Khasi socio-economic, cultural and religious life, the teachings and activities of the Ramakrishna Mission, and the changes brought about the mission in the Khasi society in the said District.

Gurdon, P.R. (1907) studied the social and cultural life of Khasis and found that the advent of the Welsh missionaries and the dissemination of English education has brought about some changes in the social, cultural and economic lives of the Khasis. About 40% of Khasis still practice the old traditional religion, culture and social life in the East Khasi Hills District of Meghalaya.

Abhedananda Swami (1944) studied the *doctrine of karma* and reported that the *doctrine of karma* alone could explain the mysterious problem of good and evil and reconcile humans to the terrible and apparent injustice of life. Those who believe in this noble doctrine are never disturbed in their minds at the sight of the inequalities of birth and fortune, or of intellect and capacities. The final end of duty is freedom and divine love. According to him, with the awakening of this love comes all knowledge. He, who has understood the duties and fulfilled them, has reached freedom, and gained divine love and divine wisdom on this earth. He transcends all the *laws of karma* or the law of compensation, and retribution and enters into the abode of everlasting existence and bliss.

Sylvester, Silber A. (1950) conducted an extensive study of the social life of primitive cultures and concluded that the economy of the primitive culture was static and not in progress. He further said that the very irregularity of man's hunting and gathering from forest made him unfit for regular and steady work which was essential for their development.

Nida, Eugene A. (1954) studied the customs and cultures and found that in each culture, technological changes occur constantly, but political and religious changes are looked upon with great suspicion. In a culture which was undergoing rapid change, not all aspects reflect the same acceleration or speed. The rate of change in any society can be accurately measured only by careful historical studies. He found that even the simplest cultures have been in debt to others for important contributions to their lives.

Samuel, V.C. (1959) conducted a study on the Ramakrishna Movement, which is known as the World Mission of Hinduism and found that the Ramakrishna Movement was primarily a religious organisation. The various activities in the field of education and social service which it carries are intended to help men and women who experience the religious truth promoted by it. The movement has claimed the superiority of Hinduism over other religions. The theology of the movement is *monistic* and the all-pervading God is the ultimate source of all work. The world and human beings are very closely allied to one another. The most fundamental affirmation of a monistic theology was that Reality is one and only one and that it has some impact on the social and cultural life of India in general and tribal life in particular.

Glover, Donald R. (1975) conducted a research on the effect of population density on infrastructure. He found that population growth have different effects on communication and economic development. Due to lack of proper communication the rural people were deprived of social and economic development.

Natarajan, Nalini (1977) in her study on the missionaries among the Khasis dealt with Khasi social, economic, cultural and religious life and the impact of both the Christian and the

Ramakrishna Mission missionaries on Khasi society. Since independence, economic and social forces at work in the country have brought about a large measure of integration of the Khasis with the rest of the country. The Ramakrishna Mission encouraged the Khasis to move towards Indianisation. The Western influence on the Khasi society has been evident in many forms such as dress, adoption of western names, economic life, modes of behaviour and Western music. Moreover, improved communication and the technologically superior Western civilisation have made a deep impression on the Khasis. It was also found that there were some changes in the Khasi political thinking due to education and the stress on the ideas of nationhood by the Ramakrishna Mission. Both Christian missionaries and Ramakrishna Mission missionaries have brought political awareness among the Khasis. With the Ramakrishna Mission assisting in the process of inculcating a broader religious outlook and a sense of being part of large nation, the Khasi ethos and worldview have been greatly enriched. The present Khasi society depicts that the synthesis of all these influences arising from missionaries' work has brought about a significant change in the Khasi attitude, thoughts, values, beliefs and culture.

Rao, T.V.S and N. Gopala (1978) examining the impact of tribal development agency programme in the district of Srikakulam of Andhra Pradesh and Ganjam & Koraput Districts in Orissa, revealed that the tribals were amenable to change through finance. The beneficiaries of agricultural development programmes showed encouraging aptitude for the use of modern inputs and most of them had significant economic gains. The study showed that economic change has an impact on their socio-cultural life.

Swahananda, Swami (1979) in his study on service and spirituality found that the visible universe, the individual and the Ultimate Reality are one and the same. *Vedanta* is man-centred but man is nothing but the embodied soul. True unity of all people and true nationhood would be a fact when an inner consciousness of the common ideal, common struggle and common feeling among the people of different cultures, languages and religions would be achieved. Each religion differs from the other in philosophy, mythology and ritual. But there is a common aspiration of transcending the limitations of life and realising itself in the highest. The Absolute manifests itself in a variety of forms in accordance with the attitude of the devotee. The different conceptions of Godhead are the symbols of the Absolute and diverse spiritual disciplines are the ways to reach it.

Bhudhananda, Swami (1980) in his study discusses the Ramakrishna Movement, its historical growth, teachings, activities and its meaning for mankind and found that renunciation and human service are the goals of each follower. *Vedanta,* the very breath of this Movement, offers to mankind the solution of human problems. The Mission bore witness to the fact that all religions are true and lead to God. Ramakrishna Pramahansa has been made the incarnation of God. The Mission work was for the uplift of the poor through education, medical care, relief operations and rehabilitation work. There is a change in the social, economic and spiritual life of human society through the teachings and service of the Ramakrishna Mission.

Bareh, Angeline (1981) in her study on the megalithic culture among the Khasis with special reference to Mawiong village aimed to discover the association of the megaliths with religious ceremonies, the feasts of the ancient heroes and the cremation of the great. She found that apart from the religious activities, the megaliths or materialistic activities of the clan as a whole and the presence of large number of memoirs and their assignments are all manifestations of a variety of social goals. Apart from the religious activities, the megaliths symbolised the corporate activities of the clan as a whole.

Vidyarathi, L.P. (1981) conducted a research on tribal development and found that development means growth and change. It involved both the material and the human factors. They seem to be under the impression that growth, as assessed in terms of such gross indicators, is a value itself. While arriving for the development of a group or an area, due emphasis has to be given to their traditional values and historical experience.

Dutta, P.N. (1982) undertook a study of the impact of the West on the Khasis and Jaintias and found that the establishment of the British rule brought to an end the isolation of the tribes and widened their outlook. Prior to the British rule, the people were extremely insecure in life and property, chiefly because of the frequent inter-tribal wars. With the arrival of the British, propitiating the evil spirits was eradicated and the spread of enlightenment and Western education has adversely affected the traditional dances, music, festivals and religious and cultural values of the Khasis.

Kharmawplang, K. (1983) evaluating the impact of the contribution of the non-Christian missionaries to the development of education in the Khasi Hills, found that education imparted to Khasis by the Ramakrishna Mission developed in them their good distinctive qualities to full extent, individually and collectively; and the service and teachings of the Ramakrishna Mission opened the windows of the world to them and brought to their very door-step the knowledge and wisdom of their races and people treasured in books. After the arrival of the Ramakrishna Missionaries, things changed in most places dramatically and in some gradually due to education. It is also reported that through education and teaching of the Ramakrishna Mission, the mode of living, the standard of living, social and cultural values also changed.

Mawthoh Iamonlang Syiem (1983) conducted a study on the emerging patterns of family relationship among the Khasis in Shillong and observed that the growing pace of urban living and new social and economic commitments placed the maternal uncle in a dilemma. In this new social situation the maternal uncle finds it increasingly difficult to perform his role to the maximum due to the strain of modern living that has affected the role of both the father and the maternal uncle. There is no doubt that dependence on the maternal side has decreased and dependence of the family on the father has increased. The change occurred when individuals acted in response to forces stronger than themselves. These forces were composed of the acts, opinions and attitudes of other individuals. The strong forces rooted in traditional values were sufficient to counteract the catalysing agents of change, but they could not remain unaltered themselves even as they lost their traditional moorings.

Das, S.T. (1986) studying the tribal life of North Eastern India observed that agriculture of the North Eastern Region is very closely associated with many social and cultural customs, patterns and even habits. Lack of technology and poor utilisation of technological tools have greatly limited agriculture production. Even the utilisation of the modern technology was poor. Post-harvest facilities like lack of marketing, lack of transport and communication facilities were some of the reasons for poor economy.

Nair, Sukumaran (1987) in his study on the tribal economy in "Transition in the State of Meghalaya" concluded that even though some households make a surplus income over expenditure, the surplus has got invested in agriculture for expanded reproduction. Much of it appears to be siphoned off into religious or social festivals on the non-formal sectors of the economy.

Romain, Rolland (1988) in his study on the life of Vivekananda and the Universal Gospel reported that there is no form of detachment where selfishness cannot find means to enter in and that there is no more repulsive form of it than the conscious or unconscious hypocrisy involved in liberation sought only for self and not for others. The Mission of Vivekananda and his followers were to rescue the great teachings of the *Vedanta* from a few privileged persons and to spread them among all sorts of human beings. Vivekananda recognised the validity of all religions. He also emphasised charity, learning and meditation. There was to be a gradual purification starting with the necessities of the body, which needs nourishment, and extending to the detached spirit of human beings absorbed in unity. Vivekananda prescribed four *yogas* (*Karma Yoga, Bhakti Yoga, Jnana Yoga* and *Raja Yoga*) to serve as direct and independent means for the attainment of liberation.

Abhedananda, Swami (1989) in his study about thoughts on "Philosophy and Religion" found that philosophy solves the problem of life and death. He also observed that all religions have tried to show the Universal Truth and that the same Eternal, Unchangeable Being is worshipped under various names by different peoples, and Vedanta philosophy does not recognise differences among people based on caste, creed, or sex. Vedanta teaches the equality and essential sameness of all human beings. Meditation is the most important step on the path of spiritual progress. *Vedanta* teaches that human beings must not separate God from the world. As long as our minds are imperfect, we are far from the central truth of blessedness.

Ksaniang, Bhakti (1990) studying the Ramakrishna-Vivekananda Movement in the Khasi and Jaintia Hills, found that the Ramakrishna Mission has contributed a lot to the development of the Khasis in the field of education and health care. The Mission does not envision a new religion in the name of Sri Ramakrishna, but its ideas were inspired with the living and dynamic *Vedanta* as offered by Sri Ramakrishna. In order to achieve a dynamic life, the message, 'work is worship' should be adopted. The Ramakrishna Mission has been working for the uplift of the Khasis through education, training, religious teachings and medical care, which shows the impact of the Ramakrishna Mission on the socio-economic and cultural life of the Khasis.

Lokeswarananda, Swami (1990) studied the religion and culture and opined that *Vedanta* is a philosophy which is not prepared to make any compromise on the question of human's identity. The perfect human being sees God everywhere. The Universal Religion, if there is one at all, has to be non-sectarian; its name is religion, which again may be called Truth, which is eternal and also universal. The Universal Religion preaches no particular creed or dogma; it rejects none either. Religion and culture cannot be separated. Every belief, every practice, every ritual may find a place in religion because it is not that important. It does not recognise any practice, ritual or belief as the only true and valid one. Truth is the Being, the Being from which all beings are derived, the Being, which is the common being of all that exist. A truly religious human being stands for peace and harmony, for he/she recognises differences in religious beliefs and practices.

Nongkhlaw, Aniema (1990) made a study on modernisation of the Khasi society from sociological perspective and found that the tradition bound Khasis have been making a steady march towards modernity, which started with the achievement of statehood. The Khasi society was backward because of the problem of communication both in the physical and abstract terms. The traditional religious festivals such as the *Nongkrem Dance* and *Behdeinkhlam Dance* though still performed, have, however, lost their religious significance. A high degree of political awareness and openness to outsiders has taken place among the Khasi youth.

Ranganathananda, Swami (1990) studying Swami Vivekananda and human excellence found that God is both form and formless, personal and impersonal. Each soul is potentially divine and spirituality is the birthright of every man and woman. The goal of life is to manifest this divine truth within by controlling nature, externally and internally. Education is the manifestation of the perfection that already exists in human beings. It is not the amount of information that is put into the brain and runs riot there all through life. It should be life building, human-making and character-building. If it does not help the common people to equip themselves for the struggle in life, it is not the right kind of education.

Lyngdoh, Mary Pristilla Rina (1991) in her study of the festivals in the history and culture of the Khasis found that in the pre-colonial period, the Khasis lived in isolation, although there were some contacts through trade with the neighbouring plains. They had their own traditional religion, culture, social, economic and political system. But all these gave way to new changes and civilisation with the coming of the British and Christianity. They introduced a new era which brought about social, economic and political changes in the district. These changes brought about by Western values and culture came as a challenge to the Khasi traditional religion and culture. But under the influence of the Indian Renaissance initiated by Brahmo Samaj and the Ramakrishna Mission, the Khasi leaders like U Jeebon Roy and U Sib Charan Roy, worked for cultural awakening in the Khasi society. These leaders under the guidance of the Seng Khasi Organisation (1899) organised group discussions on Khasi religion and culture and published books, pamphlets and journals on the socio-cultural life of the Khasis to preserve their distinct identity, rich culture, religion and social values. The study also shows that the religion and culture of the Hindu neighbours of the plains has made some impact on the cultural and religious life of the Khasis in the district.

Lyngdoh, M.P.R. (1991) in his study on inheritance, property rights and entrepreneurship in the Khasi Society found that the demand for male inheritance was started in 1961 by a young Khasi association known as *Ka Seng Iktiar Longbriew Manbriew* and by another organisation known as *Ka Syngkhong Rympei Thymmai* which was formed in 1990 at Shillong. Due to their contact with the socio-cultural and religious influences coming from outside, the Khasi society has undergone tremendous changes. Changes were brought in the socio-economic and political fields, and the Khasis who had been able to maintain social and political isolation were opened up to the outside world. However, in spite of the rapid changes, the Khasi matrilineal system of descent, succession and inheritance exist till today withstanding the forces of change. Today there is a slight change in property inheritance. Parents have a right to express their will to give a share from their property to their sons which was not there before the Bill was passed by the Meghalaya Legislative Assembly in 1984, which received the consent of the president of India.

Dev, Pallab (1992) in a study on the politico-geographical aspects of economic development in Meghalaya found that the land management system in the state is not "scientific" since the Government has no right over the land. Under the existing land tenure system in the state where the Government has no right over the land, a comprehensive planning policy for land management is very difficult to implement. The traditional socio-political institutions of the tribals play an important role in the development of the State. With changes in the political system and the reorganisation of administrative units, the political demands of the people have undergone changes and their concept of development has also changed. He suggested that there is a need for involving such institutions in the whole planning process in order to bring about sustained economic development at the grass root level by involving the people in the process.

Shantarupananda, Swami (1992) conducted a study on the fifty years of the Ramakrishna Mission Ashrama at Cherrapunji (1931-1981) and reported that it was due to the untiring zeal, spirit of self-sacrifice and love of Ketaki Maharaj, Swami Lokeshwarananda, Swami Yogeswarananda, Swami Niramayananda, Swami Pramathananda and Swami Gokulananda for the Khasi people that the Ramakrishna Mission in the East Khasi Hills had a very good impact on the different aspects of life in Khasi society. Through the educational institutions, medical service, technical training and various cultural functions, the Mission has tried to bring about social and religious transformation and an assimilation of divergent cultures of the North Eastern Region into the main stream of the Indian culture.

Synrem, H.K. (1992) carried out a study on revivalism in Khasi society and observed that Khasi revivalism took place mainly due to the threat of acculturation. The coming of the British along with Christian missionaries changed the traditional form of religious, cultural and social life. The Khasi revivalism could be exploited to convert nationalism into communalism. The Khasi revival led to regional consciousness that perpetuated political ends. Once the end is achieved, it died out. Without a serious study of Khasi religion, Khasi revivalism will remain confused and misunderstood.

O.L. Snaitang (1993) conducted a research on the role of Christianity in Social Change among the Khasi-Jaintia Hill tribes from 1841 to 1990. Christianity entered the Khasi-Jaintia hills at a time when the imposition of the British administration had so overwhelmed the people that they were unable to absorb the alien impact into their own institutions the way they had in the past. One of the effects of the new political order was to permit more extensive penetration into the area of Hindu agencies such as the Ramakrishna Mission and Brahmo Samaj as well as promoting more inter-marriage between the local people and Hindus. Christianity also played a leading role in economic, political and cultural life of the Khasis. The changed life of the individual had social consequences. The Christian ideology promoted new social relationships.

Kundu, Kamta (1993) made a critical study of the Universal Religion of Ramakrishna Paramahansa and reported that the religious philosophy of Ramakrishna is a synthesis of knowledge, devotion, action and mysticism. Truth, which is eternal, vibrated in the past and at present and will vibrate in the heart of each member of the human race in future. It is true that religion, being inevitably related to human being, is one and common to all ages. The urge for the Supreme Being is the common factor of religion in all ages. The religion, in some of its developed manifestations is universal in nature and aims at the union of the finite with the Infinite. The conflicts among people in respect to their religious beliefs arise due to an overemphasis on the superficial aspects of their religious dogmas, rituals, creeds, and manner of worship. The teaching of Ramakrishna Mission on universal tolerance gives equal status to all sects, creeds and faiths in the world. Universal Religion leads not only to universal brotherhood but also points to the root of our oneness and the fact that we all are manifestations of one living spirit. It encourages for service to humanity. It never supports mere asceticism or renunciation of the world.

Maitra, Asim (1993) studied the profile of a little-known tribe and concluded that the religious life of the Lisu was dominated by the evil spirits commonly known as *Ni*. The basic problems of the Lisu were the problems of habitat, land, identity, people, administration, education, health, communication, agriculture and energy. Because of social and geographical isolation, the Lisu have less scope for interaction or contact with any other ethnic groups. After embracing Christianity the Lisu tribe has abandoned the concept of diseases created by evil spirits and its treatments.

Sarin, Geeta (1993) in her study on urban poverty and the status of women in Shillong found that tribal women enjoy equal rights among the Khasis with men due to political, economic and social structures. There is no discrimination against women. They have the right of inheritance and succession. They have equal opportunity in work and access to education; this further enhances their economic power and has a positive bearing on their status in all other walks of life. But in spite of educational opportunities, poverty continues to increase among women. Their status in the urban areas is much better than their status in the rural areas in all spheres of life. They have to be involved in decision making bodies which is lacking.

Jairath, M.S. (1994) studying tribal economy and society observed that the tribal areas had historically remained aloof and cut off from the main stream of national development due to topographical and geographical factors. Economically, tribal society is backward due to the lack of technical education, use of scientific technology in agriculture, lack of proper communication, lack of sufficient funds and lack of proper marketing facilities.

Rajak, M.P. (1994) conducted a research on problems of poverty among the scheduled tribes in the State of West Bengal and found that illiteracy, economic problem, drinking habits, indebtedness, unawareness of competitive modern systems, sacrificial practices in ceremonies and festivals lead them to poverty. Right political approach, eradication of illiteracy, use of more developed technological tools and no discrimination in any area of tribal life is necessary for their development. Education is must for them.

Sharley, Alexander (1994) studied the social transformation in the Bhoi religion of Meghalaya and found that the spreading of education by the Christian missionaries in Meghalaya undoubtedly was one of the most important features of the social and cultural development of the Khasis. The lower a tribe's level of literacy, the less is the contact and interaction with non-tribal groups, and its social and cultural development. The traditional socio-political institutions such as *Syiemship, Lyngdohship* and *Sirdarship* hampered change in the Khasi society. The process of social transformation is affected by cultural diffusion, education, religion, urbanisation and also physical and social factors. The spread of an idea or technology is determined by a number of physical, social and cultural factors. The Christian missionaries brought about a change in the religious, social and cultural life of the Khasis through education and social service.

Caurasia, B.P. (1995) conducted a study on "Poverty: The Root Cause of Rural Misery" and found that poverty in the rural areas is due to underdeveloped agriculture, illiteracy, average growth rate, fast growing population, corruption, social and technological factors. The voluntary social service agencies have done a lot of humanitarian work in the tribal areas. The government should provide more financial help to such agencies to start more developmental schemes among them.

Syiemlieh, Joseph (1995) made a study on the funeral rites and practices in the Khasi main land and found that the morality of funeral rites and practices is a unique art and culture of a specific ethnic group which one must respect even if he does not promote it. The maternal uncle in traditional religion is the official priest. The religious rite of the final placing of bones of the dead also witnesses to a sense of sin and God's forgiveness in the religious beliefs of the Khasis. This practice also shows that there is life even after death and that the human soul is eternal in Khasi traditional religion.

Ranganathananda, Swami (1996) made a study on national integration through love and service and found that philosophy and spirituality of service of Vivekananda cuts across all communal, caste, and other differences, and shines as a universal spiritual religion or philosophy of life that is acceptable not only to all theists but also to all atheists. *Practical Vedanta* philosophy will bind all the nations of the world together since it is against discrimination based on caste, creed or sex and teaches the universal tolerance, equality and sameness of the true nature of all human beings. It is not built around any particular person, or special revelation. The nation must strengthen secularism in order to achieve total national integration through more fundamental approaches. Until political conditions are created for secular-minded members of all religious communities to represent the political, economic, and social interests of each other, and the same applies to the government servants also. According to Swami Ranganathannda, a democratic state will not be truly secular, and national integration will remain a far-away dream unless all human beings are treated equally.

Bareh, Hamlet (1997) studying the history and culture of the Khasi people with the object of presenting the history of the Khasi people from its earliest beginning to the present day has found that the greatest difficulty in reconstructing the history and culture of the Khasi people in the early period is the paucity of materials, making it necessary for historian to depend mainly on the oral traditions and legends, passed on from one generation to another. After the arrival of Christianity in Meghalaya, Khasi Christian philosophy has laid a special emphasis on the rediscovery of the cock in the person of Christ, as to be consistent with the indigenous belief. The bone burial ceremony and cremation represent the eternal re-union of the deceased with the clan. The Christian missionaries brought about changes in the dress, patterns of living, eating habits, and the musical instruments. Christians no longer observed their old religious beliefs and rituals, except for the Law of inheritance, which is still practiced. The traditional form of polity still obtains in the Khasi State with its emphasis on the law of succession, election of chiefs and the conduct of civil administration. The traditional system of education along with its consistent program of community living, were gradually changed.

The change of course, gathered momentum after 1874, when Shillong became the capital of the province of Assam. The local people who were capable of rendering such service have not handled the bulk of trade since new trade consciousness has emerged recently. In order to preserve their lands, industries, markets, traditions, and other elements of their culture, the tribes must be preserved.

Abhedananda, Swami (1999) made a study on universal religion and *Vedanta* and found that the Eternal Religion of the *Vedanta* is free from all sectarianism, bigotry and narrowness. It exists from a beginningless past and leads mankind to the path of everlasting peace, love and freedom. Matter and mind come from a common source, known as *Brahman*. God is personal and impersonal, determinate and indeterminate, *saguna* and *nirguna Brahman*. He found that God is beyond the limitations of these positive and negative categories. *Atman* is a part of God; heaven and hell are the creation of human beings and purity of heart is the precondition for God-consciousness as well as for vision of God; *Mukti* is freedom from the bondage of ignorance as human beings are enchained in the slavery of selfish desires.

Lokeshwarananda, Swami (1999) made a study on *Swami Prabhananda: His Pioneering Work in the East Khasi Hills* and found that Swami Prabhananda who hailed from Sylhet to Khasi society in September 1920, slowly won the hearts of the Khasis. He wrote a couple of textbooks in the Khasi language. He opened couple of schools in the neighbouring villages. Though he faced a lot of opposition, yet he succeeded in establishing a number of schools of various grades through which the Khasi children could have an access to education without any danger of their religious beliefs and traditions being undermined. He also found that the Mission has made an impact on the social, economic, religious and cultural life of the Khasis.

Bag, G.N. (2001) in his study on rural transformation found that improving the living conditions of the rural poor has been given top priority right from independence of our country. Agriculture is the main occupation that needs special attention in order to transform the rural life of the people in North East India to enhance agricultural productivity. Governments of different North East India states should discourage the practice of *jhuming* and ought to encourage the connected departments to provide necessary inputs like HYV seeds, irrigation, and adoption of cash crops, multiple crops and improved methods of cultivation. Development as a process will become effective only when it becomes a mass movement because if development is for the people it has to be by the people also.

Bernes, L. Mawrie (2001) in his study on the Khasis and their natural environment found that every Khasi believes that these hills and valleys are sacred and everything in them has lots of stories to tell mankind. Respect for the ancestors, which is a strong point among the Khasis, makes the love and attachment to their land even more intensive. Khasis believe in God (U Blei) as the Prime Cause of everything that has come into existence. The Khasi legends of creation show us that according to the original plan of the Creator God, humans and the rest of creation were meant to stay in perfect communion. Religion for the Khasis is neither a human affair alone nor a monopoly of human beings; nature takes part in their religious practices. Human beings are responsible for the loss of harmony in creation because of sin. The role of nature in Khasi ethics and religion is indicative of the quality and propensity of their relationship with their natural environment. It is a lamentable fact that the people living in the modern era have distanced themselves from nature. The pristine relationship that existed once upon a time has disappeared due to man's selfish attitude. The result is a sort of enmity between humans and nature. As long as this mentality is not opposed through eco-education, nothing can be done to put an end to these destructive forces.

Kolay, Swapan Kumar (2001) made a study of ecology, economy and tribal development and found that due to various welfare activities on the part of the Government, changes in the ecology and environment have taken place. The welfare schemes of the Government have not been enjoyed by the tribals. The need of the hour is that plans and programmes undertaken by the Government should be scientifically suited for the tribals in order to bring about a true economic development.

Dutta, Sujit Kumar (2002) in his study on the functioning of the Autonomous District Councils in Meghalaya, found that the *Syiem*, his ministers and other officials were holding the office but they had been divested of their real power, which was vested in the Deputy Commissioner. The objective of the study was to find out the exact role being played by the Autonomous District Councils in Meghalaya. The very purpose of creating District Councils was to protect the tribals, their cultural heritage and their socio-economic life. But on the contrary the Committee responsible for setting up such bodies failed to understand the sentiment of the local chiefs, as a result of which the conflict between District Councils and the chiefs of the 25 states started. The study showed that the existing District Councils in Meghalaya are not at all fulfilling the local needs; rather they fulfil the interest of a few affluent people. The *Syiems* were not involved in developmental programmes of the Government. They were just titular heads who enjoyed some tributes according to the desire of the local people.

Khongsdier, R. (2002) having studied fertility and mortality differentials among the War Khasis of Meghalaya found that age at marriage has a positive association with fertility behaviour among tribal women. Fertility was higher among those women who marry early after puberty. He suggested that education is a key factor of development since it has a profound influence on demographic variables and other indicators of health and nutritional status of a population. It was suggested that the best health development agenda for the developing countries is to increase investment in formal education. Female education has a significant impact on maternal and child health as it enhanced the knowledge and skills of mothers in health care, practice concerning the age of marriage, nutrition, prevention and treatment of diseases. Maternal education is related to child health because it reduces the cost of public health programmes relating to information on health technology, increases household income and productivity of health inputs.

Joshi, H.G. (2004) investigating the socio-religious, cultural and political life of the Khasis and Jaintias both in the past and present found that Khasi society has greatly been transformed by many changes which have taken place in recent times beginning with the entry of the British and the annexation first of the Khasi Hills (in 1833) and then of the Jaintia Hills (in 1835). These changes have broken down the age-old isolation of the Khasis and Jaintias and brought about far-reaching results. When a society changes from its traditional moorings into a modern society there is a gradual change in life styles and outlook on the world. Thorough changes came in the role of women in Meghalaya in general and in the East Khasi Hills District in particular. The researcher suggested that a strong women's movement is needed to highlight their rights and to cause the political authorities to grant 30 % reservation to them in order to enable them to share with manpower in the policy and decision-making process at all levels.

Shaljan, A.M. (2004) in his article (published in Economic and Political Weekly) on population, gender and development found that the symptoms of environment degradation are related to rapid population growth. This has resulted in the depletion of vegetation. The growing number of people has led to massive soil erosion, which has posed a threat to the sustainability of the Khasis and to the country's environment. The researcher suggested that the Government should start implementing programmes aimed at bringing about sustainable development.

Roy Jeebon (2005) in his study about one God wrote that Khasi religion was the most perfect, possessing the essence of all religions. Conversion to another religion, be it Hinduism, Christianity, Islam or any other religion would toss them into a cultural vacuum. Their God is the Formless Creator, Omnipotent, Omniscience and Omnipresent, who cares for all people of the universe with absolute equality. God created the world and all things in it. Only he, who obeys God's command and acts according to His will, finds happiness. Hell is the punishment for transgression and heaven is the reward for righteousness. Hell, however, is not a place of suffering.

Stephen, Abraham (2005) conducted a research on the social philosophy of Swami Vivekananda and its relevance to modern India and found that the social philosophy of Vivekananda emerged as a result of personal confrontation with the meaning of God in social life. The national disaster caused by colonialism brought the social degradation of the motherland with the material prosperity of Western society. The degradation of the Indian social situation resulted from weak-mindedness, lack of self-confidence and neglect of Hindu spirituality. He suggested that social service should be rendered in the spirit of utter unselfishness. The aim of this research was to see how far it was relevant for modern society.

From the above literature review it is very clear that a lot of studies have been done on the teachings and activities of the Ramakrishna Mission in India and on various aspects of the Khasi society. But hardly any research has been done so far on the work and teachings of the Ramakrishna Mission in the East Khasi Hills District and the changes that have been brought about in the socio-cultural and religious life of the Khasis. Therefore the East Khasi Hills District where Ramakrishna Mission has been working for the upliftment of the Khasi society was selected for the research. Next chapter attempts to have a brief historical review of the origin and development of the Ramakrishna Mission in India.

B A a b

Chapter 3

A Brief Historical Review of the Origin and Development of the Ramakrishna Mission in India

Ramakrishna Mission has been active in different parts of India in general and in North East India in particular. It is rooted in the teachings of Sri Ramakrishna Pramahamsha who stressed the equal validity of all religions, the potential divinity of humans, and service to humans, as a way of worshipping God. From its humble beginning in a haunted house in Calcutta in 1886 with a few monks and a few lay followers who did not have a square meal every day, the Movement, which is known as Ramakrishna Mission, has grown into a world organisation. It has been serving the society since 1897 through education, medical care and vocational training. This chapter is an attempt to study the historical Development and activities of the Ramakrishna Mission in mainland India.

Mission Ideology

The ideology of Ramakrishna Math and Mission consists of the eternal principles of Vedanta as lived and experienced by Sri Ramakrishna and expounded by Swami Vivekananda. This ideology, according to the Ramakrishna Mission, has three characteristics. They are: It is modern in the sense that the ancient principles of Vedanta have been expressed in the modern idiom; it is universal, that is, it is meant for the whole humanity; it is practical in the sense that its principles can be applied in day-to-day life to solve the problems of life.

Motto

The motto of the Mission was: "Doing well to the world with a spirit of worship is to pave way for one's own salvation."

General History of the Ramakrishna Mission in Main Land India

The Mission is a distinct organisation with separate management, funds, constitution and well-defined fields of activities. Having achieved considerable amount of success for his work in the West, Swami Vivekananda came back to India in January 1897. On his return to Calcutta he was welcomed by the monks and the public. He reminded the other disciples of the words of Sri Ramakrishna and spoke to them eloquently of the glory of the monastic life. Inspired by his words, they all resolved to renounce the world and became monks.[1]

Vivekananda's teachings set in motion those forces which could eventually bring in the western civilisation the needed qualitative changes.[2] For the purpose of establishing his work on a firm basis, Swami Vivekananda summoned all the monks and the lay disciples of Sri Ramakrishna to a meeting at Balaram Bose's house on 1st May 1897. He told them that he had come to the conclusion that without an organisation nothing great and solid could be achieved. He proposed that an association should be formed in the name of the master.[3]

The Ramakrishna Mission was founded on 1st May, 1897 after the passing away of Sri Ramakrishna Pramahansa in August 1886 and was registered on May 4, 1909 under the Act XXI of 1860 of the Governor General of India in Council, registration no. S/1917 of 1909-10. It was revised according to the West Bengal Act XXVI of 1961.[4] He established the monastic order with a social vision. He thus incorporated social service into Indian monasticism. Though Ramakrishna Math and Ramakrishna Mission, with their respective branches, are distinct legal entities, they are closely related to the Governing Body of the Mission which was made up of the Trustees of the Math. The administrative work of the Mission is mostly in the hands of the monks of the Ramakrishna Mission and both have their

---

[1] Swami Gambhirananda, *The Apostles of Ramakrishna*, Calcutta: Advaita Ashrama, 1995, 30.
[2] Swami Budhananda, *The Ramakrishna Movement*, Calcutta: Advaita Ashrama, 1994, 135.
[3] Swami Gambhirananda, *The Apostles of Ramakrishna*, op.cit., 66.
[4] Swami Vivekananda, "Introduction", *Ramakrishna Mission: Home of Service*, (Varanasi: Ramakrishna Mission Home of Service, 2001), 5.

headquarters at Belur Math.[5] Though both the organisations take up charitable and philanthropic activities, the former lays emphasis on religion and preaching while the latter is devoted mainly to welfare service of various kinds.[6]

The first Governing Body consisted of twenty monks. They were: Swami Brahmananda, Advaitananda, Saradannanda, Premananda, Shivananda, Akhandananda, Trigunatitananda, Subodhananda, Abhedananda, Turiyananda, Shuddhananda, Budhananda, Atmananda, Sachchidananda, Virajananda, Achalananda, Mahimananda, Shankarananda, Dhirananda and Nirbhayananda. Swami Brahmananda became the president, Swami Advaitananda Vice-President, Swami Premananda Treasurer, Swami Saradananda Secretary, and Swami Shuddhananda Accountant.[7]

After the execution of the Trust, Swami Vivekananda, the first President, stepped down from the Presidentship of the organisation in favour of Swami Bramananda. Swami Brahmananda was elected as the next president on February 12, 1901. At that time, the local municipality wanted to tax the Math premises on the plea that it was not a religious establishment, but rather a garden-house of Swamiji. The suit was contested up to the Calcutta High Court, which decreed in favour of the Math on February 23, 1901.[8]

In the opinion of Swami Vivekananda, the Mission is an institution through which the monks in co-operation with laymen and associates carry on a wide range of educational, medical and humanitarian service. He believed that the future social development of the nation depended upon the monks' self-denying activities which slowly will attract others to take part in this task.

---

[5] n.n., *Ramakrishna Math and Ramakrishna Mission: Their History, Ideals and Activities*, Hawrah: Ramakrishna Math and Ramakrishna Mission, 2007, n.p.

[6] Swami Vivekananda, "INTRODUCTION", *Ramakrishna Mission Home of Service, Centenary Memorial Annual Report (2000-2001)*, Varanasi: Ramakrishna Mission, Home of Service, 2001, 5-6.

[7] Swami Gambhirananda, *History of the Ramakrishna Math and Mission*, Calcutta: Advaita Ashrama, 1957, 144.

[8] *Ibid.*

According to the Mission report, in June 1899 Swami Vivekananda went again to the West and returned to India in January 1901. In the same year he went on a pilgrimage to East Bengal and Assam and delivered lectures at Dacca, Shillong and other places. Due to ill health he returned to the Belur Math before the annual birthday ceremony of Sri Ramakrishna in 1902. He inaugurated a centre at Varanasi in the month of July of the same year. He breathed his last on 4th July 1902.[9]

After the passing away of Swami Vivekananda, the first thing that Swami Brahmananda did was the consolidation of the Mission work at the headquarters. Swamiji made several tours in North and South India. He received inspiration from the existing centres, with the result that new centres began to spring up. He encouraged the humanitarian work. According to him, one can not do really unselfish work unless one's whole mind is given to God. As a result of his influence many young men joined the Mission.[10]

According to the Mission report, Swami Shivananda went to Benaras in the middle of 1902 and extended the activities of the Mission. The Ramakrishna Mission branch had been organised in Tamil Nadu under the Ramakrishna Sevaka Samiti by Kalipada Ghose, a disciple of Sri Ramakrishna. In 1910 another society came to be formed on similar lines by a group of South Indian devotees.[11]

In between 1911 and 1916, the work of the Ramakrishna Mission made progress. The Mission laid the foundation stone at Travancore in October 1912. The president of the Mission inaugurated another *ashrama* building at Haripad in 1913. Swami Brahmananda along with Swami Shivananda and Swami Turyananda went to Kankhal and worshipped Durga goddess. From there they went to Varanasi where the worship of Kali goddess was performed. At Varanasi Swami Brahmananda took

---

[9] Swami Gambhirananda, *History of Ramakrishna Math and Ramakrishna Mission*, Calcutta: Advaita Ashrama, 1983, 120-123.

[10] *Ibid.*, 100-101.

[11] *Ibid.*, 198.

an opportunity to reaffirm the fundamental belief of the Mission that the service it renders to suffering humanity is really a worship of God. His next visit to Varanasi was in October, 1913. He remained in North India for more than a year. During his one year visit to North India he visited different Mission centres. He returned to the headquarters on November 26, 1914. During his visit many young monks got inspiration.

A new Vivekananda Ashrama was established in 1915 by Swami Virajananda at Shyamala Tal village in Almora district. A charitable dispensary was also started there since the medical facility was not available. A third centre sprang up under the supervision of Swami Karunananda in 1916 at Kishenpur. Swami Premananda, who by his two tours in 1916 and 1917 had sown the seeds of future Ramakrishna centres, suffered from Kala-azar and epidemic influenza in 1918. Swami Adbhutananda too passed away at Varanasi on July 21, 1920.

The funds of the Mission are obtained from Government grants, public contributions, sale of literature, fees from students, etc.[12] Swami Saradananda visited Varanasi on November 25, 1919, and stayed in the Advaita Ashrama for two months helping the monks there. During his visit the Mission established centres at Kankhal, Vrindaban, Allahabad, Sargachhi and Barisal. In September, 1919, flood relief work was started in Burma under the leadership of Swami Shyanananda. He then came to Rangoon with his assistant, Swami Dhyanananda to stay at the guest house in Belur.[13]

Swami Saradananda had long been engaged in solving organisational problems. In May, 1921, Swami Brahmananda left for Madras with Swami Shivananda to open the newly constructed permanent building of the Ramakrishna Mission Students' Home, which he did on the 10th of May, 1921. From that day the home came to adolescence and started growing in structure. One of its achievements was that it started a residential high school in 1922. A training centre was also inaugurated by

---

[12] *Ibid.*, 152.
[13] *Ibid.*

Swami Brahmananda at Madras. After his return from Madras, Swami Brahmananda fell sick and died in 1922. Within four months Swami Turyananda also passed away at Varanasi.

After the death of Swami Brahmananda, Swami Abhedananda who spent many years in the west, came back to Belur Math. He had adjustment problems with other Swamis. He urged Swami Brahmananda to grant him a separate apartment in the upper room. He entrusted the responsibility to other monks and planned to visit Kashmir and Tibet. During this period there was a demand for expansion of Math and Mission. The urge for expansion was more in the Mission. But the spread of the Mission was held in check only by the shortage of monastic helpers and the need of proceeding cautiously so as not to endanger efficiency and permanence. The Mission annual report shows that the Mission opened centres at Hawrah, Varanasi, Almora, Allahabad, Mylapore, Bangalore City, Varanasi, Kankhal, Vrindaban, Muthiganj, Allahabad, Murshidabad and Barisal in between 1913 to 1922.[14]

The Vedanta Society expanded during 1924. In November, 1924, Swami Abhedananda purchased some land at Darjeeling, where a year later he established the Ramakrishna Vedanta Ashrama. Outside India in Ceylon a centre came to be organised under the Mission in 1924.[15] In July, 1925, the Society in Calcutta moved to 40 Beadon Street, where the old Swamis of the Belur Math paid him occasional visits. A charitable dispensary was started at Madras in 1925. A general meeting of the Ramakrishna Mission was held on 2nd June, 1925. It was at this meeting that the idea of a convention of all members and workers of the Math and the Mission was proposed. In the same a small centre was opened at Malda in Bengal.

According to the Mission annual report of 1925, the new centres were established in between 1920-1925 at Bankura, Garbeta, Malda, Dinajpur, Mymensingh, Faridpur, Shella and Singapore, which, in fact, were being conducted by the monks

---

[14] Ibid., 179.
[15] Ibid.

of the Order with the approval and under the guidance of the Belur Headquarters.[16]

The Vivekananda Society of Jamshedpur, originally started by some employees of the Tata Iron and Steel Company, was reorganised by the Ramakrishna Mission in 1927. The educational activities took different forms like Students' Homes for boys and girls, orphanages, general schools ranging from the Primary and Night Schools to High Schools and vocational schools. In November, 1927 the Math and Mission had entered into diverse kinds of activities according to the general programme of Swami Vivekananda, and in response to the public demand. But it is now a big educational centre with several branch schools and Students' Homes scattered over the entire city. By the end of 1927 there were not less than 17 permanent branches, 10 others for educational activities, and 8 branches for various types of social work for the uplift of the poor people. Relief and medical help were the two departments which earned a reputation.[17]

A headquarters for all the institutions of Ramakrishna Mission was established at Shillong in 1929 to accomodate Khasi boys. Swami Adyananda was put in-charge of the centre, and through his unremitting zeal, the Mission got a building of its own at 9 Norris Road, which was occupied in February, 1932. In 1933 new centres were started at Dinajpur, Bankura, Trichur, Chandipur, Mymensingh Begerhat and Garbeta.

During the leadership of Swami Shivananda, a lot of work was done to open more branches in different parts of India. During his closing years he undertook long tours, especially in East Bengal, initiating many new members into the Movement. Swamiji had a stroke of thrombosis, which paralysed his right side and made him unable to speak. He died of stroke in 1934. He was succeeded as president by Swami Akhandananda on 13th March, 1934 and Swami Virajananda became secretary on 22nd March of the same year. Swami Akhandananda was a man of vast experience. The Math and Mission expected a

---

[16] Ibid., 216.
[17] Ibid., 215

revolutionary work from him. Even the lay devotees were delighted to have him as the leader.

It was in between 1930-1938 that the new centres were opened at Bhubaneshwar, Allahabad, Dacca, Narayanganj, Sonargaon, Baliati, Jayrambati, Katihar, Midnapore, Tamluk, Contai, Sylhet, Habiganj, Perianaickenpalayam, Kanpur, Vishakhapatnam, Asansol, Silchar, Taki and Dungri near Ranchi,. The foreign centres in Europe and America, however, carried on purely spiritual work consisting in public preaching, group studies, meditation, worship, publication of religious and philosophical books, and so on. According to the general report of the Math and Mission for 1936-37, there were 50 Mission centres and 59 Math centres in India and abroad.

The work in the Khasi Hills and Jaintia Hills, under Swami Prabhananda, went on experimentally till 1936, when the Mission stepped in to assume direct responsibility. Swami Akhandananda died on February 7, 1937 and Swami Vijnananda was elected as the new President. He also did not live long. After his death Swami Suddhananda was made President on 18th May, 1938. After the death of the chief organiser, Swami Prabhananda on December 12, 1938, other Swamis carried on the work successfully. The year 1939 witnessed a new Mission centre at Lahore now in Pakistan.[18]

A decade later in between 1946-47 the number of the Mission centres was 65 and that of the Math centres was 67. During this period, the Mission was the one organisation which was always to the fore in facing any calamity befalling the nation, even from the ravages of nature.[19] The establishment of the centres at Kranchi and Vishakhapatanam was a matter of joy. The Mission constitution underwent some more important changes in 1946, though the line of development was not entirely different from what was implied in the 1937 Rules. One important change was the explicit provision for loans from the headquarters to the

---

[18] *Ibid.*

[19] Swami Budhananda, *The Ramakrishna Movement*, (Calcutta: Advaita Ashrama, 1994), 88.

branches, and from one branch to another with the approval of the headquarters. This helped many institutions to grow quickly. Social service was rendered to eradicate the hindrances that stood between human beings and their destiny.[20] Educational work took different forms like Students' Homes for boys and girls orphanages, general schools ranging from the primary and night schools to high schools and vocational schools.

After the attainment of independence by India in 1947, the Organisation received massive help from the central and state governments. This help cause phenomenal expansion of the work of the organisation. The socio-economic forces operative in the country has added new dimensions to the thinking and actions of the Order in regard to its scope of service.[21] With the growth of the work spread over the whole district, the Mission decided in 1949 to reorganise it under two separate centres- one at Shillong with its temple, preaching work, library, charitable dispensary and one primary school, and the other at Cherrapunji with its high school, hostel and other feeder institutions located in inaccessible villages near about. The Mission has been running many educational institutions to impart knowledge to all strata of society and engaged itself in social service of different kinds in order to relieve people of their physical suffering.

During 1948-1965 the Mission did a lot of relief work. In 1954 the Mission conducted Flood Relief Work in different places of Assam, West Bengal, Bihar, Orissa and East Pakistan. Such relief work was also done in 1955 in Tamil Nadu and Uttar Pradesh. In July, 1956, the Mission centre of Mumbai in conjunction with Rajkot Ashrama, started the work of building three new villages for the distressed people hit by earthquake at Anjar in Kutch.[22]

The Mission had many political and social problems after 1966. The Math and Mission had to struggle hard to keep the

---

[20] V.C. Samuel, *The Ramakrishna Movement: The World Mission of Hinduism*, Bangalore: CISRS, 1959, 1.

[21] Swami Budhananda, *The Ramakrishna Movement*, Calcutta: Advaita Ashrama, 1994, 88.

[22] n.n., *History of Ramakrishna Math and Ramakrishna Mission*, op.cit., 302-303.

work going. During this period many dedicated Swamis worked hard for the smooth running of the Mission.

In 1977 four new Mission centres at Rajpur, Gauhati, Along and Narottam Nagar were added. In 1979-80 there were altogether 119 centres under the movement. More centres were inaugurated in different parts of India during 1980-81. The latest 1994 information of the Ramakrishna Order (both Ramakrishna Math & Ramakrishna Mission) shows that excluding the headquarters at Belur Math, there were 132 branch centres and 26 sub-centres.[23]

Excluding the headquarters at Belur, there were 141 branches in all, of which 62 were Mission centres, 27 combined Math and Mission centres and 52 Math centres during 1999-2001. Out of 141 centres, 105 centres were located in India and 36 abroad. Moreover, attached to some of the branches there were 30 sub-centres, where monastic workers lived permanently.[24]

From its very inception the Ramakrishna Mission has been rendering relief services to the people suffering from natural calamities like flood, famine, drought etc. The Mission has done hundreds of relief works in India, Burma and Sri Lanka. The unselfish service rendered by the Mission centres in India through hospitals, dispensaries, educational institutions and various other ways, is being increasingly appreciated by the Government of India and the public. Today, the patients treated in the Mission hospitals and dispensaries are more than 42 lakhs. During 2006-2007 the Mission spent 5.34 crores of rupees on relief and rehabilitation work in different states of India. The total amount spent in 2007 on medical services was ₹ 26.76 crores. Today the Movement runs 153 branches.[25]

Ramakrishna Mission in North East India

The significant tour of Swami Vivekananda in North East India left a rejuvenating effect on the cultural and spiritual lives of the

---

[23] Swami Budhananda, *The Ramakrishna Movement, op.cit.,* 89.

[24] Swami Vivekananda, "Introduction", *Ramakrishna Mission: Home of Service, op.cit.,* 6.

[25] Personal Interview with the Secretary at Goal Park in Calcutta in 2006.

people. He, in course of his tour to the North East India, visited Gauhati and Shillong in April-May, 1901. During his stay at Gauhati and Shillong he delivered several spiritual lectures on Vedantic teachings. After that Swami Prabhananda was the first missionary who started his work at Shella in the East Khasi Hills District of Meghalaya. Gradually the Mission work has spread in different parts of the region. Some permanent centres have come into existence. The work in the Khasi and Jaintia Hills, under Swami Prabhananda, went on experimental basis till 1936, when the Mission stepped in to assume direct responsibility. Swami Prabhananda died in 1938 and after his death, other Swamis carried on the work successfully. With the growth of the work spread over a whole district, the Ramakrishna Mission in 1949 decided to recognise it under two separate centres. At present there are 9 affiliated centres in the whole region. They are: Shillong, Cherrapunji, Silchar, Karimganj, Agartala, Gauhati, Narottam Nagar, Along and Itanagar.[26]

The different kinds of activities like schools, medical service, hostels, libraries, computer training and vocational training are taken up by the Mission. Through these works many people are benefited educationally, culturally and economically. There are many sub-centres which are run privately by the members of the Ramakrishna Mission since 1940. These sub-centres are at Amtali, Badarpur, Barpeta, Bongaigaon, Borjhar, Dabaka, Dibrugarh, Digboi, Diphu, Dharmanagar (Tripura), Dhubri, Doom Dooma, Duliajan, Goalpara, Golaghat, Haflong, Haibargaon, Hailakandi, Hojai, Imphal (Manipur), Jorhat, Kailasahar, Kohima (Nagaland), Konaban, Lanka, Lumding, Majbat, Makum, Margherita, Nogaon (Assam), Tezpur (Assam), Bandu and Udaipur (Tripura). In these sub-centres medical services, educational work, relief works and daily religious programmes were conducted by the active members of the Mission.[27]

With regard to the service for the upliftment of the tribal communities, the Ramakrishna Mission has been at work in

---

[26] Swami Prameyananda, *"Ramakrishna-Vivekananda Movement in the North-East"*, *Golden Jubilee (1937-1987)*, (Shillong: Ramakrishna Mission, 1987), 37-38.

[27] *Ibid.*, 38-41.

Arunachal Pradesh, Assam, Maharashtra, Meghalaya, Orissa and West Bengal. The Mission came to the East Khasi Hills District in 1920 through Ketaki Maharaj of Sylhet.

Activities of Ramakrishna Mission

The Mission did not limit its service to humanity alone as the representation of God by providing temporary relief only at the hours of distress. The Mission's programme of constructive service including the spread of man-making education through establishment of necessary institutions, encouraged development of arts, sciences and industries, provided medical help to suffering people by establishing of dispensaries, help to the infirm, invalid and the afflicted, relief work among people suffering from natural or other calamities and propagation of Vedanta in the light of the life and teachings of Sri Ramakrishna through living and preaching. The following section deals with the activities of the Ramakrishna Mission:

1. Education

The Mission pays special attention to education. The activities of the Ramakrishna Mission are aimed to establish and maintain schools, colleges, orphanages, laboratories, hospitals and dispensaries. The Mission has nothing to do with politics. The Mission & the Math with their limited resources have been trying their best to provide education to the people of India so that they may play their due role in the making of a better India. In 2001 it ran 5 Degree Colleges, 5 Teachers' Training Colleges, 13 Higher Secondary Schools, 32 Secondary Schools, 7 Junior Technical Industrial Schools, 211 non-formal educational units, 3 institutes of agriculture, 5 schools of languages, 1 Sanskrit College, 2 Sanskrit Schools, 4 Polytechnics, 97 Students' Homes and 5 Orphanages throughout India. The Mission and the Math spent ₹ 72.27 crores in 2007 on educational activities in the whole country.[28] It also takes interest in the uplift of women and youth. Today the Ramakrishna Mission runs 12 Degree colleges, 20

---

[28] n.n., *The Ramakrishna Movement*, (Calcutta: The Ramakrishna Mission Institute of Culture, 2007).

Higher Secondary Schools, 31 Secondary Schools, 135 Schools of different denominations, 6 Institutes of Agriculture, 2 Schools of Languages, 1 Sanskrit College, 3 Sanskrit Schools, 4 Polytechnics, 7 Computer Training Centres, 270 Non-formal educational centres, 105 Student's home and hostels, 6 orphanages and 1 blind school. During 2003-04, the Math and the Mission spent ₹ 86.14 crores on education and 1,23,222 boys and girls received education from these institutions. The total number of students who have got their education in these institutions during 2007-08 was more than 2,16,376. During the same year, the Mission spent ₹ 90.2 crores on their education.[29]

While providing education, medical services and distress relief, the Ramakrishna Mission paid special attention to those who were weak from both material and cultural points of view. The centres in India in general and in the North Eastern states in particular pay special attention to the poor and weaker sections of the society. The aim of the Mission is to make the poor and the backward people stand on their own feet, to expose them to the main stream of Indian culture and to raise them to the status of equality with the rest of the countrymen. The Mission as propounded by Swami Vivekananda is to impart and promote the study of the Vedanta and its principles.[30]

2. Medical Service

As part of their programme of service to the sick and the dying, the Ramakrishna Mission runs indoor hospitals, dispensaries, mobile health units, old-age homes and special eye-camps. In April 1957, the Movement had 12 hospitals and 60 indoor dispensaries in India. By the end of the year these numbers were increased to 13 hospitals and 67 dispensaries. The indoor hospitals of the Mission are well equipped and the treatment given is mostly free. In 1999-2000, the Movement run 14 hospitals with 2047 beds, which served 88,185 indoor patients and 23, 82,628 out-patients. In 2003-04 the Mission had 2047 beds in 14 hospitals

---

[29] *Ibid.*, 25.
[30] Swami Gambhirananda, *History of Ramakrishna Math and Ramakrishna Mission*, (Calcutta: Advaita Ashrama, 1983), 149.

which served 1, 01,626 in-patients. In 2004-05 the Mission treated 24, 42,760 outpatients and 73,848 in-patients in their hospitals. The Mission also run 89 dispensaries. In these dispensaries 35, 93,933 patients were treated. The Mission has the capacity of 42 mobile clinics providing medical facilities to 14, 45,370 patients. The Mission spent a sum of about ₹ 26.81 crores towards medical services in 2005.[31] The number of the patients in 2007-08 has gone up. The approach to give priority to the poor, women, children and aged in hospital services has continued. In 2007-08 the number of patients treated in the Mission hospitals was 42.56,754.

3. Relief Work

Ramakrishna Mission undertook relief and rehabilitation works. The headquarters as well as some of the branches were involved in these works. Relief of evacuees and refugees and their rehabilitation work was done on a very large scale during worst national calamities. In 1954 the Mission conducted flood relief work in different places of Assam, West Bengal, Bihar, Orissa, and East Pakistan. In 1954 flood relief was given to Cooch Bihar, Dacca, Darbhanga, East & West Godabari, Faridpur, Jalpaiguri, Lakhimpur and Purnea. Such relief was repeated in 1955. On November 30, 1955, a cyclone followed by a tidal wave caused havoc in some parts of Tanjore and Tamil Nadu. The Mission Centre of Madras gave relief to the flood affected people. By February 1957, three colonies were established. In July, 1956, the Mission centre of Mumbai in conjunction with Rajkot Ashrama started the work of building three new villages for the distressed people hit by earthquake at Anjar in Kutch. The Mumbai branch spent 500000 rupees for constructing houses for the needy in that area.

The Mission branch at Madras distributed flood relief in Nellore district and riot relief in Ramnad district of Tamil Nadu. Building of new colonies and repair of damaged houses were taken up in Kutch and Surat districts in 1960. The Mission spent an amount of ₹ 8,50,000. Temporary relief work was also undertaken during

---

[31] n.n., *Ramakrishna Mission, A Report on the 95th Annual General Meeting*, 2004, 11.

the same period. A cyclone caused great damage in Andhra Pradesh and Tamil Nadu. The Mission took the rehabilitation programme after the initial distribution of relief material consisting of food grains, utensils, clothes and other essential commodities of various types.

The agriculture of Uttar Pradesh, Bihar, and some parts of West Bengal faced serious distress due to scarcity of rainfall in 1966. Flood relief was given to the people of Delhi and Midnapur in 1967-1968. The crops of these states became dry. The Ramakrishna Mission stepped into these draught-hit areas for distributing food-stuffs and other essential commodities. This way the Mission helped 79,139 people in 2149 villages.[32] The Mission spent 44,00,000 rupees during 1966. In 1971-72 relief was also distributed among the flood affected people in West Bengal and Bihar. During 1999-2000, the Mission spent ₹ 5.34 crores on relief and rehabilitation work. Public support is the principal resource on which relief work depends.

4. Rural Uplift Work

One of the concerns of the Mission has been the poor people in our country. While providing education, medical service and distress relief, the Mission pays special attention to those who are weak from both material and cultural point of view. The whole concept of integral rural development is to help the people to help themselves. That was the objective of the community development programme initiated by the Government of India. For the farm and factory labourers the Mission started a number of night schools, non-formal and high schools. According to the Ramakrishna Mission, both the headquarters and its branches provided scholarships and stipends to a large number of students. In 2003-04 a sum of ₹ 19.8 million rupees were spent by the Mission educational institutions on the uplift of the poor students in India. This amount was in addition to the huge amount spent on the medical treatment of the poor patients. The Mission also helped women of different sections of the society. It kept the

---

[32] Swami Gambhirananda, *History of Ramakrishna Math and Ramakrishna Mission, op.cit.,* 329.

males reminding of their duties towards women. Sri Ramakrishna's identification of all women as mother was borne out by his attitude towards Bhairavi Brahmani, a Vaishnava devotee of a high order and well versed in the Tantrika Sadhana.[33] Swami Ranganathananda said that India has no ideological restriction against women's development, apart from the feudal social stagnation, which is still very powerful. He also said that education would bring many other blessings like population control.[34]

The Ramakrishna Mission puts more emphasis on the education and the advancement of women and men. The development of the rural people anticipated creating in them an awareness of their surroundings and understanding of their problems.[35] The Mission believes that women could solve their own problems without the intervention of men if they are given proper education. Education will make them much more aware of the role they have to play for the betterment of their society and families. With education, they will be able to provide income to their families.[36]

5. Home for the Aged

In response to the persistent demands from the people, the Mission has started in the year 1983 a centre at Barisha near Kolkata to look after the aged. It is a complete residential home with spiritual, medical and recreational facilities.

6. Spread of Spiritual Ideas and Cultural Work

The Mission lays emphasis on the dissemination of the spiritual and cultural ideas of India. It does it through regular classes, meetings, public celebrations and publication of books. Attempts

---

[33] n.n., *Sri Ramakrishna and the Women: An In-depth Study*, (Shillong: Ramakrishna Mission Ashrama, n.d.), 12.

[34] Swami Ranganathanda, *Women in the Modern Age*, (Mumbai: Bhartiya Vidya Bhavan, 2004), 26-36.

[35] Swami Prabhananda, *Swami Vivekananda's Vision of Rural Development*, (Narendrapur: Ramakrishna Mission Ashrama, 1989), 73.

[36] Mrs. Gankhu Sumnyan, "Upliftment of Tribal Women," *Narottam*, (Tirap: Ramakrishna Mission School, n.d.), 25-26.

have been made to make the followers aware of their moral and spiritual legacy. The Mission teaches that the solution of all human problems lies in man's becoming man in all his dimensions, by manifesting his divinity. It teaches that Vedanta, the very breath of the Mission, offers to mankind the solution to all human problems. It also teaches that all human beings are potentially divine. They are also taught to respect all religions as valid paths to the same God and love all beings as their own selves. It is also noteworthy that the propagation of the master's message was taken up by the member Ashramas of the Bhavaprachar Parishads in different parts of the country.

Almost every centre of the Ramakrishna Mission maintains a shrine dedicated to Sri Ramakrishna where ritualistic worship is offered to him every day. At dusk *arti* is done along with congregational singing of hymns and *bhajans*. The most important form of spiritual service, however, is spiritual initiation given by the President or Vice-President of Ramakrishna Order to sincere spiritual seekers.

The study shows that the Ramakrishna Mission has been active in Meghalaya since 1920. It was found that the Mission has been doing a good job. Many families in India have benefited through the service of the Ramakrishna Mission. Many young people have got free education in the Ramakrishna Mission Schools.

B A a b

Chapter 4

Socio-Cultural & Religious Life of the Khasis in the East Khasi Hills District

Meghalaya lies in the extreme north eastern region of India. It is the only state in the entire north east which is matrilineal through lineage and takes the identity solely from the mother. Khasi society has a very rich cultural and religious heritage. As has already been mentioned earlier, this is a study on the Socio-Cultural and Religious life of the Khasis in the East Khasi Hills District of Meghalaya. This chapter provides a description of the Socio-Cultural and Religious life of the Khasis in the East Khasi Hills District of Meghalaya.

A Brief Sketch of Meghalaya State

The state of Meghalaya is one of the seven sister states of North East India. It is surrounded by Assam on the North and East and Bangladesh on the South and West side. Meghalaya literally means "the abode of clouds".[1]

According to Statistics Department Office Record of the Meghalaya state, Meghalaya as a fully-fledged independent state with 7 districts, 32 sub districts, 18 towns, 32 community development blocks, 5780 villages, came into existence on 21 January, 1972. The villages are small and widely dispersed which make the provision of infrastructure and social services very expensive. It is 4000 feet above the sea level.[2] The names of the 7 Districts, according to the State Government Record, are- Jaintia Hills, East Garo Hills, West Garo Hills, East Khasi Hills, West Khasi Hills, Ri-Bhoi, and the South Garo Hills district.[3]

---

[1] H.G. Joshi, *Meghalaya: Past and Present*, (New Delhi: Mittal Publications, 2004), 1.
[2] Henry Lamin, *Economy and Society in Meghalaya*, (Shillong: Har-Anand Publications, 1995), 16.
[3] n.n., *Encyclopedia of North East India: Meghalaya, Vol. IV*, ed. by H.M. Bareh, (New Delhi: Mittal Publications, 2001), 1.

The position of various administrative units in the State, according to the 2005 and 2006-07 Meghalaya Statistical Department Office Record is given below.

Table No. 4.1 Number of Administrative units in Meghalaya

Census Years	Districts	Sub-Districts	Towns	Community Development Blocks	Villages
2005-2006	7	32	18	32	5780
2006- 2007	7	32	18	32	5780

Meghalaya as a full-fledged independent state consists of 85.9 percent tribal population in 2007, according to the State Government Office Record.[4] The majority of the tribal population in the State are the indigenous tribes mainly known as Khasis, Jaintia, and Garo.[5]

Meghalaya State extends over an area of 22,429 square kilometres.[6] The total forest area in the State is 8510 sq. km. with only 993 sq km under the control of the State Government and the rest under the District Councils and private managements.[7] It lies in the North Eastern Region of India between 25^0 and 26^015 north latitude and 89^0 45 and 92^0 47 E longitudes. It has the world's wettest place- Mawsynram located 58 km away from Shillong with an annual average of 486.5 inches of rain.[8] The main tribes in Meghalaya are: *Khasi, Pnars* or *Jaintias, Achiks* or *Garos*.[9] As a matter of fact, the most common definition of the word Khasi society is that which consists of the Bhoi, the War and the Lyngngam. Although belonging to the same group of matrilineal society, the same law of inheritance does not rule them in the same way but varies from group to group.

---

[4] Henry Lamin, *Economy and Society in Meghalaya, op.cit.,* 16.
[5] n.n., *Encyclopedia of North East India: Meghalaya, Vol. IV, op.cit.,* 1.
[6] H.G. Joshi, *Meghalaya: Past and Present, op.cit.,* 6.
[7] n.n., *Encyclopedia of North-East India: Meghalaya, Vol. IV, op.cit.,* 3; see also Pocket Statistical Hand Book, Meghalaya, 2003, 16-18.
[8] G.W. Kharkongor, "Life, Religion and Culture of the People of Meghalaya," *Heritage of Meghalaya* (Shillong: Directorate of Art and Culture, n.d.), 14-20.
[9] P.R. Kyndiah, *Meghalaya: Yesterday and Today*, (New Delhi: Controller of Publications, 2005), xlvi.

Population of Meghalaya

The population of the State in 2007 was 26, 62,194. Out of the total population in the state 20, 01,969 persons (75.2 percent) live in rural areas and 6, 60,225 persons (24.8 percent) in the urban areas. It's rank was 24th among all the States and Union Territories of India. The net addition of population during the past decade was 3, 43,372 persons.[10]

The State of Meghalaya has registered +15.71 percent growth rate of population in 1911, +7.21 percent in 1921, +13.83 percent in 1931, +15.59 percent in 1941, +8.97 percent in 1951, +27.03 percent in 1961, +31.50 percent in 1971 respectively as compared to +32.04 percent growth during 1971-1981. The State growth rate of population during 1981-1991 was 32.86 percent that is higher than the national growth of +21.5 percent. The growth rate of the population in Meghalaya during 2005-2007 was +14.8. Among the Districts, Ri-Bhoi District due to non-Khasis from outside the state has the highest growth of population during 2005-2007.

Literacy Rate

The literacy rate is measured as a percentage of population aged seven years and above and as per the Census, literacy is defined as the ability to read and write the person's name. Higher literacy levels in a State denote rising socio-economic development and universal literacy is a crucial step towards achieving overall progress. The literacy rate of the state was 62.6 percent at the 2001 Census, which was significantly lower than the 73.5 percent recorded at the close of 2007. The rural urban gap in the literacy rate can be seen by the fact that against 56.3 percent literacy rate in the rural areas, 80.3 percent literacy rate was recorded in the urban areas. It may also be seen that the male and female gap in literacy is comparatively low. The literacy rate for male was 69.2 percent and for female 68.3 percent in the rural areas, while both male and female literacy rate was above 80 percent in the urban areas as per the 2007 Government Office Record. Among

---

[10] n.n., *The North-East And Sikkim*: Performance, Facts and Figures, ed. by Laveesh Bhandari, (New Delhi: Indicus, 2007), 101-102

the Districts, East Khasi Hills District had the highest literacy rate of 76.1 percent of the total population in 2007. The district wise population and literacy rate of Meghalaya State, according to Government Office Record in 2007, is shown in the following table:

Table No. 4.2 District-wise Population and
Literacy Rate of Meghalaya State in 2007

Meghalaya State	Total Population	Male	Female	Literacy Rate in Percent
State Population	26,62,194	13,50,870	3,11,324	73.5%
West Garo Hills	5,87,080	2,98,330	2,88,750	67.7%
East Garo Hills	2,97,128	1,51,153	1,45,975	73.6%
South Garo Hills	1,14,561	59,002	55,559	65.0%
West Khasi Hills	3,47,035	1,76,312	1,70,723	70.1%
East Khasi Hills	7,33,779	3,70,481	3,63,298	76.1%
Jaintia Hills	3,45,956	1,73,367	1,72,589	69.7%
Ri-Bhoi	**2,36,655**	**1,21,917**	**1,14,738**	**67.7%**

Table No. 4.2 shows the District wise population and literacy rate of Meghalaya State. The total population of the state in 2007 was 26,62,194. The population of the East Khasi Hills District in the same year was the highest (7,33,749). The literacy rate in 2007 in the whole State was 73.5 percent.

Meaning of the Term Khasi

As stated above, the term Khasi is a general name given to various tribes and sub-tribes that inhabit the Khasi and Jaintia Hills. They are- the Khynriams, the Pnars (or the Jaintias), the Bhois, the Wars and the Lyngngam. All these groups of people are commonly known as the Khasis. All of them take the title of their mother. The term Khasi has a particular significance. Etymologically, the term "Khasi" is a compound of two words, "Kha" and "Si". 'Kha' means 'born of', while 'si' means 'mother'.[11]

---

[11] Dr. C. Wolflang, "Property Rights And Entrepreneurship In A Matriliny", *The Dynamics of Family System In A Matriliny of Meghalaya*, ed. by Margaret B. Challam, (Shillong: Directorate of Printing & Stationary, 1999), 16.

Therefore, the term 'Khasi' means 'born of mother'. The origin of the Khasi is still a matter of debate among scholars.

It is relevant to add here that the various names of clans bear their mothers' name. This system of ascribing the names of clans after their mothers is intimately related to a matrilineal system of the people themselves.

Origin of the Khasis

The origin of the Khasis is still a matter of debate amongst scholars. They depended on oral traditions, which were passed on from generation to generation.[12] There is a tradition among the Khasis that they originally came into Assam via the Patkaoi range which is said to be a hill they came across on their journey. Mr. Shadwell said that the Khasis originally have come into Assam from Burma via the Patkoi range, having followed the route of one of the Burmese invasions.[13]

Gurdon states that many affinities can be traced among the Khasis and the people of the Far-East, particularly the Mon-Anam (Mon-Khmer) and on the grounds of such resemblance, he concluded that the Khasis came from the East and have used the same route of migration which was followed by other immigrants from Burma.[14]

There is a tradition that Amwi - Khasis reached their present land from the East and that their ancestors originally connected with the Mekong River in the Cambodian region.[15] Some scholars believe that they established themselves in these hills a long time ago. The migration was from East to West.[16]

According to Gait, the forefathers of the Khasis might have migrated to these hills in pre-historic times.[17] He also believes that Khasis belong to the Mon-Khmer group on the ground that

---

[12] Barnes L. Mawrie, *The Khasis and their Natural Environment* (Shillong: Vendrame Institute Pvt. Ltd., 2001), 3.

[13] P.R. Gurdon, *The Khasis*, (reprinted) Delhi: Low Price Publications, 2002, 10.

[14] Dr. Hamlet Bareh, *The History and Culture of the Khasi People*, Guwahati/Delhi: Spectrum Publications, 1997, 12.

[15] Rev. I. Laringston Kharkongngor, *The Tribal People* (Jaiaw: Shandora Press, 1994), ii.

[16] I.M. Simon, *Meghalaya*, Government of India, 1980, 31.

[17] H.W. Sten, *Meghalaya Year Book, 1980*, (Shillong: Scorpio Printers, 1980), 31.

they speak the same language.[18] Hooker asserts that the Khasis belong to the Indo-Chinese race.[19] J. H. Hutton also postulated a common origin of the Austric-speaking people either in Central Asia or South East Asia.[20] According to one tradition, the ancestors of the Khasis came to the present hills from some far away place somewhere in China.[21]

Homiwell Lyngdoh is of the opinion that Khasis came to these hills from north-eastern direction through Nowgong, Lumding and Halflong areas across the Kupli River. The original place, according to him, was somewhere in Western China, Cambodia, Burma and other regions of the East.[22]

Prof. Ernst Kuhn in 1883 to 1889 made discoveries on the connection between Mon-Khmer of Indo-China (including Khasi of Assam) and Munda of Central India but also with the non-Cowry of the Nicobars and the Sakai-Semang Orang of Malacca. He observes that both "for its vocabulary and structure and sentences, Khasi is strictly connected with Palaung-Wa dialects spoken by the tribes that live along the Central and Upper reaches of the Mekong River." The close sisters of Khasi appear to have been the Mon and Palaung-Riang-Wa dialects of Burma.[23]

J.R. Logan first revealed the discovery of the *Mon-Khmer* language spoken in Burma, Indo-China and Malesia in the middle of the 19th Century.[24]

According to him, the Khasis have a close relationship with the Mons or Talaings of Pegu and Tenasserim; the Khmer of

---

[18] E.A. Gait, *History of Assam* (Kolkata: Thacker Spink & Co., 1963), 32.

[19] Joseph Dalton Hooker, "Notes On Khasi Hills and People", *Journal of the Asiatic Society of Bengal*, Vol. XIII, 1844; see also J.D. Hooker, Himalayan Journals, Vol. II, 1985, 485.

[20] J.N. Chowdhuri, "The Khasi Conjectures About Their Origin", *The Tribes of North-East India*, (ed.), by Sebastian Karotemprel (Shillong: Centre for Indigenous Cultures, 1998), 68.

[21] W.R. Laitflang, "Glimpses of the Festivals and Music of the Khasis", *Festivals and Ceremonies in Meghalaya*, ed. by K.R. Marak & R. Wankhar (Shillong: Department of Art & Culture, n.d.), 1.

[22] H. Lyngdoh, *Ka Niam Khasi*, (Shillong: Ri Khasi Press, 1937), ii-vi.

[23] Ka Syngkhong Jingtip, *The Khasi Cultural Journal*, Vol. I, No. 1, February, 1958, 52.

[24] Mary Pristila Rina Lyngdoh, *The Festivals in the History and Culture of the Khasis*, op.cit., 19.

Cambodia and the inhabitants of Assam. He identifies a tribe called the Palaungs who inhabit the Shan State of Myanmar, as the closest kinsmen of the Khasis.[25]

As per Khasi mythology, human beings already existed with God in heaven. At the request of mother earth, God sent seven of the sixteen groups of human beings to earth to take care of the created world. David Roy says: "The seven huts or roots were seven pairs of virgin women and men created by God to marry. They formed seven houses and from them the country was filled up and rites and ceremonies were obtained."[26]

According to S. C. Sen, it is not possible to decide whether the Khasis are the result of the intrusion of a wave of Mongoloids into the Khasi Hills, where they inter-married with a settled group of Mon-Khmer speaking Proto-Australoids or whether this process took place in South East Asia after which the ancestors of the modern Khasi society were already endowed with approximately the same language.[27]

S. K. Chatterji observes that there had been several exchanges and contacts between the earliest Austrics and races of the Mongoloid family, which led to a formation of sections of Mon-Khmer speakers like the Rmen or the Mon of central and Southern Burma, the Palaung, the Wa of Upper Burma, the Khmer and other Austric speakers of Siam and Indo-China. Khasis appear to be a Mongoloid people who have adopted the language of the earlier race, the Austrics and that they became Austric while in Burma before they advanced into the Khasi Hills of Assam.[28]

Modern research scholars like Walter G. Griffith are of the opinion that the Mundas were the original settlers of this sub continent before the Dravidian and Aryan invasions. They believed that at the time of invasions, they began to migrate.

---

[25] Dr. Hamlet Bareh, *History And Culture of the Khasi People*, op.cit., 16.

[26] David Roy, "Principles of Khasi Culture", *Folk Lore*, Vol. XLII, December 1936 Collection, 30.

[27] N.C.S. Sen, *The Origin and Early History of the Khasi Synteng People* (Kolkata, 1981), 17-18.

[28] S.K. Chatterji, *Kirata-Jana-Krti: The Indo-Mongoloids, their Contribution to the History and Culture of India*, Section 20, 13.

During their migration a group of them came to the North East and settled in central Assam.[29] The funeral ceremonies of the Mundas are very much alike with the Khasis. The manner in which the body is kept before cremation, the way of lighting the fire, the collection of bones after the cremation and offering of food to the dead are some of the common characteristics of these two groups of people.[30]

According to J. N. Chowdhury, remarkable resemblances of funeral ceremonies have been found between Khasis and Mundas, who live now in Madhya Pradesh.[31] There is no denying the fact of striking similarities amongst Khasi megaliths with those of Indonesia and Burma. But it is observed that the methods of erection and the rituals connected with the Khasi megaliths differ in principle and practice with those of others.[32]

But the most accepted theory is that the Khasis came from Burma and belong to the Mon-Khmer group. However, nothing can be ascertained scientifically for reasons of absence of recorded history and documents. Anthropologists and historians continue to conduct research and try to study the origin of the Khasis.

Appearance of Khasis

The Khasis and the Pnars (Jaintias) belong to the same stock. In general, the Khasis are short in stature, having extremely muscular and developed limbs. They have a fair, yellowish complexion. The average height of males is from 5' 2" to 5' 9" and that of females from 5' to 5' 5".[33] The Khasis have broad foreheads and their cheekbones are prominent. The inhabitants of the uplands are of somewhat lighter shade and many of the women possess that pretty gypsy complexion that is found in the South of Europe among the peasants.[34]

---

[29] P.R.T. Gurdon, *The Khasis* (New Delhi: Cosmos Publications, 1975), xxi-xxii.
[30] Barnes L. Mawrie, *The Khasis and their Natural Environment* (Shillong: Vendrame Institute Publication, 2001), 6.
[31] J.N. Chowdhuri, "The Khasi Conjectures about their Origin", *The Tribes of North East India*, ed. by Sebastian Karotemprel, (Shillong: Centre for Indigenous Culture, 1998), 68-70.
[32] P.C. Chowdhuri, *History of Civilisation of the People of Assam to the 12th Century AD*, (Kolkata, 1959, 62-65.
[33] n.n., *Census of India 2001: Meghalaya*, op.cit., 9.
[34] Capt. B.S. Rana, *The People of Meghalaya*, op.cit., 68.

The Formation of Meghalaya State

Since 1932 attempts have been made to establish a Federation of Khasi States. In 1933 the Federation of States met for the first time and examined the objects of the Federation to transform the Federation of all Khasi States into an intermediary body between the Khasi states and the Government. In 1933, the Federation of the States put forward their demand in front of Lord Wellingdon for securing representation to the Khasi States in the Indian Legislature. But the Government excluded them from the Indian Chamber of Princes. The Federation did not achieve their objectives.[35]

In 1945-46, the leaders decided to revive the Khasi State Federation to regulate the administrative affairs of the Khasi States regarding the dominion Government of India. Specific provisions for the law-making power of the Federation had been laid down in the Annexed Agreement on matters like excise, forest, land and water rights, while concurrent matters were to be vested on both the Federation and either the dominion or the Assam Government.

Before 1962, there was only the State of Assam and the Union Territories of Manipur and Tripura, in North East India. The members of the Executive Committees of the Autonomos District Councils of the Garo Hills, the Khasi Hills, Jaintia Hills, the Lushai Hills and the North Cachar Hills met at Shillong on 16 June 1954. This meeting was chaired by B. M. Roy. During this meeting matters related to mutual interest were discussed. The chairman suggested that the deliberations might be confined to the formation of the separate states for the Hill Areas and the amendment of the Sixth Schedule.[36]

The Nehru plan was that the hill areas of Assam must remain within the State of Assam, enjoying 90% autonomy of a state. The remaining one percent was complete separation from Assam. The State Government opposed the Plan, because it was full of

---

[35] Dr. Hamlet Bareh, *The History and Culture of the Khasi People*, 226.
[36] V. Venkata Rao, *A Century of Tribal Politics in the North East India (1874-1974)*, op.cit., 336.

doubts and difficulties. The Government thought that the Plan would affect the democratic form of Government; it would also undermine its unity and integrity. The Prime Minister appreciated the difficulties pointed out by Chaliha, the Chief Minister.[37]

The demand for a separate State was pleaded by Hoover Hynniewta and Captain Sangma saying that there was no adequate safeguard for the preservation of the identity of the Hill people in the Sixth Schedule. But it was opposed by the Assam Government. On the 13th January 1967 the Government of India announced its decision to reorganise the State of Assam on the basis of a Federal Structure conferring upon the hill areas equal status with the rest of the State of Assam. This was the result of discussion between the Government of India and the All Party Hill Leaders Conference on 11 January, 1967.[38]

On 24 December, 1969, the Bill for the creation of the Autonomous state of Meghalaya was passed by the Lok Sabha and the Rajya Sabha with the support of almost all the members of all parties. The Prime Minister of India was requested by the APHLC on 3 September, 1970 to declare Meghalaya as a State since Manipur and Tripura had already been declared states. On 19 September the APHLC requested the Government of India to take immediate steps to declare full statehood for Meghalaya. On 21 January, 1972 the Prime Minister of India inaugurated the State of Meghalaya.[39]

The Legislative Assembly

There are 60 seats in Meghalaya Legislative Assembly. Out of 60 seats 18 are in the East Khasi Hills district, 7 seats in the Jaintia Hills, 6 seats in West Khasi Hills, 4 seats in the Ri-Bhoi District, 7 seats in the East Garo Hills, 13 seats in the West Garo Hills, and 2 seats in the South Garo Hills.[40] With the emergence of Meghalaya in 1972, a number of women showed interest in politics.

---

[37] *Ibid.*, 285-288.
[38] *Ibid.*, 435.
[39] *Ibid.*, 482.
[40] n.n., *District Statistical Handbook: East Khasi Hills District, 2007*, Shillong: Directorate of Economics and Statistics, Govt. of Meghalaya, 2007, 45-47.

Locations and Area of the East Khasi Hills District

The East Khasi Hills District is an Administrative District in the State of Meghalaya. It is surrounded by the Ri-Bhoi District in the North, Karbi Anglong District in the North-East, the Jaintia Hills District in the East, Bangladesh in the South, and the West Khasi Hills District in the West.[41] Though all Khasis (i.e., the Khasis who inhabit the central upland of the Khasi Hills, the Synteng or Pnar who occupy the Jaintia Hills, the Lyngam living in the Western portion of the Khasi Hills, the Bhoi of the low hills to the North and North-East of the Khasi Hills, and the Wars inhabiting the Southern slopes of the Khasi Hills mainly and a part of the Jaintia Hills) share basically the same language and social structure yet their culture, dialects, economy, social usage and political organisations vary to some extent due to the geographical and politico-historical differences among them.[42]

On June 4th, 1992, the East Khasi Hills was divided into two Administrative Districts: East Khasi Hills District and Ri-Bhoi District. Shillong is the headquarters of the East Khasi Hills District.[43] It lies approximately between $25°07$ & $25°41$ N latitude and $91°21$ & $92°09$ E longevity. The total geographical area of the East Khasi Hills District is 2748 sq km., which is 12.25 percent of the total area (22429 sq km) of Meghalaya State.[44] The nearest railway station is Guwahati. There is an airstrip suitable for landing aircraft at Umroi, 35 kms away from Shillong.

The widest of the study area from the north-south is 134 kms and the length from East-West is around 21 kms. This area occupies the highest part of the State. While looking from the plains of Bangladesh the hills and ranges look like a massive wall rising from the plains towards the north.[45]

---

[41] Taken from internet *http://shillong.nic.in*, 1.

[42] Pranab Kumar Das Gupta, "Land Tenure and Seng among the War Khasi", *The Tribes of North East India*, ed. op.cit., 324.

[43] Taken from internet, *http://eastkhasihills.gov.in*, 1.

[44] n.n., *District Statistical Handbook-East Khasi Hills District 2007* (Shillong: Govt. of Meghalaya, 2007), 8.

[45] H.M. Bareh, *Encyclopedia of North East India, Vol. IV, op.cit.*, 3.

Land

The economic development of a region to a great extent depends upon the availability of local resources and advancement in the socio-economic sphere. To put it in the context of the East Khasi Hills District it was explained that with a total geographical area of 2748 sq kms, 59,210 hectares of land is under cultivation.[46]

From time immemorial land has always belonged, and is still held to belong, to the people and not to the rulers. There are two types of land viz. *Ri Raid* or public land belonging to a village and *Ri Kynti* or *Ri Kur Land* or private land.

Ri Raid is community land. No person has proprietary heritable or transferable rights over such land. Every member of the community has the right of use and occupancy of the Ri Raid land without payment of land revenue. A member can not claim more land than the area he can actually occupy or actively make use of it.

Ri Kynti Land is private land acquired by a particular clan. This clan then has proprietary, heritable or transferable right over such land. Such land may also include any part of Raid land which in earlier times was given to a person, a family or a clan for certain services rendered to a particular community.

Forest is one of the valuable natural resources of the district as far as the life of the tribal people is concerned. According to the 2001 census, 6,40,151 hectares land was reserved forest and 1,22,545 hectares of land was protected forest under the Government. In the district the land as a whole belongs to the people and not to the State Government, and the land tenure system is of different categories.

Demographic Features of the East Khasi Hills District

The majority of people living in the said District are Khasis. The Khasi Hills District was divided into two Districts, viz the East Khasi Hills District and the West Khasi Hills District on the 28th October 1976. On June 4th, 1992, the East Khasi Hills District

---

[46] n.n., *States at a Glance 2006-07: The North-East and Sikkim*, ed. (New Delhi: Indicus, 2007), 7-21.

was further divided into two Administrative Districts namely the East Khasi Hills District and the Ri-Bhoi District.[47] This District having had almost 86% Khasi population is very popular for various reasons. The East Khasi Hills District has been popular for its culture and religious beliefs. Furthermore it has a history of tribal development from the time of British rule to the present day Government. The Khasis in this district have gone through various stages of transition from the primitive to the modern way of living. The demographic figure of the district is given below.

Table No. 4.3 Block-wise Area, Total Households, Population by Sex, Household Size and Sex Ratio in the East Khasi Hills District in 2001.

Sl. No	Names of Block	Area Sq.Km	House-holds	Popu-lation	Males	Females	House-hold Size	Sex Ratio
1	Nongpoh	1,317	9717	50,561	27,221	23,340	5.8	928
2	Bhoi Area	1,131	14,503	76,751	39355	37,396	5.6	950
3	Mawphlang	290	7,837	46,685	23363	23,322	5.9	998
4	Mylliem	204	32190	170,607	85897	84,710	5.3	967
5	Mawryng-kneng	293	6,326	35,914	17973	17,941	5.8	954
6	Mawkynrew	355	5,110	30,570	15587	14,983	5.9	987
7	Mawsynram	523	7,129	38,194	19445	18,749	5.6	964
8	Shella-Bholaganj	417.1	9,614	38,022	19461	18,561	6.1	954
9	Pynursla	505	9,404	47,171	2348	23,691	5.3	1009
	Total	5,196	101830	534475	270782	263,693		

Table 4.3 shows block-wise area, total number of households, total population, and population by sex, household size and sex ratio in the whole District. The total population of the East Khasi Hills District in 2001 was 5, 34,475. The total area was 5,196 square kilometres. There were 101830 households.

---

[47] Taken from internet, www.google *http://Shillong.nic.in,* 15.

Table No. 4.4 Block-wise Area, Households, Total Population, Population by Sex, Household Size, and Sex Ratio of East Khasi Hills District, in 2007[48]

Sl. No	Names of Block	Area Sq.Km	Households	Total Population	Males	Females	Household Size	Sex Ratio
1	Mylliem	204	71,416	4,29,044	2,17,508	2,11,536	5.1	971
2	Mawphlang	290	9,871	56,672	28,611	28,061	5.8	1021
3	Mawkynrew	355	5,999	35,448	17,712	17,736	5.7	1004
4	Mawsynram	523	8,276	46,736	23,624	23,112	5.5	980
5	Mawryngkneg	293	8,751	51,074	25,552	25,522	5.7	1001
6	Pynursla	505	10,847	58,622	28,961	29,661	5.2	1022
7	Shella-Bholaganj	417.1	9565	56,183	28,513	27,670	5.8	972
	Total	2,587	124,725	7,33,779	3,70,481	3,63,298	5.5	984

Table No. 4.4 showed the total population of East Khasi Hills District. The total population of East Khasi Hills District in 2006-2007 was 7,33,779[49] persons (3,70,481 males and 3,63,298 females) constituting 27.56 percent of the total population of the State. Within ten years the population of this district increased by 3,43,372. The rural population of the District was 4,31,467 and the urban was 2, 54,014. The population below 6 years was 1,29,684 of which 67,112 were males and 62,572 females. The reason behind this growth is said to be the entry of people in this district from other States and Bangladesh. The East Khasi Hills District is divided into 7 blocks. The total number of villages in the district was 899 of which 859 were inhabited villages and 40 were deserted villages. There were no forest villages because the land was in the hands of people. According to the Government Office Record (2006-07), there were 2 Head Post Offices, 63 Sub-Offices and 419 Branch Offices in the District.[50]

---

[48] Information collected from *Deputy Commissioner' Office of the East Khasi Hills District*, Shillong.

[49] n.n., *The North-East and Sikkim*, edited by Lavish Bhandari, Sumita Kale and Amaresh Dubeh, Delhi: Dorling Kindersley, 2007, 103.

[50] *Ibid.*, 44.

The East Khasi Hills District has a total literacy rate of 76.1 percent with a total male literacy rate of 76.12 percent and female literacy rate of 75.82 percent. This District has a gender ratio of 984 females per 1,000 males.

In the year 2001, the number of births per 1,000 population in India was 29.5 percent against 32.4 percent in Meghalaya and 25.7 percent in the East Khasi Hills District. According to Statistical Office Record (2007), the number of deaths per 1,000 in India, Meghalaya, and the East Khasi Hills District, was 9.8 percent, 8.8 percent and 7.2 percent respectively. Some of the most important demographic features are available from the 2007 Government record.

Table 4.5 A Comparison of Demographic Features (in 2007)

S. No.	Items	Meghalaya	East Khasi Hills	India
1	Population Growth Rate (Percent)	30.7	22.88	21.34
2	Sex Ratio (Females Per 1000)	975	984	933
3	Density of Population (Per Square Kilo meter)	103	141	324
4	Literacy Rate	76.4	80.1	65.38

According to the table 4.5, the East Khasi Hills District registered higher population growth rate (22.88 percent) compared to that of India (21.34 percent) and lower growth rate compared to that of Meghalaya state (30.7 percent) in 2001-2007. In the case of the sex ratio the East Khasi Hills District (984) is better than the State and National averages (931 and 933). In the case of density of population the figure of the East Khasi Hills District (141) remains much lower than the national average (324), but higher than the State average (103). The percentage of literacy rate in the District (80.1 percent) is higher than the average of the State (76.4 percent) and that of the national average (65.38 percent).

The total area of the East Khasi Hills District, according to Government Office Record of 2007, was 2847 sq. kms. The number of villages in the District was 899 of which 859 were inhabited villages and 40 were non-inhabited villages. All the 859 villages of the East Khasi Hills District were revenue villages and were of different sizes: big, medium and small. Some villages were very small in size where only 5 families lived. In some villages only 10 families live. Their main source of income was agriculture and forest. Now-a-days villages are not shifted to other places.[51]

Physical Features and Climate

The most important physiographic features of the district are the Shillong plateau interspersed with river valleys. The southern portion is formed by deep gorges and ravines in Mawsynram and Shella-Bholaganj, and borders on Bangladesh. The land is covered with evergreen tropical forest. Some of the well known waterfalls are: *Ka Kshaid Noh-sngi Thiang* (58 kms from Shillong), *Ka Kshaid Noh-Ka-Likai (West of Mawmluh), Kshaid Iale, Kshaid Um-diengpun (Elephant's fall),* and *Kshaid Wei-Tdem* (Sweet Fall).[52]

The climate of the East Khasi Hills District ranges from temperate in the plateau region to the warmer tropical and subtropical pockets in the northern and southern regions. Because of the considerable variations in altitude and exposure, differences in climatic conditions within the Khasi Hills can be expected. The whole of the district was influenced by the south-west monsoon which begins generally from May and continues till October. The weather is humid for the major portion of the year except for the relatively dry spell usually between December and March. The low lying hills and foothills both in the north and in the south may be as low as 5000 feet above sea level while the central range may attain heights of 1900 feet and above. The

---

[51] n.n., *District Census Handbook,* Series No. 16, 322-408.
[52] n.n., *Meghalaya District Gazeteers: Khasi Hills District, op.cit.,* 10-11.

high hills generally enjoy a salubrious climate throughout the year. The winter is very cold. The maximum temperature for Shillong is 21.2⁰ C and the minimum 12.1⁰ C. In Shella the temperature in summer is 25⁰ C and in winter around 9⁰ C or 10⁰ C. Corresponding figures for Cherrapunji are 20⁰C in summer and 14.3⁰ C in winter. The climate is pleasant in autumn and spring. From November to April, the climate remains almost dry. The Cherrapunji-Mawsynram belt on the southern slopes overlooking the plains of Bangladesh has the distinction of having the world's heaviest rainfall with an average of 16720 mm at Mawsynram in 2007 and 12989 mm per annum at Cherrapunji.[53]

The Flora and Fauna of the East Khasi Hills

Forest is one of the valuable natural resources of the East Khasi Hills District as far as the life of the Khasis is concerned. The area under forest in the East Khasi Hills District is an estimated 640151 hectares and the protected forest 1225.45 hectares.[54] Some Khasi families in the rural areas of the district depend to a great extent on the forest for their survival. The forest products are categorised into nationalised and non-nationalised products. Timber products are collected and sold in the market but non-nationalised products like firewood, bamboo and grass are used in their daily life. They do not have to purchase it from outside.

The East Khasi Hills District is rich in wildlife. Some of the existing wildlife consists of: elephant, golden cats, deer, hare, golden langurs, foxes, mongoose, leopards, black panthers, and monkeys of different kinds, flying squirrels, giant squirrels, bears, wild boar, tigers, wild-buffaloes, goats and many others.[55] There are also different kinds of birds like hornbills, geese, ducks and quails. The ancient Khasis were expert hunters and lived on this game. A few decades ago, a great number of wild life species were found in abundance in these jungles.[56]

---

[53] n.n., *The North- East and Sikkim*, op.cit., 69-150.

[54] n.n., *District Statistical Handbook: East Khasi Hills District 2002*, op.cit., 32-33.

[55] n.n., *Meghalaya: Flora and Fauna*, (Shillong: Directorate of Information and Public Relations, Government of Meghalaya, 1975), 48-80.

[56] *Ibid.*, 81-94.

The vegetation of the Khasi Hills may be classified into two types, viz. the tropical and the warm temperate types. The tropical types of vegetation cover areas up to an elevation of about 990 meters. The Khasi pines are a type of pine trees very close to the Alpine. Besides pine trees, other types of vegetation found on these hills are: chestnut, oak, teak, sal, birch, titachap, pine, gomari, bola and makrisal etc. Many types of mushrooms grow on these hills and they provide good sustenance for the people.[57] Medicinal plants and herbs like vallerina, rubia, ipecac, serpentina; chincona, terminalia and arjuna are also found in this District. Different kinds of fruits like oranges, pineapples, bananas, pears, plums, peaches, etc., are also found in these hills.

Rivers of the East Khasi Hills District

There are several small rivers in the East Khasi Hills District. **Umiam River** flows through Ri-Bhoi and turns north-east through the deep gorge until it reaches and joins the **Umsiang River**. The water of this river is dammed at a place about 20 Km. from Shillong called the Umiam Hydel Project. Wah Kynshi River has its source near Sohiong Village in West Khasi Hills.[58]

The Umtrew River rises from the western face of the Sohpetbneng Range near Lum Raitong and flows in the western direction till it meets the waters from the Umiam River further being diverted by the Umiam Hydel Project. The combined water of the Umiam and Umtrew rivers is being used stage by stage to form a continuous power potential Hydro Scheme till it reaches the plains. Umkhen River rising from the north of Shillong Peak flows northward and from the boundary between the East Khasi Hills District and that of the Karbi Anglong District. Umiew River is the principal river in the East Khasi Hills. Before it enters Bangladesh, the river flows by the important village of Shella. Wahrew River has its source at the side of the hill called Lum Swer near Dympep on the way to Cherrapunji. Umngot River has its source near the Shillong Peak. Wahrew River has its

---

[57] Barnes L. Mawrie, SDB, *The Khasis and their Natural Environment*, op.cit., 14-15.
[58] H.W. Sten, *Meghalaya Year Book*, 1977, 5.

source at the side of the hill called Lum Swer on the road to Cherrapunji.[59]

Sacred Groves

The sacred grove is a sort of divine sanctuary where the clan or a group of clans who take care of it, perform their periodical sacrifices to God. They are one of the finest instances of traditional conservation practices. They have also formed centres of cultural and religious life for people. It is from this sacred place that they converse with their Creator through rituals and prayers. The sacred grove is considered by the Khasis as a paradise of the pristine glory of creation. Every sacred grove is guarded by Ki Ryngkew Ki Basa (the deities put by God to reside in nature).[60] Sacred groves have preserved the biological diversity of that particular region which has vanished from other surrounding areas.

Besides the sacred groves, the Khasis have their sacred spots and mountains, which have become sacred to them. The mountains are not only regarded as seats of gods, but are often personified as gods. U Blei Shillong appears to be such a personification. The spirit of this mountain is considered as the most powerful among all. Due reverence is paid to him especially by the Khyrim royal family and the Nongkrem priestly clans. Sumer is another sacred hill, which figures in Khasi mythology besides Sohpetbneng. Sacrifices are made periodically to *U Blei Shillong*.[61]

The Social Life of the Khasis

Khasi society is a classless society in which all groups are considered equal. Social life of the Khasis was purely corporate; instances of which can be found even today in rural areas. Construction of houses, harvesting of paddy, erection of monoliths, construction of roads and bridges, demarcation of lands and other activities for the common good were performed together by the inhabitants. It has been pointed out that Khasi

---

[59] *Ibid.*
[60] Barnes L. Mawrie, *The Khasis and their Natural Environment*, op.cit., 143.
[61] Hamlet Bareh, *History and Culture of the Khasi People*, op.cit., 326.

society is made up of a multitude of *Kurs* (clans), each of which ascribes its origin to a primeval ancestor (*U Thawlang*) and ancestress (*Ka Iawbei*). The Khasi society is a matrilineal society. The matrilineal society involves a very close relationship between religion, social life and political life of the people. The matrilineal system in Meghalaya is where both descent and inheritance are reckoned through the female line. In a matrilineal culture, the maternal males are as motivated to protect their sisters' children as their own.[62] The *Kur* is the first social entity of the Khasis, round which every social institution revolves. The word '*Kur*' refers to all groups of people both male and female descended from the first mother of the family line, which is known as "*Iawbei*" (ancestress).

1. The Khasi Concept of Family

The basic unit of Khasi society is the *iing* or family. A Khasi family is generally nuclear in character, and consists of husband, wife and children. An important feature of the Khasi society is the reverence for the ancient female progenitor and the entire family organisation which centres on the mother.

The term family has two connotations in this context. It can mean a nuclear unit of father, mother and children as more predominant today. It is also a loose term for a kinship group comprising of two-three *iings* who are usually the descendents from the womb of one mother, grand-mother or great grand-mother. Khasis believe that God ordained and established the original family unit. According to Coralton Wolflang, family is an institution, which plays an important role in the society and on the mother's death the custodianship is passed on to her youngest daughter.

(a) The Status of Man in Khasi Society

> Khasi family is a nuclear family. Although a father has less important part to play in his wife's house, his bones on his death being restored to mother's cromlech, yet he has an important role to play in bringing up the children. In his mother's family (clan)

---

[62] n.n., *Gazetteer of India*, District Gazetteer, (Shillong: Art & Culture Department, 1991), 54.

he has the position of U Knii (uncle). He is responsible for the upbringing of children and security of the whole family.[63]

According to Khasi tradition, a man is U Nongda (protector). It is generally believed that Khasi man stands in two worlds. One is the world of his clan and another, the world of his children. The father and mother share the responsibility of earning the livelihood for the family and the grown up children are required to assist them in this respect. The father is the connecting link between his mother's clan and his wife's clan. He has plenty of powers outside his family but much less within the family. Protecting and maintaining the well being of the members of a matrilineal group is another on-going activity or role of maternal uncle (U Kni). He shares the burden especially in matters of life and death. He also functions as the spiritual mediator or priest (U Lyngdoh) of the family.[64]

(b) The Status of woman in the Khasi Family

The position of Khasi women in the Khasi family is unique. It is generally believed that women, being the fountainhead of a clan in the Khasi society, are held in high respect.[65] They enjoy a high social status in the Khasi society, and play a significant role in socio-economic matters and household management.[66] In the Khasi family, the mother reigns supreme in the management of the household. Khasi society is matrilineal, except that in special situations women have no rights in the local, political and administrative spheres.[67] In Autonomous District Councils, there have been only a few women representatives who were either elected or nominated.

---

[63] S. Rynjah, "The Khasi Family: Dynamic Role of Father and Maternal Uncle", The Dynamics of Family System in a Matriliny of Meghalaya, op.cit., 49.

[64] Dr. Hamlet Bareh, History and Culture of the Khasi People, op.cit., 302.

[65] D. Roy, "Principles of Khasi Customs", in Keith Cantlie, Notes on Khasi Laws, 88.

[66] n.n., Mega Peoples of India, Part III, (Hyderabad: India Missions Associations, 2006), 19.

[67] Mrs. Rynjah, "The Khasi Family: Dynamic Role of Father and Maternal Uncle", The Dynamics of Family System in a Matriliny of Meghalaya, op.cit., 48

2. Khasi Laws and Customs

The Khasi Customary Laws play a very important role in the Khasi society. The Khasi Customary Laws may have evolved out of the tribal social-cultural and politico-economic milieu of ancient times. In the following paragraphs the different aspects of the Customary Laws have been discussed.

(a) Marriage

The Khasis have a firm belief that God had handed over a commandment that it is not only an act of sacrilege but also an unpardonable sin if a person marries within his own clan. Both Christians and non-Christians still follow the Khasi Customary Law. A Khasi can marry his cousin (Bakha), that is the daughter of his uncle, but if an uncle is still alive marriage is not allowed. The Khasis practice the matri-local system, which means that the male has to come and stay in his wife's place for sometime. Both men and women are free to choose their partner.[68] But the most common form of marriage is *Kyntiew Kurim*, or marriage by negotiation. The process of selection of spouses begins from the male side. Usually a man selects a girl and informs his parents about his choice. If the parents approve of the choice they send a mediator or *U Ksiang* to the woman's house to convey the proposal. The mediator or *U Ksiang* meets the woman's parents and submits the proposal. On the appointed day the mediator or *Ksiang* visits the woman's house.

The Khasi system of kinship is exogamous and therefore members of the same clan can not marry. Such marriage is not tolerated by any family and state law. If any couple do marry inside the same clan, they are exiled and get no inheritance. No religious rite or ceremony can be performed for the person who commits this unpardonable sin (Marriage in the same clan). He or she is very much looked down upon by the society.

In the traditional system marriage is arranged by the eldest living uncle (Kni) who himself blesses them in a simple ceremony at the bride's residence. However, love marriage is also popular

---

[68] H. K. Synrem, *Revivalism in Khasi Society*, (New Delhi: Sterling Publishers, 1992), 33.

among the Khasis of the East Khasi Hills District. There is neither dowry nor bride price in Khasi society. The marriage is monogamous though divorce and re-marriage is permitted.[69] Adultery is not allowed for either of the sexes. The husband is at liberty to inflict any punishment on the wife, even to the extent of killing her on the spot if she is caught in the act of adultery.[70] Any family or State Law does not tolerate marriage within his or her own clan.

The sole aim of marriage for the Khasis is the procreation of children. If no issues are born, then the marriage is considered as faulty and not pleasing to God.[71] Polygamy and polyandry do not exist among the Khasis.

(b) Divorce

Although the Khasi marriage has a spiritual basis, divorce is unavoidable and was found common among the early Khasis. Divorce is finalised in the presence of relatives of both the husband and the wife and the headman of the village. The divorce must be by mutual consent.[72] The village assembly grants permission for divorce. It may have taken place for a variety of reasons, such as adultery, barrenness, and incompatibility of temperament and incurable disease.[73] But a woman cannot be divorced during pregnancy.[74] After divorce, the children remain in the custody of their mother.

(c) Widow Re-Marriage

It is believed that the Khasi laws and customs recognised the re-marriage of widows, widowers and divorcees. But Khasis

---

[69] Pariyaram M. Chacko, "Introduction", *Matriliny in Meghalaya*, ed. op.cit., 3.
[70] H.K. Synrem, *Revivalism in Khasi Society* (New Delhi: Sterling Publishers Pvt. Ltd., 1992), 33.
[71] Dr. Barnes L. Mawrie, *Introduction to Khasi Ethics*, (Shillong: DBCIC Publishers, 2005), 36.
[72] S.K. Chattopadhayay, *Tribal Institutions of Meghalaya*, (Guwahati: Spectrum Publications, 1985), 170.
[73] Leut. H.Yule, "Notes on the Khasi Hills and People", *Journal of Asiatic Society of Bengal, Vol. XII, Part II*, July-December 1894, Nos., 151-156, (Kolkata: New Series Bishop's College Press, 1894), 612.
[74] P.R. Gurdon, *The Khasis*, (Delhi: Low Price Publications, 2002), 128.

ordinarily do not approve re-marriage after the death of the spouse in the traditional Khasi society. A woman whose husband has died cannot re-marry within a period of one year. If so, it would be considered unclean and is looked down upon as an act of fornication.[75] If a spouse has a mind to re-marry, he or she must first send back the bones of the deceased partner to his/her 'kur' and also pay them some amount. The dead spouse's clan's relatives perform religious rites to cleanse him or her because the living spouse is considered to have committed adultery and in course of performance of the rites the three monoliths have to be erected.[76]

(d) Property Inheritance

The Khasi Law on Property is intrinsically bound up with the doctrine of *ka khein-kur khein-kha* which is the basic feature in the structure of the Khasi race. The principles, precepts and tenets and customary laws give the Khasi man a high position of responsibility to look after the welfare of his kur and his family. According to the matrilineal system, prevailing amongst the Khasis, the inheritance to property is from mother to daughter.[77] Inheritance is purely matrilineal in organisation. It consists of moveable and immoveable goods. There are two kinds of property: inalienable and alienable. The first type, more prevalent previously is a legacy, an ancestral property, bequeathed by predecessors of the house upon the present members who, can not dispose of it or any part from it, without the general agreement of the whole family concerned. Inalienable property belongs to the whole family and it can not be sold out without the general agreement of the whole family concerned.[78]

Property, which includes foundation house for holding celebrations of the family, is inherited by the youngest daughter. She inherits her mother's property. The mother's residential house

---

[75] P.R.T. Gurdon, *The Khasis, op.cit.,* 79-80.
[76] Kynpham Singh, "The Monoliths of the Khasi-Jaintia Hills", *Khasi Heritage,* (Shillong: U Hipson Roy, 1996), 167.
[77] M.P.R. Lyngdoh, *The Festivals in the History and Culture of the Khasis, op.cit.,* 33.
[78] Dr. Hamlet Bareh, *The History and Culture of the Khasi People, op.cit.,* 296-297.

is managed by her. Self acquired property earned by a deceased person at his wife's residence is divided among his relatives and his wife. The alienable property may be inherited by the sons and daughters.[79] The Wars on the Southern Hills are an exception to the rule where both males and females own, control and possess property.

The youngest daughter inherits the major share of the property, but other sisters also receive a share of inheritance. Any member of the family whether male or female having no source of income stays and eats with the youngest daughter, who occupies the ancestral house. The *Ka Khadduh* (youngest daughter) is debarred from such a status only when she enters into an illegal or unauthorised marriage.[80] If *Ka Khadduh* dies without any offspring, her next elder sister possesses the property. In case no daughter is left, an adopted female member called *Ka Nongrap iing* or helper of the house is kept to act as housekeeper until the birth of a female offspring.[81]

If a man brings his self-acquired property from his parent's house and sets up business in his wife's house, the earning acquired thereby will be treated as his own property. On his death such property belongs to his mother and sister. Though the whole Khasi society is a matrilineal society yet the law of inheritance is not uniform. Sons also inherit property in some villages like Shella area in the East Khasi Hills District.[82] Since Khasi society has devised and evoked the method of transmitting property through females it naturally follows that the maternal males will evince a keen interest in its management and disposal.[83]

3. Language

Khasi is the common language used in the East Khasi Hills District. It belongs to one of the Mon groups of the Austro-

---

[79] *Ibid.*, 297.

[80] The Journal of the North East India Council for Social Science Research, Vol. I, No. 1, April 1978, Shillong, 5.

[81] Dr. Hamlet Bareh, *The History and Culture of the Khasi People*, op.cit., 297.

[82] K. Cantlie, *Notes on Khasi Laws* (Shillong: Ri Khasi Press, 1971), 13.

[83] M.P.R. Lyngdoh, "Inheritance, Property Rights and Entrepreneurship in the Khasi Society", *The Dynamics of Family System in a Matriliny of Meghalaya*, op.cit., 19.

Asiatic family. But apart from the Khasi language Hindi, Bengali, and English are also used. Now the Khasi language is the spoken language of the rural and urban Khasis.

4. Traditional Political Life of the Khasis

Khasi democracy was founded in the *Durbar Raid* or the *Durbar of the Communes*, and the *Durbar Shnong* or a *Village Durbar*, which had an elected headman each at the top.[84] The will of the people was considered supreme in the Khasi political set up, and thus, the Khasi State was truly democratic, the chief was in no sense a territorial sovereign, but was merely an elected head of the village confederacy.[85]

(a) The Khasi Village

The village was the hub a round which community life centred. The size of the village differed from area to area. A village facing the East was considered to be auspicious.[86] Every Khasi village had its own local assembly known as *Durbar Shnong* (Village Durbar or Council).

The functions of the *Durbar Shnong* necessarily arose out of the socio-cultural, politico-economic milieu of rural villages. In the past, village defence was an important agenda in the *Durbar Shnong*. The village headman performed religious and ceremonial functions in the absence of the village priest. It was under his leadership the people of the village selected the village headman. The *Village Durbar Shnong* played the role of development agency in all the items of collective interest, e.g., village sanitation, water supply, health, roads, and education.

(i) Village Political Administration

Every Khasi village had its own local assembly known as *Durbar Shnong* (Village Durbar or Council). There are 5-15 members in the *Village Durbar Shnong* depending on the members of the village.

---

[84] H.O. Mawrie, *Ka Pyrkhat U Khasi* (Shillong: Ri Khasi Press, 1973), 69.

[85] A. Mackenzie, *History of the Relations of the Government with the Hill Tribes of the North East Frontier of Bengal*, (Delhi: Mittal Publications, 1979), 221.

[86] Nalini Natarajan, *The Missionary among the Khasis*, (New Delhi: Sterling Publications, 1977), 31.

The office of chief was reserved to the ruling clan of that particular area. Representatives of other clans could not be considered for the chieftainship. The ruling clan was known as *jait Syiem*. The *jait Syiem* was made up of different sub-clans and families. He acted as a judge and decided disputes among the villagers and clans.[87] The village headman or *Rangbah* is the head of the *Durbar Shnong*. It was under his leadership and enthusiasm that the village could progress and live in harmony. His power rested on his personality rather than on his position and role in the system. He was the one who organised all the functions necessary in the village. The headman was not only the administrative head of the village but he was also the fountain of justice.[88] The *Village Durbar Shnong* does the administration of legal matters in the Khasi society at the local level. Being the smallest council of people at the village level, it meets more frequently than the inter-village council. The village headman known as *Sardar*, presided at the *Durbar Shnong* or village council meeting. All the adult male inhabitants of the village were required to attend the sessions of the *Durbar*.[89] The *Durbar Hima* confirms the election of a headman.[90]

There was no representation of women in the past. Women would come to the *Durbar* only when cases or matters concerning them were discussed. They have been deprived of leadership rights in all indigenous institutions.[91] Before the coming of the British, the village headman used to exercise leadership, provide hospitality, keep up the Khasi rituals, give feasts, and generally looked after trade and welfare. It was under his leadership that the village could prosper and live in harmony. The traditional

---

[87] Dr. O.L.Snaitang, Christianity and Social Change in North East India, *op.cit.*, 14.

[88] H.K. Synrem, *Revivalism in Khasi Society, op.cit.,* 27.

[89] Juantia War, "Panchayati Raj and Traditional Khasi Institutions: A Comparison", *Power to People in Meghalaya*, ed. by M.N. Karna, L.S. Gasah & C.J. Thomas, (New Delhi: Regency Publications, 1998), 74.

[90] Dr. L.S. Gassah, *Traditional Institutions of Meghalaya: A Study of Doloi and His Administration*, (New Delhi, 1998), 3.

[91] O.L.Snaitang, "The Impact of Christianity on the Khasi Jaintia Matrilineal Family", *Matriliny in Meghalaya*, edited by P.M. Chacko, (New Delhi: Regency Publications, 1998), 60.

Durbar Shnong was entirely autonomous. By and large, the present *Durbar Shnongs* are still autonomous bodies, with some limited powers. It is the highest authority in all matters related to the village.

At present all village chiefs are placed under the jurisdiction of the District Autonomous Council. The District Council under the Act of 1959 wholly regulates the appointment and succession of chiefs and headmen. With regards to financial matters, the chief pays 1/8 of the total income to the District Council.

(ii) The Functions of Durbar Shnong

The functions of the *Durbar Shnong* necessarily arose out of the socio-cultural, politico-economic milieu of rural villages. In the past village defence was an important agenda in the *Durbar Shnong*. The village headman performed religious and ceremonial functions in the absence of the village priest. It was under his leadership the people of the village selected the village headman.[92] The *Village Durbar Shnong* played the role of development agency in all the items of collective interest, e.g., village sanitation, water supply, health, roads, and education.[93] It also functioned as village local courts to try petty cases such as land quarrels, fights, divorces, ex-communications of incestuous couples, boundary disputes, petty theft, and so on. In the case of problems outside the jurisdiction of the village, the judgement was done by the head of the *Raid* (Region). Capital punishment resulting in the death of a criminal was generally carried out outside a locality to ward off evil spirits called *Ka Tyrut Ka Smer* by the Khasis. If this was not done, the belief was that such spirits might cause depredation to the people of a locality.[94]

The Khasi concept of Law was basically abstract as they did not have written Laws. The basic foundation of Law was custom and for that reason, Laws are regarded as rigid and inviolable

---

[92] Gurdas Das, "Social Change and Traditional Tribal Political Systems in Meghalaya", *Power to People in Meghalaya*, ed. op.cit., 36.

[93] *Ibid*.

[94] Sujit Kumar Dutta, *Functioning of Autonomous District Councils in Meghalaya*, (New Delhi: Akansha Publishing House, 2002), 43.

till today. They believed that the Law must be related to morality. It was only when that condition was fulfilled that justice found its impartial application.[95] In the traditional *Durbar Shnong* there was no question of party politics in the case of elections. This is still true in present day practices by and large.

With the Administration getting out of the hands of the traditional headman, his authority was undermined. This has led to the emergence of a new leadership of the District Council and elected representatives of the Meghalaya Legislative Assembly (MLAs).[96]

(b) Inter-village Administration (Raid)[97]

Raid is a political unit under the *Syiemship* for the purpose of social control and harmonious Civil and Judicial administration.[98] A *Dorbar Raid* consists of 7-8 members from different clans. There are 4 ministers and one Lyngdoh in the Raid Dorbar. The elected headmen, *Lyngdoh* and 4 ministers manage and control the *Raid*.[99]

By the institution of *Dorbar Raid*, its headman and other elected officials settle the inter-village disputes and look after the interests of the *Raid*. At the head of this *Dorbar* there is a *Sirdar*. The king directly nominates him. An alternative person would be either a *Lyngdoh* (an administrative priest and not a ritualistic priest) or a *Doloi*. In such disputes, which arose from the encroachment of land between villages, this *Dorbar Raid* is entitled to go into the matter and bring about a peaceful solution to the problem.[100]

(c) The State Level Political Set-Up (Syiemship)

The Khasi States are formed as a result of many clans coming together. Each of the 25 Khasi States ruled by *Syiems* has a

---

[95] *Ibid.*, 44.
[96] H.K. Synrem, *Revivalism in Khasi Society, op.cit.,* 29.
[97] Raid was a potential unit comprising a number of adjacent Khasi villages organised into a political system for the purpose of social control and harmonious civil and judicial administration. This was the largest political unit under the syiemship.
[98] P.R.G. Mathur, *The Khasi of Meghalaya: A Study in Transition and Religion,* (New Delhi: Cosmo Publications, 1979), 67.
[99] n.n., *Power to People in Meghalaya, op.cit.,* 76.
[100] Dr. Barnes L. Mawrie, *Introduction to Khasi Ethics, op.cit.,* 48.

ruling clan from which *Syiemship* succession took place. Out of 25 States the Syiems ruled 15 States and the Lyngdohs, Sirdars or Wahadadars ruled 10 States. The names of the twenty States are: Khyrim Syiemship, Mylliem Syiemship, Nongstoin Syiemship, Nongkhlaw Syiemship, Maharam Syiemship, Myriaw Syiemship, Malai-Sohmat Syiemship, Rambrai Syiemship, Nongspung Syiemship, Mawiang Syiemship, Sohiong Syiemship, Nobosohphoh Syiemship, Mawsynram Syiemship, Langrin Syiemship, Nongpoh Syiemship, Langrin Syiemship, Bhowal Syiemship, Nongwah Syiemship, Sohra Syiemship, Sohbar Syiemship, Shella Confederacy, Dwara Nongtyrnem, Jirang Syiemship, Jyrngam Syiemship and Sutnga Syiemship(Jaintia Kingdom).[101]

(i) Durbar Hima

The Durbar Hima was the supreme authority of the state. In addition to the chief and Ki Bakhraw, the State Durbar included representatives of the Raid and Village Councils. The cultural integrity of the state centred on the Durbar Hima. It maintained law and order. It was the keeper of the traditional Customary laws and exercised power in maintaining the law and order.

The founding clans play an important role in the Khasi States, not only having the privilege of electing the *Syiem* but also being entrusted with the Government of the State with other officials through the *Durbar Hima*. The *Syiem* is elected from a certain family and the heirship to the *Syiemship* is from the female side and the line of succession is uniform in all cases except in *Khyrim* State. An electoral college consisting of elders and representatives from every family chose the *Syiem* as the administrative head.[102]

The number of the members of *Durbar* differs from State to State. At first the five Lyngdohs were electors of the Syiem in Maharam Syiemship. Later on Sirdars and Myntris of inferior status were added to the electoral Assembly. Altogether there

---

[101] Captain D. Herbert, *Succession to Syiemship in the Khasi States*, (Shillong: Directorate of Art & Culture, Govt. of Meghalaya, 1991), 73.

[102] V. Venkata Rao, *A Century of Tribal Politics*, (New Delhi: S Chand & Company, 1975), 114

were 30 Myntris (ministers), 13 Sirdars, and a Basan.¹⁰³ In Khyrim State there were 31 members, 1 Lygskor, 6 Lyngdohs, and 21 Myntris. The *Syiem* with the assistance of 3 Lyngdohs (Priests), 12 Myntries and 15 Sirdars of the villages ruled the Khasi States. The *Syiem* was the guardian of the Law and the authority with regard to the moral laws. All the *Raid* officials like M*yntries*; *Basans* and *Lyngdohs* elected from different clans under the *Syiemships*, were the members of the *Durbar Myntri*.¹⁰⁴ They were collectively known as noblemen.¹⁰⁵

The *Syiem* as the head of the state performed administrative, military, religious and judicial functions in consultation with the members of the *Durbar Myntris* (ministers) along the desired line of the *Durbar Hima*. His was the highest court in the State.¹⁰⁶ All unsettled disputes either at the village level or at the *Raid* level and all serious cases involving severe punishment like life imprisonment and death were referred to his Court.¹⁰⁷ In criminal cases, the *Syiem* and his *Durbar* could inflict great punishment on the culprits. Murder or homicide was punishable by beating the offender to death. Adultery also carried with it a heavy punishment. The punishment was usually life imprisonment or a heavy fine of ₹ 1100 and a pig.¹⁰⁸

The main sources of income of the State were State subscriptions, market tolls, judicial fines and registration fees. The principal source of income of the *Syiem*, however, in all the Khasi States was the toll (*Khrong*), which he collected from those who sold their goods at the markets in his territory.¹⁰⁹

Following the British annexation of Assam in 1826, its policy underwent a drastic change from one of non-interference to intervention.¹¹⁰ The British administration had tremendous effects

---

[103] Captain D. Herbert, *Succession to Syiemships in the Khasi States*, (op.cit., 35).
[104] H.O. Mawrie, *The Khasi Milieu*, (New Delhi: Concept Publishing Company, 1981), 93.
[105] *Ibid.*
[106] P.R.T. Gurdon, *The Khasis*, op.cit., 69.
[107] *Ibid.*
[108] *Ibid.*, 93.
[109] *Ibid.*, 247.
[110] David R. Syiemlieh, *British Administration in Meghalaya*, (New Delhi: Heritage Publishers, 1989), 66.

on the traditional institutions in general and the powers and functions of the chiefs in particular among the various tribes of Meghalaya. With regards to their policy towards the traditional chiefs of the different areas, the British were very particular to see that such indigenous institutions be made useful tools in their hands for the furtherance of their imperialistic interests in such a difficult hilly terrain.

Until its annexation by the British (1833), the Khasi Hills had maintained a fair degree of isolation to condition its political system according to its needs and environment. The institution of *Syiemship* was considered as an ancient one. The ruler combined in himself the fiscal, legal, administrative and military powers. The system as such was, however, an aristocracy or limited monarchy as the *Syiems* were from special clans. The scope of election was also limited as the law of succession was clear and limited by the eldest of the uterine brothers of the deceased *Syiem* and failing this, by maternal cousin brother, or son of the sister. In course of time, the elements of feudalism and capitalism had infiltrated into the system as the *Syiems* had the privileges of controlling the vest crown lands and the command of the service of the people.[111]

In 1874, the new Province of Assam was created with Shillong as its capital. Around 1895, there was a spirit of nationalism among the Khasis. In 1904, the merger of Assam with the United Province of East Bengal, Shillong became the headquarters. The year 1923 saw the formation of the Khasi National Durbar and in the years 1934-1935, the Khasi States Federation. The traditional pattern of polity went side by side with modern systems in which members of the Parliament; Legislative Assembly, District Council and Municipality were returned on modern universal adults' suffrage without any consideration to the hereditary basis. In fact, modern institutions contain more elite than the traditional state form of polity.[112]

---

[111] Dr. Jatanta Bhushan B., "The Changing Khasis: An Historical Account," *The Tribes of North East India*, 338.

[112] Nalini Natarajan, *The Missionary among the Khasis*, op.cit., 140.

Since independence, the political, economic and social forces at work in the country have brought about a large measure of integration of the Khasis with the rest of India. In 1953, in the wake of independence under Article 244 and the Sixth Schedule of the Constitution of India, District Councils were set up. The *syiemship* is continued subject to the provisions of the Sixth Schedule. All the powers and functions exercised by the Deputy Commissioner over the *syiems* were transferred to the District Council and the State Government. The chiefs or *syiems* have to carry all the orders issued to them by the Autonomous District Council. The Khasi Hills District Council framed a Law regulating succession of the syiems and headmen.

The united Khasi Jaintia Hills Autonomous District Act, 1959, made the provisions not only for its authority to appoint the chiefs and headmen, but even the removal and suspension of the offices by the Executive Committee of the District Council if in its opinion the chiefs and headmen violate the terms and conditions of their appointment. Further, the Khasi Hills Autonomous District Council in its amendment of the Principal Act on Appointment and Succession of syiems and headmen, 1980, went even to the extent of passing an Act debarring the chiefs, deputy chiefs, acting chiefs, in taking any part in politics and elections either of the State or of the District Council. This is another way of control enforced by the District Council over the traditional chiefs.[113] Moreover, the District Council should confirm the appointment of the *syiems*. This is the outside influence, which has led the Khasi society to adopt a new political system in the East Khasi Hills District.

Nowadays with the existence of the District Councils and the Judicial Courts in the State all disputes are referred to them for final decision. With the administration getting out of the hands of the traditional headmen, their authority has been undermined. This has led to the emergence of a new leadership of District Counsellors (MDCs) and elected representatives of the Meghalaya Legislative Assembly (MLAs). In 2007, there were 15 *gramsevak circles*, 2 Syiemships, 2 Legislative Assembly

---

[113] Dr. S.K. Chattopadhayay, *Tribal Institutions of Meghalaya*, 46.

Constituencies and 2 District Council Constituencies in the said Block. C.B.Syiem was the Chief Executive Member of the Autonomous District Council of the East Khasi Hills District.[114]

(5) The Khasi Hills Autonomous District Council

The Autonomous District Council is a corporate body, having perpetual succession and a common seal with the right to sue and to be sued. The Council consists of representatives elected by adult franchise to administer the functions, and exercise the powers entrusted to it. It was at the cabinet mission's advice that the Constituent Assembly of India set up an advisory committee on January 24, 1947 regarding the formation of Autonomous District Council. The committee later on constituted two sub-committees on February 27, 1947. This committee is known as Bordoloi Committee. This committee studied the administrative set up carefully. The Bordoloi Committee recommended the setting up of the administration of the tribal areas, based on the concept of regional autonomy in all matters affecting their customs, laws of inheritance as well as administration of justice, land and forest. The sub-committee's report was submitted on 28 July, 1947. The Constituent Assembly accepted the recommendations of Bordoloi Committee and incorporated them in the Sixth Schedule.[115]

By Act 1935, the Tribal Areas in Assam were kept as 'Excluded Areas' in the Constitution of India, 1950, and provision was made for the constitution of Autonomous District Councils. This was done in such a way that the tribal people could be in a position to enjoy some rights of self-government for socio-economic development.[116] The first District Council, created under the provisions of the Sixth Schedule was inaugurated in 1952. The District Council consists of representatives elected by adult franchise to administer the functions, and exercise the powers entrusted to it. It shall consist of elected and nominated members.[117]

---

[114] District Statistical Hand Book: East Khasi Hills District, *op.cit.,* 46-48.
[115] Sujit Kumar Dutta, *Functioning of Autonomous District Councils in Meghalaya,* New Delhi: Akansha Publishing House, 2002, 8.
[116] *Ibid.,* 9.
[117] V. Venkata Rao, *A Century of Tribal Politics, op.cit.,* 216.

Its jurisdiction was then the whole of the United Khasi & Jaintia District with the exception of the normal Government area of Shillong Municipality. Since 1964, Jaintia Hills has had its own Council. All the chiefs are now under the Jurisdiction of District Councils. The District Councils under the Act of 1959 wholly regulate the succession and appointment of chiefs and headmen. In such circumstances the autonomy of the tribal institutions is jeopardised. The Supreme Court of India observed in 1960 that Syiem was a functionary under the District Council. The Councils have certain control over the budget of the chiefs. At present the Khasi Hills Autonomous District Council is divided into 29 constituencies. The number of nominated number is one. The total number of Constituencies in Jaintia Hills is 19. The District Councils have three functions like legislative, executive and judiciaries.[118] The Syiems opinion about District Councils was not very good. The Durbar Syiem, which is partyless democracy, is very much opposed to this.

In 1952, under Article 244 and the Sixth Schedule of the Constitution of India, the Autonomous District Councils in Meghalaya were first introduced in the United Khasi-Jaintia Hills District and the Garo Hills District along with other Autonomous District Councils in Assam believing that it would be able to protect their interests and identity. A separate District Council for the then Jowai sub-division (now known as Jaintia Hills District Council) was created in 1964 under the Sixth Schedule (Under the Act of 1959).

The total number of the Council members was reduced to 29 and one nominated member. The District Council functions under the supervision of the Chief Executive Member. Out of 29 members 6 or 7 are Executive members. Two members of the Autonomous District Council are elected from Shella-Bholaganj Block.[119]

Under the Autonomous District Rules of 1951 the District Council elects a Chairman and Deputy Chairman from among themselves. The Chairman has his own office with a small staff under the control of a Secretary. The term of the Council is ordinarily 5 years.[120]

---

[118] Sujit Kumar Dutta, *Functioning of Autonomous District Councils in Meghalaya, op.cit.,* 5-13.

[119] Julius L.R. Karak, "Traditional Institutions of the People of Meghalaya", *Heritage of Meghalaya,* (Shillong: Directorate of Art & Culture, Govt. of Meghalaya, n.d.), 9.

[120] V. Venkata Rao, *A Century of Tribal Politics in North East India, op.cit.,* 216.

The executive functions of the District Council are entrusted to the Executive Committee. Each member of the Executive Committee is given a responsibility. The Council elects the Chief Executive Member but the other members are appointed by the Governor on the advice of the Chief Executive Member from amongst the members of the District Council.[121]

The District Council has the power to establish, construct or manage primary schools, dispensaries, markets, cattle, ponds, ferries, fisheries, roads, and waterways. It also has power to determine the language and the manner in which primary education should be imparted in the primary schools within its jurisdiction.[122] The District Council has power to constitute village courts for the trial of suits and cases in which both the parties are tribal. The overall impact of the British rule was that although the *Syiem* and his *ministers* and other officials remained in their offices, they were divested of their real power, which was then vested in the Deputy Commissioner.[123]

(a) The Pattern of Land Holding

According to the 2007 State Government Record, the total geographical area of the district was 2748 sq km. The East Khasi Hills District being predominantly a hilly region, land on the plain is very limited. There were two kinds of land: *Ri Kynti* and *Ri Raid*. *Ri Kynti* Land is the ancestral property of a clan.

Ri Raid is land belonging to the community as a whole. The management and control of this land lies within the jurisdiction of the community concerned. It may be a group of villages comprising a *Raid* for the *Ri Raid* land of the *Raid* excluding such lands, as is already part of a village, which is a member of that *Raid*. The traditional system of forest management in the East

---

[121] B. Pakem, "The Socio-Political System of the Jaintia Tribe of Assam: An Analysis of Continuity and Change", *Tribal Situation in India*, ed. by K Suresh Singh, Simla, 1972, 353-357.

[122] Sujit Kumar Dutta, *Functioning of Autonomous District Councils in Meghalaya*, (New Delhi: Akansha Publishing House, 2002), 1-6.

[123] Dr. L.S. Gassah, *Traditional Institutions of Meghalaya: A Study of Doloi and His Administration, op.cit.,* 7.

Khasi Hills District differed from area to area depending upon the culture that the people represent and their indigenous faith.[124]

In the East Khasi Hills, the forest is divided into seven classes based upon the ownership and traditional system of management. They are: The private forests; the *Ri Kynti* forests; the *Raid* forests; the community forests; the sacred grove; the clan forests; and the village forests. The Ri Kynti forest, the second category of forests, is very similar to the privately owned. The only difference between the two is in the extent of the holding and the area where the systems have been practised. The size of private forest is always below 20 hectare or so, whereas the Ri-Kynti forest may extend up to 500 hectares or more. Owners of Ri Kynti forests used to issue temporary *patta* to the tenants for the purpose of cultivation by way of *jhum* shifting cultivation.

Raid forests are owned and managed by the people of a particular *Raid*. In case of community forests the management is in the hands of the community *Durbar*. The clan forests are owned and managed by the particular clans only. During the earlier days the head of the clan used to be very powerful. No one dared to challenge his authority on any matters relating to the clan.[125]

There are many sacred groves locally known as *Law Lyngdoh* and *Law Adong*. These forests are believed to be the abode of gods and goddesses. They have been protected and preserved through a religious taboo. They like to propitiate the gods by maintaining the sanctity of these sacred forests. However, in the wake of materialism getting dominance over spiritualism, peoples' conscience started disappearing. Accordingly, the sense of fear among the Khasis seems to be on the decline.

The clan forests are owned and managed by the particular clans only. During the early days the head of the clan used to be very powerful. He acted as an arbitrator in all matters

---

[124] R.T. Rymbai, "*The Pattern of Landholding*", Tribal Institutions of Meghalaya, (ed.) (Guwahati: Spectrum Publications, 1985), 189.

[125] Krishan Kumar Gaur, "Traditional Management System of Forests in Meghalaya: Some Reflections", *Environment Forest and Tribes: Anthropological Concomitance*, (New Delhi: Himanshu Publications, 2000), 157.

pertaining to the clan and the clan forest. The clan head is empowered to decide about the distribution of the land among the members.

(b) The Economy of the East Khasi Hills District

As a whole the economy of the people in the East Khasi Hills District revolves around agriculture. The traditional rural communities in the district were largely dependent on a very primitive mode of agriculture. Agriculture was an important economic activity of the people of this district. Most of the Khasis in the district are primarily producers, sellers and middlemen, taking most of the produce to the markets located in the various places in the hills. They practiced the *jhuming* method of cultivation and the festivities and ceremonies connected with *jhuming* form a part of their religious and social culture.[126] The soil of the district is light to heavy in texture, ranging from acidic soil to soil which is rich in organic matter, though generally poor in phosphorus while the potash content varies.

Fishery, piggery and fruit and vegetables are the main source of income. Fishery development in the District has received very little attention so far. This was due to the fact that most of the available natural fishery resources and potential water areas are not directly under the control of the Government. They either belong to the District Council or Local Authorities. In the district the available fishery resources are either in natural ponds or rivers. The traditional and old-fashioned method of fish culture has to be modified. The Government of Meghalaya distributed 256,530 seedlings to the people in 2001. In 2007 the Meghalaya Government distributed 384,000 seedlings. But very few Khasis have fisheries in the Shella-Bholaganj Block. People hardly produce fish for sale. Only a few Khasis bring their fish to market for sale. The fish in the market comes from outside Meghalaya.[127]

Apart from these the coal-mining industry experienced a temporary boom in early 2001. The coal is found in Mawmluh

---

[126] Hugh R. Page, "Khasi", *Encyclopedia of World Culture: South Asia, Vol. III*, ed. by Paul Kockings, (G.K.Hall & Co. Boston, 1992), 122-124.

[127] Quoted from the Office of the Director of Industries, Government of Meghalaya, Shillong.

and Mawsynram area. The production in 2007 was 4143 metric tonnes. In Laitryngew village, coal deposits cover an area of 31 sq. kms. And the inferred reserve of about 4,29,173 tonnes at the middle seam and 3208966 tonnes at the bottom seam. In Cherrapunji coal deposits cover an area of about 36 sq. kms. The inferred reserve is 19.0 million tonnes. In Pynursla and Lyngkyrdem coal deposits cover an area of about 2 sq. kms. The total production of coal in the district during 2005-2006 was 83,000 tonnes. In 2007 it has increased to 86,700 tonnes in the whole district.[128]

The cement factory at Cherrapunji may be regarded as a modest beginning for the utilisation of the vast mineral resources of the Khasi Hills. In 2007 it produced 1,18,000 metric tonnes of cement and gave employment to 700 people. The industry is almost entirely an undertaking of the State Government, which contributed ₹ 640.43 lakhs to its working capital. Today the Cement Industry earns ₹ 495 crores per year for the owners and the government of Meghalaya.[129]

Limestone is found in the Cherrapunji, and Mawmluh-Mawsmai hills. The area is about 1.40 sq. kms. The total proved reserves in the Mawmluh-Mawsmai Hills comes to 31.15 million tones. Limestone is also found in Shella on the west bank of the Umiew River. An area of about 2.76 sq. kms was covered. The total production of limestone in the District during 2007 was 2,08,000 tonnes.

In terms of economic value, of course, cattle play a very important role. Piggery is an important vocation of the rural population. Poultry keeping is easily the most popular side occupation both among the rural and urban population. The majority of rural Khasis keep poultry for their own limited needs. According to the 2001 Census, 84,447 pigs, 45,253 goats, 56,604 cows & Mithuns and 5,664 sheep, were produced in the District. According to the East Khasi Hills District Office Record 2007,

---

[128] Quoted from the Office of the Director of Industries, Government of Meghalaya, Shillong.

[129] Quoted from the Office of the Cherrapunji Cement Factory Record, Cherrapunji.

the total production of livestock was 192,224 of which pigs form 43.93 percent, goats 23.54 percent, cows and mithuns 29.44 percent and sheep 2.94 percent of the total livestock population of the district. The East Khasi Hills District also produced 3,66,763 hens in the same year.[130]

The early Khasis made rudimentary bamboo and cane handicrafts. Mats made from the skin of cane or long grass, were used as containers for harvested crops and for storing paddy and water. Basketry was simple and utilitarian while carpentry was rudimentary.

(c) Agriculture

The important crops are rice, maize, and vegetables. The rice is produced only in the lower area of the district. Farmers have been quick to adopt improved and better seeds. The sources through which such seeds are obtained and distributed are: the State Research Stations, the National Seed Corporation, and the I.C.A.R. Institutions. The fertilisers and manure are of special importance in high altitude regions, which have to rely heavily on them. All types of soil in the district are deficient in natural nitrogen and phosphates and only artificial application of these nutrients has been able to help in increasing the yields of many crops and plants.[131] According to the 2007 Deputy Commissioner's Office Record, altogether there were 3,43,827 total workers out of which 2,62,185 were main workers, 54,913 cultivators, 23,446 agricultural labourers, 3,283 household industry workers and 3,16,232 non workers in the district.[132]

The agricultural land in the district was fertile for producing potatoes and vegetables but the whole economy does not meet the requirements of the daily life of the Khasi people. In the most interior part of the hills, communication was not possible and on the steep slopes, hoeing, or ploughing will result in washing away of the fertile soil. *Jhuming* and slash-and-burn methods were extensively carried out.

---

[130] Quoted from the Office of the Deputy Commissioner of the East Khasi Hills, Shillong.
[131] n.n., *Meghalaya District Gazetteer: East Khasi Hills District*, 69-71
[132] Quoted from the Office of the Deputy Commissioner, Shillong.

(d) The Production of Important Crops in the East Khasi Hills District

Varieties of crops were produced in the East Khasi Hills District. The main vegetables were: potato, sweet potato, papaya, cabbage and cauliflower.[133] The list of the area and important crops produced in the District are mentioned below:

Table No. 4.6 List of Crops and Production in the East Khasi Hills District

Name of Crops	2005		2006-2007	
	Area (Hects)	Production (Tonnes)	Area (Hects)	Production (Tonnes)
1	2	3	4	5
Rice	5,379	10,043	5,484	10,357
Maize	1,900	3,084	1,940	3,443
Millet	457	290	459	487
Potato	10,854	85,635	10,829	944,29
Arecanut	4,568	4,734	4,602	4,524
Sweet Potato	890	3,136	892	3,449
Banana	662	8,644	672	9,122
Turmeric	60	372	61	389
Soyabean	194	154	190	163
Chillies	92	52	94	59

Table 4.6 shows that the most popular cash crops in the market, were: rice, potatoes, bananas, maize, millets, turmeric, betel-nut and chillies.

(e) Tourism

It is another source of income for the society in the district. According to the District Statistical Office Record, this district has attracted many tourists from different parts of India and abroad. In 2007 altogether 2,390 foreigner and 178,697 numbers of tourists from different parts of India visited the East Khasi Hills District. But most of the tourists visited Shillong and did not go beyond it. Around 12 crore rupees were earned for the

---

[133] Nalini Natarajan, *The Missionary among the Khasis*, op.cit., 33.

district through tourism. Some tourists went to visit Cherrapunji. The rural people did not earn much income from tourism.[134]

(f) Transportation

Transportation stands as indispensable activity for the agricultural operation and marketing. Transportation comprises freight services together with supporting and auxiliary services by all modes of transportation i.e., rail, air and sea for the movement of goods and international carriage of passengers and goods. Transport facilitates movement of raw material to the place of production and the finished product from factories to the place of consumption. Along with the transport facility, there is also a need for communication facilities so that producers, traders and consumers may exchange information with one another. Without proper transportation and communication facilities, no community can develop truly.

(g) Power Resources

Electricity was a very important item for living even in the early days. The development of Hydro projects in the state as well as in the Districts has been the responsibility of the Electricity Department. Power plays a vital role in the economic development. Apart from providing the various amenities of modern life, the supply of cheap electric power constitutes an essential infrastructure to the rapid industrialisation of the economy. The State has four Hydro projects, viz. the Umtru Hydro Project, the Umiam Hydro Project Stage I, the Umiam Hydro Project Stage II, and the Umiam Hydro Project Stage III. The State earned several crores of rupees revenue from power and electricity and 2,478 people were given employment in 2007.[135]

The three stages of the Umiam Hydro Project produced 114.00 megawatts. Another Hydro project in the District is the Umtrew Hydro Project, which has a capacity of 11.2 megawatts. In 2007, the Umiam Hydro Project produced 185.2 megawatts and as a

---

[134] Recorded from the District Tourism Department Office, Shillong.
[135] Recorded from the Meghalaya State Electricity Department, Shillong.

result, 73.2 percent of villages of Meghalaya were electrified in 2001 and in 2007, about 95 percent of villages were electrified in the whole district.[136]

(h) **Medical Care**

The ancient Khasis lived in communion with the earth. The ancient Khasis did not have qualified physicians. They did not have hospitals and dispensaries. But they used herbal medicines to cure some special kinds of diseases like abnormal behaviour, epilepsy, and somnambulism, which were thought to be caused by the evil eye or the evil spirits. In order to get rid of these sicknesses, they appeased the spirits by offering animal sacrifices. But due to this ignorance, many people lost their lives. Along with the medical practices, the village medicine man also followed some kinds of magical practices to cure diseases.

Initially the Christian missions did not plan to become involved in medical ministry since they believed that this would interfere with their primary task of evangelism. However, when confronted with the suffering of the people the missionaries began to treat the diseases as best as they could. In 1879, Rev. Griffith opened a dispensary at Mawphlang. The people at first were reluctant to take the medicine offered by the missionaries. But, as they saw the result of medicine they gained confidence in the treatment offered to them.

Even though qualified doctors like Dr. Grifiths and Dr. Hughes had begun medical work earlier, it was not until Dr. G. Roberts arrived in 1913 that a major medical mission among the Khasi-Jaintia people was begun. The Christian missionaries also opened a hospital for the Khasis in 1922. Today, it runs 2 hospitals with competent doctors. They educated the people in different fields. Besides the hospital, the Mission also opened dispensaries at Laitkynsew. The medical service opened the eyes of many Khasis about the need of the medicine. Instead of offering sacrifices to the spirits for their treatment they have started approaching the doctors for treatment.[137]

---

[136] Recorded from the Office of the Chief Engineer's Office, Shillong.
[137] Nalini Natarajan, *The Missionary among the Khasis, op.cit.,* 69-71.

A Hospital in Jawai was inaugurated in 1953 under the leadership of a local Khasi Christian medical graduate; Capt. Dr. Homiwell Lyngdoh Nonglait. He was the only local person who was given the position of missionary by the Welsh mission in 1938.[138]

It was only in 1964 that the Civil Hospital was raised to the status of a largely self-sufficient major hospital with 150 beds. The old Civil Hospital served only a small number of patients. When the Welsh Mission opened a hospital in 1922, most patients preferred treatment there. The Ganesh Das Hospital for Women and Children was started in 1935. Till 1949, the hospital was managed entirely by the women's medical service. Nazareth Hospital at Laitumkhrah was set up in 1959 with 60 beds. It caters to the need for general internal medicine, surgery and gynaecology. Nongpoh Hospital was upgraded from a dispensary to a full-fledged hospital in 1974. In 1979, the number of beds was raised to 400. Bhoilymbong hospital was started with 10 beds in 1980. Civil Hospital, Nongstoin was set up after 1980 with 10 doctors and 12 nurses. There were more than 17 Government dispensaries functioning in different Districts of Meghalaya. In Shella-Bholaganj Block, only 30.47 percent people had medical facilities till 2001. It means more than 69 percent of total population had no access to medical facilities. In 2001, there were 181 qualified doctors, 218 nurses, 34 pharmacists, 70 A.N.M., 10 health visitors and 18 Lab-technicians in the East Khasi Hills District. 180,745 patients were treated in different hospitals and dispensaries of the East Khasi Hills District in 2007 as against 106,540 patients in 2005.[139]

The Ramakrishna Mission runs three dispensaries at Shillong, Cherrapunji and Shella. The first dispensary was established at Shella in 1924. The second dispensary was established at Shillong in 1952. The third dispensary was established at Cherrapunji. The number of qualified doctors in 2007 at Shillong was 14. This

---

[138] J.F. Jyrwa, The Wondrous Works of God: A Study on the Growth and Development of the Khasi-Jaintia Presbyterian Church in the 20th Century, 1980, 83.

[139] Recorded from the Office of the Ramakrishna Mission, Cherrapunji.

dispensary served the rural and urban Khasis free of cost. The Mission's Mobile Dispensary offered service to the rural Khasis. The Mission has been serving the Khasis in the deep interior areas through its Mobile Dispensary. In 2007 the Mission has two Mobile Dispensaries. In the whole district 66,433 patients were treated by the Ramakrishna Mission in 2007. In Shella-Bholaganj Block alone 20,877 patients were treated by the Ramakrishna Mission which is 38.6 percent of the total population in the block.[140]

Table 4.7 Number of Hospitals, Dispensaries, Public Health Centres and Health Sub Centres & Mobile Dispensaries in Meghalaya, East Khasi Hills District and Shella-Bholaganj Block in 2007[141]

Sl No.	Particulars	Meghalaya State	East Khasi Hills District	Shella Bholaganj Block
1	Hospitals	10	5	nil
2	Dispensaries	38	13	3
3	P.H.C.'s	88	19	2
4	C.H.C.	12	1	2
5	Maternity & Child Welfare Centres	1	1	nil
6	Sub-Centres	413	70	6
7	Mobile Clinics	5	3	0
	Total	567	114	14

Table 4.7 indicates the total number of hospitals, dispensaries, public health centres, community health centres, maternity & child welfare centres, sub-centres and mobile clinics in Meghalaya State, East Khasi Hills District and Shella-Bholaganj Block. In the East Khasi Hills District there were 899 villages but medical facilities were fewer. All the five hospitals in the district were

---

[140] Quoted from the Ramakrishna Mission's Office, Cherapunji & Shillong.
[141] Quoted from the Office of Deputy Commissioner of the East Khasi Hills District, Shillong.

found in Shillong only. In the Shella-Bholaganj Block there was no hospital as such to get good medical treatment.

(i) Education

Long before the Khasis were exposed to orthography in the Khasi Hills, they were given some kind of ritualistic education and technical education, which could be identified in the socio-economic structure of the Khasi society throughout the Khasi and Jaintia Hills. There was no school as such, at that time. Even though the Khasis were deprived of formal education during this period, every Khasi home was an informal school, where the children were taught moral, physical, technical and spiritual education through folk songs, pastoral melodies, proverbs and maxims. We can say that education was carried over from one generation to another by word of mouth only.[142]

The first Christian school in the Khasi land was established the Serampore Mission. It did not continue when that Mission withdrew in 1838. The Welsh Christian missionaries opened a new chapter for scientific education in Meghalaya when the first missionary of the Welsh Presbyterian Mission, Rev. Thomas Jones arrived in 1841. Lieutenant Lewin, a government officer gave him a warm welcome at Cherrapunji. The first three Christian Mission schools were opened at Mawsmai, Mawmluh and a place called Cherra. Slowly, more Christian missionaries came and opened more schools and colleges to spread education among the Khasis.

The Christian missionaries from Wales first came to Meghalaya on June 22nd, 1841. Rev. Thomas Jones and his family also arrived at Cherrapunji. Lieutenant Lewin welcomed him. Rev. Jones put down the Khasi language to the Roman alphabet. Education has had due emphasis from the beginning. The dialect spoken at Cherrapunji became the standard language for all sections of the Khasi-Jaintia people.[143] In the 1850's more schools were established

---

[142] Kharmawphlang, *A Study of the Contribution of Non-Christian Missionaries to the Development of Education in Khasi Society*, M.A. Thesis, Submitted to the North East Hills University, 1988, 27.

[143] Dr. O.L.Snaitang, Christianity and Social Change in North East India, *op.cit.*, 113-114.

in Shella, Nongkroh, Nongwar, Sohbar, Mawnai, Lamin, Tyrna, Nongrmai, Mairang, Laitdom, Nongthymmai and Jowai. Till the end of 1973, the Khasi-Jaintia Presbyterian Church had 520 primary schools, 22 middle schools, 8 high schools, and a college. The Christian mission had made a very good contribution in the field of education. The adoption of the Roman script since the 1840's made it comparatively easy to proceed to the study of English which immediately became popular. According to the 2001 Khasi Presbyterian Church record, 44 High Schools, 74 Middle Schools and 240 Primary Schools and a college were run by K.J.P Synod Mihngi and 50 High Schools, 103 Middle Schools, 319 Primary Schools and 4 Colleges by the K.J.P. Synod Sepngi. In the East Khasi Hills District, there were 180 schools run by the Presbyterian Church where over 25000 students got education till 2007.[144] The Roman Catholic Church runs around 800 schools and 3 colleges in the whole of Meghalaya state. The Church of God runs around 40 schools in different parts of Meghalaya. Most of the schools were located either in the towns or in the developed villages. In the Shella-Bholaganj Block the number of schools run by the church was less.

With the advent of Christianity and western education, transformation in social life became inevitable. The new converts abandoned their former religious rites, beliefs and rituals. While accepting Christian teachings and observing Christian ways and collaborations, Khasis maintained their laws of inheritance, their household usages and observed the age-old Khasi cultural and political customs. Funeral ceremonies, ancestor-worship and other animistic celebrations were abandoned in Christian areas but orthodox Khasis continued to preserve their socio-religious and cultural way of life.

In 1920 Ramakrishna Mission entered the Khasi Hills and opened schools to educate them. Ramakrishna Mission has concentrated in the deep rural areas of the East Khasi Hills. Till 2007 the Mission had 58 schools in the East Khasi Hills District

---

[144] Recorded from the Khasi Presbyterian Church Assembly Office.

alone. Over 9000 students have been enrolled in the Ramakrishna Mission schools.[145]

According to the 2001 Census, the literacy rate in the East Khasi Hills District was 76.1 percent. The male literacy rate was 78.12 percent and female literacy rate was 75.82 percent. The rural & urban literacy rate in the District was 63.72 & 88.65 percent. The literacy rate of Meghalaya in 2001 was 63.31 percent. In the same year the male and female literacy rate in Meghalaya was 66.14 & 60.41 percent. The literacy rate in 2007 in the East Khasi Hills District was 81 percent.

Table No 4.8 Descriptions of the Educational Institutions in Meghalaya; East Khasi Hills District & Shella-Bholaganj Block in 2007.

S. No.	Schools & Colleges	State	East Khasi Hills District	Shella-Bholaganj Block
1	L.P./ U.P. Schools	4,679	786	110
2	Middle Schools	922	201	55
3	Secondary/Higher Schools	448	135	12
4	Colleges/Teachers' Training Colleges	33	17	1
5	Universities	1	1	nil
6	Total	6,083	1,140	175

Table 4.8 deals with the educational institutions in Meghalaya State, the East Khasi Hills District and the Shella-Bholaganj Block.

Cultural Life

Corporate Khasi cultural life was in consonance with other aspects of their social life. Graham Wallas, an English sociologist defines culture as "an accumulation of thoughts, values and objects". It is the social heritage acquired by us from proceeding generation through learning as distinguished from the biological

---

[145] Recorded from the Office of the Ramakrishna Mission, Cherrapunji.

heritage passed on to us automatically through genes.[146] According to Basil Pohlong, culture as a way of life includes many components like customs, folklores, faith, language, art, laws, music, ornaments, dance, and so on.[147]

The Khasis have their distinct history, culture, traditions, customs and beliefs, which are treasured as their most cherished heritage. They love music, dancing and songs. They observe many festivals and ceremonies. One of the striking features of the Khasi culture is the megalithic culture where they erect the megaliths.[148]

1. The Food of the Khasis

The Khasis of the East Khasi Hills District eat varieties of food. They take boiled rice with dried or fresh fish, potato or wild herbs, which are well fried with spices.[149] They also eat a variety of meat like pork, mutton, beef, chicken, deer, wild pigs and pigeons, which are prepared in different ways. They eat millet and maize. Some Khasi clans observe food taboos, for example the Kharumnuid clan does not take pork.[150] They also prepare various fruit salads by mixing sour and sweet fruits with proportionate quantities of mustard leaf and the leaf of the Arun plant.[151] The Khasis take two meals a day.[152]

2. House and Architecture

The people were connected with megalithic culture, so they must have had more stone dwellings in the past. Houses differ in style, structure, and shape, according to the climatic and topographical conditions.[153] The Khasi houses were usually oval

---

[146] C.N. Sankar Rao, *Sociology*, (New Delhi: S. Chand & Company, 1997), 217.

[147] Basil Pohlong, *Culture and Religion: A Conceptual Study*, (New Delhi: Mittal Publications, 2004), 92-93.

[148] Dr. C. Woltflang, "The Megalithic Culture of the Khasis," *Heritage of Meghalaya*, op.cit., 24.

[149] K.S. Singh, *People of India: Meghalaya, Vol. XXXII*, (Kolkata: Anthropological Survey of India, 1994), 19.

[150] Mary Pristilla Rina Lyngdoh, *The Festivals in the History and Culture of the Khasi*, op.cit., 24.

[151] H.M. Bareh, *Encyclopedia of North East India, Vol. IV*, op.cit., 96-98.

[152] Pranab K. Das Gupta, *Life and Culture of Matrilineal Tribe of Meghalaya*, op.cit., 66.

[153] *Ibid.*, 318.

type, which had one small opening resembling a window. As there was no chimney, the smoke had to find its way out as best as it could. Grass was used for thatching. Other materials used were bamboo, reeds, dry grass, mud and stones. Each house had two main apartments, the floor being either of stone blocks or tamped earth. The building site was not considered safe if two or three roads meet at one spot. The entrance of the house had to face the East. Brass utensils, copper pots and earthenware were used for cooking. Bamboo containers were commonly used to store water and other articles like betel leaves and nuts, coins and cowries. The old type of Khasi house was usually divided into three rooms, a porch, a centre room and a retiring room. The floor of the centre room and the sleeping room were covered with planks. The roofs were covered with thatch obtained from the neighbouring forest. In such houses there was only one door in front and a window or a small opening on one side.[154]

It was 'taboo' to build a house on the summit of a peak. The houses were made of hardwood and most superior timbers like jackfruit, Champa, Enginaia Tetragona, Oak, and Pine. They considered it taboo to use Makria Sal wood in any part of the house due to the irritant present in the wood.[155] Before the missionaries came to the East Khasi Hills, the Khasis considered nails 'sang' or 'taboo' and used only a certain kind of timber for the fender that surrounds the hearth. The hearth was the place where the family members both young and old gathered together after a day's hard work. They sat together around the fire that was right in the centre of the room. It was the best opportunity for parents to teach their children about their culture, tradition, customs and manners.[156]

It is said that people helped each other for the construction of the houses free of cost.[157]

---

[154] R. Gopalakrishnan, *Meghalaya: Land and People*, op.cit., 70-71.
[155] Caot. B.S. Rana, *The People of Meghalaya*, op.cit., 71.
[156] Silbi Passah, "Sawdong Ka Lyngwiar Dpel," *Heritage of Meghalaya*, (Shillong: Directorate of Art and Culture, n.d.), 26.
[157] *Ibid.*

Khasi buildings were mostly of stone, corroborating the view that the ancient Khasis were among the original authors of stone culture in Assam, including the phallic fertility cult. Other specimens of early Khasi architecture consist mainly of important palatial or royal and public buildings as well as megaliths, bridges, and fortifications. The ancient Khasis also knew sculpture and painting.[158]

3. Script

The general belief is that the Khasis had no original script of their own. But oral legends narrate that the Khasi script was lost in the very early days when they were crossing a river. In the pre-British period, important records of Khasi history were preserved in manuscripts written in Bengali, Assamese and Arabic.[159]

4. Dress

As regards the male Khasi dress of olden days, Khasi dress may be divided into two divisions, ancient and modern. The Khasi males of the interior wear a sleeveless coat or *jymphong* (a wrapper) which is a garment leaving the neck and arms bare, with a fringe at the bottom, and with a row of tassels across the chest. This coat, however, may be said to be going out of fashion in the East Khasi Hills. Coats of European pattern have taken its place in the more civilised centres. They also wear a cap with earflaps. The elderly men, members of noble families and also those who belong to the priestly class wear a turban usually of yellow colour with maroon prints either of geometrical design or animal motifs made of a valuable silk.[160]

The old traditional dress of women is still worn, but with some modification, both in the urban and rural areas. Next to the skin is worn a garment called '*ka Jainpien shad*', which is a piece of cloth worn round the body and fastened at the loins

---

[158] Nalini Natarajan, *The Missionary among the Khasis*, op.cit., 25-26.
[159] *Ibid.*, 23.
[160] Rev. I. Kharkongor, *The Preparation for the Gospel in Traditional Khasi Belief*, (Shillong: Ri Khasi Press, 1973), 12.

with a kind of cloth belt, and which hangs down from the waist to the knee or a little above it.[161] A skirt is used for women called *Jympien*. A mantle is draped from over the shoulders, its two ends being tightened at the chest. Over this is worn a long piece of cloth, sometimes of *muga silk* called *ka Jainsem*. It hangs loosely from the shoulders down to a little above the ankles, and is not caught in at the waist. It is kept in position by knotting it over both the shoulders. Over the *Jainsem* another garment called *ka Jain kup* is worn. This is thrown over the shoulders like a cloak, the two ends being knotted in front, and it hangs loosely down to the ankles. Over the head and shoulders is worn a wrapper called *ka tap-moh-khlieh*. Khasi women also wear a long sleeve velvet blouse (known as Ka Sopti-Kti) with rows of button on the front and lace decoration around the neck.

5. Ornaments

Khasis wear different kinds of ornaments. Khasi women wear gold necklaces, and silver chains. The Pansngiat (a silver crown adoring the head), 'Siar Kynthei (worn on both sides of their ears, which is something like an earring) and Shanryndan (a gold or red coral necklace).[162]

6. Music and Musical Instruments

The Khasis were very fond of songs since music is a part of their life. They have the habit of singing while they work in the fields. They used different musical instruments. The different Khasi musical instruments were: *Ka Bom ka Nakra Bad Tasar* (It is big drum and is used for different purposes at a celebration of a marriage, or during a dance festival), *Ka Ksing Bom* (it is a smaller drum used during a funeral ceremony of grown up people), *Ka Duitara* (a sitar used as an accompaniment for the singing), *Ka Tangmuri* (it is wind instrument used among the Khasis),[163] *Ka Sarong* (It is very close to *Ka Duitara*. It is played on any joyful

---

[161] *Ibid.*, 18-19
[162] *Ibid.*
[163] P.R. Kyndiah, "A Peep into Khasi and Jaintia Music," in *Khasi Heritage* (Shillong: n.p., 1979), 132.

occasion.),[164] and *Ka Besli* (a Flute which is played for fun and not for any official ceremonies).

7. Festivals and Dances

The festivals and ceremonies were the connecting link between the past and the present, and they reflect the socio-economic, cultural and political life of the people.[165] The Khasis are an agrarian community and therefore their lives are centred around the agricultural activities, namely the tilling of land, sowing and planting of seeds, the harvesting of grains and the thrashing and cleaning of the gathered crops. Harvesting is the most popular among them. Harvest is dependent on God who is able to bring His blessings in the form of crops. Harvest dances are expressions of man's prayer to God for a good crop, or a curse in the form of a famine.

In some parts of the study area, there were dances performed before or after the sowing of seeds in the field. The sowing dance like Ka Shad Kylla Mohkhiew, symbolises the happiness of the people after the heavy work of ploughing and sowing is done. It also expresses the hope and expectation of the people after having sown the seed.

There were several popular festivals and dances adopted by the Khasis. These festivals or dances were held at different times, and in different places. The most important Khasi festivals are: *Ka Shad Suk Mynsiem, Ka Shad Nongkrem, Ka Sajer Ka Raid Nonglyngdoh* and *Behdeinkhlam*.[166]

(a) Ka Shad Nongkrem

This festival is celebrated annually in the month of November, at Smit, the capital of the Khyrim Syiemship near Shillong.[167] It was started during the British period, when a need was felt to preserve the traditional culture of the Khasis due to the threat caused by the process of westernisation. This is a very famous

---

[164] Barnes L.Mawrie, *The Khasis and their Natural Environment, op.cit.,* 97.

[165] n.n., *Festivals and Ceremonies in Meghalaya,* ed. by K.R. Marak & R Wankhar, (Shillong: Directorate of Art and Culture, 1994), Preface.

[166] Barnes L. Mawrie, *The Khasis and their Natural Environment, op.cit.,* 103.

[167] n.n., *Meghalaya Hills Gazetteers: East Khasi Hills District,* Shillong, 1991, 59.

annual festival of the Khyrim Syiemship of Nongkrem. This is a type of religious dance in which the Queen Mother inaugurates the dance herself. The King also takes part in the dance and together with him, all his ministers, heads of Raids (regions), and chiefs of the villages. The participants in the dance are both male and female. The female dancers have to be unmarried (virgin), while their male counterparts do not have such restriction.[168]

The dance takes place after a week long-celebration of religious ceremonies. During this festival, the people thank God for all His blessings during the year that has passed and invoked His blessings for the coming year for a bountiful harvest.[169] It is also an invocation to bring in prosperity and peace to the people. Men are active cultivators, not only in planting the seed, but also in protecting and looking after the off-shoots until the harvesting of crops.[170]

The dance is meant to promote solidarity in the kingdom. Performance of the dance before sowing season highlights the relationship between human beings and the earth. This dance is also an expression of invoking the blessing of God on mother earth for a good harvest in the whole kingdom.[171]

(b) Ka Shad Suk Mynsiem

Although the origin of this dance is still obscure, some writers are of the opinion that it had its origin from Ka Pah Syntiew, the legendary ancestress of the Hima Shyllong (Shillong Kingdom). While she was a virgin, Ka Pah Syntiew loved to sing and dance and also taught others the art of dancing. *Ka Shad Suk Mynsiem* is similar in content and style to *Ka Shad Suk Nongkrem*. It is an annual thanksgiving dance held in Shillong in the month of April.[172] This dance is performed only by virgin girls. This festival is celebrated annually under the religion of the Khasis to

---

[168] n.n., A.K. Nongkynrih, "The Khasi Folk Dances: A Sociological Perspective", *Festivals and Ceremonies in Meghalaya* (Shillong: Directorate of Art and Culture, 1998), 32-33.

[169] *Ibid.*

[170] *Ibid.*, 19.

[171] *Ibid.*

[172] n.n., *Meghalaya Hills Gazetteers: East Khasi Hills District*, Shillong, 1991, 59.

commemorate the memory of the founder ancestors of the *Hima*. It is a state religious festival of the Khyrim Syiemship. It is held to honour and respect the ancestors, the founders of the state and religion, and to invoke God's blessings for a bountiful harvest and general prosperity of all people. This dance is held in the month of April after the harvest. During this time, all the political units known as *Raid*[173] who are under the Khyrim Syiemship also take part to show their respect and political unity.[174] This religious festival is held for five days continuously every year.[175]

After gathering the people, a proclamation is made that all should observe complete silence and no one should come in or go out. Then all are asked to pray silently. After this the *Syiem* takes off his turban and kneels down and prays aloud to God, the Creator to bless and give him and the members of the Durbar, wisdom and strength to enable him and the *Ministers* to look after any problem between rich and poor, powerful and weak, men and women and that there may be peace and happiness in the state. After that, one of the elderly persons kneels down and prays to God for His blessings on the *Syiem*, the *Ministers*, the people and the State as a whole.[176]

(c) Ka Sajer Ka Raid Nonglyngdoh

Ka Sajer is another popular festival of the Khasi and Jaintia Hills. This festival is observed in the month of December or January. It is a religious celebration of the whole *Raid Nonglyngdoh*. It is connected with agriculture and cultivation. It is a thanksgiving festival to God for all the blessings that He has showered upon the people. There are important rites, which are associated with cultivation and agriculture in the Khasi and Jaintia Hills.[177]

---

[173] Raid is a political unit in the Khasi kingdom. It consists of number of component villages and usually administered by Basan or Lyngshkor, who is elected by the people and assisted by his durbar.

[174] Mary Pristilla Rina Lyngdoh, *The Festivals in the History and Culture of the Khasis*, op.cit., 72-73.

[175] Capt. B.S. Rana, *The People of Meghalaya*, op.cit., 85-86.

[176] Mary Pristilla Rina Lyngdoh, *The Festivals in the History and Culture of the Khasis*, op.cit., 74-75.

[177] D.T. Laloo, Ka Sajer, Ka Raid Nonglyngdoh, Vol.I, (Shillong: Bynta I, 1982), 27-31.

(d) Ka Behdeinkhlam

This festival is celebrated in the month of July after the sowing is done and attracts a lot of participants and tourists as well. It is a very old Khasi festival and has been given by God Himself to the *Hynniew Trep*. Behdeinkhlam literally means to drive away the plague. It is not only a festival to drive away plague and other evil spirits, but also to invoke God's blessings for the well-being of the people, for a beautiful harvest, for prosperity of the trade and other works of the people, for the increase of the family and also to ask God's forgiveness for all sins. During this festival the relatives and family members who live far away to earn their livelihood come back home to join their family members in common worship of their gods.

There are other dances like harvest dance and sowing dance. Harvest dance is an expression of human's prayer to God for a good crop, and prosperity in the land. The sowing dance symbolises the happiness of the people after the heavy work of ploughing and sowing has been done. It also expresses the hope and expectation of the people after having sown the seeds.[178]

8. Wine

In the East Khasi Hills, distilled liquor is the most commonly used drink at present among the Khasis. The Khasis are in the habit of regularly drinking considerable quantities of rice or millet beer, which is of two kinds (1) *Ka'iad hiar*, (2) *ka'iad um*. Both of them are made from rice or millet and in some places from the root of a plant called *U Khawiang*. Rice beer is a necessary drink for practically all traditional Khasi and Pnar religious ceremonies since it is the custom for the officiating priest to pour out libations of liquor from a hollow gourd to the gods on these occasions. Distillation of liquor was first introduced in the Khasi Hills about the middle of the 19th century. Before the introduction of this kind of liquor, the Khasis used "*Iad-Um*" or "*Iad-Hiar*". *Iad-Um*, which is extracted from fermented rice.

The use of wine is very common in the rural areas. Wine is served in the traditional Khasi social and religious functions.

---

[178] *Ibid.*

Even among the Christians, some young and old take wine. Due to the bad habit of drinking wine and other intoxicating drinks many incidents of murder, rape, robberies, thefts and kidnapping took place in between 2001-2007 in Meghalaya in general and in the East Khasi Hills District in particular. In 2007, 50 murders, 6 rapes, 21 kidnapping, 21 dacoity, 64 robberies, 145 thefts and 24 cheating cases took place in the East Khasi Hills District due to the use of wine. During 2001 and 2007 the number of murders, robberies, thefts, rapes and kidnappings in the adopted and non-adopted villages of the Shella-Bholaganj block was as follows:

Table 4.9 A List of Crimes in Adopted & Non-adopted Villages

Sl. No.	Particulars	2001		2007	
		Adopted	Non-adopted	Adopted	Non-adopted
1	Murder	1	2	1	2
2	Rape	1	3	2	3
3	Robbery	2	4	1	3
4	Theft	2	4	3	4
5	Kidnapping	0	1	0	0
	Total	6	14	7	12

Figure in parenthesis indicates percentage

Table 4.9 shows the social crimes record of murder, rape, robbery and theft incidents of 2001 and 2007 in the adopted and non-adopted villages.

9. Khasi Architecture and Painting: The ancient Khasis also knew sculpture, painting and architecture. The main sculptural designs consisted of human figures like warriors, horse riders and animal figures. Other specimens of early Khasi architecture consist mainly of important palatial or royal and public buildings as well as megaliths, bridges, and fortifications.[179] The images of deities were rare, as the Khasi religion prohibited the making of

---

[179] Nalini Natarajan, *The Missionary among the Khasis*, op.cit., 25-26.

these. There were clay pots with floral designs, ornamental lime pots and vessels covered with floral decorations and painting.[180]

10. Script

Language is generally an important factor in creating a sense of common identity among the people. All big or small states did not have a standard language understood by all. Each state has its own dialect. It is generally believed that the Khasis did not have a script of their own till the coming of the missionaries and the introduction of the Roman script to the Khasi language by Rev. Thomas Jones of the Welsh Mission in 1841, known today as the father of Khasi literature. Nevertheless there was a belief among the people that at one time they had a single language. There is an old belief that they had a script but it was lost in a deluge. This indicates the migration of the Khasis to this land from an unknown time and place.

This is expressed in their folklore. Prior to the middle of the nineteenth century language was spoken, not written. There are a number of folktales like "The Seven Huts of Ancient Days" (Ki Sngi Barim U Hynniew Trep) and "The Cavern" (Ka Krem Lamet Ka Krem Latang) that suggest the contribution of language to a sense of common identity. All sixteen families including God Himself spoke one language.[181] The Cavern folklore tells that once upon a time when all creatures in this world were honest and spoke only one language, the thanks-giving dance was arranged. The dance continued for the whole day and by late afternoon the crowd began to disperse. Just then the Sun and the Moon, as a sister brother, arrived to participate in the dance. During this dance there was a great uproar of scornful laughter because a sister and a brother were dancing together. Due to that the Sun was overcome with shame and fled to the cavern. It shows that there was a spoken language in the primal Khasi-Jaintia community.[182]

---

[180] *Ibid.*, 26.
[181] Dr. O.L.Snaitang, Christianity and Social Change in North East India, *op.cit.*, 22-23.
[182] *Ibid.*, 23.

11. Sports

Archery is not merely a game, the bow and arrow were also part of the day-to-day life of the Khasis and the arrow is the symbol of a life long companion to a person. Archery is the manifestation of the character of the Khasis. In-grained in archery is the spirit of tolerance, even if one loses a contest. Even swordsmanship was the most popular game linked with the use of war-like arts.[183] Archery as traditional game still figures prominently. Among other games high jump, long jump, wrestling and butting, the javelin, the spear and stone weighing were other important games.[184]

12. Megalithic Culture

In the East Khasi Hills District we can see a group of upright stones, table stones and other stone structures. The practice of megalithic culture seems to represent the concept of unity and of human power in their society. These stones were erected in honour and memory of their deceased fathers besides showing their power and strength by performing these activities for future generations. Khasis believed that for a peaceful and prosperous life they must practise this culture. They expect to gain a peaceful life and good luck by doing so. These memorial stones indicate the belief of the people in supernatural powers. All these megaliths have social, religious, economic and political significance. Some of them are connected with religious rites; others are erected in memory of the dead. The upright stones are known as male stones. Megalithic erections are also connected with cremation, bone collection and depository ceremonies.

Other stones are the *Mawumkoi*, which are erected when the bones of those who died of unnatural death are washed in a pool known as the *umkoi umsham* to free them from defilement and that their spirit could go to the house of God. Before this ceremony their bones are kept in a separate stone known as *mawbah*. After their bones have been washed followed by certain rites and ceremonies, they are placed in the right place.

---

[183] Nalini Natarajan, *The Missionary among the Khasis*, op.cit., 3.
[184] Dr. Hamlet Bareh, The History and Culture of the Khasi People, *op.cit.*, 305.

Religious groups: Christians, animists, Hindus and Muslims are the major religious communities of different origin living in the urban areas of the district. But in the rural areas of this district Khasi Christians and traditional Khasis were the majority. Now some Khasis have adopted certain Hindu cultural and religious elements to some extent. Along with the Hindu Bengalis many Khasis are also absorbing the language and the culture of the Hindus.

Religious Life of the Khasis in the East Khasi Hills District

The essence of Khasi religion is that nothing falls outside its sphere be it social, political or economical. Aniema Nongkhlaw in her book title "Modernisation of the Khasi Society: A Sociological Study" says that religion is at the core of the tribal culture and there is no dichotomy between the sacred and the secular in their lives. It deeply influences the Khasi way of life and in fact, Khasi culture itself revolves around it.[185] The essence of the Khasi religion is that nothing falls outside its sphere. It starts within the *Kur* and religion plays a predominant role not only in the social life of the people but in the political life as well.

The Khasis believe that their religion is given by God, and is not founded by human beings.[186] They believe that their life and action, thought and speech are very much controlled by a deep sense of religion. They were highly conscious of the role of God in their lives.[187] The close relationship between humans and religion is depicted in the rituals carried on right from the time when the baby is conceived up to the time when a human being is to be cremated. The religious rites and ceremonies of a *Kur* must be performed within the boundary of the *Kur* and cannot be performed by another *Kur*.[188]

---

[185] Miss Aniema Nongkhlaw, *Modernisation of the Khasi Society: A Sociological Study*, Unpublished M. Phil. Thesis Submitted to the North Eastern Hill University, 1990, 46.

[186] H.O. Mawrie, *The Essence of Khasi Religion, op.cit.*, 40.

[187] Dr. Barnes L. Mawrie, *Introduction to Khasi Ethics, op.cit.*, 19.

[188] U. Hipson Roy Kharshing, *The Land where Women are Women and Men are Men*, ed., Shillong, n.d., 36.

The Khasi religion does not preach any superiority over other religions. According to them, God has given each form of worship or religion to glorify Him. One of the fundamental beliefs of the Khasi religion is that the human beings come into this world to learn truth and righteousness.[189]

1. Myth

The word 'myth' is derived from the Greek 'Muthos'. Muthos in its meaning is the word for a story concerning gods and super human beings. Thus, a myth is an expression of the sacred in words.[190] Walter F. Otto states that in any original myth, there is God's revelation within His immediate living surroundings; this God is the whole essence of the world.[191]

(a) The Sohpetbneng Myth

It is true that primal religions are usually rich in myths and legends. This mythology explains the arrival of human beings on earth. After making heaven and earth, God created 16 families at the beginning. They were created to be with Him for a social co-existence. These 16 families were divided into two groups. One consisted of nine families and the other seven. The former was genderless and was called **Khyndaitrep** (nine families), and the latter called **Hynniewtrep** (seven families). There were many mountains and hills of which one was *Sopetbneng*. It is a bare dome-like hill, about 13 miles to the north of Shillong. *Sopetbneng*, in Khasi dialect, means the centre of heaven. God drew up a suitable covenant that was sealed between Him and the seven huts. The covenant was sealed so that if you remain faithful to it, you shall live happily here on this earth but if you break it or you cut down the Diengiei Tree, the relation between heaven and earth shall become null and void and thirty sins and thirty troubles shall fall upon them.[192] The gods who lived in heaven

---

[189] U. Hipshon Roy, "My Faith", *Khasi Heritage*, ed. by Hipshon Roy, (Shillong: Ri Khasi Press, 1979),119.

[190] Kees W. Bolle, "Myth", In *Encyclopedia of Religion, Vol. 9*, ed. by Mircea Eliade, (New York: Macmillan Publishing Company, 1987), 261.

[191] J. Wardenburg, *Classical Approaches to the Study of Religion*, (Paris: Mouton & Co., 1973), 632.

[192] Rev. Kharkongor, *I La Pyndep*, (Shillong: Ri Khasi Press, 1969), 6.

watched the beauty of this earth and used to think of coming down for a while.[193]

It is said that on the top of U Sohpetbneng Peak grew a tree, which served as a ladder of communication between God and human beings. That was then the Golden Age after the creation.[194] God granted peace and prosperity to the seven huts. God made a covenant with them that He would be with them always. The covenant stated that as long as human beings would preserve this tree they would enjoy peace and immortality, but if the tree was cut down, sin and suffering of all kinds would invade the world.

One day human beings fell into the trap of the evil one who, in the form of a big snake who deceived a human being, and tricked him into cutting down the tree. It is believed that God Himself planted the symbolic tree.[195] Communication broke down after the disappearance of the golden ladder from the Sohpetbneng Peak.[196]

(b) The Diengiei Myth

It is believed that communication broke down after the disappearance of the golden ladder on Sohpetbneng Peak. It is said that soon after the fall there grew on the top of the Diengiei Peak another tree, which was big and tall, and its over-spreading branches and leaves became so thick as to overcast the earth with darkness. This darkness signifies the spiritual crisis of human beings.[197] The whole earth was covered by darkness. Finally human beings turned to God in repentance. For the Khasis this symbolises the spiritual crisis that fell upon man after the fall of the golden ladder.[198] The myth speaks of one thing; and that is

---

[193] G.K. Ghosh & Shukla Gosh, *Fables and Folk Tales of Meghalaya*, (Kolkata: Firma KLM Private Ltd., 1998), 36-37.

[194] Joseph Puthenkurakal, "Christianity and Mass Movement among the Khasis: A Catholic Perspective" *Christianity in India*, ed. by F. Hrangkhuma, (New Delhi: ISPCK, 1998), 196.

[195] G. Costa, *Ka Riti Jong Ka Ri Laiphew Syiem*, (Shillong: St. Antony's College, 1936), 1-3.

[196] H.O. Mawrie, "God and Man", in *Khasi Heritage*, (Shillong: Seng Khasi, 1979), 87.

[197] *Ibid.*, 87.

[198] Mrs. Rafy, *Khasi Folk Tales*, (Guwahati: Spectrum Publications, 1985), 9.

man's transgression and man's fall. The separation from God inevitably led to the reign of darkness and sin in the world as symbolised by the great tree that covered the whole earth.[199]

2. Concept of God

God is the secret ground that becomes the foundation stone of the Khasi religion. The holiness and conception of God is kept secret and so the people never used the term "God" in their daily life. However, the holiness of God does not mean that God is unimportant.[200] God, according to the Khasis, is the Creator and the Sustainer of this universe.[201] Being all in all He is above gender. God, according to them, has no sex, and never grows old. They believe that He is the Supreme Spirit who permeates the whole universe, the Giver and Sustainer of our life and universe.[202] He is Omnipotent, Omnipresent, Omniscient and All-Powerful, and Him only should humans fear and worship.[203]

The Khasis feel free to address God in the language of their liking. U Sib Charan Roy said that God for the Khasis is above sex, gender and form. As the Creator of life and of all beings, He is known as *U Blei Nongthaw*. He also said that God is good, kind, forgiving, and the unfailing one.[204] In fact the position of the Supreme Being and the Author of creation has not been so much removed from the affairs of the human beings who still seek His consent to the institution and pacification of other spirits and who, when pressed by afflictions and sufferings, leave everything to His will.[205] According to H.O. Mawrie, the word 'Nongthaw' means Creator. But this word is preceded by the word 'Nongbuh' which implies that God is the 'Planner' or 'Designer.'[206]

---

[199] H.O. Mawrie, "God and Man", *Khasi Heritage*, op.cit., 87.
[200] T. Nongsiej, Khasi Cultural Theology, (Delhi: ISPCK, 2002), 27.
[201] R.T. Rymbai, "The Concept of God", *Golden Jubilee Commemoration Souvenir* (Shillong: n.p., 1987), 47.
[202] Sib Charan Roy Jaid Dhkar, *Ka Niam-Ki Khasi Ka Niam Tip Blei Tip Briew*, (Shillong: Ri Khasi Press, 19.
[203] *Ibid.*, 47.
[204] CFR Mawrie & H. Onderson, "God And Man", *Khasi Heritage*, ed. op.cit., 83.
[205] Dr. Hamlet Bareh, The History and Culture of the Khasis, op.cit., 341.
[206] H.O. Mawrie, *The Essence of Khasi Religion*, op.cit., 41.

On the eve of cremation, the people address to their deceased saying "go in peace and partake at the feast of betel-nuts in the House of God," which indicates that they strongly believe in the world here-after which is identified with the House of God.[207]

Khasis believe that God is Self-sufficient, Self-existent, and Self-sustaining. He does not require any sacrifice from human beings.[208] God is the Dispenser of everything in this world.[209] Some scholars suggested that sometimes the conception of the Godhead is female (*Ka Blei*). He is both Transcendent and Immanent. He is within all human beings, when we love fellow human beings we love God.[210] His nature, his purposes, and way of behaving are not subject to any change, either for better or for worse.[211] It is the firm belief of every Khasi that God reveals Himself and His desires through the things of nature. S. Barkataki wrote: "The Khasis invoke God when there is suffering or in times of trouble. He is not actually worshipped."[212] They pray to Him as the goddess of health (*Ka Lei Longspah*) to bless their business or trade ventures. He is the Defender of the village and State from their enemies.[213] He is the cause of goodness and prosperity.

God, according to the Khasi traditional faith, is a personal God but He is the unseen one. He is not co-existent with something else. He has the power to bless the home and the clan so that they flourish and multiply. He never takes the form of one of His creatures.[214] Apart from being the Creator, He is also the Inner Principle of life and growth. He gives new life and also

---

[207] Dr. Hamlet Bareh, The History and Culture of the Khasis, *op.cit.*, 341.

[208] Rabon Singh, Ka Niam Khasi, (Shillong: Re-Khasi Press, 1960), 14.

[209] Khynpham Singh, "Khasi Religion and Khasi Society", *Religion and Society of North East India*, ed. by Sujata Miri, (New Delhi: Vikas Publishing House Pvt. Ltd., 1980), 42-45.

[210] Sib Charan Roy Jaid Dhkar, *Ka Niam Ki Khasi Ka Niam Tip Brew Tip Blei*, (Shillong: Ri-Khasi Press, 1979), 3-8.

[211] Mary Pristilla Rina Lyngdoh, *The Festivals in the History and Culture of the Khasis*, *op.cit.*, 26.

[212] S. Barkataki, *Tribes of Assam*, (New Delhi: National Book Trust, 1969), 36.

[213] R.T. Rambai, "The Khasi Concept of God", *Golden Jubilee Souvenir, op.cit.*, 48.

[214] H. Lyngdoh, *Ka Niam Khasi, op.cit.*, 14.

sustains it.[215] Khasis also believe that God is within and around them.[216] It is human beings who try to distance themselves from God who is always closer to them.[217] 98.7 percent respondents believe that God is one.

3. Spirits

Belief in the existence of spirits was very much prevalent in Meghalaya State in general and in the East Khasi Hills District in particular. The Khasi traditions tell that Khasi religion became corrupt as a result of an inherent fear of fiends, ghosts and malevolent spirits who had to be propitiated.[218]

Sacred groves which are preserved well indicate the existence of jungle spirits. The cutting down of trees is taboo, and it is an offence to cut trees therein for any purpose other than performing funeral rites. The sacred trees are believed to be the abodes of both good and evil spirits and hence cutting them was prohibited. The most important trees of this type among the Khasis are the *Symbud* and *Khnong*.[219]

Besides the sacred groves, the Khasis too have their sacred spots and similarly deify mountains that become sacred to them. The mountains are not only regarded as seats of gods, but are often personified as gods. The evil spirits, which were in need of sacrifices, tormented the people with sickness and natural calamities. These evil spirits are the souls of those people who died without earning righteousness in this world. They are unworthy to join their ancestors in heaven. So they continue to roam the length and breadth of this world and inhabit the mountains, the rivers, the lakes, the stones and the trees in the forests. These evil spirits torment the people with sicknesses and misfortunes.[220] The sacrifices were performed during the autumn

---

[215] Pascal Malngiang, *Aspects of Khasi Philosophy*, (Shillong: Seven Huts Enterprise, 1991), 18-19.
[216] Kynpham Singh, "Khasi and Jaintia Religion", *Khasi Heritage*, ed., Shillong, 1978,97.
[217] R.T. Rambai, "U. Hynniewtrep Bad U Blei," in *Sawian S.S..* ed., (Shillong: Seng Kut Snem, 1998), 37.
[218] Personal Interview with Kharwanlang on 17.5.2006 at Shillong.
[219] K.L. Bhowmik, *Tribal India*, (Kolkata: The World Press Pvt. Ltd., 1971), 144.
[220] *Ibid.*, 326-327; also see Mrs. Rafy, *Khasi Folktales*, (Guwahati: Spectrum Publications, 1985), 18.

time when different clans participated. Whenever the river was to be crossed in those days, the travellers confessed their sins.[221]

Khasis also believe in the existence of good spirits, whom the almighty God has put on earth to be its guardians. These good spirits are not worshipped as God by the Khasis. They are seen as guardians appointed by God. These spirits are seen as the extension of God who is Omnipresent and Omniscient. They also believe that as long as a person fears God and does not violate His commandments, they will be looked after and protected by these good spirits.[222] 95.4 percent of the respondents were of the opinion that traditional Khasis worship the spirits of their ancestors. They appease the spirits by offering animal blood. They also believe in two kinds of spirits known as malevolent and benevolent spirits.

4. Concept of World

The Khasis believe that God is the ultimate creator and originator of all things in this world. He caused all things to be and to grow.[223] They believe that the orderliness and harmony that exists in the world is the intelligent design of the creator God.[224] He is the one who keeps watch over the whole creation and supports it with everything that they need for their sustenance.[225] Khasis also believe that in the evolutionary process, God is always the efficient and final cause.[226]

According to traditional Khasi belief, in the beginning the world was perfect and without sin (pap). Heaven and earth were very near to each other, and human beings had direct and free communication with God.[227] Although the Khasis do not articulate clearly the concept of ex-nihilo creation, yet implicitly they uphold this idea. In fact the word "Thaw" in its strict sense

---

[221] R.T. Rymbai, "U Hynniewtrep Bad U Blei," in *Sawian S.S.*, (ed.), *op.cit.*, 37.
[222] Barnes L. Mawrie, *The Khasis and their Natural Environment*, (Shillong: Vendrame Institute Publications, 2001),134.
[223] Jeebon Roy, *The Book about One God*, (Shillong: Ri Khasi Enterprise, 2005), 23.
[224] H.O. Mawrie, "God And Man", in *Khasi Heritage*, (Shillong: Seng Khasi, 1979), 83-84.
[225] Barnes L. Mawrie, *The Khasis and their Natural Environment, op.cit.*, 32.
[226] Sib Charan Roy, *Ka Niam Ki Khasi Ka Niam Tip Blei Tip Briew, op.cit.*, 36.
[227] Rev. I. Kharkongngor, *The Preparation for the Gospel in Traditional Belief, op.cit.*

means to create out of nothing. On the other hand, the word "nongshna" is used to refer to a person who makes something out of an existing material like *u nongshna iing* (house builder), *u nongshna baje* (watch maker), etc.[228] U Sib Charan Roy, a prominent Khasi thinker, in his book called *Ka Niam-Ki Khasi* explained that God created everything out of the matter that already existed in the world. He said that God gave life to the living bodies out of the life already in existence.[229]

5. Concept of Human Being

According to the Khasi belief, human beings are said to have come into the world as designed and decreed by God. The human being is a created being but a creature above all other creatures. In the great plan and design of God the human being has a place and an allotted part to play. They believe that God made human beings as a full-fledged humanity to inhabit this world. For this reason they have the moral obligation to live a righteous life and earn righteousness.[230] However, in the Khasi creation story, no mention is made as to when the human being was created. The mythology states that human beings already existed with God in heaven. At the request of Mother Earth, God sent seven of the sixteen groups to earth to take care of the created world. The human being is placed as a steward and keeper of the earth and everything in it. Humans become mediator between the Creator and the created things.[231] Humans are to propagate truth and to procreate and ensure the continuity of his/her own race.[232] One comes to this world with a divine cause and his or her life has a purpose, value and direction.[233]

The Khasis also believe that human beings have free will.[234] They believe that when human beings walk in consonance with

---

[228] Barnes L. Mawrie, *The Khasis and their Natural Environment*, op.cit., 29.
[229] Sib Charan Roy, *Ka Niam Ki Khasi Ka Niam Tip Blei Tip Briew*, op.cit., 23.
[230] *Ibid.*
[231] *Ibid.*
[232] Khynpham Singh, "Khasi and Jaintia Religion," *Khasi Heritage*, op.cit., 98-99.
[233] Mawrie H.O., "A Short View of the Khasi Religion," *Where lies the Soul of Our Race*, edited by Hipson, (Shillong: Re Khasi Press, 1982), 66-67.
[234] Dr. Barnes L. Mawrie SDB, *Introduction to Christian Ethics*, op.cit., 15.

God's will, God is with them at every moment in their lives to guide them in all activities.[235] The God-man relationship, according to the Khasi belief, can be understood and appreciated if we have a look at the relationship between the mother and her child.[236]

6. The Concept of Soul

The Khasis believe in the existence of the soul. They believe that the soul is immaterial and immortal.[237] God has created it. They also believe that the souls of the dead become linked with the spirits of their predecessors. They compare life on earth to dewdrops hanging from a leaf. As the most beautiful dew drops glitters and sparkles with an excellent colours of the rainbow, so also soul. Therefore funeral ceremonies are carefully performed in the belief that by doing so the soul of the deceased will go straight to the house of God without any obstruction by evil spirits. The soul comes with a purpose, and when the purpose is over it goes back to where it comes from. It exists in itself and does not owe its existence to any other material reality like the body. They also believe that all human beings are equal.[238] At death the body of a human being disintegrates but the soul and identity of that person will continue to live.[239] About 99 percent of the respondents from Christian and non-Christian communities believe that soul is eternal.

7. The Concept of Sin (*Pap*)

The Khasis believe that crimes and transgressions committed, not only adversely affect the person responsible but they also bring misery and misfortunes to the family members as well. The folklore concerning sin clearly portrays that it was a human being who broke his or her relationship with God by cutting down the tree, which symbolises that relationship between God and human beings, is cut off.[240]

---

[235] Jaitdkharm U Sib Charan Roy, *Ka Niam Ki Khasi*, (Shillong: Ri Khasi Press, 1979), 5.

[236] R.T. Rymbai, *Meghalaya: Yesterday and Today*, op.cit., 96.

[237] Dr. Hamlet Bareh, *The History and Culture of the Khasi People*, op.cit., 323-330.

[238] Jaitdkharm U Sib Charan Roy, *Ka Niam Ki Khasi*, op.cit., 33.

[239] P.R. Kyndiah, *Meghalaya: Yesterday and Today*, op.cit., 96.

[240] R.T. Rymbai, *The Origin and Settlement of the Khasi-Pnar*, (Shillong: 1979), 34.

Streamlet Dkhar says that *Pap (sin)* is the making of oneself equal to God, the personal breaking, alienating or turning away from God, which is both an act of omission and commission.[241] The Khasi Code of Conduct describes the whole duty of human and any breaking of it is *pap(sin)*.[242] Sin is a transgression against the covenant that God made with human beings from the beginning of time.[243]

The essence of sin lies not in isolated acts of transgression, but in the depths of man's being. The most formidable and abominable sins, which cannot be forgiven by God, are incest and marriage within the same clan.[244] The sinners who commit such two kinds of sins cannot find peace even in the future state, but roam in the world like ghosts (*snaiap*). The souls of those who are wicked or whose funeral ceremonies have not been duly performed or have died under the ban of sang (taboo) will go to a place known as the abode of devil.[245] Gurdon says that the Khasis apparently do not believe in the punishment after death, and there is no idea of hell. God can forgive them through intercessory prayers, divination and sacrifices.[246] 97% respondents also believe that there are two kinds of sin in Khasi traditional religion- forgivable and unforgivable. In their opinion the souls who have married in their own clan or committed a murder will not go to the house of their forefathers after death.

8. Salvation

Traditional Khasi religion believes that salvation is an eternal state of happiness and fellowship. The Khasis believe that those who act justly and righteously on earth will go to join the nine-hut in heaven. The good person goes to eat betel-nut in God's

---

[241] Streamlet Dkhar, *Ka Jinglong Marwei U Briew Kat Kum Ki Khasi Drama*, (Shillong: Streamlet Dkhar, 1986), 33.

[242] n.n., *People of India: Meghalaya*, ed. by K.S. Singh, et. el., (Kolkata: Seagull Books, 1994), 22

[243] R.S. Berry, *Ka Jing Sneng Tymmen, Part II*, (Shillong: Ri Khasi Press, 1960), 20-21.

[244] T. Nongseij, *Khasi Cultural Theology*, (Delhi: ISPCK, 1998), 198.

[245] *Ibid.*, 22.

[246] Joseph Puthenpurakal, "Christianity and Mass Movement among the Khasis: A Catholic Perspective", *Christianity in India*, (New Delhi: ISPCK, 1998), 198.

house. Salvation is for those Khasis who earn righteousness.[247] They rarely make offerings and sacrifices to God, either as a token of gratitude or to propitiate Him. They believe that God does not need offerings because He has created all things.[248] Even 98.5 percent households have the same opinion about the concept of salvation in Khasi traditional religion.

9. Life after Death

The traditional Khasis strongly believe that there is life after death. They consider earth as a temporary place and are more concerned with their life after death in the house of God.[249] They glorify their dead as they have become supernatural beings and are ordained of the deity to assist the living ones to obtain blessings.[250]

They believe that death is not the end of life. They also believe that any person who dies goes to join the ancestors who have gone ahead to God's abode.[251]

In the Khasi practice the body of the person from traditional religion is cremated after death. The bones and ashes are collected. The depository ceremony has its origin in the life after death.[252]

The task of the human is to earn righteousness by fulfilling one's duties sincerely and faithfully. According to their faith, those who live a righteous life will go to the abode of their forefathers (heaven).[253] In their belief the enjoyment of such souls with the ancestors in heaven will depend on receiving proper death rites at the hands of the members of their clan. The elaborate final ceremony, covering five days, is important.[254] It is believed

---

[247] H.W. Sten, *Khasi Poetry: Origin and Development*, (New Delhi: Mittal Publications, 1990), 48.
[248] Kynpham Singh, "Khasi and Jaintia Religion," *Khasi Heritage*, op.cit., 99-100.
[249] S.C.Roy Dkhar, *Ka Niam Ki Khasi Ka Niam Tip Blei Tip Briew*, op.cit., 9.
[250] *Ibid.*, 9.
[251] Radhon Singh Berry, *Ka Jingsneng Tymmen* (The teachings of Elders), Translated by Bijoya Sawian, (Shillong: Ri Khasi Press, n.p.), x.
[252] Dr. Dominic Jala, "The Khasi Christian Concept of Death and After Life," *Impact of Christianity on North East India*, ed. (Shillong: Vendrame Institute Publications, 1996), 176-185.
[253] Kynpham Singh, "Khasi and Jaintia Religion," *Khasi Heritage*, op.cit., 98-99.
[254] H.G. Joshi, *Meghalaya: Past and Present*, op.cit., 195.

that when the individual's bones were finally resting with those of the antecedents in the *mawbah*, they enjoy a state of endless bliss.[255]

However, the bones of a person who has lived a sinful life on this earth, and for whom sacrificial and religious rites have not been performed, are not kept in *mawbah*; the spirits of such persons will not go to the house of God.[256] It is also believed that the just person would reap a good harvest while those who have committed sins would suffer the fruits of their evil deeds.[257] One, who works honestly, justly, diligently, is worthy of the life God has given.[258] He will eat betel-nut in the house of God, which expresses the supreme state of happiness enjoyed by him/her who has gone to the house of God as a result of his/her good life in this world. 98.6 percent households also believe that there is life after death.

10. Belief in "*Thlen*" and Practice of Human Sacrifice

The Khasis have no idols or temples. One curious feature is related to the belief about snake *(thlen)*. The tradition runs that there was once in a cave near Cherrapunji a gigantic snake *(thlen)*, which caused great havoc among human beings and animals.[259] According to some scholars, Khasi offered human sacrifices to the gigantic snake, U *Thlen*. The worshippers of such *thlen* were supposed to prosper. The thlen is believed to possess the power of conferring great riches upon the families who offer human sacrifices to it.[260] 99.7 percent respondents believe that there was 'Thlen'. The Khasis offered human sacrifices to him.

---

[255] Hugh R. Page Jr., "Khasi", *Encyclopedia of World Culture: South Asia*, Vol. III, ed. by Paul Kockings (Boston G.K. Hall & Co., 1992), 122-124.

[256] Pascal Malngiang, *Aspects of Khasi Philosophy*, (Shillong: Seven Huts Enterprise, 1991), 46-47.

[257] Miss Aniema Nongkhlaw, *Modernisation of the Khasi Society: A Sociological Study*, M.Phil. Thesis Submitted to the North East Hill University, Shillong, 1990, 45-46.

[258] R.T. Rymbai, "Some Aspects of Khasi Culture and Religion", Ki Symboh Na Ka Seng Kut Snem, (Shillong: Ri Khasi Press, 1988), 32.

[259] S.N. Barkataki, *Tribal Folk-Tales of Assam Hills*, (Guwahati: Publication Board Assam, 1970), 151.

[260] B.C. Allen, et el., *Gazetteer of Bengal and North-East India*, (New Delhi: Mittal Publications, 2001), 488.

Moreover, the people associated with *thlen* usually preserve for one year the liquor, which is prepared of *thlen's* sweat, which is ejected during the swallowing of the victimised person to help them to remain audacious for kidnapping and criminal practices.[261] While the thlen (snake) strangled the victim to death, the associated person with the thlen cuts off the eye-brows, nostrils, lips, and finger-nails of the victim to offer to the *thlem*.

Traditional Khasis believed that feeding the *thlen* required a big ceremony. If the *thlen* is not fed with human blood, he will come out of his abode and put the keepers in shame. Although his favourite form is that of a snake, he can also take on different forms like that of a lizard, fish, cat, worm, and so on.[262]

11. Ancestor Worship

Ancestor worship was an important feature of the traditional Khasi religion. Bareh says that the conception of ancestor worship maintains the link with the dead by the continued observance of funeral ceremonies.[263] The glorification of the dead consisted of the appeasement of the deceased ancestors with offerings of food and other material presents. Respect and love for the dead ancestors was of utmost importance. This is the reason why they perform a sacrifice with a cock at the death of a person.[264] They also believe that the cock will act as a guide for the departed soul of a person. The Khasis have great respect for the dead, as they believe that although they are no longer here on this earth, yet they live in another world in the house of God.[265] 100 percent households opined that traditional Khasis worship the spirits of their ancestors. They appease the spirits of their forefathers by offering sacrifices to them.

Among the important spirits are those of the first ancestors of the *kur or clan*, who could inflict much pain and sufferings upon the living, if the entire funeral and other rites are not

---

[261] Dr. Hamlet Bareh, *The History and Culture of the Khasi People*, op.cit., 324-325.
[262] *Ibid.*
[263] H. Bareh, *A Short History of Khasi Literature*, Shillong, 1962, 10.
[264] H. Lyngdoh, *Ka Niam Khasi*, op.cit., 3-4.
[265] Personal Interview with Rev. Sampliang on 10.2.2005 at Shillong.

performed. They offer sacrifices in front of the monoliths, which are erected in their memory. The offering of food to the dead ancestors is known as *ka Ai Bam* and it is performed in order to protect the living from evil spirits and to obtain material prosperity.[266] By offering them some kind of food, and building monoliths in their names as outward signs and symbols of their reverence to their departed, they show them respect.[267] Kympham Singh denies the worship of the ancestors by the Khasisi. According to him they only performed duties as simple tokens of remembrance. 96.5 percent households believed that the traditional Khasis offer animal sacrifices to the ancestors' souls. They also worship ancestor spirits.

12. Religious Rites and Rituals

Lot of rituals were practiced in the traditional Khasi religion. In the East Khasi Hills District rites and rituals performances differ from place to place.[268] The funeral rites among the Khasis differ from village to village. The difference may be due to the long keeping of a corpse among the Lyngngams. Rituals play an important role in the religious life of the Khasis and have both social and supernatural sanctions. Rituals concerned with economic activities, social structure and with the life of human beings.[269] The Khasi rituals connected with birth, naming, puberty, marriage and death commonly gave expression to their social structures.

When a baby boy was born in a family, three arrows *nam jer* and a bow formed part of the naming ceremony. The first arrow is designed to guard oneself, the second arrow for guarding the family and clan, and the third arrow to guard the territorial rights. In the Khasi traditional religion the word 'myth' has a relevant meaning. It is an important word for studying the origin

---

[266] N.C.S. Sen, *The Origin and Early History of the Khasi Synteng People*, (Kolkata: 1981), 17-18.

[267] Maham Singh, "Nongkrem Dance," *Khasi Heritage,* ed. Shillong, 1979, 148.

[268] P.R. Gurdon, *The Khasis, op.cit.,* 116-118.

[269] Mary Pristilla Rina Lyngdoh, *The Festivals in the History and Culture of the Khasi, op.cit.,* 29-30.

of human history and belief. The sources that provide insights about the understanding of God are myths and legends.[270]

The birth of a baby was not an occasion for much ceremony as when someone died. Cremation rites were important. The funeral ceremonies had to be carefully performed so that the spirit of the dead would not be obstructed by evil spirits on its journey to the house of God. Death ceremonies were elaborate. This ritual began with the sacrifice of the cock and ended with an offering of the betel leaf and nut sent to the body.

13. Divination, Priesthood and Animal Sacrifice

The term divination is derived from the Latin word 'deus' or 'divus', which means 'a god' or 'divine'. It is believed that divination is the phenomenon related to foretelling or interpreting the future with supernatural aid. It is also used to detect the cause for past events. It is believed that the practice of divination became a common practice among the Khasis due to their belief in evil spirits. Breaking of eggs has been one of the most popular methods adopted by the Khasis for divination.[271] 97.6 percent respondents were of the opinion that traditional Khasis practised divination and animal sacrifices and that they are practised even today by the traditional Khasis.

The Khasis have their institution of priesthood. But they, unlike the Hindus have no *Purohit*, or priest to perform the family ceremonies. Such duties fall to the lot of the head of the family or clan, who carried them out generally through the agency of the *kni*, or maternal uncle. The propitiation of the spirits is carried out by the Lyngdoh or by an old man who is knowledgeable in the art of communicating with the spirits of the dead. The office of the priest was both hereditary and elective. The priest offers various sacrifices as prescribed on behalf of the individual or the family. The priest was both mediator as well as diviner.[272]

The Khasis have several sacrifices that are performed in various ways. Cock sacrifice occupies an eminent place in the Khasi

---

[270] P.S. Nianglang, "Evolution of Riangsih Sirdarship", *Heritage of Meghalaya*, (Shillong: Directorate of Art and Culture, n.d.), 15.

[271] Henry H. Presler, *Primitive Religions of India*, (Chennai: C.L.S., 1971), 66.

[272] Dr. Hamlet Bareh, *The History and Culture of the Khasi People*, op.cit., 339.

tradition. All sacrifices are performed by the diviner. The diviner is believed to be ordained by God himself. The diviner has the gift of interpreting the signs that are portrayed in the sacrifices. The common people simply accept whatever the diviner tells them afterward. The Lyngdoh, who is always appointed from a special priestly clan, holds his office for life, and may be one of several within a State being the chief functionary of the community cults. He also has certain duties in conjunction with marital laws and household exorcism.[273]

The idea of sacrifice, according to a Khasi myth, came to man only after a covenant had been made between God and the cock in the divine assembly in heaven. According to the covenant, the cock agreed to give his life for the sins of human beings. Sacrifice of cocks occupies an important place in the Khasi religion. Therefore rules concerning sacrifice of the cock and the breaking of eggs were framed following the cock's offer to give his life for the sake of human beings. Because of sin, human beings were not able to talk to God as before, but the cock restored communication between God and human beings.[274] During life on earth, sacrifices for purification are means to obtain God's forgiveness, which one can acknowledge through its manifested signs; such as recovery from an illness and obtaining financial help.[275] The Khasis offer pigs, goats, cocks, fowls and pigeons to different deities. However, the cock has been given special place as a sacrificial offering.[276]

14. Totem

A totem is usually a species of animal, or of plant, or insect, or bird and is very rarely a class of inanimate objects, or very closely related to a group in that the group is believed to descend from an animal or any of the species mentioned above. Some early

---

[273] Hugh R.Page Jr., "Khasi", *Encyclopedia of World Culture: South Asia, Vol III, op.cit.,* 124.

[274] Rabon Singh, *Ka Kitab Niam Khein Ki Khasi*, (Shillong: Ri Khasi Press, 1950), 9.

[275] Joseph Syiemlieh, *The Funeral Rites and Practices in the Khasi Mainland: An Anthropological Study*, Ph.D. Unpublished Thesis Submitted to North Eastern Hills University, Shillong, 1995, 15.

[276] H. Onderson Mawrie, *The Essence of the Khasi Religion, op.cit.,* 34-37.

Khasi tribes believed that in the distant past, their forefathers had an intimate relation with the totem of a clan; the idea was that the life of a particular clan was bound up with that of the totem. Some tribes consider the monkey, the tortoise, and the tiger as their totem. Some Khasi tribes consider even a pumpkin or an orange type of fruit as totem. They never kill these animals and cut down such types of trees. They believe that if they kill these animals and cut such trees they will have very serious sickness, which can take away their life.[277]

15. Taboos (Sang)

The term taboo is taken from a Polynesian dialect, and introduced into English by Captain James Cook, who on his third voyage around the world in 1777 found in Polynesia that their priests placed a *taboo* on the site of Captain Cook's observatory for his convenience. Captain Cook found the system of *taboo* entrenched in the islands, forced by law and religion alike, and constituting the chief means of government functioning.

The Khasi word *Ka Sang* is expressed partially by the word *taboo*. *Taboo* means something forbidden by the society. The *Taboo* is a common phenomenon among primitive societies. The Khasi society also believed in *taboos*.[278] If a person committed a sin against *sang*, he had to appease deities by offering special sacrifices. Some *taboos* are: (4.2.10.14.1) to cut a house with stonewalls on all four sides; (4.2.10.14.2) to cut trees from sacred forest; (4.2.10.14.3) to step over someone's body; (4.2.10.14.4) to build a house near the rock; and (4.2.10.14..5) to use iron nails or any metal, or to hold up the structure for it was considered *taboo*.[279] *Taboos* concerning food and marriage are also observed by the Khasis.[280] Some parents, who were prohibited from accompanying funeral processions, or putting a thatching on the ridge of the house, are meant to observe these *taboos*.[281]

---

[277] Nalini Natarajan, *The Missionary among the Khasis*, op.cit., 27.
[278] Dr. Barnes L.Mawrie SDB, *Introduction to Christian Ethics*, op.cit., 38.
[279] Kynpham Singh, "The Khasi-their Houses and Housewarming Customs," *Khasi Heritage*, op.cit., 173.
[280] Ibid., 28.
[281] Kynpham Singh, "Khasi Religion and Khasi Society," *Religion and Society of the North East India*, ed. (New Delhi: Vikash Publishing House, 1980), 42-45.

16. Witchcraft

Witchcraft and sorcery were prevalent among certain sections of the early Khasi society. The Traditional Khasis are said to believe in magic to some extent.[282] Evil spirits known as *Ka Taro, U Thlen* and *Ka Shwar* were invoked. In the beginning of the twentieth century, there were several cases when murders were reported to have taken place both in the deep interior and even in the cities. The victims were reported to have been offered to deities. The rulers had to exorcise and clear the atmosphere in order to make ineffective the evil powers connected with this type of magic.[283] But now the practice of witchcraft and sorcery is seen mainly in the rural areas only. 80 percent households opined that the traditional Khasis believed in witchcraft.

17. Fertility and Death Rites

The traditional Khasis observe fertility rites associated with dances and songs. Conception and pregnancy is looked upon as biological facts, but occurring because of the will of God. They are not ignorant about the facts of paternity. Elderly and experienced women of the vicinity assist during the delivery. Most women return to work next day. This is perhaps due to illiteracy in the early traditional Khasi society.[284]

The Khasis also observe death rites. After death, the dead body is washed with a new piece of white cloth. Relatives and friends are informed so that they can attend the funeral. The dead body is kept in the house for two days at the most. During these two days some food is offered to the dead body. On the day of cremation, the relatives and friends make a bamboo bier. A little mustard oil is applied on the head of the dead body by relatives and friends before they carry it in procession for cremation. The children of the dead person and other relatives lit the pyre. After cremation, the bones of the dead are collected

---

[282] Personal Interview with Dr. J.W. Lyngskor at Sohbar on 15.5.2005.

[283] Kynpham Singh, "Khasi Religion and Khasi Society," *Religion and Society of the North East India, op.cit.,* 56.

[284] U.R. Ehrengfels, "Khasi Kinship Terminology in Four Dialects", *Anthropos, Vol. 48,* 1953, 396-412.

in an earthen pot. The bones are placed in the clan repository in the nearby jungle.[285]

British Rule

The people of the East Khasi Hills first became known to the civilised world in 1765, when the East India Company established its stations in Bengal. Initially the British had no interest in extending their political and administrative control over the hill areas, except to the extent necessary to maintain stability. This was because of heavy expenditure for administering that area. But due to several reasons they had to adopt a policy of annexing and controlling the Khasi-Jaintia area. One of the reasons was direct communication between Sylhet and the Brahmaputra Valley through the Khasi hills.[286] By the time the East India Company took possession of Sylhet, relations between the local Sylhet people and the Khasis were not at all good. On several occasions, the Khasis were victims of Sylhet traders and in exasperation they often carried away hostages to the hills and threatened their victims with starvation if they misappropriated their money. The Khasis are very true and honest by nature.[287]

With the object of opening direct communication between the two, the Governor General's agent, David Scott, negotiated with the Khasi chiefs for the opening of a road across the hills. The first Burma war of 1824 was the first occasion for the British to enter Khasi territory in order to march to the Assam plains from Sylhet. David Scott the Governor-General's agent marched through the Khasi and Jaintia Hills. At the end of war, by the treaty of Yandabo in 1826, Assam was annexed and there arose an administrative need to connect Sylhet and the Assam plains through the Khasi Hills. David Scott negotiated a treaty with the Syiem of Nongkhlaw for building a road from Sylhet to Gauhati. The attack on a British survey party by the people of Nongkhlaw in 1829, resulted in heavy casualties, which led to harassments

---

[285] *Encyclopedia of North East India: Meghalaya*, Vol. IV, op.cit., 278.
[286] Dr. O.L.Snaitang, Christianity and Social Change in North East India (Kolkata: Vendrame Institute Firma KLM Private Limited, 1993), 43.
[287] H.G. Joshi, *Meghalaya: Past and Present*, op.cit., 7.

of the Hillman by the British, which culminated in the British annexation of the Khasi Hills by 1833 and the establishment of a cantonment and headquarters at Cherrapunji.[288]

The Jaintia Hills became an entirely British territory in 1835. When the British entered upon the affairs of the Khasi area, the fragmented nature of the traditional political system became apparent in their inability to put up a united resistance. In November 1858, the Government of Great Britain took over the political interests of the East India Company and the Queen proclaimed that all treaties and engagements made with them or under the authority of the East India Company are accepted by the Government and will scrupulously be maintained. Until 1859, the relations between the Khasi chiefs and the British were regulated only by agreements. The isolation of this area was breached by the advent of the British and the advent of Christianity in the nineteenth century.[289]

The *Syiemship* was a gift in the hands of the British, which they could always use to their advantage.[290] As soon as the Khasi Hills came under the control of the British, the need was felt to formalise succession to *Syiemships* through the Principal Assistant Commissioner in Cherrapunji. Where a claimant appeared in the dependent States and represented himself to be the heir of a deceased *Syiem*, he was required to state his right. When the officer was satisfied on the point, a proclamation was issued to all the inhabitants desiring them to state whether they accepted the right of the claimant. If objections were raised the people were called to vote whether they would or would not have the claimant. The Principal Assistant Commissioner confirmed the candidate.[291]

---

[288] John Hughes Morris, *The Story of our Foreign Mission*, Aizawl: Synod Publication Board, 1930), 16.

[289] T. Nongsiej, *Khasi Cultural Theology, op.cit.*, 4-5.

[290] S.K. Chattopadhyaya, *Tribal Institute of Meghalaya*, ed. (Guwahati: Spectrum Publications, 1985), 16, 61.

[291] D.R.Syiemlieh, "Colonialism and Syiemship Succession: A Study of Cherra State (1901-1902)," *Proceedings of the North East India History Association*, ed. by Jayanta Bhushan Bhattacharjee, Shillong, 1983, 147-157.

Khasi Syiems were placed under the control of the Deputy Commissioner. They were deprived of the powers to try cases in which their subjects were not involved. It is very clear from the facts stated above that before 1947 Khasi chiefs had very limited powers and the appointment of the *Syiems* required the confirmation of the British Government through the Crown's representative.[292] After independence the British Government lost power and 15 chiefs (Khyrim, Mylliem, Nongkhlaw, Nongspung, Mawsynram, Malaisohmat, Langrin, Bhowal, Jirang, etc.) established a Federation.[293]

Christian Missionaries

The Khasi Hills felt gentle breezes of change with the arrival of the British missionaries in the early nineteenth century. Along with British rule came the evangelical work of the missionaries from the Great Britain. The Welsh Calvinistic Methodist Mission formed the new branch. They preached Christ as the only Saviour to the Khasis. Salvation could be attained by faith in Christ through grace. The Gospel of Christ was preached to the Khasis for transforming the Khasi society. Along with preaching, teaching (education) and healing (medical care) ministry was also started by the Christian missionaries in the said district. Through education and medical ministry the Khasis gave up the worship of spirits and expensive animal sacrifices. The close personal relationships between government officers and the missionaries strengthened the impression of close co-operation.

Around 60 percent Khasis have embraced this new faith and have given up the old Khasi traditional faith. Priesthood is no longer hereditary; but now any person fit for this ministry can become a priest among the Khasi Christians.

Major Church Denominations in East Khasi Hills District

This section deals with Christian faith and missionary activities in the East Khasi Hills District of Meghalaya. Khasi Christians are divided into many denominations. But this section deals with only general Christian belief.

---

[292] S.K. Chattopadhyaya, *Tribal Institute of Meghalaya, op.cit.,* 64-65.
[293] *Ibid.,* 66.

1. The Presbyterian Church

The first missionary was a Bengali named Krishna Chandra Pal, who was converted by William Carey in 1793. Under this mission, a translation of the New Testament and some Khasi books in the Bengali Script were prepared. At the time that its presence in Khasi hills began to secure strong foothold, it eventually abandoned its works in 1838. The Welsh Calvinistic Methodist Mission, (later known as the Welsh Presbyterian Foreign Mission) was the first to set foot in the Khasi Hills. Rev. Jacob Tomlin came to Cherrapunji in 1840 on a chance visit during a journey to China. After his stay at Cherrapunji for nine months, he reported to his home church.[294]

On 22nd June, 1841 the first foreign missionary of the Welsh Presbyterian Mission, Rev. Thomas Jones and his family arrived at Cherrapunji. Lieutenant Lewin, a Government officer, gave Rev. Thomas Jones a warm welcome at Cherrapunji. He also gave a part of his house to Rev. Thomas Jones until the Mission bought a suitable place. He had to undergo a painful experience when his wife died while delivering a baby. He started the first school at Mawsmai near Cherrapunji in 1842, heralding the beginning of education and educational institutions in the Khasi Hills. Another school was set up at Mawmluh. The third school was opened in Cherra.[295] The Khasi teachers were Lurshai, Mising and Jam. The Khasi Book read in the school in 1842, was *Kot Kitab Nyngkong* followed by *Rhodd Mam* (Mother's Gift).[296]

Growth was slow in the beginning. As the missionary work made a progress among the Khasis, certain superstitions that held a grip on the Khasi mind were shaken. The courageous stand taken by one of the new converts Ka Nabon and the sufferings she had to face certainly impress anyone who has read the early history of the Welsh Presbyterian Church in the Khasi Hills.[297]

---

[294] Nalini Natarajan, *The Missionary among the Khasis, op.cit.*, 62.

[295] John Hughes Morris, The Story of our Foreign Mission, (Aizawl: Synod Publication Board, 1990), 26.

[296] *Ibid.*, 64

[297] John Huges Morris, *The History of the Welsh Calvinistic Methodists' Foreign Mission*, (Carnavon: C.M. Book Room, 1910), 102-110.

Owing to the paucity of workers, the missionary work had been confined to Cherra and the villages around. The work was extended to Shella, which is 14 miles South West of Cherra. The main Mission work was concentrated around Cherrapunji till 1850. In 1851 a new school was started at Shella. By the end of 1851 five schools were opened at Cherra, Nongsawlia, Mawsmai, Mawmluh and Shella. As the result of the visit of Judge Mills of Calcutta, in 1853, the attention of the Government was drawn to the missionary's educational efforts. The British Government donated ₹ 50 per month to the Mission for its educational work. The educational enterprise was not quite successful in the early years due to poverty. Secondly, to a certain extent, the indifference of the natives including some Rajas to schools who favoured the Bengali script instead of the Roman Script contributed towards the slow progress of education at that time.[298]

Despite the opposition, the Welsh mission gradually expanded its work to other areas of the hills. Looking at the progress of the educational activities of the missionaries, the British Government communicated its decision to grant five pounds financial help to the missionary institutions through the agency of a religious organisation to spread education in Khasi Hills. Every school was a centre of evangelism as well as educational work.[299] By the end of 1857 the missionaries had opened sixteen schools. From the humble beginning of three schools in 1842 with only 14 students, the number of schools rose to 65 with about 2000 students in 1866. In 1891 the number of students was 4,625.[300] From 1870-1880 remarkable progress was made in every branch of the work. Seven stations, with resident missionaries, had also been opened by the year 1880. They are: Nongsawlia, Jowai, Shella, Shillong, Mawphlang, Nongrymai and Cherrapunji. A new Theological Institution was established at Cherrapunji in 1887 with Rev. John Roberts as principal.[301]

---

[298] *Ibid.*
[299] Rev J. Fortis Jyrwa, *The Wondrous Works of God*, (Shillong: Mrs. M.B. Jyrwa, 1980), 23.
[300] John Hughes Morris, *The Story of Our Foreign Mission, op.cit.*, 31-33.
[301] *Ibid.*, 37-40.

The beginning of medical service goes back to 1878 with the arrival of Dr. G. Griffiths who opened the first dispensary at Mawphlang, moved to Cherrapunji in 1891 and finally to Laitlyngkot in 1897. Dr. Griffith Griffiths served faithfully from 1878 till 1902 battling bravely against superstitions, which prevailed at that time. Dr. A. D. Hughes arrived and became the pioneer of medical missions in the Jaintia Hills. The Shillong Welsh Mission Hospital (now KJP Synod Hospital) under the surgical genius of Dr. H. Gordon Roberts, who was replaced by Dr. R. Arthur Hughes, won fame throughout the erstwhile State of Assam.[302]

It is pointed out that the main object of medical missions was to express the church's concern for the welfare of the whole human being, irrespective of caste and creed. Medical work had been entirely in the hands of missions until 1968. Today the Khasi Presbyterian Church looks after it.[303]

The educational institutions connected with the mission made excellent progress during these years, and contributed largely to the success of the work by providing better equipped leaders and teachers. The Shillong High School had also made striking progress.[304] Towards the end of the year 1904 the joyful news of the great revival in the churches of Wales reached the mission field. The accounts of the remarkable effects, witnessed in the homeland, reported month by month in the **Nongialam Khristan**, aroused the churches in the Khasi hills to a state of great expectancy.[305]

In 1912 seven hundred names were on the roll. Prior to 1920, the majority of persons in the Government High School at Shillong were non-tribals. But due to the efforts of the missionaries, there was noticeable increase in the figures of tribals. According to the statistics for 1929 there were a total of 304 Presbyterian Schools and 14,006 students. In 1931-1932 the Presbyterian Church ran

---

[302] *Ibid.*
[303] J.F. Jyrwa, *The Wondrous Works of God*, op.cit., 78-84.
[304] Nalini Natarajan, *The Missionary among the Khasis*, op.cit., 68-69.
[305] John Hughes Morris, The Story of Our Foreign Mission, (Aizawl: Synod Publication Board, 1990), 47.

a total of 6 middle schools and 247 primary schools.[306] According to 1945 statistics, there were 7 middle schools and 267 primary schools.[307] The schools continued growing until 1970. The emphasis was given on the girl's education, since girls were not allowed to go to school. In 1972 the Presbyterian Church Mission established 1 higher secondary school, 6 high schools, 29 middle schools, 275 primary schools, 1 teachers training centre, 1 theological college, 1 general college and 1 printing press. It run 436 Primary Schools, 78 Middle Schools, 30 High Schools and 1 College in 1988 in Khasi-Jaintia and Ri-Bhoi areas. It was reported that in 2007 there were around 2100 schools run by different churches and 1200 schools of different levels by the Presbyterian Churches in Meghalaya state.[308] The Mission also undertook several other programmes for the advancement of the rural poor and needy.[309]

It is through revival and not through enticement that Christianity spread in Meghalaya. The missionaries preached Christ to the Khasis in western garb, which led them to give up cultural values in many ways. The missionaries should have preached the Gospel in Khasi culture, which would have strengthened different aspects of their culture. In 1985 the total number of believers in the Presbyterian Church of Meghalaya went up to 163,593 and in 1995 it went up to 387,357.[310] It is believed that the last decade of the nineteenth century was a turning point in the history of Christianity among the Khasi-Jaintia people.

With the advent of the Welsh Mission, adaptation of a script for the Khasi language was completed by the introduction of the Roman alphabet, which fitted well with its simple, uniform, and legible order.[311] The history of conversion began with the Welsh

---

[306] *Ibid.,* 72.
[307] *Minutes of the 7th Session 1946, Ramakrishna Math & Ramakrishna Mission*, Kolkata, 18-19.
[308] Personal interview with Rev. Dr. J.F. Jyrwa at Aizawl.
[309] Personal interview with Rev. Dr. J.F. Jyrwa at Aizawl.
[310] F. Hrangkhuma, *Christianity In India, op.cit.,* 206.
[311] *Ibid.,* 115.

Presbyterian Mission, and a big number of the Khasis embraced Christianity.

2. The Catholic Church

The first band of four Catholic missionaries, belonging to the Society of Divine Saviour, came to Shillong in 1890. Prior to 1890, there was hardly any Roman Catholic contact with the Khasis despite the fact that there were Catholic communities in the region like in Rangamatti, Bondashil and Mariamnagar well in the 18th century. The area was made the missionary responsibility of a new German order, the Catholic Teaching Society which later came to be known as the Society of the Divine Saviour. Fr. Broy, who had worked among Catholics resident in the Assam valley for a number of years had established a small chapel at Shillong in 1881 but undertook no missionary work because of the dispute. Shillong was contested between different Catholic orders and jurisdictions. The Roman Catholic Church as the second largest of the Christian sects in the East Khasi Hills started its work at Laitkynsew village in Shella area in 1890.[312] The Catholic Church has spread to most other parts of the Khasi Hills.[313]

The Catholic missionaries established a Teachers' Training School and the St. Mary's College in Shillong. They were more tolerant of Khasi culture and traditions than the Presbyterian Mission.[314] The Catholic missionaries established a Teachers Training School in St. Mary's College. As of 1990, the Catholic Church ran in Khasi-Jaintia hills 879 elementary schools, 50 High Schools and 3 colleges with a number of boarding and hostels in its parishes and centres in the region.[315] Slowly the number of believers increased. It was reported that by 1944 the number of Catholic believers in Meghalaya was 50,000.[316]

---

[312] Dr. O.L.Snaitang, Christianity and Social Change in North East India, *op.cit.*, 78.
[313] *Ibid.*, 380.
[314] *Ibid.*
[315] *Ibid.*, 114.
[316] Nalini Natarajan, *The Missionary among the Khasis, op.cit.*, 77; see also Dr. O.L.Snaitang, Christianity and Social Change in North East India, 78.

Presently the Catholic Church runs more 900 schools of different grades, a homeopathic hospital, a general hospital, and a Teacher's Training School. The Catholic Mission did not object to the Khasi dances, and in fact traditional dances have been encouraged but rituals and religious ceremonies are discouraged. In addition to academic schools, Christian Missions and churches introduced technical education as well.

Catholic Church has also been playing a significant role in the development of higher education in the region. The church saw education as one of the practical means of preaching the Gospel among the Khasis.

3. The All Saints' Church

An old missionary sect started its work in Shillong in 1876. The first clergyman to visit this place was Rev. A. Garstin, Chaplain of Sylhet in 1841. The new Church was opened around 1876. In 1966, Bishop Cotton of Calcutta became very interested in the efforts of Welsh Presbyterian Mission to make the Khasis civilized. It was established to meet the spiritual need of the believers. There are nearly 15 churches with 1000 members belonging to this tradition in the Khasi Hills.[317]

4. The Church of God

In 1902 Rev. J. J. M. Nichols-Roy, an influential person from Shella started the Church of God in Khasi Hills. He was a forceful and popular leader. He won the hearts of many Khasis. Mr. Wholley Mohan Roy Laitphlang, Mr. Joy Mohan Roy, Mr. Jobin Roy Khain and Mr. E. Dhorum were the founding members of the Church of God.[318]

The Church of God, which was originally formed as a Baptist type of church, has under Mrs. Nichols-Roy's Pentecostal influence turned into some kind of being charismatic. The Church of God undertook much the same sort of work as other churches. It runs more than 50 Primary Schools, 3 Middle Schools and 2 High Schools. It carries out evangelistic work in Khasi-Jaintia

---

[317] *Ibid.*, 79-84.
[318] Dr. O.L.Snaitang, Christianity and Social Change in North East India, *op.cit.*, 84.

area, among the Karbis and among the Nepalese. This church also runs many schools in different villages in the East Khasi Hills District.[319]

5. The Seventh Day Adventists Church

It was started in Khasi Hills in 1935 by Rev J.F. Ashlock.[320] Though he established some schools in the East Khasi Hills District yet he failed to win many believers. It undertook missionary work in the form of schools, literature, technical, agricultural and social welfare schemes. At present the Seventh day Adventist Church has become very weak due to the paucity of workers.

6. The Impact of Christian Missionary Activities on the Khasis

The main agency of change in Meghalaya beginning in the 19th century was the British Government. It provided the political power to bring change. One of the acts of the British Government was to give permission to the Hindu agencies like Brahmo Samaj and the Ramakrishna Mission to penetrate into the land and also promote more inter-marriage between the local people and the Hindus.[321]

The contribution of the Christian missionaries to the development of the Khasis has been many and varied. The influence of missionary work and teaching could be seen in every corner of Khasi life. Education brought by the Christian missionaries played an important role in socio-economic, religious and cultural transformation of the Khasis. Thus, this system of education broke down the traditional Khasi system of education and opened a new world to the Khasis. By 1867 the work of the missionaries had covered all parts of Cherrapunji area and extended into other areas.[322] By the end of the nineteenth century Christianity had expanded into all the geographical areas of the Khasi Jaintia Hills.

---

[319] Nalini Natarajan, *The Missionary among the Khasis, op.cit.,* 82.
[320] Dr. O.L.Snaitang, Christianity and Social Change in North East India, *op.cit.,* 83.
[321] *Ibid.,* 179.
[322] Meghalaya District Gazetteers: Khasi Hills District, *op.cit.,* 292

Changes like construction of more hygienic house, improving the water supply, regular bathing and washing of clothes took place. A new material culture was being built on the old. While virtually all Christian Khasis had a positive attitude towards the changes in the material and political culture, there were some among them that did not agree with the comprehensive missionary condemnation of the traditional religion of the Khasis. The missionaries did not oppose the traditional political structures. The missionaries also supported for the traditional kinship system which continued to function for the strengthening of the culture which contributed to a sense of tribal identity. The old polity based on hereditary chieftainships and State Durbars while maintained to a certain extent in some areas, was nevertheless reduced to relative importance. Through the Christian missionary work the traditional religion of the people and social practices related to it were changed.[323]

The new faith set the people free from fear of the unseen spirits which were considered to be the source of all kinds of troubles. It was this teaching about Supreme God which most appealed to the people and accounted for embracing new faith. Belief in demons was not totally eradicated among those who became Christians. A written language provided the basis for the introduction and development of Khasi literature. A standard language promoted through education, worship and literature that helped to create a new sense of cultural community among all the members of the tribe.[324]

The synthesis of all the influences arising from Christian missionary work has brought about a change in the Khasi society and culture and has removed outdated, irrelevant and superficial values that had to be discarded in the context of the modern, rational world and at the same time has enriched the substantial core factors in the society that required to be preserved and nurtured.[325]

---

[323] *Ibid.,* 180.
[324] *Ibid.,* 147.
[325] Nalini Natarajan, The Missionary among the Khasis, *op.cit.,* 192.

It is true that the growth of Christianity in the East Khasi Hills District was a challenge to some of the Khasi cultural norms.[326] As the missionaries rejected the religious elements in traditional Khasi culture it was assumed that there was a complete change in attitude towards culture on the part of those who adopted the new faith. The progress of Christianity in Meghalaya including East Khasi Hills District was considered as a challenge to traditional culture of the Khasis by some intellectual non-Christian Khasis.[327] This situation has made a section of the Khasi intellectuals to resort to certain measure for the preservation of their religion and culture by inspiring the Khasis to be proud of their rich heritage. This cultural awakening found its expression through the Seng Khasi Organisation, initiated by some educated Khasis who may be regarded as the apostles of the Khasi renaissance leading to the establishment of the Seng Khasi Organisation in 1899. Since it is not an attempt to deal with the impact of Christianity on the Khasi society we will not study in detail the changes brought about by Christianity in the Khasi society of the East Khasi Hills District.

With the advent of Christianity and Western education, transformation took place in the social and political life of the people. The converts abandoned their former religious rites, beliefs and rituals, and accepted the Christian teachings. The impact of Christianity on the Khasis has been profound. In 2007 the Khasi community had a very high level of literacy (61.3 percent) in the state. Christianity has made an important contribution to the education of women. There were several schools run by the church for the education of women in the Khasi Hills. The spread of education and the use of the Roman script for the Khasi language have together encouraged the vernacular. The Christian missionaries were also concerned about medical care.[328]

---

[326] Bhattacharjee J.B., "The Messenger of Khasi Heritage", edited by U Hipson Roy, Khasi Heritage: A Collection of Essays on Religion and Culture, Shillong: Seng Khasi, 1979, 3.

[327] *Ibid.*

[328] n.n., *Encyclopedia of North East India: Meghalaya, Vol. IV*, ed. *op.cit.*, 247.

They taught against the social evils that were prevalent in the society. They introduced them to scientific education. They also taught them about human values. About 90 percent of the households from the Ramakrishna Mission and the Seng Khasis said that Christian missionaries have destroyed Khasi culture.

Another important element in the new cultural synthesis provided by Christianity was the development of relationships between the tribals and the peoples in other parts of India. Their traditional relationship was limited to a clan or state. An intra-tribal conflict and the raiding on the plains of Bengal indicated, little value was placed on people other than those who belonged to the small group that established the limits of social relationship. Schools, medical institutions and church organisation contributed to the development of this new understanding of relationships. The missionaries created self-consciousness among the Khasis so that they could understand the value of socio-cultural identity.[329]

With the arrival of the British, the Khasis started feeling a gentle breeze of change, which led to the transformation of the society. Changes began when the location of the capital of Assam was shifted to Shillong in 1874, and many outsiders entered Shillong and married with Khasi young women. Conversion started, the Khasis were introduced to formal education and their language was put into writing. The Christian missionaries made great contribution to the hills, as it was through their efforts and endeavors that literacy made rapid progress and Khasi literature has since then developed. They also contributed to the richness of the social life of the Khasis.[330]

Sickness was regarded as having religious causes. The medical service of the Christian missionaries transformed the old belief system. Though there was opposition to the new medical techniques, when the Khasis found that the missionary medical service has healed their sicknesses, they lost their confidence in rituals.

---

[329] Fredrick S. Down, *Essays on Christianity in North East India*, (New Delhi: Indus Publishing Company, 1994), 193-196.

[330] Mary Pristila Rina Lyngdoh, *The Festivals in the History and Culture of the Khasi*, op.cit., 174.

The history of conversion of the Khasis began and a large number of Khasis were converted to Christianity. They placed several restrictions on the new converts such as performance of indigenous religious rites, participation in the festivals and dances, which had religious connotations. All these had been prohibited as contrary to the teachings of Christianity. Christianity with its teachings about a loving God liberated the people from fear of evil spirits which were traditionally believed to be the source of all kinds of troubles and all kinds of enslavement.[331]

Education played an important role in socio-cultural transformation of the Khasis. The Welsh Presbyterian Mission started schools and medical services. Higher education exposed Khasis to the external world. Christianity gave the Khasis a sense of being a people with their own history and identity. Religion is but one of the focal points in trying to define the framework within which cultural and social changes took place. In the field of education, the Welsh Mission encountered initially severe opposition from the local tribes against evangelisation.[332] But Christianity followed the same rules of inheritance and succession with the result that some of the political institutions still survive.[333] There is no denying the fact that in Christian areas, old usages of meghalithic erections, household and community religious celebrations and festivals have been obliterated. Christianity has also caused reversals in marriage, funeral rites, house building and village ceremonies.

The pioneer, Thomas Jones, introduced the Roman alphabet. With the advent of the Christian missionaries in Meghalaya, the presence of alien rulers effected Khasi society. Thus, inevitably, contact with an alien ruler, and an alien religion involved the Khasi individual and the Khasi society deeply. The Mission imparted regular training in singing on tonic solfa notation. The Missionaries also educated Khasi women.[334]

---

[331] Dr. O.L.Snaitang, *Christianity and Social Change in North East India*, op.cit., 162.
[332] Nalini Natarajan, *The Missionary among the Khasis*, op.cit., 122.
[333] *Ibid.*, 136.
[334] *Ibid.*, 91.

The education imparted by the missionaries left its trace on Khasi living too. A change took place in house style. Earlier the houses were oval-shaped, low, thatch-roofed and dark. Now their houses are Assam type dwellings with lighter walls made of bamboo mats or reeds with plaster. Even the housing ceremonies connected with house building are observed on a much smaller level. Most Khasi Christians do not break an egg to see if the site will be lucky or not. The Christians no longer observe their old religious beliefs and rituals except some in the rural areas.

Through Christian missionaries the Khasi economy also changed, though not entirely. David Scott introduced the cultivation of potatoes, pears and cabbages, which earned them money. A superior quality of livestock was also introduced. The Khasis started catering cows, pigs, cocks, geese and ducks. The missionaries also taught carpentry, tailoring, baking and printing. The Christian missionaries who worked for the advancement of the Khasis in the East Khasi Hills District of Meghalaya have influenced the socio-cultural and religious life of the Khasi society. Beliefs in superstitions, witchcrafts, taboo, black magic and sorcery have nearly died down among the Khasi Christians. Some Christians in rural areas still respect the covenant as they think that it was the faith of their forefathers. However, some Christians and traditional Khasis in the rural areas still believe in black magic and sorcery.[335] While the Khasi Christians generally agreed with the negative attitudes of the Christian missionaries towards traditional Khasi religion, there were some Khasi Christian believers like Rabon Singh Kharsuka from Mawmluh, who did not agree with the negative attitude towards the Khasi traditional religious practices. The rituals and practices Rabon Singh advocated were those practiced at Mawmluh and the Cherrapunji area. U Saso Tham was another Christian leader who had respect for the traditional religion.[336]

On the other hand, Christian missionaries preached the Gospel in European garb. Perhaps many local people found it difficult

---

[335] *Ibid.*, 133.
[336] Dr. O.L.Snaitang, Christianity and Social Change in North East India, 134-137.

to adjust. Since many Khasi mothers died at child-birth because of superstitious ideas and lack of medical care, the missionaries realised the importance of medical care and started giving medical aid, although it was not sufficient.[337]

With the change of religion several social traits and other aspects of cultural heritage have also been forgotten. The consolidation of the British administration opened up the isolated Khasi and Jaintia Hills by linking it up with the centers of different cultures in the neighborhood.

There is no denying of the fact that Christianity has caused reversals in marriage, funeral, house building and village ceremonies. The Christian impact was also seen in Khasi law. The traditional values and systems were thoroughly depreciated and the process of social change as a result of the new impact was bound to disturb their traditional society. On the other hand, the question of changes due to change in religion, did affect their cultural values and social norms to some extent. Converts were deprived of their rights to property and cremation rights. But, on the other hand, Christian missionaries brought inter-tribal solidarity since there was fighting between different Khasi headmen. Prof. Kapila Chatterji said that it was the British policy in these hills not to take up any direct project of education or medical care, so that the only agency for education and medical work was the Christian mission. Through their service the majority of Khasis realised that their true benefactors were the Christian missionaries.[338]

The Church in Meghalaya in general and in the East Khasi Hills District in particular has not really attempted to relate Christ to Khasi culture and to express Christian faith and life in terms of the rich heritage of Khasi thought and traditions. Indigenous music has been relegated to a place outside the mainstream of worship. The church has denied the social and cultural aspects

---

[337] Padmashri S.S. Shastri, *Tribal World in Transition*, (New Delhi: Anmol Publications, Pvt. Ltd., 1995), 180-187.

[338] Prof. Kapila Chatterji, "Christianity in Meghalaya-Trends and Reactions", *Vivekananda Kendra Patrika*, Vol. 8, No. 2, August, 1979, 217.

of traditional dance and festivals. Only the laws of inheritance and some Khasi cultural and political customs are still maintained. One important factor that has helped to retain some elements of Khasi customs is kinship ties.[339]

Brahmo Samaj

The movement of the Brahmo Samaj in Bengal had for some time actually received the magnitude of a social revolution. Waves of the Brahmo Samaj Movement entered East Khasi Hills District in 1828. It happened when the Khasis of Shella wrote a letter to the Brahmo Samaj in Calcutta asking to send more missionaries to them.[340] In response the Sadharan Brahmo Samaj sent Nilomani Chakravarty as their representative to the Khasi Hills in 1875.

Adi Brahmo Samaj also had sent a representative to the Khasi Hills in the person of Prasanna Kumar Majumdar who lived at Laban. The two people succeeded in initiating a large number of Khasis to the Brahmo faith. The Sadharan Brahmo Samaj was engaged in Cherrapunji, Shella, and Nongkhlaw. Adi Brahmo Samaj was engaged in and around Shillong. The Brahmo Movement played an important role in the field of social reforms.[341]

Along with the shifting of the Secretariat of the State on 23rd March 1874, came the Brahmos to Shillong. The first Brahmo who came to Shillong came with an intention to preach the message of the Brahmo Samaj. Later on Hemanta Kumari established the first Mahila Samity for moral and spiritual improvement of the women in 1887. The Brahmo Samaj then established a school for children on Jail Road. The aim of the Brahmo Samaj leaders was to educate the Khasis in the East Khasi Hills District by imparting education to them and also to uplift the status of Khasi women.

Long before the British came in contact with the hills of Meghalaya, the Bengalis, particularly from the district of Sylhet had made their way into the Khasi Hills. They brought Hindu

---

[339] M.P.R. Lyngdoh, *The Festivals in the History and Culture of the Khasis, op.cit.,* 191.
[340] Dr. Jayanta Bhusan B., "The Changing Khasis: A Historical Account", *The Tribes of North East India,* ed., 340.
[341] *Ibid.,* 342.

culture and civilisation to the Khasis. Some Khasi families in this area adopted the Hindu way of life. There are several Khasi families even today who have followed Vaishnuism. Many families have adopted the culture of the plain people.[342]

With the increase of the outsiders, there soon developed a schism between the Brahmos and the Orthodox Hindus. The Orthodox Hindus had a majority and they preferred to celebrate the festivals and religious ceremonies. On the other hand, the Brahmo Mission was established to propagate the Brahmo faith among the Khasis. The Shillong Brahmo Samaj in 1884 established their centre at Mawkhar. Nilmoni Chakravarty after learning Khasi language wrote some pamphlets on the Brahmo creed and widely distributed it among the Khasis. He who came from Sadharan Brahmo Samaj established his headquarters at Cherrapunji; this was already a centre of the Welsh Mission. He started his homeopathic practice and continued the missionary work in a humble way. With the help of some other Brahmos from Calcutta he could even extend his activities to Shella, Mustoh, Mawlong, Mawsmai and other villages in the neighbourhood of Cherra.[343]

Rohini Kanta Roy continued to conduct Brahmo prayers on Sundays at Mawkisyiem Prayer Hall. He enjoyed the support of some doctors and the simple villagers. Through his service hundreds of Khasis were influenced. Many Khasis started attending their prayers.[344]

In September 1899, Nilmoni along with Jacob Solomon arrived at Cherrapunji. Nilmoni took with him U Tham Singh, a young man of Cherra, and went to Shella to meet the Khasis who asked for Brahmo preacher. The Syiem of Cherra, Hajom Manick Syiem gave Nilmoni Chakravarty a plot of land at Mawkisyiem for building a school and a prayer hall, the foundation stone of which was laid in June 1882. Within a short period they established sixteen centres in different villages. A committee was

---

[342] H.M. Bareh, *Encyclopedia of North East India: Meghalaya, Vol. IV, op.cit.,* 167.
[343] *Ibid.,* 173-179.
[344] *Ibid.*

formed to implement the programmes of the Samaj as decided in the conference held in December 1892.³⁴⁵ Hemanta Kumari, wife of Raj Chandra established a school for moral and spiritual improvement of women. A school for children was also established there at Laban. The school was upgraded to Middle School level. Jail road and Laban were the two localities where Brahmos lived.³⁴⁶

With the establishment of the Brahmo Samaj Mandir at Shella, the Durbar office bearer rendered all possible assistance. The English Medium School was inaugurated in 1924 at Shella. But religious differences remained the great dividing line between the Bengalis and the Khasis.³⁴⁷

The Brahmo Samaj movement at Shillong was mostly confined to the upper class Bengali office goers and professionals, totalling about 200 in number with a handful of Khasi and Assamese elites. At the southern slope of the Khasi Hills it became essentially a Rural Social Reform Movement. A number of schools were also opened in different parts of Khasi Hills like Sohbarpunji, Mawsmai, Nongthymmai, Upper Cherrapunji, Mawlong and Laitkynsew. Brahmo Samaj established a building in 1921 in Police Bazaar with library facilities. Brahmo Samaj helped not only in educating the people but also in raising the moral standard of the people.³⁴⁸

There are three branches in Brahmo Samaj. They are: (4.5.1) Adi Brahmo Samaj (Debendranath's Group that practiced Hindu Customs); (4.5.2) Sadharan Brahmo Samaj (Those who were against Keshub); and (4.5.3) Nava Vidhan Brahmo Samaj (Founded by Keshub).

It seems that the differences in the beliefs of the three branches were minor. Both the missionaries from Brahmo Samaj were not

---

[345] W. Kharmawphlang, *A Study of the Contribution of Non-Christian Missionaries to the Development of Education in Khasi Hills*, M.A. Unpublished Thesis, submitted to the North Eastern Hills University, Shillong, 1994, 110-111.

[346] n.n., *Encyclopedia of North East India: Meghalaya Vol. IV, op.cit.*, 174-175.

[347] *Ibid.*

[348] W. Kharmawphlang, *A Study of the Contribution of Non-Christian Missionaries to the Development of Education in Khasi Hills, op.cit.*, 5-9.

on good terms. They worked in Cherrapunji. They helped people in distress with money, medicines and clothes. During the peak of this Movement there were nearly 150 Brahmo Khasis and of these, the followers of Sadharan Brahmo Samaj were only about 50. After the death of Roy in 1930 Nilmoni Chakravarty also died in 1941. And all Bengali Brahmo informants said that one Rohini Roy tried to continue the Movement after the death of Binod Bihari Roy, but he failed due to paucity of funds.[349]

In the beginning the Brahmo Missionaries had very strong opposition from the Seng Khasis and the Khasi Christians. But the admirable service rendered by the Brahmo Samaj to the Khasis, pleased the Khasis. Atulananda Das from the Indian Forest Science opened Lady Keane College in Shillong. It was the Bengali Brahmos who for the first time tried to build a bridge of understanding between the Khasis and the Bengalis. The close rapport that existed between the local Brahmo Samaj and the Khasi Unitarian Church was able to generate a good deal of communal harmony.[350] Due to their internal problems and lack of proper leadership the Brahmo Samaj could not survive. Ramakrishna Mission has taken over the work of the Brahmo Samaj in the East Khasi Hills District.[351]

The Seng Khasi Organisation

At first Khasis accepted and welcomed the changes due to modern education, a new faith, a new way of life, and other factors of modernisation. Later on they found that there was a danger in their political and economic life. A large number of people came from outside as employees in the Central and State Government, as businessmen, contractors, as employees of private and public establishments and other menial services. The penetration of various religious movements and the influence of different cultures in the East Khasi Hills, paved the way for a reform movement within the Khasi society. They were afraid of losing their social, cultural and religious identity. The people started appreciating their indigenous way of life, such as their festivals,

---

[349] *Ibid.*
[350] *Ibid.*
[351] *Ibid.,* **116.**

dances, songs and musical instruments; their basic customs and traditions. It is this appreciation of the past that led to a revivalist Movement known as Seng Khasi Organisation.[352]

The Seng Khasi Organisation is a socio-cultural organisation of the Khasis, who have continued to stick to the traditional monotheistic Khasi religion based on the belief in God (U Blei) and respect for the ancestors.[353] It was established on November 23, 1899 when sixteen Non-Christian Khasi young men met together in the Brahmo Samaj Hall at Mawkhar to form an association in order to revive the moral, religious and cultural life of the Khasis.[354] U Rash Mohon Roy was the first chairman of the Seng Khasi Organisation. U Babu Jeebon Roy was the leading spirit behind the formation of the Organisation. This Organisation began to function in the same year.[355]

According to P.R.G. Mathur, the Seng Khasi Organisation was the primary agent in providing a religious basis for the Khasi tribal effort to establish solidarity in the face of change. The Seng Khasi Organisation has continued to work through education, cultural celebration and social service. U Jeebon Roy and U Rabon Singh played a very important role in founding this organisation. The tradition set by U Jeebon Roy was followed by a section of the illustrious Khasis individually and collectively.[356] Because of the challenge posed by the western missionaries, actively supported by the British Government, the hearts of some enlightened Khasis were disturbed by a feeling of insecurity.[357]

---

[352] Mary Pristila Rina Lyngdoh, *The Festivals in the History and Culture of the Khasi*, op.cit., 190.
[353] Dr. Jayanta Bhusan Bhattacharjee, "The Messenger of Khasi Heritage," *Khasi Heritage*, Revised and Enlarged Edition, (Shillong: Ri Khasi Press, 1996), 1.
[354] Soumen Sen, "Seng Khasi and Idealisation of Khasi religion," *Proceedings of North East India History Association*, op.cit., 239.
[355] Dr. Jayanta Bhusan Bhattacharjee, "The Messenger of Khasi Heritage," *Khasi Heritage*, op.cit., 11-15.
[356] Dr. Jayanta Bhusan B., "The Changing Khasis: A Historical Account", *The Tribes of North East India*, op.cit., 332-348.
[357] Soumen Sen, "Seng Khasi and Idealisation of Khasi religion," *Proceedings of North East India History Association*, Seventh Session, Pasighat, 1986, 239.

Seng Khasi Organisation emerged at the time when the progress of modernisation and westernisation posed as a challenge to the traditional religion and culture of the Khasis. It aroused the consciousness of the Khasi to be proud of their cultural heritage and to preserve the religious and cultural norms.[358]

The Seng Khasi Organisation with some nationalist minds like U Tirot Singh Syiem and others shaped and intensified the ideological direction of Khasi reformation. The Reformists' motive was nationalism. A major feature of Khasi revivalism was the influence of Gandhiji, Raja Ram Mohan Roy and several others.

(a) Objectives of the Seng Khasi Organisation

The aims and objectives of this organisation are as follows: i) To foster a sense of brotherhood among the Khasis who still retain their socio-cultural and religious heritage; ii) To create consciousness of God.; iii) To work for the advancement in the field of education, welfare, sports, and moral and social code of conduct; iv) To earn righteousness through service and to respect one's own fellowmen with the sense of humanity and divinity; v) To work for the development of fellow human beings.[359]

(b) Functions of the Seng Khasi Organisation

This organisation works for the development of Khasi education. The first free morning school was established in 1921. Today the organisation runs several schools and a college. This organisation also works for the preservation of Khasi culture. It also works for the preservation of Khasi religion. It has helped the Khasis to revive and preserve their traditional festivals and dances. Today it has emerged as a more effective association than in subsequent years by extending its activities in the rural areas of Meghalaya. It has struggled hard since its inception to safeguard the customs, traditions and religious beliefs of the Khasis from the onslaught by other religious groups. It had been able to promote its ideals by creating cultural consciousness among the Khasis.[360]

---

[358] Mary Pristilla Rina Lyngdoh, The Festivals in the History and Culture of the Khasi, op.cit., 179.
[359] Personal Interview with Rony Kharpiang on 17.5.2005 at Shillong.
[360] Dr. Jayanta Bhusan Bhattacharjee, "The Messenger of Khasi Heritage," *Khasi Heritage, op.cit.*, 15-16.

Ramakrishna Mission in East Khasi Hills District

The Ramakrishna Mission is primarily a religious organisation. The various activities in the field of education and social service which it carries on, are intended to help men and women experience the religious truth promoted by it.[361] The Mission started its activities in the East Khasi Hills under the leadership of Swami Prabhananda (known as Ketaki Maharaj) from Sylhet in 1924. The Mission opened its first primary school with a homeopathic dispensary at Shella (in East Khasi Hills District) in the same year. The activities of the Mission were gradually extended to different villages like Cherrapunji, Sohbar, Kalibari, Laitryngew, Laitdiengsai, Nongwar, Majai, Mawmluh, Mawlong, Mawkhar, Mawsmai, Mylliem, Shella, Umwai etc.[362] The Mission has been serving the Khasis of the East Khasi Hills District of Meghalaya through education, medical care, and other programs for their uplift. The Mission runs 58 schools and three hostels, 3 medical dispensary, 2 mobile clinics, 2 vocational training centres and 2 computer centres attached with libraries for the needy people in the East Khasi Hills District.

Conclusion

In conclusion it can be said that Khasi society is a matrilineal society where both descent and inheritance are reckoned through the female line whereas authority and power is vested in male's hand. The main occupation of the Khasis is agriculture. This system empowers only females to have authority on property and not males. Reverence for female progenitors diminished in importance although the mother's clan continued to be adopted by children as before. The Christian missionary support for the traditional kinship system also constituted a major affirmation with the traditional culture that has contributed to a sense of tribal identity. Matrilineal inheritance also continued but women depended less on the male relatives of the *Kur*. They managed

---

[361] V.C. Samuel, The Ramakrishna Movement: The World Mission of Hinduism, Bangalore: CISRS, 1959, 1.

[362] n.n., The Ramakrishna Mission Shillong, Meghalaya, Shillong: Ramakrishna Mission, 2007, 3-6.

their affairs either independently or with the help of their husbands. Now the role of the maternal uncle has been taken over by the father. The change of religion from *Khasi Niam* to Christianity was perhaps the most important reason for this. The challenge has come from growing exposure and interaction with patriarchal cultures of the neighbouring people. Education has played an important role in socio-cultural and religious transformation of the Khasis.

Before the British took control over Meghalaya, the *Durbars* were considered by the people to be the institutions of divine origin. The Christian missionaries did not reject the traditional political structures that continued to function but with limited authority. Under the British Government, the composition and sanctity of the institution of *Durbars* was in the first instance diluted by inclusion of the elders and leading men of the State who had no divine or hereditary right to the honour. Radical changes had occurred in the character and power of these two traditional institutions of the Khasis, namely, the Syiemship and the *Durbar*. The political system before the formation of the District Autonomous Councils was not democratic enough. Although the franchise is controlled by men yet the youth have fewer rights to speak on tribal matters. Moreover, women have no participation in political matters. Not only the chiefs, but even the *Durbars* declined in importance as an institution.

The main purpose of creating Autonomous District Councils was to protect the Khasis with their cultural heritage as well as their socio-economic life and living. But the committee responsible for setting up such bodies failed to understand the sentiments of the local chiefs as a result of which the conflict has been going on between Autonomous District Councils and the Syiems that have been set up. The gap between the District Councils and the States may further take a violent form. The District Councils do not get sufficient co-operation from the Syiems although they have been given magisterial powers to function with limited capacity. The new political system has reduced the power of the traditional rulers. Prior to the British entry into Meghalaya, the consent of the people was the basis of political and social activities.

Since independence, the political, economic and social forces at work in the country have brought about a large measure of integration of the Khasis with the rest of India. Western influence on the Khasi society is evident in many forms such as dress, adoption of western names, western music, dance and religion. The spread of enlightenment has adversely affected the traditional dances, music and festivals. The dances during festivals were an essential part of the social life of the people. But the Christian converts on the advice of the missionaries refused to join the community in the dances and music. Among the Christians, the European dresses and apparels came into use.

The traditional Khasis still believe in *taboo*. Originally when they constructed their houses they did not use nails because nails were regarded as *taboo*. Prejudice against the use of nails started disappearing. Building houses on a European pattern became fashionable.

The problem of inheritance continues into the present. In the olden days, there was no problem of self-acquired property. The people mostly carried on agricultural pursuits and the mother or the clan invariably inherited through wives or daughters, and in the case of the Pnars inherited all their earnings. With the rapid expansion of economy under the British rule, the people adopted various professions or trades and became rich. They gained properties independent of their families or clans. The rapid progress of Christianity among the Khasis had also brought about changes in the form of marriages, house patterns, health, education and ways of life.

In the early days the sense of common good was very strong among them all. The study shows that there is a growing dissociation of the Khasis from their natural environment. The pristine relationship that existed once upon a time has disappeared due to human's consumerist attitudes, which has resulted in a sort of enmity between humans and nature. This was due to their ignorance about the elements of nature and the cultural heritage related to nature handed down to them from their ancestors. Unlike western countries where ecology has become a common subject about which every one talks and discusses, in

India the majority of the people are still strangers to this issue. The forest is rapidly disappearing and the landscape quickly degrading, there may not be left behind even the slightest trace of the past history of humanity's closeness with nature.

Education has played a very vital role in shaping the attitudes of people right from an early age. The educational institutions must give importance to the subject of ecology which has become a global problem.

The study also revealed that the Khasis have many important festivals and dances which are performed either before the sowing or after the harvesting is done. Khasis have a rich cultural heritage, their history is preserved through the ages in the form of festivals, folk songs, folk tales and folk dances. They glorify their God as the souls of the departed ones have become supernatural beings and are ordained of the deity to assist the living ones to obtain blessings. It is believed that souls that earned a righteous life go to the house of God and become united with their predecessors. But bad souls will suffer here before the sacrifices are offered on their behalf. Sacrifices are still practiced by traditional Khasis.

The Seng Khasi Organisation has also played a very important role in preserving the Khasi traditional religion and culture. One of the main objects of the Seng Khasi Organization was to encourage national sports like archery and preserve Khasi culture and religion. It has been successful to achieve its object and in getting the traditional Khasis united.

The Next chapter deals with the work of the Ramakrishna Mission in the East Khasi Hills District of Meghalaya.

B A a b

Chapter 5

The Work of the Ramakrishna Mission in the East Khasi Hills District

History of the Ramakrishna Mission in East Khasi Hills District

It was in 1924 after the visit of Swami Vivekananda to Assam, a band of dedicated workers headed by Swamiji Prabhananda started the work in North-East India. The Mission which came into existence through the service of needy and poor people has been maintaining its motto till today by undertaking relief works in North-East India in general and in Meghalaya in particular. The fifth chapter deals with the historical development, social activities and teachings of the Ramakrishna Mission in the East Khasi Hills District of Meghalaya.

1. Ramakrishna Mission at Shella and Cherrapunji

Ketaki Maharaj was responsible for starting the work of the Ramakrishna Mission in East Khasi Hills District. While undergoing teacher's training at Dacca, he learnt that many Khasis of Assam were keen on sending their children to new schools in the hills without the influence of any religious propaganda. The suggestion was made from several quarters that the Ramakrishna Mission should undertake this work. If Ramakrishna Mission would take up this work, it will get the support of all sections of society irrespective of their religious persuasion.[1] Ketaki Maharaj subsequently became a monk in the Ramakrishna Mission with the name Swami Prabhananda and stepped into a small village called Shella of the East Khasi Hills

---

[1] Swami Lokeswarananda, "Swami Prabhananda: His Pioneering Work In The Khasi Hills," *Golden Jubilee Souvenir* (Shella: Ramakrishna Mission, 2005), 4.

District and opened a school and a homeopathic dispensary at Shella.[2]

The Khasi Chiefs granted his school some financial help of ₹ 500.[3] Other schools also grew up at Nongwar, Mawshamok, and many other neighbouring villages around Cherrapunji. Many parents did not like to send their daughters to school. It was in 1975 when they began to feel the need of education and from that time onwards girls were admitted into different schools. When the Ramakrishna Missionaries came to the Khasi Hills there was no transport facility. They also found it very difficult to communicate their message to the Khasis due to language problem.

When the Ramakrishna missionaries established their schools, they asked their parents to send their children to school. Parents found it difficult because most of the children supplemented the family income by working in the fields. Therefore, the said schools had to spend a lot in educating the Khasi children since most of them were poor.[4]

Ketaki Maharaj observed that as a result of the work of the Christian Missions, many Khasis had been converted to Christianity but a large number of them only nominally and these were still loyal to their Khasi traditional religion and traditions; nevertheless they were being influenced by Christian dogmas. He found that there was already much erosion of their ancient customs and traditions going on as a result of various influences to which they had become exposed following the British conquest of their territory. He blamed the Christian missionaries for not only converting the Khasis to Christianity but also denationalising them in spite of the fact that they themselves claimed to belong to the Aryan stock.[5] According to Swami Gahanananda, Vice-President of Ramakrishna Mission,

---

[2] Swami Lokeshwarananda, *An Unknown Young Man's Pioneer Work in the Hills of Assam*, (Delhi/Kolkata: Prabudh Bharti, 1968), 419.

[3] Personal interview with Swami Brahmonanda on 15.10.2005 at Shillong.

[4] Personal interview with Seng Khasi Leaders on 25.5.2005 at Shillong.

[5] Swami Gambhirananda, *History of the Ramakrishna Math and Mission*, (Kolkata: Advaita Ashrama, 1983), 273.

"Christian missionaries not only converted the simple and illiterate poor people, but also they denationalised them."[6]

In those days of British rule, most of the hill areas in Assam were sealed off from the people of the plains. There was real danger for the entire Khasi community life since Christian missionaries were attacking their religious beliefs and traditions, social habits and customs.[7]

The contact of the Khasis with the different socio-religious influences coming from beyond their boundaries had a shaking effect on various aspects of their traditional ethos. The Khasi society on the one hand was enjoying a new air of change and on the other hand traditional religion, social customs and cultural elements were at the brink of collapse. The Christian converts gave up their former religious rites and beliefs. Funeral ceremonies, ancestor worship, and other animistic celebrations were completely abandoned.[8]

Ketaki Maharaj also observed that the textbooks, which the Khasi students used, taught only Christian theology. He decided to write books from the traditional Khasi perspective. Within a short span of time he published some books.[9]

He was struck by the fact that the Khasis, otherwise a charming people, suffered from the peculiar complex that they regarded every non-Khasi as an "outsider" with whom they did not maintain healthy relations. He realised that this happened because they had for centuries lived in isolation and also because of their unpleasant experiences whenever they came in contact with people from the outside world.[10]

---

[6] Swami Gahana, "Message from Revered Gahananandaji Maharaj," *Diamond Jubilee Souvenir (1937-1997)*, Shillong: Ramakrishna Mission, n.d), Cover Page.

[7] Swami Lokeshwarananda, "Swami Prabhananda: His Pioneering Work in the Khasi Hills," *Golden Jubilee Souvenir*, *op.cit.*, 3.

[8] Miss Bhakti Ksaniang, "Contributions of the Ramakrishna-Vivekananda Movement to Khasi Society," *Golden Jubilee Souvenir*, (Cherapunji: Ramakrishna Mission Higher Secondary School, 2001), 17.

[9] I. Kharmawphlang, *A Study of the Contribution of the Non-Christian Missionaries to the Development of Education in Khasi Society*, M.A. Thesis submitted to the North East Hills University, Shillong, 1994, 55.

[10] Swami Lokeshwarananda, "Swami Prabhananda: His Pioneering Work in the Khasi Hills," Golden Jubilee Souvenir, *op.cit.*, 18-19.

While Ketaki Maharaj sought to bridge relationships he also cautioned the Khasis against losing their identity as a race. He wanted them to be progressive. Slowly the people started realising that he was different from other outsiders. The traditional Khasis had faith in him. Gradually people from different villages approached him to open schools in their villages. Ketaki Maharaj worked very hard for their development.[11]

He realised that the Khasi people had for centuries lived in isolation, therefore in order to make them more progressive he took them on tours to different parts of the country. He also picked up some intelligent boys and girls and sent them to Calcutta for their education.[12]

When he almost gave up hope of being able to start a high school at Cherrapunji, one Khasi gentleman donated a piece of land for the school. But the *Syiem* of Cherrapunji had given a notice to both Ketaki and the intending donor of the land saying that they were not to proceed towards starting the school building. The members of the committee felt insulted because the *Syiem* tried to place a ban on this good work. They took up the cudgels on behalf of Ketaki and fought the *Syiem* until they were able to win his favour to start a high school at Cherrapunji.[13]

Moreover, Seth Harakh Chand & Moti Chand of Kathiawar donated a sum of ₹ 1,50,000 for the construction of the school building. With the financial help from Seth Harakh Chand & Moti Chand, the high school building at Cherrapunji took its full shape.[14] Both Ketaki Maharaj and Swami Archananda decided to serve a wider circle of Khasis from Cherrapunji and to save them from foreign cultural conquest by spreading the light of national and liberal education and holding up the greatness of Khasi culture before the people. They helped the Khasis to

---

[11] I. Kharmawphlang, *A Study of the Contribution of the Non-Christian Missionaries to the Development of Education in Khasi Society*, M.A. Thesis submitted to the North East Hills University, 1988, op.cit., 54.

[12] Swami Lokeshwarananda, "Swami Prabhananda: His Pioneering Work in the Khasi Hills," *Golden Jubilee Souvenir*, op.cit., 11.

[13] Ibid., 7.

[14] n.n., *Golden Jubilee Souvenir*, (Shillong: Ramakrishna Mission, 1982, 10.

preserve and develop their culture.[15] They opened schools in the surrounding villages, which was only a drop in the ocean as compared with the vast organised efforts and resources of the Christian missionaries. The monks had won the hearts of the people, and this small effort succeeded in engendering among the Khasis a faith in themselves and a spirit of resistance to alien cultures and religious faiths.[16]

They encouraged the villagers towards education. Under the guidance of the young Swami, hundreds of young Khasis and other young tribals were educated.[17] Leaders of neighbouring villages approached him to start similar schools in their villages. Ketaki Maharaj visited those villages, and agreed to start schools in those villages only where the villagers really felt the need of education.[18] Soon he had a network of schools, covering many villages with Shella as their centre. Although he was the moving spirit of this work, he had local committees appointed which shouldered the responsibility of running those schools. Meanwhile, the school at Shella had been raised to the status of a middle school.

Slowly the Swami got the support of the local people and the local administration. The *Durbar* of the Shella confederation gave a grant of ₹ 500 to those schools run by the Ramakrishna Mission. Another orthodox Khasi donated land for additional schools. Opposition from the *Syiem* was also overcome. A committee of the leading men of Cherrapunji belonging to different religions was formed to take decisions regarding the running of the schools. Another monk also offered help in this matter.[19]

When Ketaki Maharaj from the Ramakrishna Mission started establishing schools in order to impart education to the Khasi children, a few Christian leaders wrote to the District authorities

---

[15] Kapila Chatterji, "Ramakrishna Mission in the South Khasi Hills," *Golden Jubilee Souvenir*, (Shella: Ramakrishna Mission, 1982), 10.
[16] n.n., *Diamond Jubilee Souvenir (1937-1997)*, (Shillong: Ramakrishna Mission, 1997), Front Page.
[17] H.M. Bareh, *Encyclopedia of North-East India: Meghalaya, Vol. IV, op.cit.,* 175.
[18] n.n., *Diamond Jubilee Souvenir, (1937-1997), op.cit.,* 17-37.
[19] Ibid.

complaining that under the pretext of giving education to the Khasi children, he was preaching hatred against the British. This was in the days when anti-British feelings ran very high in the country. The District authorities naturally took alarm and the Deputy Commissioner went to Shella for enquiries. But the Deputy Commissioner did not find any fault with him; he asked Ketaki to continue his service to the society.[20]

In March 1960, the Cherrapunji Centre developed enormously from its early condition to its present state. Under the guidance of Swami Subodhananda, this Centre took up a new programme of extension by opening new branches throughout the East Khasi Hills.[21]

The Ramakrishna Mission also started a technical school to train the tribal boys and girls in carpentry, tailoring, embroidery, weaving, knitting, welding, and typewriting. It also ran a Students' Home for 120 boys at Cherrapunji. Help was also given in cash and kind to the poor Khasi students and Khasi people to stand on their own. A mobile dispensary also served the rural Khasis through which many poor people got free treatment. The Mission also began to help the poor Khasis by establishing a dairy farm. A poultry farm was also set up to meet the needs of the local people in this area.[22]

During the tenure of Swami Gokulananda, a dynamic monk with uncommon missionary zeal, the centre at Cherrapunji saw again some remarkable development. He mastered the Khasi language within a short period and started publishing books in Khasi. Among his achievements the publication work may be rated at the top.[23]

---

[20] Swami Lokeshwarananda, "Swami Prabhananda: His Pioneering Work In The Khasi Hills," *Golden Jubilee Souvenir, op.cit.,* 17-35.

[21] Swami Aparananda, "A Few Years at Cherrapunji," *Golden Jubilee Souvenir,* (Cherrapunji: Ramakrishna Mission Ashrama, 1982), 22.

[22] Swami Gambhirananda, *History of Ramakrishna Math and Mission,* Third Revised Edition, *op.cit.,* 108-111.

[23] Swami Shantarupananda, "Fifty Years of the Ramakrishna Mission Ashrama at Cherrapunji- A Flash Back (1931-1981)" *Golden Jubilee Souvenir,* (Sohbar: Ramakrishna Mission, 1982), 8.

The Cherra Mission had also undertaken the noble national task of reviving the glories of the Khasi religion, and teaching the Khasis their nearly forgotten Khasi cultural and religious heritage. The initiative of Swami Gokulananda in this work was really commendable and exemplary. The Government of India also sanctioned him funds for the scheme for the dispensary building, library-cum-reading room and doctors' residence.[24]

The great and silent national and educational worker of the Khasi Hills, Miss Margaret Barr of Kharang has praised the noble service of Ramakrishna Mission in acting like a saviour of Khasi religion and culture from foreign inroads.[25]

The students who have come out with a brilliant educational culture from this institution have been holding important positions, and have earned a name for their discipline and sincerity. The avenues for future growth and development are always open. Today Swami Sumedhananda is the secretary of Cherrapunji Ramakrishna Mission, which controls the education in the whole East Khasi Hills District. In 1984 there were 28 teachers and 625 students. IN 2007-08, there were about 1,000 students with very competent teachers in the Cherrapunji Higher Secondary School.[26]

2. Ramakrishna Mission in Sohbar

Sohbar is an interior village and was cut off from the main stream. Due to the hilly jungles, this village had no proper communication facility. At that time Tarani Kumar from Dacca-Dakshin village (now in Bangladesh), being inspired by the books of Swami Vivekananda, dedicated himself to the service of the poor and needy. He visited many villages along with his friends and opened schools, and taught the villagers how to make clothes. He was expert in spinning and weaving. In 1926 Swami Sivanandaji at Belur Math ordained him for priesthood. The

---

[24] Ibid.
[25] Kapila Chatterji, "Ramakrishna Mission in the South Khasi Hills," *Golden Jubilee Souvenir, op.cit.,* 12.
[26] Personal interview with the Principal of the Ramakrishna Mission School, Cherrapunji at Cherrapunji on 26.4.2008.

following year he met Swami Saradeshananda in Sylhet and the meeting changed his life.[27]

In April 1928 Mr. Tarani Babu crossed the hills and reached Shillong. After a few days he went to Cherrapunji and opened a school in a rented house at Pdengshnong. This school was upgraded up to 7th Standard. Since this school was established in a deep rural area it educated over 300 children. By the third week of April, Babu came to Sohbar and expressed his desire to the villagers. When he arrived at Sohbar, he found that the Christian missionaries had imposed on the Khasis of the East Khasi Hills District an alien culture. This was the main reason for welcoming the Ramakrishna missionary, Tarani Babu, in Sohbar village.[28] He looked for a spot where he would be left in peace to carry on with his work. He started a free primary school at Sohbar in the fourth week of April 1928. In December 1929, the school was shifted to a new house. Swami Cinmayananda of Ramakrishna Mission also opened a school at Nongjri village in 1929.[29]

When the school started to grow, another problem cropped up. It happened that most of the students from other local schools joined the New India School. They stirred the minds of some fanatic people who complained against him to the Government. The Government machinery was in no mood to allow a school like the New India School. In February 1931 the Inspector and Deputy Inspector of schools came to Sohbar village, and asked him to hand over his school to them. The pressure was so strong that even the monthly donation from Shillong was discontinued. Tarani Babu also faced opposition from the imperialist British Government and the authorities of the local Welsh mission school. But in spite of all these problems he did not give his consent. Margaret Barr of the Unitarian Church who worked among the Khasis from 1936-1973, stood behind Tarani Babu in these

---

[27] n.n., *Golden Jubilee Souvenir (1928-1978)*, (Sohbar: Ramakrishna Mission, 1979), 17.
[28] Ranjit Nag, "One Man's Dream Come True," *Golden Jubilee Souvenir*, (1928-1978), (Sohbharpunji: Ramakrishna Mission Ashrama, 1979), 9.
[29] Personnel interview with Mr. Nikhil Kumar Gosh on 27th April 2006 at Sohbhar.

difficult days. Through the Ramakrishna Mission, her dream came true.[30]

The Ramakrishna Mission has had special concern for the health of the Hill tribals. At first a small homeopathic dispensary was established in 1930. A centre and a school at Sohbarpunji were established in 1940 by Tarani Purkayastha.[31]

During that time there was no medical facility available in that area. Due to the lack of medical facilities people had to suffer. When Tarani K. Purkayastha, a homeopathic practitioner, saw the physical suffering of the Khasis, he felt the need to help the people. He opened a dispensary in the village. His information was that Khasi herbal medicine was not found to be so effective. They found homeopathic medicine to be easily available and cheap. The rural people found that Tarani had come to live in their midst to help and heal them. U Lad Singh, a local leader and his sister Ka Tewmala, donated a house for the school. Slowly he got the support of many local leaders.[32]

The New India School with the two hostels, one for girls and other for boys, is now a complete unit. The school was upgraded to middle school level in 1933. In the same year the Ramakrishna Mission Asharma was named as *Vivekananda Kutir*. A centre at Sohbarpunji was established in 1940. The school was affiliated to the School Board of Assam in 1949.[33] In 1950 Babu undertook a project to construct a road in the village. In November 1952 weaving, tailoring, embroidery, cane and bamboo works and bee-keeping sections were introduced to the trainees. Babu used to visit the houses in the village regularly and taught the people basic principles of hygiene. Every Saturday he, along with the students and their guardians, used to do community cleaning.[34]

In 1954 weaving formed a separate section to impart vocational training for the local people. Every year 15-20 men

---

[30] n.n., *Golden Jubilee Souvenir*, op.cit., 7.
[31] Personnel interview with Headman at Sohbar on 25.4.2007.
[32] n.n., *Golden Jubilee Souvenir*, op.cit., 41.
[33] n.n., "The Milestones," *Golden Jubilee Souvenir (1928-1978)*, op.cit., 15.
[34] Personal interview with Mr Akhil Kumar Ghosh at Sohbar on 25.4.2006.

and women passes out from the institution. So far over 600 people have been trained in the vocational training centre run by the Mission at Sohbhar. In the same year a poultry-farm was also started in the same school building for the development of the villagers. It was taken over by the Ramakrishna Mission on March 31st, 1959. Today the school has been upgraded upto the 10th standard. There are 407 students and 16 teachers in this school. This school is under the direct supervision of the Cherrapunji Ramakrishna Mission. Sohbar Asharma teaches the people to be self-reliant and self-supporting by means of cottage industries.

3. Ramakrishna Mission in Mylliem

Ramakrishna Mission established a Primary School in 1987 at Mylliem, which was upgraded to high school level in 2000 and to secondary level in 2003. There were 600 students and 18 teachers working in the school in 2007-08.

The rural children of this area were given free education. Apart from education, the Mission has launched some socially beneficial programmes. This Mission is given credit by many elite Khasis of all religious sects, for promoting a sense of nationhood among the Khasis and also a secular outlook like the Unitarians who taught to treat everyone alike.[35]

For efficient management of work in Khasi Hills, the institutions of Cherrapunji, Shella and Nongwar were integrated with the Ramakrishna Belur Mission, with effect from the 1st January 1949. Cherrapunji as the branch centre came under the supervision of Swami Subodhananda.[36]

4. Ramakrishna Mission in Shillong

The history of Ramakrishna Mission, Shillong was a history of gradual growth and development.[37] The work was started at Shella with a primary school in 1924. The work of the Mission gained popularity and dimension day by day and spread further

---

[35] Nalini Natarajan, *Missionary among the Khasis*, op.cit., 87.

[36] n.n., *Golden Jubilee*, op.cit., 52.

[37] Shahadhar Bhattacharjee, "Reminiscences of Sri Ramakrishna Mission Shillong," *Diamond Jubilee Souvenir (1937-1991)*, Shillong: Ramakrishna Mission, 1997, 15-17.

over the Hills bringing into existence some schools in places like Nongwar, Mawlong, Mawkhar, Umwai and Jowai.[38]

With the expansion of work the Swami understood that it was becoming difficult for him to move among the entire place regularly. He decided to have an Ashrama at a central place from where he could supervise the activities of the Mission. He chose Shillong to be the proper place and laid the foundation of an ashrama here. Dr. Manoranjan Goswami, a homoeopathic practitioner had his practice in Shillong in 1937. Swami Bhuteshanandaji came to Shillong and started his work. The Shillong centre originally started functioning on a humble scale in 1929 and the Ramakrishna Mission officially recognised it in 1937. From 1929-1934 the *ashrama* was run in a rented house at Laban, Mawkhar. The 12th President of the Ramakrishna Mission, the late Swami Bhuteshananda, was its first secretary. Vigorous attempts to procure a plot of land for the *ashrama* came to a success when a part of the present site of the Mission at Laitumkhrah was purchased in February 1934. The *ashrama* is located on Ramakrishna Mission Road, Laitumkhrah, Shillong.[39] The Mission workers stand by the people during their suffering caused by natural calamities or the like.

In 1938 a temple was constructed at Shillong. This temple was renovated in 1970.[40] Swami Prabhananda was the founder of both the Shillong and Cherrapunji Ashramas. Swami Saumayananda was the head of the *ashrama* in 1958. Swami Saumayananda had proficiency in classical music. He invited eminent artists like Kumud Goswami on the occasion of Durga Puja.[41]

Today Ramakrishna Mission, Shillong runs the following programmes: (a) A dispensary with moderate facilities. (b) A library facility. (c) Computer training. (d) Cultural programmes.

---

[38] Swami Baneshananda, "Ramakrishna Mission Shillong: A Glimpse of Its Growth", Golden Jubilee (1937-1987), (Shillong: Ramakrishna Mission, 1987), 22.

[39] n.n., *A General Report on the Ramakrishna Math and Ramakrishna Mission for 1956*, Kolkata; Ramakrishna Math and Ramakrishna Mission, 1957, 30.

[40] n.n., *Golden Jubilee Souvenir, op.cit.,* 33.

[41] Swami Bhaskarananda, "My Reminiscences of Shillong Ashrama," in *Diamond Jubilee Souvenir*, (Shillong: Ramakrishna Mission, 1997), 15-18.

(e) A student's home. (f) Arts and painting competitions. (g) Spiritual classes and medical service.[42]

3. Ramakrishna Mission at Nongwar

Ramakrishna Mission started its work at Nongwar by opening a school. Swami Prabhanandaji opened the school at Nongwar village in the year 1928. It was a free primary school and later it was raised to 8th standard in 1949. The Ramakrishna missionaries also explained to the Khasis of Nongwar village the conditions on which the Mission insisted before agreeing to work in a particular area. The Ramakrishna Mission received financial assistance from the Central Government to run lower primary and middle schools, a medical dispensary and technical training programme. It also received grants from the State Government to run lower primary schools under its management. Step by step the primary school became a high school in 1991. Today it provides educational facilities to 400 students and jobs to 20 educated Khasis of Nongwar and the surrounding area. Children get education free of cost.[43]

The objective of the Ramakrishna Mission was to cater to the well-being of the Khasi people, and give them education so as to enable them to become progressive in their march towards modernisation without losing their cultural identity. The Khasis of this area, even though they were poor and dependant only upon their agricultural products, gladly came out to help the Mission in its endeavour.[44]

Apart from education, the Ramakrishna Mission provided the people free medical aid through a mobile clinic. In the neighbouring villages the Ramakrishna Mission rendered free medical service to the Khasis.

4. The Ramakrishna Mission Work at Laitryngrew

Ramakrishna Mission, Cherrapunji established another school in 1969 at Laitryngrew, five kilometres away from Cherrapunji in

---

[42] n.n., *A General Report on the Ramakrishna Math and Ramakrishna Mission for 1956*, Kolkata, op.cit., 30.

[43] I. Kharmawphlang, *A Study of the Contribution of Non-Christian Missionaries to the Development of Education in Khasi Hills*, op.cit., 76.

[44] n.n., *A General Report on the Ramakrishna Math and Mission*, 1992.

order to help the rural children. At the beginning it was a primary school. It was upgraded to middle school level in 1981. Today 407 students are getting an educational facility in this school free of cost. Most of the teachers in this school are Khasis. The expenditure of the school is borne by the Mission. Free medical facility is also available to the people of this village.[45]

5. The Ramakrishna Mission Work at Mawmluh

The Ramakrishna Mission established this school in 1958. At the beginning it was a lower primary school with around 35 students. Today the school has been upgraded to a high school level with 450 students and 13 teachers.[46] The children of Mawmluh village and other surrounding villages get free education in this school. The Mission provides books and uniforms free of cost. There is another school in the village run by the Presbyterian Church. But the school run by the church has not been able to attract many children because of heavy expenditure. Many parents find it difficult to send their children to Christian schools because they cannot afford the fees. The Ramakrishna Mission School gets funds from the Central Government to pay the salaries of the teachers and to construct a school building.[47]

Slowly the Mission has opened more schools in the deep interior villages like Mawshamok, Mawkynring, Mawrah, Majai (Bhola-Bazar), Laitdengsai, Laitkroh, Pyrkan, Umblai, Umthli, Rudu, Swer, Umwai, Wahlong, and so on- all in the said district. In these schools except for a few non-Khasis, the majority of teachers are Khasis. The Ramakrishna Mission runs 9 secondary schools in the same district.[48]

The Attitude of the Khasis towards Ramakrishna Mission

While most of the Khasis welcomed the Christian missionaries, some of them did not like them because they undermined the Khasi culture. But they learnt that the Ramakrishna Mission had

---

[45] Personal interview with the Headmistress of Laitryngew Ramakrishna Mission School on 22.4.2005 at her Office.
[46] Personal interview with Mrs. A.B. Lyngdoh at Mawmluh Mission School on 22.4.06.
[47] Personal interview with a group of people at Mawmluh on 25.6.2006.
[48] Taken from Cherrapunji Ramakrishna Mission Office.

come to the Khasi Hills to educate them and make them more progressive. The leaders of the Ramakrishna Mission realised that the Khasis have felt the need of maintaining their culture and traditions. Education is the only means to improve their cultural and social standard. This, therefore, was one of the main reasons for welcoming the Ramakrishna Mission. Moreover, Khasis found that the aim of the Ramakrishna Mission was not to destroy Khasi culture.[49]

The activities of the Ramakrishna Mission in the East Khasi Hills District

The activities of the Ramakrishna Mission are based on a distinct work ethic.[50] One of the abiding concerns of the Mission from its inception has been to carry the light of education to the poor, neglected and tribal communities. In regard to the service for the uplift of the tribal people, Ramakrishna Mission has been active. Besides educational activities, Ramakrishna Mission lays emphasis on humanitarian service.[51] The Mission extends social, cultural, moral, religious, educational and spiritual services to the local people as well as to others in every way possible.[52] The service it gives is open to all, irrespective of caste, creed, and language. According to Swami Vivekananda, service to humanity is a social expression of religion.[53]

The philosophy of human service seeks to lift human beings out of a stunted ineffective state and put them on the road to growth and creativity. And this kind of service, said Swami Ranganathananda, will restore human beings to their dignity and strength.[54] Swamiji coupled the spirit of the monks regarding

---

[49] I. Kharmawphlang, *A Study of the Contribution of Non-Christian Missionaries to the Development of Education in Khasi Hills*, op.cit., 76.

[50] Swami Bhajananda, "Rural Development Work in the Perspective of Swami Vivekananda's Social Philosophy," *Souvenir of Ramakrishna Mission High School 2000*, (Asansol: Ramakrishna Mission, 2002), 10-16.

[51] Swami Ranganathanda, *National Integration through Love and Service*, (Mumbai: Bhartiya Vidya Bhavan, 1996), 12.

[52] n.n., *Administrative Report of Ramakrishna Mission Sevashrama*, Lucknow, 2001, 1.

[53] n.n., *Vedanta Concept and Application*, (Kolkata: The Ramakrishna Mission Institute of Culture, 2000), 333.

[54] Swami Ranganathanda, *The Philosophy of Democratic Administration*, (Kolkata: Advaita Ashrama, 2003), 32-35.

renunciation with the ideal of service. He held that service to humankind is the best form of worship. This idea became the foundation of the Mission's gospel of social service.[55] The Ramakrishna Mission has restored traditions to a great extent among the tribal people. This has helped bring them back to the mainstream of national life and heritage.[56]

Health Care

The charitable dispensary and hospital run by the Ramakrishna Mission have continued to retain their popularity in different parts of India.[57] The Khasis in Meghalaya were practically unacquainted with hygienic ways of living, proper dietary habits, and medical care before the advent of Christianity.[58]

The Ramakrishna Mission began with medical care in Shella, Cherrapunji and Shillong. The charitable dispensaries with well-equipped clinical and pathological laboratories, X-Ray, surgical sections, and homeopathic departments have been serving the local population in Shillong, Mylliem, Shella and Cherrapunji. Khasis have been given better facilities for the treatment of diseases and through education their sanitary system has improved. Ramakrishna Mission's medical service has been very significant for the rural Khasis in the East Khasi Hills District.

The present Shillong charitable dispensary, the foundation of which was laid in 1951, was formally opened on 2nd February 1952. Another dispensary was set up in Shella in 1930. The third dispensary was set up at Cherrapunji in the 1950s. In these charitable dispensaries over 49,218 patients were treated during 2004-2005.[59] The mobile dispensary at Cherrapunji, which started

---

[55] Swami Bhajananda, "Global Ethics and Vivekananda," *Swami Vivekananda: His Global Vision*, ed. by Santi Nath Chattopadhayay, (Kolkata: Punthi Pustak, 2001), 167-204.

[56] Swami Gahanananda, "Message From Revered Gahananandaji Maharaj," *Diamond Jubilee Souvenir*, (Shillong, n.p., n.d), 13

[57] n.n., *The Forty Seventh General Report of Ramakrishna Mission and Math*, (Mumbai: Ramakrishna Mission, 2002), 21.

[58] Sumit Mukherjee, "Geomedical Aspects of Acute Respiratory Infection Diseases in Meghalaya," *Tribal Studies in North East India*, ed. by Sarthak Sengupta, (New Delhi: Mittal Publications, 2002), 161-175.

[59] n.n., *Annual Report and Account of the Ramakrishna Mission*, (Shillong: Ramakrishna Mission, 2002), 86-87.

functioning from 1960, serves the Khasi population in 70 villages of Shella-Bholaganj Block.[60] Through the mobile clinic 20,000 patients were treated during 2001and 32000 patients in 2007-08. Altogether 2,71,620 patients were treated in the Government hospitals, dispensaries, public health centres and sub-centres in 2007-08. The Ramakrishna Mission has given free treatment to 66,433 patients in the district during 2007-2008.[61]

(2) Educational Facilities

In a rapidly changing situation, education is indispensable for the people in the East Khasi Hills District. The Ramakrishna Mission has special concern for the education of the people in Meghalaya. Since education in rural areas has been neglected, Swami Ranganathananda said, only proper education can bring about a true change in the lives of the rural people.[62] It's plan was to help the Khasis to help themselves through the right type of education without injuring their religious belief and traditional mores and norms.[63] The Ramakrishna Mission organises value educational courses to create awareness about values in the field of education.[64] The list of the educational institutions in the East Khasi Hills District, according to the 2007-2008 record, was as follows:

The work has spread to Bholaganj, Kalatok, Kalibari, Khahmalai, Ladmawphlang, Laitduh, Laitmawsiang, Laitryngrew, Laitkroh, Maraikaphon, Mawrah, Mawsmai, Mawkynring, Mylliem, Mawmluh, Mawshamok, Majai, Khliehshnong, Kalatek, Jatap, Nongwar, Nongkynrih, Nongsteng, Pomsohmen, Pyrkan, Rengua, Rumnong, Rudu, Swer, Sohbarpunjee, Shella, Umdiengpoh, Umblai, Umploh, Umthli, Wahlong, and Cherrapunjee.[65] In all these villages the

---

[60] *Ibid.*, 47.
[61] Quoted from the Ramakrishna Mission Annual Report, Cherrapunji.
[62] Swami Rangananthanda, *Role & Responsibility of Teachers in Building up Modern India*, (Mumbai: Bhartiya Vidya Bhavan, 2004), 2-11.
[63] Miss Bhakti Ksaniang, "Contributions of the Ramakrishna Vivekananda Movement to Khasi Society," *Golden Jubilee Souvenir* (1928-1978), *op.cit.*, 18.
[64] n.n., *Vivekananda: His Call To The Nation*, Compiled, (Kolkata: Advaita Ashrama, 2001), 49.
[65] Quoted from Cherrapunji Ramakrishna Mission Office Record.

Ramakrishna Mission has established schools to educate the rural Khasis. Most of these schools were established after 1980. Apart from education, the Mission has started doing some socially beneficial programmes such as the distribution of rice, clothes, etc.

In his annual report Swami Devamayanandaji Maharaj, the Secretary of the Ramakrishna Misssion Ashrama, Cherrapunji, reported that the Mission runs 58 schools in the East Khasi Hills District.[66] Table 5.3 shows the accounts of the schools run by the Ramakrishna Mission in this area. Over 9,000 students every year got free scientific education from these schools in 2007-2008. Most of these children are Khasis.

Table No. 5.3: A List of the Ramakrishna Mission Schools in East Khasi Hills District[67]

Higher Secondary School	1
High Schools	9
Middle Schools	14
Primary Schools	34
Total Schools	58

According to the Ramakrishna Mission, eradication of poverty and meeting the basic needs of life are the pre-conditions for imparting spirituality in ordinary people. Poverty can be eradicated through proper education.[68]

(3) The Students' Home

The Ramakrishna Mission has concern for poor children. The Mission established a home for poor children at Shillong in 1949. This home was shifted to the new place in 1956. This home is just across the Mission's main compound on the Ramakrishna

---

[66] Personal Interview with Swami Vedamayanandaji Maharaj at Cherapunji on 23.4.2005.
[67] Swami Devamayananda, *A Brief History*, (Cherapunji: Ramakrishna Mission Ashrama, n.d.), 4-5.
[68] Dr. Ajit Sarkar, "National Integration in the Light of Swami Vivekananda's Ideas," Vivek Jivan, Vol. XXXIV, No.7, January, 2003, 22.

Mission Road. It can accommodate 30 students. The majority of students kept in the Students Home are from the rural areas of this district. Another home was established at Cherrapunji where 200 children are accommodated. These children come from poor families and enjoy the facility of free boarding and lodging.[69]

It is found that not all the Ramakrishna Mission schools provide hostel facilities to the pupils. In many places like Ramakrishna Mission schools at Nongwar and Mawshamok, there is no need of hostel facility as most of the students live in these villages.[70]

4. The Advancement of Women

Ramakrishna Mission has special concern for the development of women. Young people are educated to recognise the equality of men and women, and to strengthen the dignity of the individual and the unity of the nation.[71] The Mission encourages rural industrialisation for the eradication of rural poverty. According to Swamis, the children of the rural areas did not have the chance to go to schools and colleges due to poverty and their low social and economical condition in the society.[72]

The Mission teaches that due to the lack of proper educational facilities women did not have the chance to go out to expose their talents. Both Christian missionaries and the Ramakrishna Mission have contributed a lot to educate Khasi women and to bring them out of their old social and cultural boundaries. The Ramakrishna Mission has been providing them some kind of financial assistance and short technical training in different areas to make them be the earning members of the family.[73]

Swami Vivekananda held the males responsible for the oppression of women. He never liked their meddling into the

---

[69] Personnel interview with Swami Gokulananda at Cherrapunji on 25.5.2006.
[70] Personnel Interview with Sohbhar Village Council Members on 24.5.2005 at Sohbar.
[71] Swami Ranganathanda, *Role & Responsibility of Teachers in Building Up Modern India*, (Mumbai: Bhartiya Vidya Bhavan, 2004), 10.
[72] *Ibid.*, 12.
[73] Personal Interview with village Councils of Umkhabaw, Mawrah, Phong, Rngimawsaw village council Members on 26-27 November, 2006.

affairs of women. He fought all his life tooth and nail for the emancipation of women. Ramakrishna looked upon every woman as the living embodiment of the goddess of the universe. He gave very high place to women in the society.[74]

The centres and sub-centres of the Ramakrishna Mission conduct special programmes for youth and women. Besides their village welfare schemes, the Mission also gives training to the Khasi women for dairy, cottage industry, agriculture, poultry, weaving, and tailoring in order to make them valuable and contributing members of their communities.[75] After training the women, the Mission helps them to conduct welfare activities in their villages with the assistance of the villagers that creates a sense of social awareness.[76] Swami Vivekananda also invoked new India to arise through education and human development of the Indian masses.

According to the Ramakrishna Mission, Khasi rural women have been facing a lot of hardships. They carry heavy loads of firewood on their back, the load held fast by a sling spread across their foreheads. They clear the weeds from their fields; in every household woman's duty is cooking, washing, fetching water, nursing the children and taking care of the household.[77]

The Ramakrishna Mission has totally rejected intellectualism because it well knew that spiritual excellence was infinitely superior to intellectual excellence. The Mission also taught men to love and worship God as mother. The Mission opined that Khasi women have to be drawn into administrative work by making them the members of *Durbar Shnong, District Autonomous Councils, Raid* and the members of the Legislative Assembly.[78]

---

[74] Santwana Dasgupta, *Social Philosophy of* Swami Vivekananda, Kolkata: The Ramakrishna Mission Institute of Culture, 2005, 433.
[75] Swami Someswarananda, "The Ramakrishna Math & Ramakrishna Mission Among Common Men," *Souvenir*, (Kolkata: Ramakrishna Mission, 1980), 109-111.
[76] Swami Tapasyananda, *For Enquirers About Ramakrishna Math and Ramakrishna Mission*, op.cit., 37.
[77] Personal interview with a group of women on 30.12.2006 at Laitryngew.
[78] Swami Brahmeshananda, "Holy Mother and Women Empowerment," *Bulletin of the Ramakrishna Mission Institute of Culture*, Vol. LVI, No. I, January 2005, 7

The Khasi women are famous for their arts, their weaving of exquisite shawls, traditional coats, mats, and in their running of business. The Mission trains the Khasi women for these trades and encourages them to have proper workshops that will ensure the displaying of their artistry in the market.[79]

According to the Ramakrishna Mission, the educational institutions must ensure that the content and process of education reflects gender equality. All changes begin in the minds of men and women. At first, when the Ramakrishna Mission established these schools in the East Khasi Hills District, most parents did not allow their daughters to go to schools. They proclaimed that girls do not need education. But the Ramakrishna Mission has concern for the education of the girls. The Mission knows that education could liberate them and make them aware of the role they have to play for the betterment of their society. They will also know about the vital aspects of family planning and the importance of keeping the population under control.[80]

5. The Computer Training Centre

This project aims at providing computer training to educated Khasi youths to help them in getting professional knowledge for employment in government or private sectors. Many Khasi students have benefited through this scheme. Today the Ramakrishna Mission runs three computer-training centres in the East Khasi Hills District.[81]

6. Rural Development

The different centres are engaged in the rural development work. The aim is to make the poor and the backward people stand on their own feet, and to expose them to the mainstream of Indian culture, and to raise them to a status of equality with the rest of their countrymen.[82] Swami Vivekananda said: "So long as the millions live in hunger and ignorance, I hold every man a traitor

---

[79] *Ibid.*, 25-26.
[80] *Ibid.*, 14.
[81] *Ibid.*
[82] Swami Budhananda, *The Ramakrishna Movement, op.cit.,* 142-143.

who, having been educated at their expense pays not the least heed to them."[83]

The Mission too in its humble way entered the fields, helping the sufferers to rebuild their houses, supplying them with food and agricultural implements, and encouraging them to restart their religious practices. The Mission has laid special emphasis on the socio-economic, cultural and religious advancement of the Khasis in order to fulfil the dream of the founder. The Mission helps some of the Khasis financially to start their own work.[84]

7. Relief Work

Rural and tribal welfare work has come to occupy a prominent place in the scheme of services rendered by the Mission. With its limited funds and workers, the Mission has been doing its utmost for serving the poor and needy wherever any natural calamity takes place. The Mission also helped the Khasis when earthquake took place in Meghalaya. The Ramakrishna Mission spends some amount of its income on the flood affected people.

Teachings of the Ramakrishna Mission

According to the members of the Ramakrishna Mission, it is truly the Mission of the divine in the world. The Mission teaches freedom from religious bigotry, intolerance, hatred, superstition, social and racial prejudices, and also encourages freedom of thought, and the articulation of different philosophical concepts like God, the world, human being, *maya*, sin and salvation.

1. Religious Teachings

Religion, according to the Ramakrishna Mission, is the science of the knowledge of a human being's real nature. It is the perception, realisation, and manifestation of a human being's real nature, which is divinity itself. It is one in substance, pure existence, and

---

[83] Swami Ranganathanda, *Social Responsibilities of Public Administration*, (Mumbai: Bhartiya Vidya Bhavan, 2000), 20.

[84] Swami Shantarupananda, "Seventy Five Years of the Ramakrishna Mission Ashrama at Cherapunji- A Flesh Back (1931- 2006)", *Souvenir*, (Sohbar: Ramakrishna Mission, 2006), 5-9.

pure bliss, which is universal. The Universal Spirit expresses itself through infinite aspects, in infinite forms, modes, and media.[85]

At the same time religion is said to be a set of beliefs, symbols, and practices, which is based on the idea of the sacred and which invites believers into a socio-religious community.[86] Ramakrishna said that, "God has made different religions to suit different aspirants, times, and countries."[87] He also said that religion is the relationship between God and soul.[88]

Swami Vivekananda taught that all religions of the world are equally true, leading to the same goal. In every religion there are three parts, namely, philosophy, mythology and ritual. Each religion presents the fundamental doctrines, the goal and the means of attaining it. To him, philosophy was the basis of religion. He defined religion, as "the manifestation of the divinity which already exists within human beings."[89] He also defined religion as "the eternal relationship between the soul and the eternal God."[90] He said that for Christians and Muslims there is no need to renounce their faith to become Vedantists. Vivekananda thus gave a *vedantic* dimension to every human being's faith.[91] Similarly Swami Lokeswarananda defined religion as "a science of the self."[92] Swami Ranganathananda said, "Primarily religion is a value which is deeply personal."[93]

Swami Abhedananda said that "the religion of the twentieth century needs a conception of God who is personal, impersonal,

---

[85] Swami Nitya-Swarupananda, *Education for Human Unity and World Civilisation*, (Kolkata: The Ramakrishna Mission Institute of Culture, 2003), 7 & 111.

[86] Personal interview with Swami Davamayananda on 24.4.2005 at Cherrapunji.

[87] Hossainur Rahman, *Sri Ramakrishna: The Symbol of Harmony of Religions*, (Kolkata: The Ramakrishna Mission Institute of Culture, 2000), 31.

[88] Shanti Kumar Gosh, *Universal Value, op.cit.,* 62.

[89] Swami Ranganathanda, *Democratic Administration In The Light of Practical Vedanta*, (Chennai: Sri Ramakrishna Math, 1996), 80.

[90] n.n., *Reflection on Swami Vivekananda*, (ed), New Delhi: Sterling Publishers Pvt. Ltd., 1993), 65.

[91] R.K. Dasgupta, *Swami Vivekananda's Neo-Vedanta*, (Kolkata: The Asiatic Society, 1999), 36.

[92] Swami Lokeshwarananda, *Science and Religion*, (Kolkata: The Ramakrishna Mission Institute of Culture, 2000), 15.

[93] David Chander, "A Dialogue On Politics," *Vedanta*, No. 325, Sept-October 2005, 238.

and beyond both, whose supreme aspect will harmonise with the Absolute Reality of the universe, called by different names."[94] The purpose and task of religion is to tame and subdue the forces of hatred and violence in human beings.[95] Due to the mixing of religion with non-religious elements and much superstition, religion has fallen into decay, and ceased to be a character-forming force; it has become increasingly dogmatic, irrational, narrow, sectarian and unsuited to the modern scientific age.[96]

The followers of the Ramakrishna Mission who are influenced by Ramakrishna Pramahansa believe religion to be a kind of science open to study and investigation. The Ramakrishna Mission teaches about the concept of God, world, man, soul, *maya*, sin, and salvation. The same will be highlighted below.

(a) The Concept of God (Brahman)

Ramakrishna's approach to interpret the nature of Ultimate Reality is very similar to that of Ramanuja as he says that there is no contradiction between two aspects of Brahman known as *nirguna* and *saguna*. The Ramakrishna accepts *Brahman* as the Highest and the only Reality, which in essence is a principle of intelligence.[97] Ramakrishna realises that the Ultimate Reality can be comprehended both as *nirguna* or as *saguna*, the two aspects of the same reality. In the religious philosophy of Ramakrishna, God the Absolute and God the Personal are one and the same.[98] Ramakrishna realised that the Ultimate Reality can be comprehended both as *saguna and nirguna*, the two aspects of the same Reality. God with qualities is equally real as *nirguna* Brahman as both are one and same Reality. God without any quality can never be known to anybody.[99]

---

[94] Swami Abhedananda, *Religion of the Twentieth Century*, (Kolkata: Ramakrishna Vedanta Math, 1968), 7.
[95] *Ibid.*
[96] Swami Ranganathanda, *Children: Humanity's Greatest Assets*, (Mumbai: Bhartitya Vidya Bhavan, 2004), 2.
[97] Swami Tapasyananda, *Sri Ramakrishna: Life and Teachings*, (Kolkata: Sri Ramakrishna Math, n.d.), 206.
[98] n.n., *Sayings of Sri Ramakrishna*, (Chennai: Sri Ramakrishna Math, 1975), 266.
[99] Dr. Mamta Kundu, A Critical Study of Universal Religion of Ramakrishna Paramahansa, (Kolkata: Dev Sahitya Kutir Private Limited, 1993), 75-76.

According to Ramakrishna, Brahman is not the five elements. He is not the senses, nor the mind, nor the intelligence, nor the age—He is beyond all categories. To get up to the roof a person has to leave below all the steps of the staircase one by one. In order to reach the highest principle, the Absolute, one will have to proceed step by step in and through the process of denying the unreal in search of the Real. Unless Real is attained the process goes on.

He also says that God is both *Brahman* and *Ishvara*. He is not only the Immanent Principle but also the sum total of the universe, and on this ground, the view that the world is an illusion, seems to be meaningless. But it would be wrong to think that God is exhausted by the world because the world is the manifestation of God. All other things apart from God, said Sri Ramakrishna, are like zeros. It is Brahman that gives value and reality to the world.[100] He conceives Brahman as the Universal Spirit and the Inner Ruler of all souls. He is the Supreme Self, the Infinite, manifesting through everything in the universe.[101]

According to Swami Vivekananda, *Brahman* is the real Absolute.[102] He also said that *Brahman* in the Upanisads is Consciousness and the Self of all things.[103] In Vivekananda's teaching, Brahman is the only Truth, the goal of life. The Absolute Reality of an impersonal God is beyond human comprehension but impersonality can be known only through personal gods such as *Saguna Brahman*.[104]

Vivekananda believed that Brahman is in everything and so embraces the whole of the universe without making any

---

[100] Dr. Mamta Kundu, *A Critical Study of Universal Religion of Ramakrishna Paramahansa*, (Kolkata: Dev Sahitya Kutir Limited, 1993), 119-120.

[101] n.n., *The Condensed Gospel of Sri Ramakrishna*, (Chennai: Sri Ramakrishna Math, 1978), 118.

[102] n.n., *The Complete Works of Swami Vivekananda, Vol. 2*, (Kolkata: Advaita Ashrama, 1999), 210.

[103] John B. Chethimattam, "Vedanta As A Method for Inter-Religious Theology," *Vedanta: Concepts and Application*, (Kolkata: The Ramakrishna Mission Institute of Culture, 2000), 200.

[104] Abrahman Stephen, *The Social Philosophy of Swami Vivekananda: Its Relevance to Modern India*, Delhi: ISPCK, 2005), 81.

discrimination. God (Brahman), for him, is the ground of all existence as an Omnipresent Impersonal Power.[105] According to him, this Impersonal Principle or Spirit runs through the universe as a divine force as well as the source of existence of everything.[106]

Swami Vivekananda also said that Brahman is ever unchanging, immortal, and fearless. Impersonal does not mean less than personal, but rather without the limitations of personality. Everyone is a manifestation of that Impersonal God.[107] In a practical sense, the impersonal *Brahman* is known only through the personal gods. However, the idea of personal God is not a true and final conclusion because such a God can never be universal; therefore, one must go on to the highest stage where God is Impersonal. At the highest stage the personality of God vanishes, replaced by impersonality.[108]

He also said that this Impersonal Principle or Spirit is both the subject and the object. He is the "I" and the "You".[109] The Impersonal God becomes Immanent as different objects and the invisible unknowable One turns visible and becomes knowable as the many. If a person is in ignorance he or she will see God as many.[110]

According to Swami Ranganathananda, God is one in the many, and, though one, sages call it by various names.[111] This Divine Being dwells in all human beings.[112] According to Swami Jagadatmananda, the Ultimate Reality is the Universal

---

[105] n.n., *The Complete Works of Swami Vivekananda, Vol. 4*, (Kolkata: Asvaita Ashrama, 1999), 234.

[106] n.n., *The Complete Works of Swami Vivekananda, Vol. 5*, (Kolkata: Asvaita Ashrama, 1999), 3.7.

[107] Swami Vivekananda, *Lectures From Colombo to Almora*, (Kolkata: Advaita Ashrama, 2003), 129, 188.

[108] *Ibid.*, 8.

[109] n.n., *The Complete Works of Swami Vivekananda, Vol. 1* (Kolkata: Asvaita Ashrama, 1999), 217.

[110] *Ibid.*, 363.

[111] Swami Ranganathanda, *Eternal Values for a Changing Society, Vol. I*, (Mumbai: Bhartiya Vidya Bhavan, 1994), 41.

[112] n.n., *The Complete Works of Swami Vivekananda, Vol. 3 & 8*, (Kolkata: Adviata Ashrama, 1999), 123.

Consciousness- *Saccidananda,* the Ultimate Principle that is eternal and does not decay nor die.[113] He also said that God, the true philosopher's stone, answers every prayer, and lays hidden deep within every heart.[114]

Swami Abhedananda wrote in his book with the title "The Philosophy of Progress and Perfection" that the Absolute is not without but within us. He is the soul of our souls. So it is vain to seek the Absolute outside.[115] However, he acknowledged that God appears as personal to a dualistic or monotheistic worshipper and as impersonal to a qualified non-dualistic believer or one who believes in the immanence and transcendence of God. As one master of the house appears in various forms, being father to one, brother to another, and husband to third, so one God is described and called in various ways according to the particular aspect in which He appears to His particular worshipper.[116]

Thus in general, God, according to the Ramakrishna Mission, is the ground of all existence. He is one without a second, yet He is hidden in every being. He gives to all being's the fruits of their actions. God fully enjoys His own transcendent sweetness in the incarnation.[117] Neither the fire exists apart from its burning power; nor can its burning power be thought of apart from the fire. God or Absolute cannot be thought of apart from the idea of God with attributes.[118] The Ramakrishna Mission teaches that God is internal and external, spiritual and material. It teaches that universal God is the God of oneness; our partial knowledge causes differences, and, of course, it can cause disharmony too. According to the Mission, God the Absolute and God the

---

[113] Swami Jagadamananda, *Gospel of the Life Sublime, Vol. 1,* (Singapore: Ramakrishna Mission, 1998), 203.

[114] Swami Yogeshananda, *The Visions of Sri Ramakrishna* (Mylapore: Sri Ramakrishna Math, n.d.), 108.

[115] Swami Abhedananda, *The Philosophy of Progress and Perfection* (Kolkata: Ramakrishna Vedanta Math, 1994), 248.

[116] n.n., *Teachings of Sri Ramakrishna, op.cit.,* 5-6; see also Dr. Anindita Niyogi Balslev, *Religious Tolerance Or Acceptance?* (Kolkata: The Ramakrishna Mission Institute of Culture, 1987), 29.

[117] n.n., *The Complete Works of Swami Vivekananda, Vol.4,* 234.

[118] n.n., *Teachings of Sri Ramakrishna, op.cit.,* 4-5.

Omnipotent and Personal are one and the same. According to Ramakrishna Mission, you and I are personal gods. According to Swami Saradananda, God is within all and He is without all this world of phenomena.[119]

According to Swami Lokeswarananda, God is in all men, but all men are not in God.[120] God is manifested in the whole world, in all men, and in all incarnations.[121] This is the God of *Vedanta* and His heaven is everywhere.[122]

Ramakrishna Mission teaches that *Brahman* Himself is Pure, Undifferentiated Consciousness; but each of these qualities represents a stage in progress the differentiation by which the one becomes seemingly many. On the other hand, God the Absolute is the independent Reality. He is the only one power, which is God, and our mind is nothing but a reflection of that.[123]

(b) The Concept of World

The world in the teachings of the Ramakrishna Mission is the manifestation of the dynamic aspect of Reality. The infinite universe emanates from the Infinite Brahman. God is the material cause of the universe.[124] God alone is the agent of the action of creating the world.[125]

---

[119] Swami Saradananda, The Vedanta: Its Theory & Practice, Kolkata: Udbodhan Office, 2002, 8.

[120] F.Max Muller, "Sri Ramakrishna," *World Thinkers on Ramakrishna-Vivekananda*, ed. by Swami Lokeshwarananda, (Kolkata: Ramakrishna Mission Institute of Culture, 1983), 5; see also Swami Tapasyananda, *Sri Ramakrishna: Life and Teachings*, (Mylapore: Sri Ramakrishna Math, n.d.), 136; See also Swami Paramananda, *Concentration and Meditation*, (Mylapore: Sri Ramakrishna Math, 2002), 17.

[121] J.N. Farquhar, *Modern Religious Movements of India*, (Delhi: Munshi Ram Manohar Lal, 1967), 203.

[122] Swami Ashokananda, *When the Many Become One?* (Kolkata: Advaita Ashrama, n.d.), 45.

[123] Dr. Mamta Kundu, *A Critical Study of Universal Religion of Ramakrishna Paramahansa*, op.cit., 38.

[124] n.n., *What Religion is in the Teachings of Swami Vivekananda?* ed. by Swami Vidyatmananda, (Kolkata: Advaita Ashrama, 2004), 109.

[125] n.n., Ramakrishna Math and Ramakrishna Mission Convention, (Kolkata: Ramakrishna Mission Ashrama, 1980), 64.

Ramakrishna said, "The whole world is nothing but a part of the Supreme."[126] He also calls it a *Lila*, an aspect of *Brahman* and hence real, though not eternal. It is like ice crystals appearing on water and again dissolving back in water. The ice crystals are as real as water, but do not endure permanently.[127]

Vivekananda said that *Vedanta* does not say that the world is false; he says that it is what it is, what you find it to be.[128] According to him, the whole universe is an external symbol of God, and behind that stands His grand name.[129] Each particular body is a form, and behind that particular body is its name. Out of this material He creates the universe, and at the end of a cycle His body becomes thinner, it contracts; and at the beginning of another cycle, it becomes expanded again, and out of it evolves all these different worlds.[130] The Absolute is the only existence and the universe is but a speck in that infinite ocean of knowledge and bliss.

Vivekananda reconciled the two views of the universe; the one in which it dissolves in illusion, and the other in which it is one with God.[131] According to Baladev, the creation of the world is a spontaneous act of the Lord.[132] Swami Ranganathananda said that the world is a mixture of good and evil, happiness and misery. There will never be a perfectly good or bad world, because the very idea is a contradiction in terms.[133]

(c) The Concept of Man

According to Ramakrishna Mission, a human being is the owner of infinite power and is the abode of divinity. For this reason a

---

[126] Dr. Mamta Kundu, *A Critical Study of Universal Religion of Ramakrishna Pramahansa*, op.cit., 78.

[127] Swami Harshananda, *Philosophy of Ramakrishna*, (Bangalore: Ramakrishna Math, 2000), 15-16.

[128] n.n., *The Complete Works of Swami Vivekananda*, Vol. 8, 3-30.

[129] Swami Vivekananda, *Bhakti or Devotion*, (Kolkata: Advaita Ashrama, 1989), 10.

[130] n.n., *What Religion is in the Words of Swami Vivekananda*? Ed. by Swami Vijayamananda, Kolkata: Advaita Ashrama, 2004), 109.

[131] n.n., *The Complete Works of Swami Vivekananda*, Vol. I, 95.

[132] Swami Harsananda, *The Three System of Vedanta: An Introduction*, (Bangalore: Ramakrishna Math, 2001), 46.

[133] Swami Ranganathanda, *Swami Vivekananda on Universal Ethics and Moral Conduct*, (Mumbai: Bhartiya Vidya Bhavan, 1995), 36-40.

human alone can think of God, can think of the Infinite, of which no other creature can think. He regards human as the topmost creation of God.[134]

According to Swami Vivekananda, the law of causation does not bind a human being. Pain and misery do not affect the soul, they are but as a passing cloud throwing its shadow over the sun, but the cloud passes, the sun is unchanged; and so it is with a human.[135] Vivekananda teaches that the apparent man is known as *Jiva*, which stands for *atman* in bondage and the real man is the perfect Eternal *Atman*.[136]

Thus, in general, the Ramakrishna Mission believes that God is the creator of human beings. It believes in the equality of all human beings. All are the sons and daughters of the same God.[137] There is, therefore, no essential distinction between man and man, high and low, a priest and a sweeper.[138] A human being is the epitome of the cosmos. The Mission holds that a human being is not simply an economic being or a political creature, but is *Atman* or Universal Spirit also.

The Ramakrishna Mission teaches that there is one spirit in everyone; that there is God in every human being. Since every human being has the same divinity in God, we can worship Him by serving human beings.[139]

He manifests Himself in every being, but He is only visible and recognisable in a human being.[140] Swami Lokeswarananda said that only a human being could morally and spiritually

---

[134] n.n., *The Ramakrishna Movement*, (Kolkata: The Ramakrishna Mission Institute of Culture, 2000), 3.

[135] n.n., "Swami Vivekananda On the Hell and Heaven in Man," *Prebudha Bharata, Vol. 109*, July 2001, Cover Page.

[136] n.n., *The Complete Works of Swami Vivekananda, Vol. 2*, 254-262.

[137] Romain Roland, *The Life of Vivekananda and the Universal Gospel*, (Kolkata: Advaita Ashrama, 1988), 166; see also Swami Swahananda, *Service and Spirituality*, (Mylapore: Sri Ramakrishna Math, 1979), 178.

[138] Swami Jitatmananda, *Immortal India*, (Rajkot: Sri Ramakrishna Ashrama, 2002), 2.

[139] Santana Dasgupta, *Social Philosophy of Swami Vivekananda*, (Kolkata: The Ramakrishna Mission Institute of Culture, 2001), 45.

[140] Swami Vivekananda, *Bhakti Or Devotion, op.cit.*, 11.

develop so as to be second only to God. A human is truly an image of God. This is why serving humans is like serving God.[141]

(d) Maya

Maya is considered to be the veil that keeps God hidden from our sight. Ramakrishna compares it as to a small patch of cloud that can hide the big sun from our view.[142] However *Maya* is not to be superficially interpreted as illusion. Vivekananda said: "Maya is not illusion as it is popularly interpreted. *Maya* is real, yet human being does however acknowledge that the root of *Maya* is "ma" meaning that which leads to the idea of illusion or appearance.[143] Therefore some people interpret the term *"Maya"* to mean that which truly is not, but appears to be.[144]

Maya acting in human produces the sense of duality.[145] This means that from the practical point of view this world is real as a temporal phenomenon but not in the sense of eternal reality. One who knows the real sees in *Maya* not illusion, but Reality.[146]

Ramakrishna says there is a certain rift in the universe which puzzles the human mind. Swami Vivekananda calls it the 'contradiction' riddling human existence. According to Ramakrishna Paramhamsa, *Maya* is of two kinds- one leading towards God *(Vidya-Maya)* and other leading away from God *(Avidya-Maya)*. The former consists of non-attachment. Vidya Maya belongs to the realm with the help of *Vidya-Maya* souls surrender themselves to the mercy of God. *Avidya-Maya* consists of lust, anger, avarice, inordinate attachment, pride, and envy.

---

[141] Swami Lokeswarananda, *Vedanta In Practice*, (Kolkata: Sri Ramakrishna Mission Institute of Culture, 2001), 45.

[142] Swami Harshananda, *Philosophy of Sri Ramakrishna*, (Bangalore: Ramakrishna Math, 2000), 13.

[143] L.Thomas O'Neil, *Maya In Sankara: Measuring the Immesurable*, (Delhi/Varanasi: Motilal Banarsidas, 1980); see also n.n., *The Complete Works of Swami Vivekananda*, Vol. 6, 92.

[144] n.n., *A Dictionary of Advaita Vedanta*, Compiled by Nirod Baran Chakraborty, (Kolkata: Ramakrishna Mission Institute of Culture, 2003), 129.

[145] Nalini Devdas, *Sri Ramakrishna*, (Bangalore:/CISRS, 1966), 65; see also *Adi Kathamrata*, Vol. 3, ed. by Shyamal Basu, (Kolkata: College Street, 1983), 249.

[146] n.n., *The Complete Works of Swami Vivekananda*, Vol. 6, 92.

This kind of *Maya* gives rise to the sense of "I" and "Mine" and serves to keep men chained to the world.[147]

(e) The Concept of Sin

The Vedanta recognises no sin but recognises errors. And the greatest error, says the *Vedanta*, is to say that you are weak.[148]

While Vivekananda does not subscribe to the Christian understanding of sin, he says that selfishness is the chief sin. According to him, ignorance, wickedness and weakness are the dirt and dust that are on the mirror of the heart of a sinful person due to selfishness. This sense of ego makes us think of ourselves as separate from all others. Sins are very low degrees of self-manifestation.[149] According to Swami Vivekananda, it is selfishness and greed that lead the human towards all evil doing. As long as we do not know our real nature we remain selfish.[150] Ignorance is evil.[151] Living in ignorance we are bound to make mistakes.[152]

Swami Srikantananda stipulates that there are many factors like attachment, grief, anger, greed and lust, which delude the intellect and make us lose the power of discrimination.[153] According to Swami Ranganathananda, the ego in man is the cause of all errors (sins) and the origin of all false values. He says that selfishness and greed are the two basic infirmities of the human mind. But selfishness that is thinking of oneself is the chief sin.[154] It is desire that makes men injure others. These desires, when remain unfulfilled, lead to frustrations and complexes.[155]

---

[147] n.n., *Teachings of Sri Ramakrishna Mission, op.cit.,* 13.
[148] n.n., *The Complete Works of Swami Vivekananda,* Vol. 2, 295; see also Swami Gokulananda, *Some Guidelines to Inner Life,* (Mylapore: Sri Ramakrishna Math, n.d.), 105.
[149] n.n., *Vivekananda Writes To You, op.cit.,* 26.
[150] Swami Vivekananda, *Lectures from Colombo to Almora,* (Kolkata: Advaita Ashrama, 2003), 47, 56.
[151] n.n., *The Complete Works of Swami Vivekananda,* Vol. 8, 15-16.
[152] Swami Abhedananda, *Religion of the Twentieth Century,* (Kolkata: Ramakrishna Vedanta Math, 1968), 28.
[153] Swami Srikantananda, *The Intelligent Way to Yoga,* (Mylapore: Sri Ramakrishna Math, 2000), 19-20.
[154] Swami Vivekananda, *Salvation and Service,* (Kolkata: Advaita Ashrama, 1998), 92.
[155] Swami Harshananda, *Relevance of Ramakrishna to Modern Life,* (Bangalore: Ramakrishna Math, 2000), 12.

Swami Tejasananda observed that God is in all human beings, but all human beings are not in God and that is the reason why they suffer.[156]

(f) The Concept of Atman or Soul

According to the Ramakrishna, the *Jivatman* and *Paramatman* are one and the same, the difference between them being only one of degree. For, one is finite and limited while the other is infinite; one is dependent while other is independent.[157] The jivas are the manifestation of the Supreme Self having a separate individual existence of their own though possessing a basic unity with the Supreme. The relation between the two has been expressed by Ramakrishna in his utterance that the union of the *Jivatman* and *Paramatman* is like the union of the hour, minute and second of a watch. They are inter-related and interdependent and though usually separate, they may become united as often as favourable opportunities occur.[158]

According to Vivekananda, the nature of atman or self has two levels. One, the lower self, enjoys the fruits of the earth. The other, the higher self, manifests aloofness from sensuous enjoyment and has equipoise of spirit, calm and majestic. The *Atman*, according to Vivekananda, is neither body nor mind, but beyond both. He said that the soul is the only existence in the human body that is immaterial, and it cannot be a compound.[159] He also said that human soul is eternal, immortal, perfect and infinite, and death means only a change of centre from one body to another.[160] The self is indestructible, is beyond death, because it is immaterial and immortal.[161] That which is immortal can

---

[156] Swami Tejasananda, *A Short Life of Sri Ramakrishna*, (Kolkata: Advaita Ashrama), 1999), 125.

[157] n.n., *Sayings of Sri Ramakrishna, op.cit.*, 33.

[158] *Ibid.*, 32.

[159] Swami Ranganathanda, *The Approach to Truth in Vedanta*, (Kolkata: Advaita Ashrama, 2004), 31; see also Swami Pramananda, *The Problem of Life and Death*, (Mylapore: Ramakrishna Math, n.d.), 9.

[160] Swami Vivekananda, *State Society and Socialism*, (Kolkata: Advaita Ashrama, 1998), 44.

[161] n.n., *The Complete Works of Swami Vivekananda, Vol. 3, op.cit.*, 7.

have no beginning because everything with a beginning must have an end.[162]

Swami Vivekananda further elaborated, "Each soul is eternally divine. In every being there is infinite knowledge, infinite power, and infinite divinity. The human being is the highest among all beings. He is the visible manifestation of God."[163] He also said that the only God to worship is the human soul in the human body. Of course all animals are also the temple of God, but the human being is the highest.[164] Similarly Swami Paramananda held that the body dies, but the self is deathless; the body is limited, but the self is unlimited; the body has form, but the self is formless. Each soul is really not just a part of the Infinite, but actually is the Infinite *Brahman*.[165]

Swami Abhedananda said that each soul, being a spark of the huge bonfire of divinity, is of a similar nature. Each individual soul may be called potentially divine. Whatever has a beginning must have an end. Everything that has form must have a beginning and an end. The body dies because it has a form, but the soul is deathless because it has no form.[166] It is beyond time, space and casualty.[167]

Swami Ranganathananda said that the Infinite *Brahman* is *Atman*.[168] The Self is never created nor destroyed.[169] Love, existence, and knowledge are not the qualities of the soul, but its essence. The goal is to manifest this divinity within by controlling nature, external and internal.[170]

---

[162] n.n., Selections From The Complete Works of Swami Vivekananda, (Kolkata: Advaita Ashrama, 1993), 150.

[163] Swami Jitamananda, *Immortal India: Short Plays on India's Spiritual Heritage*, (Rajkot: Sri Ramakrishna Ashrama, 2002), 2.

[164] Swami Prabhananda, "Vivekananda's Approach to the Upliftment of the Masses," *Report On Ramakrishna Math and Ramakrishna Mission Youth Convention 1985*, (Kolkata: Ramakrishna Mission, 1985), 55.

[165] n.n., *The Problem of Life and Death*, (Mylapore: Sri Ramakrishna Math, 2001), 8.

[166] Swami Pramananda, *The Problem of Life and Death*, op.cit., 8.

[167] Ibid., 8.

[168] Ibid., 10

[169] Swami Ranganathanda," Swami Vivekananda and Today's Youth," *Report on Ramakrishna Math and Ramakrishna Mission Youth Convention 1985*, op.cit., 206.

[170] Swami Lokeswarananda, *Science and Religion*, Kolkata: Sri Ramakrishna Mission Institute of Culture, 2000), 15; see also Swami Pramananda, *Reincarnation and Immortality*, (Chennai: Sri Ramakrishna Math, 1974), 11.

Thus in general, according to Ramakrishna Mission, the soul is self-shining, self-existent, immutable, free, and pure. It must be one with the Supreme Being.[171] The *Atman* or the soul is one without a second, is deathless and indestructible. The law of beginning and end cannot bind it.[172] The difference between *Jivatman* and *Parmatman* is only one of degree. For one is finite and limited while the other is Infinite.[173] The *Atman* is a constant entity and it is unchangeable amidst of all changes.[174] The body is limited, but the self is not. All these births and rebirths, coming and goings are the figments of *Maya*.[175]

(g) The Transmigration of Soul

The Ramakrishna Mission teaches that desires lead a person to the transmigration of soul.[176] Swami Vivekananda taught that all selves are parts of the Infinite Self known as *Paramatman*. But owing to ignorance, most people are not familiar with this fact.[177] He further states that ignorance, inequality, and desire are the three causes of human misery, and each follows the other inevitably.[178] The *Atman* in bondage is called *Jiva*. According to him, each work we do, each thought we think, produces an impression, called in Sanskrit *Samskara*. The sum total of the *Samskaras* is the force, which determines a man's direction after death.[179] The *Jiva* comes to lower and higher states. This is the

---

[171] Swami Vireswarananda, *Religion and Spiritual Life*, (New Delhi: Ramakrishna Mission, 1982), 4.

[172] n.n., Selection From *The Complete Works of Swami Vivekananda*, (Kolkata: Advaita Ashrama, 1993), 150.

[173] Swami Abhedananda, *Thoughts on Philosophy and Religion*, (Kolkata: Ramakrishna Vedanta Math, 1989), 27.

[174] n.n., *The Gospel of Sri Ramakrishna*, translated by Swami Nikhilananda, (Mumbai/Chennai: Sri Ramakrishna Math, 1964), 1016-1017.

[175] n.n., *The Complete Works of Swami Vivekananda*, Vol. 1, 403.

[176] n.n., *The Complete Works of Swami Vivekananda*, Vol. 9, 543.

[177] Swami Bhajananda, "Rural Development Work in the Perspective Swami Vivekananda's Social Philosophy," *Souvenir 2002*, (Asansol: Ramakrishna Mission High School, 2002), 14.

[178] Swami Vivekananda, *State, Society and Socialism, op.cit.*, 100.

[179] n.n., Selection *From the Complete Works of Swami Vivekananda*, (Kolkata: Advaita Ashrama, 1993), 152-155.

well-known law of reincarnation; and this law binds all creation.[180]

Karma proves to be the cause of bondage as long as human beings cling to the temporal, but when one turns to the eternal; *karma* opens the way to freedom.[181] Death does not mean an absolute break with this life and entrance into a wholly unaccustomed state.[182]

(h) The Concept of Liberation or Salvation

The liberation of the self and the good of the world is the ideal of the Ramakrishna Mission.[183] The ultimate goal of a person's life is to manifest the divinity hidden within.[184] All the evils, all the bad *samskaras* or impressions are finally destroyed, burnt away in the fire of spiritual knowledge, leading to spiritual self-realisation, and hence this cycle of births and deaths ceases.[185]

According to Swami Ramakrishnananda, God is the only one who can free us from desires and fears; hence He is called the Purifier.[186] Vedanta prescribes no set path of liberation but offers three main paths of salvation like *Karma* (Action), *Bhakti* (Devotion) and *Jnana* (Knowledge).

i. Salvation through Action

The Ramakrishna Mission teaches that the doctrine of *karma* is the fundamental principle of philosophy and religion of *Vedanta*.[187] Karma-Yoga is the science of right action by which, according to

---

[180] Swami Vivekananda, *Is Vedanta the Future Religion?* (Kolkata: Advaita Ashrama, 1993), 18.

[181] Swami Satprakashananda, *How is a Man Reborn?* (Kolkata: Advaita Ashrama, 2000), 7-8.

[182] Swami Pramananda, *Re-incarnation and Immortality*, (Chennai: Ramakrishna Math, 1974), 72.

[183] Swami Tapasyananda, *Ramakrishna Math and Ramakrishna Mission*, (Mylapore: Sri Ramakrishna Math, n.d.), 4.

[184] Swami Srikantananda, *The Intelligent Way to Yoga*, (Mylapore: Sri Ramakrishna Math, 2001), 18.

[185] Swami Ranganathananda, *Proceedings of the Question Answer Session in Chicago*, (Kolkata: Advaita Ashrama, 2002), 15.

[186] Swami Ramakrishnananda, *God Divine Incarnations*, (Mylapore: Sri Ramakrishna Math, 1947), 27.

[187] Swami Vivekananda, *Practical Vedanta, op.cit.*, 93.

Vivekananda, one realises one's own divinity through works.[188] All good actions are God's work by which we all are simply working out His Will. The desire to do good deeds is the highest divine motivating power, and it tends to embrace universal humanity. The Super Divine Strength is the only way.[189] The basic idea of *Karma-Yoga* is that the doer surrenders to God and engages in selfless service. The only unbound work is to work as free beings to give up all work unto God.[190]

According to Swami Abhedananda, we create by our actions the causes of good and evil and receive reward or punishment as the reactions of our thoughts and deeds by the law of compensation.[191] Through *karma-yoga* a man realises his own divinity.[192] By work the effects of the work can be nullified.[193] The object of selfless work is to remove the ignorance which hinders a soul to have the true knowledge of the Brahman. The Mission teaches that through selfless work the mind gets purified. After the mind becomes pure, there arise knowledge and devotion in it.[194] The Mission also teaches that any work that stands in the way of God-realisation and increases discontent is bad work.

There are two kinds of actions- *pravrtti* and *nivrtti*. *Pravrtti* leads to earning a name and gaining fame. It makes a person selfish. On the other hand *nivrtti* leads a person away from selfishness. This *nivrtti* is the fundamental basis of all morality and all religion.[195] According to Vivekananda, it is renunciation of this trivial organic-centred ego that makes for one's life-

---

[188] n.n., Complete Works of Swami Vivekananda, Vol. 5, 292.

[189] n.n., Complete Works of Swami Vivekananda, Vol. 2, 7.

[190] n.n., Complete Works of Swami Vivekananda, Vol. I, 104.

[191] Swami Abhedananda, *Doctrine of Karma*, (Kolkata: Ramakrishna Vedanta Math, 2000), 28.

[192] n.n., *Meditation and Its Methods: According to Vivekananda*, ed. by Swami Chetanananda, Kolkata: Advaita Ashrama, 1998), 93.

[193] Swami Prabhavananda, *Spiritual Heritage of India*, (Chennai: Sri Ramakrishna Math, 2000), 346.

[194] n.n., The Apostles of Ramakrishna, Kolkata: Advaita Ashrama, 1995, 195.

[195] Swami Ranganathananda, *Swami Vivekananda on Universal Ethics and Moral Conduct*, op.cit., 24.

expression in the mood and act of service.[196] He said that freedom or salvation is only possible to the being that is beyond all conditions, all laws, all bondages of cause and effect.[197]

According to Swami Paramananda, we must work with sincerity, faith and earnestness to reach the same state as the great ones have attained.[198] A person, who attains to perfection, possesses the qualities of *Sattva* or goodness. The fear of death or of disease will cease to exist in the state of liberation.[199]

ii. Salvation through Devotion (Bhakti-yoga)

Bhakti-yoga is a devotional discipline of intensively searching love for God. According to the Mission, it is an earnest effort to search for the truth which leads to the experience of God.

The Ramakrishna Mission emphatically pointed out that devotion to the personal God brings divinity within easy access of men and women everywhere.[200] Human beings can realise Him in this very life. True *Bhakti* or devotion never seeks material benefits. If anyone seeks such prosperity through religion he called their religion "shop keeping religion". *Bhakti* is always directed to God and first and foremost thing is to want God honestly and intensely. He argued," If a person uses all his/her mental energy in seeking to satisfy his/her body and its wants, shows the difference between him and an animal. Bhakti is a higher thing, higher than even desiring heaven.[201]

In true devotion there is a rejection of personal cravings and an acceptance of God as the entire fulfilment of one's desire. *Bhakti* or devotion is a means of satisfying the emotional side of a person and family. It ends in God, in the experience of perfect love. *Bhakt-yoga* or devotion is love which is directed towards

---

[196] Swami Ranganathananda, *Democratic Administration in the Light of Practical Vedanta*, (Mylapore: Sri Ramakrishna Math, 1996), 34.
[197] Swami Vivekananda, *Life After Death*, (Kolkata: Advaita Ashrama, 2002), 9.
[198] Swami Pramananda, *The Problem of Life after Death*, (Mylapore: Sri Ramakrishna Math, 2001), 2.
[199] Swami Pramananda, *Vedanta in Practice*, (Chennai: Sri Ramakrishna Math, 1974), 35-36.
[200] Richard Schiffman, *Sri Ramakrishna: A Prophet for the New Age*, (Kolkata: The Ramakrishna Mission Institute of Culture, 1994), 207.
[201] n.n., Complete Works of Swami Vivekananda, Vol. V, 267.

the only object worthy of receiving that love, that is *Isvara*, the personal God; and *Bkakt-yoga* or devotion is the means of attaining that ideal love.[202]

According to Swami Tapasyananda, "Single-hearted love for God is the aim and object of renunciation."[203] A true devotee understands that God is manifested as pure love in the human form, and so God as love is not an abstract concept, but rather a divine living being. God as love is approachable. He is also an attainable being in this world.[204] After one realises God, the world seems to be a mere appearance like the mirage. There is nothing in it that can attract one. What really comes in the spiritual domain in this unswerving faith- faith in the words of the Guru, in the Lord and in the scripture? In a *Bhakta's(disciple)* primary stage a guru or teacher is necessary to help the disciple's inner thirst for God. There is no use in uttering thousand names of God without turning the mind to Him. The practical instruction of Swami Vivekananda was that "instead of hearing foolish things, we must hear about God; instead of talking foolish words, we must talk of God."[205] He also said that the memory of God will not come to the selfish man. The more we come out and do good to others, the more our hearts will be purified, and God will be in them. Happiness is only found in the spirit.[206]

Swami Pramananda, in his book on *Concentration and Meditation* wrote: "He who has given up all attachment, all fear and all anger, he whose soul has gone unto the Lord, he who has taken refuge in the Lord, whose heart has become purified, with whatsoever desire he comes to the Lord, He will grant that to him."[207]

---

[202] n.n., Complete Works of Swami Vivekananda, Vol. III, 31-36.

[203] Swami Tapasyananda, *Sri Ramakrishna: Life and Teachings* , (Kolkata: Sri Ramakrishna Math, n.d), 144.

[204] Abraham Stephen, The Social Philosophy of Swami Vivekananda: Its Relevance to Modern India, (Delhi: ISPCK, 2005), 202.

[205] n.n., Complete Works of Swami Vivekananda, Vol. IV, 9.

[206] Swami Ranganathananda, *Swami Vivekananda on Universal Ethics and Moral Conduct*, op.cit., 35.

[207] Swami Paramananda, *Concentration and Meditation*, (Mylapore: Sri Ramakrishna Math, 2002), 123.

Swami Abhedananda says that the souls that have reached the spiritual realisation, are conscious of God the Absolute, and lose the sense of 'I,' 'me' and 'mine'. That is salvation.[208]

iii. Salvation through Knowledge (Jnana-yoga)

According to Swami Vivekananda, *jnana-yoga* is the rational method which follows the way of knowledge to the realisation of the divine self. He said that the discipline of *jnana-yogi* is a negative way of positively discovering and critically assessing one's own ability, leading to the realisation of oneness in self.[209]

Avidya or Maya, said Swami Vivekananda, deludes the mind with the sense of plurality giving rise to the consciousness of the ego as a separate and independent existence. The *Atman* in bondage is called *Jiva*.[210] In order to achieve oneness the *jnana-yogi* must give up all worldly attachment and all empirical objects. The knowledge of reality can be achieved by the elimination of ignorance. The devotee realises that he/she is *Brahman* only when his/her ignorance is removed. A *jnani* has to realise "I am not the body, I am not the mind, I am not thought, I am not even consciousness; I am the *Atman*."[211]

According to Swami Ranganathananda, spiritual knowledge is the only thing that will eliminate our suffering forever. All perfection is there already in the soul but this perfection has been covered up by ignorance.[212] Sri Ramakrishna says that studying the scriptures alone cannot attain salvation.[213] It is the guidance of the *guru* who helps the student to realise the truth of the scriptures and thereby attain the knowledge of the true self and of salvation.

---

[208] Swami Prajananda, *The Philosophy of Progress and Perfection*, (Kolkata: Ramakrishna Vedanta Math, 1994), 193.

[209] Abraham Stephen, The Social Philosophy of Swami Vivekananda: Its Relevance to Modern India, 210.

[210] Swami Vivekananda, *Is Vedanta the Future Religion*, op.cit., 18.

[211] n.n., Complete Works of Swami Vivekananda, Vol.VIII, 4.

[212] Swami Ranganathananda, *Swami Vivekananda on Universal Ethics and Moral Conduct*, (Mumbai: Bhartiya Vidya Bhavan), 1.

[213] Swami Ranganathananda, *Eternal Values for a Changing Society, Vol. I*, (Mumbai: Bhartiya Vidya Bhavan, 1994), 412.

The Ramakrishna Mission teaches that meditation on the real nature of things (as taught by the guru with the instrumentality of the scriptures) can pierce through the outer coverings and fix the aspirant's mind on their real essence.[214] The goal of each soul is freedom from the slavery of matter and thought, mastery of external and internal nature.[215]

According to the Mission, egoism is so injurious to human beings that as long as it is not eradicated there is no salvation for them.[216] Meditation on the real nature of things can pierce through the outer coverings and fix the aspirant's mind on their real essence.[217] Sri Ramakrishna said that one must practice meditation by concentrating the mind on Him.[218] He also taught that the way of purifying the mind is to retire into solitude, control all cravings and engage oneself in contemplation and meditation.[219]

The Mission teaches that for the *jnani*, different religions are not the issues because a devotee extracts the essence from all religions. His/her aim is to seek oneness in diversity, and such an "Abstract unity" is the foundation of *Jnana-yoga*. When a *jnani* has reached that state of absolute "oneness", he/she is known as *jivanmukta*.[220]

Vivekananda taught that the way of knowledge is the creedless path because it is beyond all creeds, and finally" all creeds should lead to *jnana* (knowledge of Atman) and become one. The first and the foremost mark of the true *jnana-yogi* is the

---

[214] Swami Hitananda, *Worship of Sri Ramakrishna*, (Kolkata: Sri Ramakrishna Math), 14-17.

[215] Swami Vireshwarananda, *Religion and Spiritual Life*, (New Delhi: Ramakrishna Mission, 1982), 6-7; see also Swami Tapasyananda, *Ramakrishna Math and Ramakrishna Mission*, (Mylapore: Sri Ramakrishna Math, n.d.), 4

[216] Swami Tapasyananda, *Sri Ramakrishna: Life and Teachings*, (Kolkata: Sri Ramakrishna Math, n.d.), 144.

[217] Swami Hitananda, *Worship of Sri Ramakrishna*, (Mylapore: Sri Ramakrishna Math, 1999), 13.

[218] C. Rajagopalachari, *Sri Ramakrishna Upanishad*, (Chennai: Sri Ramakrishna Math, 1981), 21.

[219] Swami Ranganathananda, *Spiritual Life of the Householder*, (Kolkata: Advaita Ashrama, 2005), 46-55.

[220] n.n., *The Complete Works of Swami Vivekananda*, Vol. 8, 5.

ability to control the mind perfectly in order to break all selfish desires for fixing the mind firmly on the divine self. Through this knowledge of the spirit the lack of right knowledge is annihilated forever, ignorance will disappear, the bonds will break, and the soul will be free.[221] True knowledge will cure the soul by taking the person to the other side.[222]

Another requirement of a true *jnani* is *Sraddha* or faith. A devotee must have strong faith in God. Unless one has it, one can not aspire to be a *jnani*. The *jnani* must also be able to practice *samadhana* which means constant work to hold the mind on God. He/she must also reach the stage of *nityanitya* in which one must discriminate between the transitory and the eternal, the unreal and the real Eternal One with whom he/she seeks to unite.[223]

The last quality of a *jnana-yogi* is that of *mumuksutv*, the intense desire to be free without any attachment. Therefore, a real mark of *jnana-yogi* is the renunciation of all fruits of work and all enjoyments in his/her life, except God as the free divine self.[224]

(i) The Concept of Guru

Ramakrishna Mission teaches that faith in the scriptures is not enough. They believe in the scriptures because they are revealed truths; they come from saints and sages who have realised the truth written therein. But we need to receive these truths directly from a living *guru*. They become living truths in the hearts of the students.[225] A real guru is one who is born from time to time as a repository of a spiritual force, which he transmits to future generations through successive links of *gurus* and disciples.[226] Both Sri Ramakrishna and Vivekananda also represent God as *guru*. A human *guru* is treated as the symbol of that Supreme

---

[221] Swami Vivekananda *Lectures From Colombo to Almora*, op.cit., 31.
[222] n.n., *The Complete Works of Swami Vivekananda*, Vol. 9, op.cit., 543.
[223] n.n., *The Complete Works of Swami Vivekananda*, Vol. 1, 407-409.
[224] *Ibid.*, 407-411.
[225] Pravrajika Sevaprana, "The Power of Faith," *Prabhudda Bharata*, Vol. 109, October 2004, 40-48.
[226] Swami Tapasyananda, *The Nationalistic and Religious Lectures of Swami Vivekananda*, (Kolkata: Advaita Ashrama, 1990), 196.

Guru. In spiritual life of *bhakti* or loving devotion, and in *Jnana (knowledge)*, a time comes when a person feels the need for guidance of a *guru*. The Supreme *Guru* is hidden in every heart.

(j) The Concept of Sacrifice

The Ramakrishna Mission does not speak about animal sacrifice. According to Vivekananda, there is but one life, one world and one existence. Everything is one; the difference is in degree and not in kind. The *Vedanta* also denies the difference between the souls of animals and the souls of human beings.[227] Vivekananda said that animal sacrifice is a superstition and God is only a superstition invented by the priests.[228] Animal sacrifice never leads to eternal happiness. It may earn some materialistic profits but spirituality can never be attained unless all the materialistic ideas are given up.[229]

(k) Magic and Superstition

The Ramakrishna Mission condemns magical practice. Magic is superstition. According to Vivekananda, only reason can save society from the power of superstition that is faith in old traditions without enquiry into their truth, which keeps men bound hand and foot. He had the courage to attack the superstitions that accumulated around the Vedic traditions.[230] These superstitions never encourage interest in miraculous powers, as it is a great obstacle to spiritual progress. According to Swami Ranganathananda, our country had become lost in the darkness of ignorance and superstition.[231]

(l) The Harmony of All Religions Through Advaita Vedanta

It is true that Sri Ramakrishna recognised the differences among religions but showed that, in spite of these differences, they lead to the same Ultimate Goal. This is the meaning of his famous

---

[227] Swami Vivekananda, *Practical Vedanta*, op.cit., 14-17.

[228] n.n., *The Complete Works of Swami Vivekananda, Vol. 8*, op.cit., 98-99.

[229] n.n., *The Complete Works of Swami Vivekananda, Vol. 1*, op.cit., 462.

[230] R.K. Dasgupta, *Revolutionary Ideas of Swami Vivekananda*, (Kolkata: Ramakrishna Mission Institute of Culture, 2000), 33.

[231] Swami Ranganathananda, *The Essence of Indian Culture*, (Kolkata: Advaita Ashrama, 1996), 134; see also R.K. Dasgupta, *Swami Vivekananda's Vedantic Socialism*, (Kolkata: Ramakrishna Mission Institute of Culture, 1995), 52.

maxim, Yato Mat, Tato Path, "As many faiths, so many paths." Apart from this, Swami Vivekananda also held that the religion of the world is expressions of one eternal universal religion. Since Vedanta contains all the basic principles and laws of the spiritual world, Swamiji regarded Vedanta as the eternal universal religion. That is to say, Vedanta can serve as the common ground for all religions.[232]

In the present context, the harmony of religions is very much a world problem. National integration depends upon social norms, political integration, economic development, and cultural unity. The transition from the fragmented to a unified social organisation involves not merely a reshaping of the social order, but a restructuring of social relations and the development of new social norms. In communalism religion plays an entirely extraneous role or the role of a mask. It is from the stand point of *Vedanta* that all religions can be harmonised.[233] Harmony of religions is both a global as well as an Indian problem.[234]

Swami Vivekananda envisaged national unity within international unity, which would bring about a lasting global peace. He also said that religious difference is a basic element of communal violence.[235]

Many international groupings of religions at the global level and many religious institutions belonging to individual religions have been working for religious harmony. The Ramakrishna Mission emphasises the harmony of all religions. It tolerates all religions and accepts them all to be true.[236]

---

[232] n.n., Ramakrishna Math and Ramakrishna Mission: their History, Ideals and Activities, *op.cit.*

[233] Swami Lokeswarananda, "Benoy Sarkar: And The Ramakrishna-Vivekananda Movement," *Bulletin of the Ramakrishna Mission Institute of Culture*, Vol. LI, No. 2, February 2000, 64.

[234] Santana Mukherji, "Swami Vivekananda's Sociological Ideas of Integration," *Swami Vivekananda: His Global Vision*, ed. by Santi Nath Chattopadhyay, (Kolkata: Punthi-Pustak, 2001), 329-340.

[235] Bipen Chandra, *Communalism in Modern India*, (New Delhi: Vikas Publishing House, 1989), 158-190.

[236] George M. Willium, "The Ramakrishna Movement: A Study in Religious Change," *Religion in Modern India*, ed. by Robert D. Baired, (New Delhi: Manohar Publications, 1998), 76-77.

Swami Prabhananda in his article on a fresh look at Swami Vivekananda said, "To thwart the wicked British policy of 'divide and rule', Indian national leaders made efforts to weld India into unity on a liberal, humanistic, secular and democratic base."

Ramakrishna declared that his religion stood for the whole humanity. Knowledge, love, and wisdom have always moulded the minds of many.[237] Without this concept of harmony of religions and toleration of all creeds, the spirit of national consciousness could not have been established in India, which is full of diversities.[238]

Ramakrishna's spiritual experiences of the mysteries of different religions led him to a realisation of the harmony of all religions. He taught that different religions are so many forms of one undying Eternal Religion. Different religions and opinions have come into existence through the will of God.[239] A lot has been written of the founder's practice and realisation of *samadhi* through the paths of Islam, Christianity, and many other schools of Hinduism.[240]

Swami Vivekananda was more concerned with the essence of a religion than its practices. He also said that Truth is one but scholars define it differently.[241] He taught that the worst problem that stands in the way of establishing peace and harmony in the world is an attitude of intolerance, of selfishness, of sectarianism and of dogmatism.[242]

Swamiji said that there is a need to take humanity to a place, where there is neither the Vedas, nor the Bible, nor the Koran.

---

[237] Hossainur Rahman, *Sri Ramakrishna the Symbol of Harmony of Religions*, (Kolkata: The Ramakrishna Mission Institute of Culture, 2000), 20-31.

[238] Prof. Kedarnath Labh, "Swami Vivekananda's Visit to the West; the Impact on the Indian Mind," Souvenir, Kolkata, Ramakrishna Mission Ashrama, 1997), 38.

[239] n.n., *The Gospel of Ramakrishna*, Vol. I, (Chennai: Sri Ramakrishna Math, 1985), 3-73, 306, 540.

[240] n.n., *Studies on Ramakrishna*, (Kolkata: The Ramakrishna Mission Institute of Culture, 1998), 70.

[241] Sri Harsha Datta, "Swami Vivedananda's Concept of Oneness," Souvenir, 1997, (Patan: Ramnkrishna Mission, n.d.) 50.

[242] Swami Purnatmananda, "Swami Vivekananda's – Gift to the West, "Swami Vivekananda: His Global Vision, ed., by Santinath Chattopadhayay, Kolkata, Punth Pustak, 2001), 141-145.

It is to be accomplished by a synthesis of the Vedas, the Bible and the Koran. We are to teach mankind that the so-called religions are parts of that invisible Eternal Religion.[243]

Advaita Vedanta transcends all forms of religion in a unifying vision of the One Absolute. It teaches that each soul and this whole universe are the reflections of the Infinite Brahman.[244]

The Ramakrishna Mission emphasises the practical Vedanta, which teaches service to all in all human beings. When *Vedanta* becomes practical in everyday life, tremendous social transformation will take place. Human dignity, human freedom, human equality, a spirit of service, capacity for different types teamwork, will all become heightened in society.

Conclusion: The study shows that the Ramakrishna Mission has been trying to uplift the Khasi society through education, medical service and some other training programmes. Through the service of the Ramakrishna Mission thousands of the Khasis have been benefited educationally and medically. Service to mankind according to the needs of the society in conjunction with lay disciples and workers to look upon all, irrespective of caste, creed or colour, as envisioned by the founder, has been carried out by the Mission in different parts of India in general and in the East Khasi Hills District of Meghalaya in particular. The Mission should continue to work for the upliftment of the rural Khasis where proper education and health care is lacking. Through the social service the Ramakrishna Mission should work to unite the Christian and traditional Khasis and not to preach hatred.

The Ramakrishna Mission preached the harmony of all religions. But in reality Swami Vivekananda and many other Swamis argued that neo-vedanta is the only rational religion to lead humanity to perfection. Will it be possible to make harmony of all religions through the service of the Mission a reality when

---

[243] Sri Harsadatta, "Swami Vivekananda's Concept of Oneness," Souvenir, (Patna: Ramakrishna Mission Ashrama, 1997), 7.

[244] n.n., *The Complete Works of Swami Vivekananda, Vol. 5, op.cit.,* 282, 285 & Vol 8. 137.

the other religions are placed at lower level and Christianity, which is the faith of the majority in Meghalaya state, is considered as a foreign religion?

Next chapter will attempt to study the socio-cultural and religious changes in the Khasi society through the Ramakrishna Mission.

B A a b

Chapter 6

Socio-Cultural and Religious Changes through the Ramakrishna Mission in the Khasi Society

This chapter is an attempt to find out the changes being brought about by the Ramakrishna Mission in the socio-cultural and religious life of the Khasis in the East Khasi Hills District of Meghalaya.

Ramakrishna Mission has emerged as an alternative development strategy to promote the common interest of the weak, particularly the rural poor. At present, the Government of India is making strenuous efforts to remove the defects in the rural structure and is attempting rural reconstruction of solving social, economic and cultural problems of the rural masses. It was believed that through the Ramakrishna Mission rural development has taken place.

Effective functioning of the Ramakrishna Mission may lead to the development of the family and the community at large.[1] Development is a subjective and value-loaded concept and hence there cannot be a consensus as to its meaning. The term is used differently in diverse contexts. It means 'unfolding' 'revealing' or 'opening up' something, which is latent when applied to human beings. It therefore means 'unfolding' or 'opening up' their potential powers. The term development implies a social, economic and cultural change. The Mission gave emphasis on education, social service to uplift the rural Khasis in the said District.[2]

The Ramakrishna Mission's main emphasis has been on the East Khasi Hills District, which has been chosen for the study.

---

[1] Dr. Jatanta Bhusan B., "The Changing Khasis: An Historical Account," *The Tribes of North East India, op.cit.,* 343.

[2] n.n., *Ramakrishna Math and Ramakrishna Mission,* Hawrah: Ramakrishna Math & Ramakrishna Mission, 13.

At the beginning, the attitude of the Khasis towards the Mission was not so positive because the Khasis were afraid of their identity loss. Slowly they felt that the Ramakrishna Mission had come to live in their midst to help and heal them. Today, the Mission runs 58 schools, 3 dispensaries, 3 technical training Schools, 2 orphanages and 3 libraries in the District.[3] The following section attempts to study in brief the activities of the Mission in the Shella-Bholaganj Block of the East Khasi Hills District.

(1) Sample Structure of the Selected Households

Before examining the changes being brought about by the Ramakrishna Mission in the study area it is necessary to have a general idea about the basic demographics and educational standard of the sample households from selected sample villages in terms of the family size, age distribution, literacy rate, occupation, marital status and religious status. Data collection was done through questionnaires. Questionnaires were given to the knowledgeable members of the families or other elderly members of the households, who were capable of furnishing all the relevant information.

Table No. 6.1 Detail Description of Head of Rural Households in Selected villages

N = 280, AH = 156, NAH = 124

Sr. No.	Particulars	Selected Rural Households		Over all performance of both the groups
		Adopted Villages	Non-adopted Villages	
1.	Total No. of Selected Rural Households	156 (100.00)	124 (100.00)	280 (100.00)
2.	Age composition of the head i) Less < 15 years	2 (1.28)	3 (2.42)	5 (1.78)
	ii) 15-30 years	65 (41.67)	50 (40.32)	115 (41.07)
	iii) 30-45 years	50 (32.05)	45 (36.29)	95 (33.93)
	iv) 45-60 Years	32 (20.51)	22 (17.74)	54 (19.29)
	v) 60 & above years	7 (4.49)	4 (3.23)	11 (3.93)

---

[3] Quoted from Shillong Ramakrishna Mission Office Record.

Contd., Table No. 6.1 Detail Description of Head of
Rural Households in Selected villages

Sr. No.	Particulars	Selected Rural Households		Over all performance of both the groups
		Adopted Villages	Non-adopted Villages	
3.	Religious Composition of Head of Households			
	i) Christian	74 (47.45)	54 (43.55)	128 (45.71)
	ii) Khasi Hindus	5 (3.20)	3 (02.42)	8 (2.86)
	iii) Other (Traditional Khasis)	77 (49.35)	67 (54.03)	144 (51.43)
4.	Educational level of the Head of Households			
	a. Illiterate	31 (19.87)	50 (40.32)	81 (28.93)
	b. Literate	125 (80.13)	74 (59.68)	199 (71.07)
	i) Primary	25 (16.02)	27 (21.77)	52 (18.57)
	ii) Secondary	27 (17.31)	23 (18.55)	50 (17.86)
	iii) High/Higher Secondary Education	30 (19.23)	14 (11.29)	44 (15.71)
	iv) Graduate	25 (16.03)	7 (5.65)	32 (11.43)
	v) Post Graduate & above	18 (11.54)	3 (2.42)	21 (7.50)
5.	Marital Status			
	i) Married	120 (76.93)	110 (88.70)	230 (82.14)
	ii) Unmarried	34 (21.79)	12 (9.67)	46 (16.43)
	iii) Widow/widower	2 (01.28)	2 (1.61)	4 (1.43)

Figures in parenthesis indicates percentage.

Table 6.1 indicated the sample structure of the selected households. The data showed that the highest number of family members were in age group of 15-30 years. The Christian percentage was 60.26 percent in the adopted villages and 59.68 percent in the non-adopted villages. The traditional Khasis and others were 36.54 percent in the adopted villages and 37.90 percent in the non-adopted villages. The Christian population was higher in the adopted and non-adopted villages than that of the traditional Khasi households. Literacy rate was higher in the adopted villages than the non-adopted villages. The literacy rate in the adopted and non-adopted villages was 80.13 percent & 59.68 percent. The illiteracy rate in both adopted and non-adopted villages was 19.87 percent & 40.32 percent respectively. In the marital status, the married samples from adopted and non-adopted villages were more than the unmarried samples. The main purpose of studying the religion of the respondents was to find their religious status and if there is an impact on them from outside. The most important was how religious beliefs and practices affect social, economic and cultural lives and their relationship with the people of other faiths.

(2) Structure of the sample families

Family size is one of the important parameters of the social characteristics of any specific population group. It has an important role in the social and economic life since it is related to the pressure of population on land. It has a significant bearing on the economic and educational level of the family and on the level of intra and inter family interactions with a particular village. The size of the family depends on education, medical facilities, age of marriage & fertility, types of marriage and economic conditions. Family size is one of the important parameters of the social characteristics of any specific population group. It is believed that gender and family size issues bring about a convergence of culturally imbued interest and socio-economic and religious purpose among different categories of people in the society. Family size provides social security to the family in case of emergency and otherwise generates the supportive tendencies. The rural Khasis, mainly agriculturists and laborers in the non-adopted villages like to have larger families due to illiteracy, superstitious faith and poverty. The sample of the rural households in the adopted and non-adopted families is presented in table 6.2

Table 6.2 Structure of Sample Families in Different Rural Households

N= 280, AV= 156, NAV= 124

Sr. No.	Particulars	Selected Rural Households		Sample Average for both the groups
		Adopted Villages	Non-adopted Villages	
1.	Average size of family	6.20(100.00)	6.03(100.00)	6.12(100.00)
2.	Sex Composition of the Family a. Male	3.01(48.55)	3.02(49.52)	3.01(49.03)
	b. Female	3.19(51.45)	3.01(50.48)	3.11(50.97)

Contd., **Table 6.2 Structure of Sample Families in Different Rural Households**

Sr. No.	Particulars	Selected Rural Households		Sample Average for both the groups
		Adopted Villages	Non-adopted Villages	
3	Age-wise Composition of Family			
	a. Below 15 Years	0.99(15.98)	1.20(19.93)	1.08(17.65)
	b. 15-59 Years	4.47(72.05)	3.91(69.05)	4.22(68.95)
	c. 60 & above Years	0.74(11.97)	0.66(11.02)	0.82(13.40)

Figures in parenthesis indicate percentage

The table 6.2 indicated that a percentage of female population was higher in comparison to male population in adopted villages. The data also indicated that the maximum numbers in the selected rural households fell in the age group of 15-59 years in both the groups. The average size of family in adopted and non-adopted villages was 6.20 and 6.03 members respectively.

(3) Literacy

Literacy is defined as the ability to read and write the person's name and to form simple sentences. Higher literacy levels in a particular society denotes rising socio-economic and cultural development and universal literacy is a crucial step towards achieving overall progress.

Literacy of the respondents was also inquired into. It has been generally realised that the adoption of new technology brings development with education. Education bringing with it the promise of many openings of positions has attracted young Khasis a great deal. However, facilities were very limited as compared to the demands. In Meghalaya education was widely accepted as a necessary tool for the attainment of developmental goals, and as a social process it attempts to create an awareness to make individuals or a community more responsive to the needs of development, and to equip them with necessary knowledge and skills.

Table 6.3 Detail Description of Literacy of Sample Households
N= 280, AH= 156, NAH= 125

Sr. No.	Particulars	Selected Rural Households		Sample Average for both the groups
		Adopted Villages	Non-adopted Villages	
1.	Average size of family	6.03(100.0)	6.20(100.00)	6.12(100.00)
2.	Literacy Rate	4.83(80.13)	3.70(59.68)	4.27(68.71)
3.	Educational level			
	a. Primary	2.11(35.00)	1.95(31.48)	2.03(33.24)
	b. Secondary	1.51(25.00)	1.13(18.20)	1.32(21.50)
	c. Graduate & above	1.21(20.00)	0.62 (10.00)	0.92(15.00)
4.	Illiteracy	1.20(19.87)	2.50(40.32)	1.85 (31.29)

Figures in parenthesis indicates percentage

Table 6.3 indicated that the literacy percentage is considerably higher in adopted villages as compared to non-adopted villages. The illiteracy percentage is higher in non-adopted villages. The percentage of literate is more than that of illiterate in both the groups. The data showed that 80.13 percent households from adopted villages and 59.68 percent households from non-adopted villages were literate. However, 19.87 percent households from adopted villages and 40.32 percent households from non-adopted villages were illiterate. Nevertheless, the percentage of literate was higher in the adopted villages and the percentage of the illiterate was higher in the non-adopted villages.

(4) Occupational Distribution

The respondents have different occupations including agriculture. Some households have just one occupation. Some households have two occupations and many have more than two occupations. Table 6.4 given below deals with the occupational distribution of households.

Table 6.4 Occupational Distributions of Selected Rural Households

N= 280, AH= 156, NAH= 124

Sr. No.	Particulars	Selected Rural Households		Sample Average for both the groups
		Adopted Villages	Non-adopted Villages	
1	Total Number of Samples	156(100.00)	124(100.00)	280.00(100.00)
2	Occupational Distribution			
	a. One Occupation	35.00(22.43)	30.00(24.19)	65.00(23.22)
	b. Two Occupation	41.00(26.29)	35.00(28.23)	76.00(27.14)
	c. More than Two Occupation	80.00(51.28)	59.00(47.58)	139.00(49.64)

Figure in parentheses indicates percentage

The Table 6.4 clearly shows the occupational distribution of the households in adopted and non-adopted villages. The table shows that many households in adopted and non-adopted villages followed more than two occupations since they have limited holding and they cannot thrive only with it. Therefore, they go into other occupations for employment. It was also important to note that the households in adopted villages were following more than two occupations. 22.43 percent household respondents from adopted villages and 24.19 percent households from non-adopted villages have one-occupation. 26.29 percent households from adopted and 28.23 percent household respondents from non-adopted villages have two occupations. However, 51.28 percent households from adopted and 47.58 percent households from non-adopted villages have more than two occupations.

(5) House Style

The house is very important for living. Housing is a major health resource, which can protect individuals from physical and mental ill-health. Alternatively, it can increase their vulnerability, depending on the standard, location and type of accommodation they live in. Like food and eating, poor housing affects health directly through physiological processes. Homes can be a major source of personal wealth. The Table 6.5 given below shows what type of houses the Khasis lived in. The standard of the houses depends on the income of the family. Many families in the adopted villages have Government or private jobs or they are involved in industry or trade and have a better income due to education imparted by the Ramakrishna Mission or the Church. They have a better standard of living too. Their house condition was far better than those households living in the non-adopted villages

Table 6.5 Distribution of House Resources in Selected Households

N=280, AH= 156, NAH= 124

Sr. No.	Particulars	Selected Rural Households		Sample Average for both the groups
		Adopted Villages	Non-adopted Villages	
1.	Total No. of Samples	156(100.00)	124(100.00)	280(100.00)
2.	Types of Households			
	a. Kachha Houses	110(70.51)	106(85.48)	216(77.14)
	b. Pucca Houses	46(29.49)	18(14.52)	64(22.86)

Figures in parentheses indicate percentage

The table 6.5 clearly showed the house condition of the households in the adopted and non-adopted villages. It was found that 70.51 percent *kachha* and 29.49 percent *pucca* houses were in the adopted villages and 85.48 percent *kachcha and* 14.52 percent *pucca* houses were in the non-adopted villages. The data clearly showed that the standard of houses in the adopted villages was much better than the standard of houses in the non-adopted villages. The percentage of *pucca* houses was higher in the adopted villages than in the non-adopted villages, which shows the impact of education and income on the society.

6. Changes in Khasi Society

The changes have its impact made into various spheres of social life and culture. This is also due to the exposure of the society to contracts from outside. While the change was innovative in certain respects, it had affected some of the ancient incentives and industries.[4] The main agency of change in the nineteenth century was the British Government, which was followed by Christian missionaries. It provided the political power to effect change that the earlier Sanskritic contact had lacked. In addition to the traditional contacts in the market places, Hindus were brought into the hills as workers of the government. The influx was in no small measure due to the fact that Shillong was made the capital of the entire province of Assam. Due to this there was more contact with the Hindus during the nineteenth and twentieth centuries than ever before. One of the effects of the new political order was to permit more extensive penetration into the area of Hindu agencies such as the Brahmo Samaj and the Ramakrishna Mission. This more extensive penetration encouraged the intermarriage between the local people and the Hindus. Ramakrishna Mission is next to the western missionaries who have been able to bring about social, cultural and religious changes in the Khasi society of the East Khasi Hills District. The next section of this chapter deals with the social, cultural and religious changes brought about by the Ramakrishna Mission in the adopted and non-adopted villages of the East Khasi Hills District.

7. Social Change

Khasi society has been transformed by many changes, which have taken place between 2001 and 2007. Social change means a change in social behaviour, social structure, and social values. For Srinivas, "Social change arises only when the quantum, comprehensiveness and time span of change are such as to induce or result in significant alterations in the social structure, the institutions, norms, symbols and values associated with older generations."[5] M.E. Jones states: "Social change is a term used to describe variations in or modifications of any aspect of social processes, social patterns, social interaction or social organisation."[6]

---

[4] H.M. Bareh, Encyclopedia of North-East India: Meghalaya, Vol. IV, 110.
[5] H.K Rawat, *Sociology: Basic Concepts*, (Jaipur: Rawat Publications, 2007), 270.
[6] *Ibid.*

Social changes were more phenomenal among the Khasis than among their neighbours as they came into contact first with the British Government and Christian missionaries in 1860s and then through their contact with the Ramakrishna Mission missionaries since 1920.[7] In this connection, the retrospective effects from the process of urbanisation, spread of Christianity, administrative orientation, emergence of new trade, structures and new social contacts from outside led to a social transformation. Earlier Khasis were famous hunters, fighters and raiders. Their life was originally primal and isolated with not much exposure to the outside world because of lack of communication and their fear of demons.

In spite of that the Ramakrishna Mission has been able to bring about social change through education and medical care among the Khasis of the Shella-Bholaganj Block. Though the Ramakrishna Mission taught the traditional Khasis to maintain their social, cultural and religious values, yet it also preached the equality of genders and importance of family. It taught the people not to embrace the western social way of living but rather to maintain their social and cultural values. It has been successful to some extent.

(a) Changes in Khasi Family

The word 'family' has been taken from the Roman word, 'famulus', meaning a servant and a Latin word 'familia', meaning 'household'.[8] In other words, family is a group of people united by ties of marriage, blood or adoption, constituting a single household interacting or inter-communicating with each other in their respective social roles of husband and wife, mother and father, son and daughter, brother and sister creating and maintaining a common culture.[9] Elliott and Merrill defined family as "a biological social unit composed of husband, wife and children."[10] It has generally been accepted that the present Khasi

---

[7] H.G. Joshi, *Meghalaya: Past and Present*, (New Delhi: Mittal Publications, 2004), 212.
[8] S.R. Myneni, *Sociology*, (Faridabad: Allahabad Law Agency, 2006), 240.
[9] *Ibid*, 241.
[10] *Ibid*.

family is still matri-centred in nature. It may be difficult to describe the Meghalaya family situation.

The traditional pattern of the family has been undergoing gradual change. The large joint family has slowly disappeared. However, the nuclear family structure has become more common especially with the invention of new technological education and economic change through Christianity and the missionaries of the Ramakrishna Mission. Christianity has brought to Khasi society a view that the family relationship is something deeper than purely social bond. The dignity of a woman, as life partner and as mother is a repeated theme in Christian teachings. All the Khasi families are nuclear in adopted and non-adopted villages. A new dimension has been added to the earlier status of Khasi women, particularly of the educated and economically independent women. While, the matriarchate is still a living and active institution, the *iing* (family) has become smaller owing to families migrating on a scale larger than before.

Earlier due to lack of communication, illiteracy, shifting cultivation, poor agriculture, lack of proper marketing and their family standard was not high. The Ramakrishna Mission has taught about the importance of equality of genders and population control. The Mission has also taught about family planning and the need for fewer children in this area in order to provide them better educational and medical care.[11]

The Ramakrishna Mission teaches that over-crowding and inadequate housing facilities lead to unpleasant situations in families. In such a house environment, children are found to be restless and wish to stay away from home very often. The study showed that due to over-crowded and inadequate facilities in the house, the members of the family are deprived of healthy life. It compels them to live in an unhygienic environment. There is a difference between the behaviour of the children of the adopted and non-adopted villages. In the adopted villages the size of the family has started decreasing while in the non-adopted villages the size of the family has not decreased, which shows the lack

---

[11] Personal interview with B. Lyngdoh at Cherrapunji on 23.5.2005.

of proper education and medical facilities in the non-adopted villages.

Therefore, a change has been brought in the family, income of the family, standard of living, cultural values, religious beliefs, and behaviour towards nature and to their fellow human beings in the adopted villages, and much less change was seen in the non-adopted villages.[12] On the other hand, the life span of the Khasis in the non-adopted villages is shorter due to lack of development, superstition, illiteracy and want of modern medical facilities.

The Ramakrishna Mission has also been instrumental in the educational and economic change of the Khasi family in the study area. Through education, many members of Khasi families have learned to find better sources of income. Since there were many children to be looked after in the family of the non-adopted villages, the parents could hardly give love and proper guidance to their children. The children were deprived of their rights to education due to poverty and illiteracy. Many families live below the poverty line. The families with a low income were unable to meet all their children's needs. Although the Central Government has launched some schemes to eradicate poverty, yet poverty has not been eradicated. It was because those schemes have not reached them practically.

Table No. 6.6 showing an attitude on:
"A Change has taken place in the Khasi Family"

N= 280, AH= 156, NAH= 124

Sr. No.	Particulars	Selected Rural Households		Sample Average for both the groups
		Adopted Villages	Non-adopted Villages	
1	Total No. of Households	156(100.00)	124(100.00)	280(100.00)
	a. Agree	60(38.46)	40(32.26)	100(35.71)
	b. Disagree	92(58.98)	80(64.52)	172(61.43)
	c. Undecided	4(2.56)	4(3.22)	10(03.57)

Figures in parentheses indicates percentage

---

[12] Personal interview with a group of teachers at Sohbhar on 24.5.2006.

Table 6.6 indicated that 38.46 percent households from adopted villages, 32.26 percent households from non-adopted villages opined that a change has taken place in Khasi family of the adopted villages through the Ramakrishna Mission. Likewise, 58.98 percent households from adopted villages and 64.52 percent households from non-adopted villages opined that no change has taken place in rural Khasi families through the Ramakrishna Mission alone. The Church has played a major role in bringing about a change in the Khasi family. However, 2.56 percent households from adopted villages and 3.22 percent households from non-adopted villages remained silent. The study indicated that the Ramakrishna Mission has been instrumental to some extent in bringing about change in the Khasi families.

(i) **The Change in Khasi Male Status**

The ancestral maternal uncle 'U Suidnia' is the one who formally established and sealed the sacred pact between God and man in family worship and rituals, including the ceremonial internment of bones in the 'mawbah'. The role of the father in matrilineal societies was an ambiguous one because the maternal uncle was seen as the figure of authority. The Khasi matrilineal system in the present day has come under criticism in the light of the dominance of the nuclear family which has become all the more strong with the spread of education, modernisation, urbanisation and the teachings of other religions like Christianity and Hinduism.[13] The impact of modernisation, education and other religions on the Khasi society has led to the dwindling of the role of the maternal uncle while that of the father has increased.[14]

The struggle in Khasi society today to strengthen the position of man in the family and to foster the care for and the equal rights of the boy child is based on the awareness of the basic equal dignity of the human person, whether boy or girl, man or woman.[15] The lack of this awareness on the part of male boy as well as on the parts of the leaders of the family also lies at the

---

[13] Pascal Malngiang, "A Critique of the Khasi Matriliny," *The Dynamics of Family System in a Matriliny of Meghalaya, op.cit.*, 10.
[14] H.M. Bareh, *The History and Culture of the Khasi People, op.cit.*, 404-406.
[15] Philomath Passah, "Impediments to Entrepreneurship in Matrilineal, Societies of Meghalaya," *Dynamics of Family System in a Matriliny of Meghalaya*, ed. by Margaret B. Challam, 1999, Shillong, 27-29.

root of the lack of a sense of direction in male society. However, Christianity being patriarchal in nature, never sought to destroy the matrilineal culture of the Khasis. At the same time, the call of Christianity to respect the equal dignity of every human being, challenges any society where injustice prevails. The present issue questioning the matrilineal society is not the product of Christianity alone. Even the Ramakrishna Mission has created an atmosphere of patriarchal system. Even men acquired a new sense of confidence about themselves. Father's authority among the Khasis even in rural families has become dominant.[16]

Most probably, the basic philosophy of the Syngkhong Rympei Thymmai (SRT) or Association of the New Hearth was to work for changing the system from matrilineal to patriarchy. Probably such a group owes its strength to the frustration of the people with regard to the concentration of authority and power at the hands of the mother besides the principle of inheritance of the property by the females.[17]

Both Christianity and the Ramakrishna Mission have been able to influence the minds of many male and female Khasis even in the Shella-Bholaganj Block. Many Khasi women in place of their maternal uncles want their husbands to be the head of their households.[18] Table 6.7 pointed out the opinion of both male and female respondents regarding the head of the household.

Table No. 6.7 Showing an attitude on:
"The Husband should be head of the Family"

N= 280, AH= 156, NAH= 124

Sr. No.	Particulars	Selected Rural Households		Sample Average for both the groups
		Adopted Villages	Non-adopted Villages	
1	Total No. of Households	156(100.00)	124(100.00)	280(100.00)
	a. Agree	52(33.33)	30(24.19)	82(29.28)

---

[16] T.B. Subba, Wonder that is Culture, 105.
[17] Pascal Malngiang, "A Critique of the Khasi Matriliny," *The Dynamics of Family System in a Matriliny of Meghalaya, op.cit.,* 12.
[18] Dominic Jala, "Christian Values Encounter Family in Meghalaya," *Matriliny in Meghalaya, op.cit.,* 97.

Contd., **Table No. 6.7 Showing an attitude on:**
"The Husband should be head of the Family"

Sr. No.	Particulars	Selected Rural Households		Sample Average for both the groups
		Adopted Villages	Non-adopted Villages	
	b. Disagree	94(58.75)	90(72.58)	174(62.14)
	c. Undecided	10(6.41)	4(3.22)	14(05.00)

Figures in parentheses indicates percentage

Table 6.7 showed that 33.33 percent households from adopted villages and 24.19 percent households from non-adopted villages opined that husband should be the head of the Khasi households and not the maternal uncle. However, 58.75 percent households from adopted villages and 72.58 percent households from non-adopted villages were of the opinion that the husband should not be the head of the household. The pattern that is followed today should continue. Only 6.41 percent households from adopted villages and 3.22 percent households from non-adopted villages remained undecided.

Majority of the respondents were against changing descent patterns. However, the absence of codification of traditional laws and the decrease in power of the maternal uncle in a fast changing society have created a hiatus and confusion about who really owns or controls property. Except in Shella-Bholaganj Block and nearby villages the sons are not given a share in the family property except through the will of the parents.[19]

In the Khasi matrilineal society, the father who should be the leading member of the family has become less significant because of his role as an uncle on the one hand and the incompatibility of his clan code with that of his wife on the other hand. His status in the house of his sisters is still supreme up to the present time. Children take their mother's title. This system was healthy and suitable as long as the society was in isolation.[20] Nevertheless,

---

[19] Patricia Mukhim, "Crisis of Authority in the Khasi Matrilineal Society," *The Dynamics of Family System in a Matriliny of Meghalaya, op.cit.,* 35.

[20] *People of India: Meghalaya, Vol. XXXII, op.cit.,* 20

when it began to be exposed with other communities of the neighbouring people its family foundation has appeared to be questioned. There are different views on children taking the father's surname.

Table 6.8 Showing opinion on:
"Children should be given Father's Surname"

N= 280, AH= 156, NAH= 124

Sr. No.	Particulars	Selected Rural Households		Sample Average for both the groups
		Adopted Villages	Non-adopted Villages	
1	Total No. of Households	156(100.00)	124(100.00)	280(100.00)
	a. Agree	40(25.64)	40 (32.26)	80(28.57)
	b. Disagree	110(70.51)	80(64.52)	190(67.86)
	c. Undecided	6(3.85)	4(3.22)	10(3.57)

Figure in parentheses indicates percentage

Table 6.8 projected the views on children taking the father's surname. The data showed that a majority of the households opined that Khasi children should not take their father's surname. They should take mother's title since it has been accepted by the Customary Laws. 25.64 percent households from adopted villages and 32.26 percent households from non-adopted villages opined that Khasi children should take their father's surname and not their mother's surname. The higher percentage of the respondents favouring father's surname in the non-adopted villages was because the male in the family in the rural areas are fed up with their rights in the property. On the other hand, 70.51 percent households from adopted villages and 64.52 percent households from non-adopted villages opined that Khasi children should take their mother's title. In this regard many scholars believe that this influence is from outside. It was perhaps the Ramakrishna Mission and Christianity that have contributed to the change in attitude. One possibility is that both the Ramakrishna Mission and Christianity have awakened them to patriarchy because both have a male dominated structure. Some

Khasi women prefer the patriarchal system. Their children have demanded their fathers' title. Some of the respondents from adopted and non-adopted villages feel that matriliny should not undermine the authority of the father.

(ii) The Change in the Status of Women

It is commonly assumed that women's status in the Khasi society is higher than the patrilineal societies. It was considered very important to have a female child in Khasi family because otherwise the parents will have no one to look after them in their old age. Moreover, without a daughter, complications arise concerning the inheritance of a clan property and the continuity of a family name.[21]

Prior to the introduction of scientific education in the region by the Christian missionaries and the Ramakrishna Mission, women took care of the nursing and rearing of children and of other household activities. Khasi folklore considered that women were physically weak. Therefore, they did not participate in any political decision-making process.[22] Why women were not allowed to have an access to education was due to socio-cultural and religious factors.[23] However, education in the district came with the church and the Ramakrishna Mission. Both agencies despite their male dominated structures gave importance to girls' education. Education generates new ideas and ambitions, economic independence bestowed further freedom. Despite their matrilineal system, a social bias favouring men existed already among the Khasis. The successful entrance of women into education and employment has given them new status. Due to the education rendered by the church and the Ramakrishna Mission, women enjoy a higher status.

---

[21] Dianghunmon Rynjah, "Khasi-Jaintia Women-Their Changing Role and Status," *Changing Status of Women: North Eastern States*, (New Delhi: Mittal Publications, 2009), 43.

[22] V. Venkata Rao, "Development of Local Self-Government in Meghalaya," *Tribal Institutions of Meghalaya*, ed. (Guwahati: Spectrum Publications, 1985), 316.

[23] Cerilla Khonglah, "Khasi Women and the Indigenous Question, "*Changing Women's Status in India: Focus on the North East*, ed. (Guwahati: North East Social Research Centre, 2002), 169.

Currently, women in Meghalaya in general and in the East Khasi Hills District in particular, have come up in every field such as professional studies, trade, civil services and other fields. Today Khasi women have access even to university level education. Education has given women the possibility of becoming aware of their right to equality.[24] It has promoted the building of personality and leadership in every sphere of life for Khasi women. A new dimension has been added to the earlier status of women particularly of the educated and economically independent women. Whether they gain equality in practice or not depends on whether their society and the culture is open enough to grant them such equality. However, Khasi women in the rural non-adopted villages were very backward in education. There were very less high and higher secondary schools in the rural areas of this district and so they have to go many miles on foot to get higher secondary and college level of education.

Moreover, matrilineal system provides considerable importance to women in comparison to other tribal women. Freedom, in the matter of sex, marriage, and economic pursuits is not something new to them. Literacy is directly related to the status of women, and her decision-making power and capability to have access to health care services.[25] Literacy not only increases women's self-confidence but also makes them exposed to information and thereby altering the way others respond to them. Both the Ramakrishna Mission and leaders of the Seng Khasi began to think about what the girls would be later on if they are not given education. It was later on through the efforts of the Ramakrishna Mission and Christian missionaries that Khasi parents began to feel the need of women's education in rural areas of this district. In addition to academic education, Christian missions and the Ramakrishna Mission schools introduced technical education. The graduates of these technical and training centres either set up small business or were employed in government and private enterprises.

---

[24] H.G. Joshi, *Meghalaya: Past and Present*, *op.cit.*, 215-218.
[25] n.n., *People of India: Meghalaya, Vol. XXXII*, ed. by K.S. Singh, *op.cit.*, 21.

According to the 2001 Census, the female literacy rate of the East Khasi Hills District was 76.1 percent. According to District Headquarters Office Record (2007), the male and female literacy rate of the district was 77.12 percent and 76.3 percent. Khasi women now assume control of important family business concerns. According to 2007 Shella-Bholaganj Office Record of the adopted villages, out of 169 salary holders 98 were women, 71 were men. From the non-adopted villages 12 out of 20 salary holders were women. It was due to education that women in the East Khasi Hills District have become advanced in every sphere of life.

Education has brought a new life style to the Khasi women. The education imparted by the Ramakrishna Mission developed in them their good distinctive qualities to their full extent, individually and collectively. It has opened the windows of the world to them and has brought them to the very doorstep of the knowledge and wisdom of other races.

Khasi women have begun to work as doctors, nurses, teachers, magistrates and other top Government officers. Even in business and other private jobs, the majority of women have now become involved. It was largely due to education imparted by the Christian Church which has brought a major change in the status of the Khasi women in the East Khasi Hills District. The Ramakrishna Mission missionaries have also brought some changes in the social status of the Khasi women in the study area of this District. Although society has remained matrilineal, the women do not act under as many safeguards as before from their maternal uncle and elder brother.

In spite of the advancement of the Khasi women on different fronts, one may wonder why there were only a negligible number of women representatives to the Meghalaya Legislative Assembly, Autonomous District Councils, *Hima, Raid* and village *Durbar Shnong*. There was also an insignificant representation of women in the various decision-making bodies of the Government. Now there are localities particularly in the urban areas where women are allowed to attend *Durbars* and to express their views. There are local *Durbars, which* have co-opted women as members of its

Executive Committee. Unfortunately, women in the rural areas have no representatives in *Durbar Shnong*, District Councils and Legislative Assemblies. Interestingly, all the political parties in Meghalaya have their women candidates for legislative Assembly elections, but not many in terms of numbers. They have also started participating in politics.

6.9 Showing opinion on: "A Change has taken place in the Status of Khasi Women in the study area"

N= 280, AH= 156, NAH= 124

Sr. No.	Particulars	Selected Rural Households		Sample Average for both the groups
		Adopted Villages	Non-adopted Villages	
1.	Total No. Of Households	156(100.00)	124(100.00)	280(100.00)
a.	Agree	75(48.08)	30(24.19)	105(37.5)
b.	Disagree	78(50.00)	90(72.58)	168(60.00)
c.	Undecided	3(3.84)	4(3.23)	10(3.57)

Figures in parentheses indicates percentage

Table 6.9 indicated that 48.08 percent households from adopted villages and 24.19 percent households from non-adopted villages opined that a change has taken place in the status of Khasi women through the Ramakrishna Mission. On the other hand, 51.92 percent households from adopted villages and 72.58 percent households from non-adopted villages opined that no change has taken place in the status of Khasi women through the Ramakrishna Mission alone. It is due to the service of Christian missionaries and the Ramakrishna Mission that the change in women status has taken place. However, 3.84 percent households from adopted villages and 3.23 percent households from non-adopted villages did not express their opinions.

(iii) A Change in the Gender preference among the Khasi Parents

In the Khasi culture, the importance of a female is unquestioned. Right from the birth a baby girl among the Khasis got preferential treatment. To her, due attention has been paid. There must be a girl in the family to inherit ancestral property. This implied that a female child was naturally preferred in traditional Khasi society. A family could not continue without a female. The birth of a female child was hailed with greater joy than that of the male child. The male children do not stay with their parents. Such ideas were galore but seldom substantiated. Presently many parents have felt the need to give equal status to their sons too. There is a change in the attitude of the Khasi parents towards their sons.[26]

Even educated Khasis, influenced by the movement fighting against the matrilineal system prefer the patriarchal system in the Khasi society. There is a clear indication that male children are also preferred by the parents. The usual answer one gets from the male respondents is like this: "The sex of the child does not make any difference for a man because a man does not lose or gain anything. The child does not take the father's surname." The son has to leave his parent's house and stay in his mother-in-law's house. Usually old age security is the most important reason for preferring a female child, followed by the continuation of lineage. The sense of old age insecurity seems to be stronger among women than men and the sense of responsibility regarding continuation of lineage is more heavily borne by women than by men. This change in the attitude of the parents towards sons may be due to the teachings of the Ramakrishna Mission or the church since both are patriarchal based. No particular change has been brought about by the Ramakrishna Mission in the Khasi parents' attitude towards the preference of the male child.

Table 6.10 Showing opinion on:
"Male Children are preferred by Khasi Parents"

N= 280, AH= 156, NAH= 124

Sr. No.	Particulars	Selected Rural Households		Sample Average for both the groups
		Adopted Villages	Non-adopted Villages	
1.	Total No. of Households	156(100.00)	124(100.00)	280(100.00)

---

[26] Margaret B. Challam, "Introduction," *The Dynamics of Family System in a Matriliny of Meghalaya, op.cit.,* 1-6.

Contd., **Table 6.10 Showing opinion on:**
"Male Children are preferred by Khasi Parents"

N= 280, AH= 156, NAH= 124

Sr. No.	Particulars	Selected Rural Households		Sample Average for both the groups
		Adopted Villages	Non-adopted	
	a. Agree	30(19.23)	10(8.06)	40(14.29)
	b. Disagree	120(76.92)	110(88.71)	230(82.14)
	c. Undecided	6(3.85)	4(3.23)	10(3.57)

Figures in parentheses indicate percentage

Table 6.10 showed that there was a gender preference in the Khasi society, which slowly changed due to outside influence on the parents. The data shows that 19.23 percent households from adopted villages and 8.06 percent households from non-adopted villages were of the opinion that Khasi parents prefer male children. This change is due to the influence of the outsiders. At the same time 76.92 percent households from adopted villages and 88.71 percent households from non-adopted villages opined that Khasi parents prefer both sons and daughters equally. Parents of adopted and non-adopted villages who preferred male children were mixed parents or some educated Khasi Christians. The data clearly showed that Khasis still prefer the mother's title for the children. Therefore, the Ramakrishna Mission and other agencies have not been able to bring about a change in this regard. The church in Meghalaya has already accepted the matriliny system and property inheritance.

(b) Educational Change

Education is one of the essential factors for any positive change or development (both human resources development and socio-economic development). The persons whether engaged in any traditional occupation need education so as to adopt the new technology which has been developed in different occupations, be it agriculture, animal husbandry, health, household industry, Government or private jobs and even business. To make profit from any type of occupation, it is necessary to understand not only the modern technology but also the management and marketing of the same and for this education is the only answer.[27]

The traditional pattern of education laid stress on practical and all-round training in which men were acquainted with warfare, oratory, arts, sports, hunting, mountaineering, iron-smelting, carpentry, crafts, divination and sacrifices. The greatest defect was the absence of modern technology-based vocational schools in the educational curriculum.[28]

The modern system of education no doubt has broken such traditional-biased instructions. Christian education, bringing with it the promise of many openings of new positions, has attracted young Khasis a great deal. The British Government gave education grants to the Christian missionaries for spreading education among the Khasis. The Presbyterian Church runs 1200 schools in the whole state and more than 200 schools of all categories in towns and advance villages of the East Khasi Hills District.[29] In order to work for the advancement of the Khasis the Ramakrishna Mission missionaries also felt the need for enabling them to have education so that a new social solidarity might be established. They knew that education was the only means through which the Khasi standard of living could improve. The Ramakrishna Mission has also contributed towards education of the Khasis in the study area of the East Khasi Hills District.[30]

The Khasis in the adopted villages have a better source of income due to education. But the Khasis of the non-adopted villages do not have a good source of income due to illiteracy. Their standard of education was found low. The high school facility was not available in all the non-adopted villages. Due to bad communication and heavy rainfall, they find it difficult to go to distant villages for their further studies. Poverty is one of the major reasons for children dropping out of school.

---

[27] Swapan Kumar Kolay, *Ecology, Economy and Tribal Development*, (New Delhi: Mohit Publications 2001), 169-70.
[28] H.G. Joshi, *Meghalaya: Past and Present*, op.cit., 218.
[29] R. Tokin Roy Rymbai, "Evolution of Modern Khasi Society," *Khasi Heritage*, (Shillong: Ri Khasi Press, 1979), 63.
[30] Dr. Jatanta Bhushan B., "The Changing Khasis: An Historical Account," *The Tribes of North East India*, op.cit., 343.

The Ramakrishna Mission pays special attention to the education of the rural Khasis in the block. It tried its best to provide education with its limited resources so that they may play their due role in the making of better community. It runs 51 schools in the Shella-Bholaganj Block where more than 8000 students get free education.[31] The table 6.11 gives an account of the educational activities of the Ramakrishna Mission in the said Block.

Table No. 6.11 No. of Schools in Shella-Bholaganj

Sr. No.	Particulars	Total No. of Schools on District & Block Level					
		East Khasi Hills District			Shella-Bholaganj Block		
		2001	2005	2007	2001	2005	2007
1.	Total No. of Schools	52	55	58	50	51	51
2.	Total No. of Students	8000	9000	9000	7000	7800	8230

Table 6.11 indicates that the Ramakrishna Mission has a good contribution to educate the Khasis in both the East Khasi Hills District and the Shella-Bholaganj Block. The Mission runs 52 schools in 2001, 55 schools in 2005 and 58 schools in 2007-08 in the District. In Shella-Bholaganj Block, the Mission runs 50 schools in 2001, 51 schools in 2005 and the same number of schools in 2007. The data also revealed that in 2001 the Mission admitted 8000 students, 9000 students in 2005 and 9000 students in 2007 in the East Khasi Hills District. It has good contribution in the Shella-Bholaganj Block too. The Ramakrishna Mission has been providing education to 7000 students in 2001, 7800 students in 2005 and 8230 students of the Shella-Bholaganj Block in 2007. The data clearly indicates the progress of the Mission in the field of education.

Wherever there were the Ramakrishna Mission schools, they were influential. These schools have won the hearts of the rural Khasis in the rural areas of this district. Education changed the living standard in this district. It also changed their mode of

---

[31] Quoted from the Cherrapunji Ramakrishna Mission Headquarters.

living, religious values, their occupation and social atmosphere.[32] Many Khasis of this district appreciate the education rendered by the Ramakrishna Mission. It may be because Government schools have failed to render quality education to the Khasi children.[33] Many parents find it difficult to bear the expenditure. The Ramakrishna Mission schools are able to attract the people because the education in these schools is free. Books and uniforms are provided free of cost.[34]

Table 6.12 Showing attitude on: "Ramakrishna Mission is helping the Khasis in education in the study area"

N= 280, AH= 156, NAH= 124

Sr. No.	Particulars	Selected Rural Households		Sample Average for both the groups
		Adopted Villages	Non-adopted	
1.	Total No. of Households	156(100.00)	124(100.00)	280(100.00)
	a. Agree	100(64.10)	60(48.39)	160(57.14)
	b. Disagree	50(32.05)	60(48.39)	110(39.29)
	c. Undecided	6(3.85)	4(3.22)	10(3.57)

Figures in parentheses indicate percentage

Table 6.12 revealed that 64.10 percent households from adopted villages and 48.39 percent households from non-adopted villages opined that the Ramakrishna Mission has been helping the Khasis in their education. 32.05 percent households from adopted villages and 48.39 percent households from non-adopted villages were of the opinion that no help is given by the Ramakrishna Mission to the Khasis in their education. Only 3.85 percent households from adopted villages and 3.22 percent households from non-adopted villages did not give their opinions on the statement.

A question was asked to the respondents on "Whether or not Ramakrishna Mission has any impact on the educational life of

---

[32] Personal interview with a group of Khasis at Laitryngew on 23.6.2006.
[33] Personal interview with the Secretary of Mawsmai Village on 20.5.2005.
[34] Personal interview with Swami Devamayananda at Cherapunji on 18.4.2006.

the Khasis?" There were different opinions on the issue. Table 6.13 gives an idea about the change brought about by the Ramakrishna Mission in the Khasi educational life.

Table 6.13 Showing opinion on: "Do you agree that Ramakrishna Mission has made any change in Educational Life of the Khasis in the study area?"

N=280,AH=156,NAH= 124

Sr. No.	Particulars	Selected Rural Households		Sample Average for both the groups
		Adopted Villages	Non-adopted	
1.	Total No. of Samples	156(100.00)	124(100.00)	280(100.00)
a.	Agree	120(76.92)	70(56.45)	190(67.86)
b.	Disagree	30(19.23)	50(40.32)	80(28.57)
c.	Undecided	6(3.85)	4(3.23)	10(3.57)

Figures in parentheses indicates percentage

Table 6.13 revealed that 76.92 percent households from adopted villages and 56.45 percent households from non-adopted villages opined that a change has taken place in the educational life of the rural Khasis in the adopted villages. Likewise, 19.23 percent households from adopted villages and 40.32 percent household respondents from the non-adopted villages opined that no change has taken place in Khasi educational life through the Ramakrishna Mission. However, 3.85 percent households from adopted villages and 3.23 percent household respondents from the non-adopted villages did not express their opinions on the question. It is very clear from the data that a majority of household respondents from adopted and non-adopted villages have witnessed a change in Khasi educational life.

(c) Change in Physical Health through Medical Service

Health and family welfare are crucial inputs into the well-being of the population and the expenditure by the Government in this sector indicates how seriously this commitment is taken. Expansion of education makes people more health conscious. The Ramakrishna Mission with its limited resources pays special attention to the health of the rural Khasis by running dispensaries

SOCIO-CULTURAL AND RELIGIOUS CHANGES 227

in the rural areas. The Mission runs three dispensaries and 2 mobile clinics in the East Khasi Hills District.[35] The following table 6.14 gives an account of the medical service rendered by the Mission in the District.

Table 6.14 Number of Dispensaries or Health Units Run by the Ramakrishna Mission

Sr. No.	Particulars	Total No. of Dispensaries/Mobiles clinics and Patients Attended					
		East Khasi Hills District Level			Shella-Bholaganj Block Level		
		2001	2005	2007-08	2001	2005	2007-08
1.	Total Dispensaries	3	3	3	2	2	2
2.	Total No. of Mobile Clinics	1	2	2	0	1	1
3.	Total No. of Patients	42600	54800	66433	12820	20877	22436

Table 6.14 revealed that the Mission has been rendering good medical service to the rural Khasi masses. The Mission had 3 dispensaries in 2001, 3 in 2005 and the same number of dispensaries in 2007 in the East Khasi Hills District. In Shella-Bholaganj Block, the Mission started its work with a dispensary at Shella. There were 2 dispensaries in 2001 and the same number of dispensaries in 2005 and 2007 in the Shella-Bholaganj Block. The data showed that the Ramakrishna Mission in the whole district attended 42600 patients in 2001, 54800 in 2005 and 66433 patients in 2007. The Mission gave medical service to 12820 patients in 2001, 20877 patients in 2005 and 22,436 patients in 2007 in Shella-Bholaganj Block.[36]

Education is generally considered a key factor in health development. It has a profound influence on demographic variables and other indicators of health and nutritional status of a population. Expansion of education makes people more health conscious. This can be partly due to relatively inadequate health

---

[35] *Annual Report and Account* (2007-08), Shillong: Ramakrishna Mission, 2-5.
[36] n.n., Annual Report and Account, (Shillong: Ramakrishna Mission, 2001, 2005, 2007-08)

facilities available in the district. It is believed that female education has a significant impact on maternal uncle and child health.[37] A Government, which looks after the health of the people, satisfies their deepest need in the field of health. Moreover, health improves productivity by increasing the man-hours of work as well as by improving the quality of work. Until 2001, there were reports of the incidence of epidemics such as fever, small-pox, cholera and anthrax, malaria, Gastro-enteritis, rickets, respiratory problem, tuberculosis, inflammation and ulceration and black-water fever in the District. In the non-adopted villages, such diseases were found even more than in the adopted villages in 2007.

The health condition has improved in the adopted villages. Though India has made a considerable progress in spreading health facilities, yet there is a lack of health facilities in the rural areas of the country in general and in the rural areas of the East Khasi Hills District in particular. There is also absence of awareness on the teaching of health problems in the rural areas. The problem of health acquires dimensions when viewed in the context of the poor and underprivileged sections of the society.[38] A particular malignant form called *Khieshoh rih* is ascribed to the malevolent influence of the demon u ***Rih***. Thus, the overall health status of any tribal community is the manifestation of several interrelated factors including the natural habitat, genetic and hereditary elements, cultural and behavioural aspects, traditional perception of health and diseases.

It was noticed that the rural areas as a whole were not adequately served by Government hospitals. They used their indigenous medicines and magic for healing their diseases. In many villages due to non-availability of qualified modern medical practitioners, the people approach the traditional medicine men and magico-religious practitioners. In each non-adopted village and even adopted villages, these kinds of people are found.[39]

---

[37] Dr. Jatanta Bhusan B., "The Changing Khasis: An Historical Account," *The Tribes of North East India, op.cit.,* 343-344.

[38] Anand Kumar Yogi, *Development of the North-East Region,* (Guwahati: United Publishers, 1991), 34.

[39] Walter Fernades & Sanjay Barbora, *Modernisation and Women Status in North East India,* (Guwahati: North Eastern Social Research Centre, 2002), 92-102.

Death, due to non-availability of modern medical care, is not uncommon in the non-adopted villages. These facilities are invariably concentrated in urban areas, leaving the rural areas high and dry. But due to the speedy efforts by the Ramakrishna Mission in the adopted villages and to some extent in the non-adopted villages the death rate has come down. The death rate of girls was higher than the death rate of boys in East Khasi Hills District.

During 2001 the Ramakrishna Mission served 12,820 patients in the Shella-Bholaganj Bolck and 48,151 patients in the whole District. While in 2007, it provided free treatment to over 20,877 people in the said Block and 66,433 patients in the East Khasi Hills District. In the whole District 180745 patients were treated in the Government hospitals, dispensaries and primary health centres during 2007. In the same year 66,433 patients were treated in the Ramakrishna Mission dispensaries in the East Khasi Hills District.[40] It means out of total 247,178 patients treated in 2007 in the District 26.9 percent of the total patients in the whole District and 38.4 percent of the total population of the Shella-Bholaganj Block were treated in the Ramakrishna Mission dispensaries and the Ramakrishna Mission mobile clinics, which has improved their physical health. The data clearly shows the impact of the medical service of the Ramakrishna Mission on the Khasi health.

Table 6.15 showing opinion on: "Do you agree that a change has taken place in Khasi Physical Health through the service of the Ramakrishna Mission in the study area?"

N=280, AH= 156, NAH= 124

Sr. No.	Particulars	Selected Rural Households		Sample Average for both the groups
		Adopted Villages	Non-adopted	
1	Total No. Of Households	156(100.00)	124(100.00)	280(100.00)
a.	Agree	80(51.28)	40(32.26)	120(42.86)
b.	Disagree	72(46.16)	80(64.52)	152(54.29)
c.	Undecided	4(2.56)	4(3.23)	8(2.86)

Figures in parentheses indicates percentage

---

[40] Quoted from Ramakrishna Mission Dispensaries at Shillong and Cherrapunji.

Table 6.15 showed that a change has taken place in Khasi physical health through the Ramakrishna Mission. 51.28 percent households from adopted villages and 32.26 percent households from non-adopted villages believed that a change has been seen in Khasi physical health through the service of the Ramakrishna Mission. However, 46.16 percent households from adopted villages and 64.52 percent households from non-adopted villages opined that this change has not taken place in Khasi physical health of the rural Khasis through the Ramakrishna Mission alone. The Church and the Government of Meghalaya have also played an important role in improving the physical health of the Khasis in the study area. Nevertheless, 2.56 percent households from adopted villages and 3.22 percent households from non-adopted villages did not express their opinion.

The data clearly indicated that the Khasis of non-adopted villages have been benefited much less through the medical service of the Ramakrishna Mission. The medical facilities in the non-adopted villages were available at the distance of 10 to 55 kms. The road condition was also not good in the non-adopted villages. There was no proper transportation facility available in the non-adopted villages due to the bad condition of roads. Moreover, the rural Khasis of the non-adopted villages used old traditional methods of medical treatment.

(d) The change in Birth and Death Rate

The factors influencing high death rate are malnutrition, lack of safe drinking water, lack of proper sanitation, lack of health care facilities, epidemics and disasters. The social and cultural factors like age at marriage, joint family system, social traditions and religious beliefs, lack of medical facilities, lack of family planning facilities and education always alter the fertility of a woman. Infant fertility rate is defined as the total number of deaths of infants i.e. less than one year of age, in a given year to thousand live births in that given year.[41] Life expectancy is defined as the

---

[41] I.J.S. Jaiswal & S.S. Datta Choudhuri, "Biological Demography in North East India, "The Pattern and Problems of Population in North-East India, (New Delhi: Uppal Publishing House, 1986), 318-19.

average number of years a child at birth is expected to live if the current mortality rate persists

Education is generally considered a key factor of development. It has a profound influence on demographic variables and other indicators of health and nutritional status of a population.[42] Through field study, it was found that female education has a significant impact on maternal and child health as it enhances the knowledge and skills of mothers in health care practices concerning age at marriage, contraception, nutrition, prevention and treatment of diseases. This also means that the higher infant and child mortality rate among the poorly educated mothers was due to their poor hygienic practices and lack of access to modern medical facilities. Moreover, maternal education was related to child health because it reduced the cost of public health programmes relating to information on health technology, increases household income and the productivity of health inputs.

Female education is also important in exerting a negative effect on fertility. Educated women are likely to have more voice with regard to lightening the burden of repeated pregnancies because they have more control over household resources and personal behaviour. Moreover, educated women have higher aspirations for the better achievements of their children, which is conducive to a reduction in a desired family size. They often have a higher age at marriage, which in turn affect fertility rate though not necessarily in uneducated families and families believing in superstitious things.

In rural areas of India in general and in Meghalaya in particular an early age for marriage was prevalent before the passing of the Child Marriage Restraint Act. It was considered to be a religious and sacred duty. But even now the age of marriage in rural areas of the East Khasi Hills is lower than the urban societies. Due to the low age of marriage the death rate is also high. At present the male should be 21 and the female 18 at the time of marriage. But usually the Khasi rural girls get married at an early age in comparison with the urban Khasi girls

---

[42] S.R. Nyneni, *Sociology*, Faridabad: Allahabad Law Agency, 2006), 296-297.

who marry at the age of 18-25. The age of marriage followed in 2007 by the rural Khasi women was 15-20 and they had 8-10 live births, whereas women who marry at the age of 18-25 had 6-9 live births. Those who marry at 30-35 have only 3-4 children.[43] As the age of marriage increases the fertility of a woman decreases. On the other hand, as the duration of marriage increases the tendency of women having more births also increases. The older age group of women always had a tendency to have fewer births than younger women.

Religion also plays an important role in birth and death rate. To the Khasis, children are the gifts of God. Therefore, the birth of a child is a happy occasion in the family. The traditional Khasis still believe that the will of God was supreme in connection with children. Most of the early taboos relating to pregnancy were observed in the non-adopted villages and less in the adopted villages. It was because life was held sacred. There are certain rituals, which are connected with the birth of a child. Besides, the children were considered as a source of help and security. Declining rates of infant mortality was the most important influence on increasing life expectancy.[44] The infant mortality rate tends to increase with the increasing age group of the mothers, and lack of education and lack of health facilities. The study shows that both infant and juvenile mortality rates decrease with the increasing educational levels for both the Christians and non-Christians. Concerning religion, the fertility and mortality rates are more or less the same in both the religious groups, though they are slightly lower among the Christians than the non-Christians.

Different factors like poverty, illiteracy, negligence of the government, superstitious faith, house condition, lack of medical facilities and lack of health awareness and drinking water facilities contributed to a high death rate.[45] Their houses, due to humidity, were not fit for healthy living. Because of illiteracy and blind

---

[43] Personal interview with knowledgeable persons of several villages in the study area on 20-27 December, 2005.

[44] Nalini Natarajan, *The Missionary among the Khasis*, 111.

[45] A.N. Agarwal, *Indian Economy*, (New Delhi: Viswa Prakashan, 1997), 80.

faith, they were not able to follow the standard for healthy living. Famines and epidemics stalked the land, which caused a high death rate. The house environment in the non-adopted villages due to damp conditions affected Khasi children. Both children and adults who were exposed to the high levels of damp and mould growth, had higher level of irritability, affecting the nervous system, bringing depression, and unhappiness. Moreover, Christians were healthier than the non-Christians who believe in superstition and witchcraft. The people learnt about decent living and kept their houses neat and clean through education. However, in the non-adopted villages this impact was not found much.[46]

Table 6.16 Showing opinion on: "A change has taken place in Birth and Death Rate." (per 1000)

N=280, AH= 156, NAH= 124

Sr. No.	Particulars	Selected Rural Households		Sample Average for both the groups
		Adopted Villages	Non-adopted	
1	Total No. of Samples	156(100.00)	124(100.00)	280(100.00)
2	Birth Rate in 2001	32.5	40.6	36.55
3	Birth Rate in 2007	28.5	36.60	32.23
4	Death Rate in 2001	15.6	18.6	17.1
5	Death Rate in 2007	9.2	13.10	11.15

The table 6.16 showed that the birth rate in 2001 in the adopted and non-adopted villages was 32.5 and 40.6 per thousand. Consequently, the gap between high birth and falling death rate widened with the passage of time. The birth rate in 2007 in the adopted and non-adopted villages fell down to 28.5 and 36.60 per thousand. This was due to better medical facilities, more health awareness programmes, better communication and education and less belief in superstitious faith. The death rate in the adopted and non-adopted villages in 2001 was 15.6 and 18.6 per thousand. But the death rate in 2007 in the adopted and non-adopted villages fell down to 9.2 and 13.10 per thousand.

---

[46] H.G. Joshi, *Meghalaya: Past and Present, op.cit.,* 215.

The birth rate in 2001 and 2007 in the East Khasi Hills District was 42.0 and 38.2 per thousand. The death rate in 2001 and 2007 in the same district was 8.9 and 6.8 per thousand respectively. Thus, the death rate due to the want of medical facilities in this district in the beginning of the century was very high. The steep fall in death rate was the result of the provision of a better diet, pure drinking water, and improved medical facilities.[47] The Ramakrishna Mission and church have been playing an important role by providing better medical facilities, health awareness and the need of smaller family. The result of their services in the field of physical health and education was visible in the adopted villages and in the non-adopted villages to some extent. Due to better medical facilities rendered by the Ramakrishna Mission and the church to the people of study area, the death rate has fallen very fast.

It was also found that the help the Ramakrishna Mission and the church gave to the poor rural Khasis reached them since there was no corruption among their workers.[48] It was due to the teaching on family planning, medical service and scientific education to the Khasis of this block by the Ramakrishna Mission and Christian missionaries that the birth rate and the death rate have fallen very fast in the adopted villages than in the non-adopted villages.

(e) Change in Property Inheritance

Christianity accounts for considerable changes. Christianity no doubt has caused reversals in marriages, naming, funeral, house building and village ceremonies. It has not materially changed the laws of inheritance.[49] The concept of property inheritance has not changed but individual property (as against clan property) has acquired a new importance because of changing times.[50] The changes took place whereby the youngest daughter can make a claim to the family properties as a legal heir. This change was

---

[47] Ibid.
[48] Personal interview with a group of Khasis at Cherrapunji on 26.12.2006.
[49] H.M. Bareh, Encyclopedia of Religion: Meghalaya, Vol. IV, Delhi: Mittal Publications, 2001, 112.
[50] Personal interview with S. Mazao at Cherrapunji on 24.5.2007.

facilitated during the British rule when courts made wrong interpretation of the local custom. This greatly helped the youngest daughter to successfully manipulate and treat the property as personal or self-acquired and dispose them, as she liked. While the power of the youngest daughter has increased beyond custodianship, the customary role and power of the maternal uncle has declined beyond measure. Maternal uncle's role has become less significant. As the education came and spread among the Khasis, the efficacy of the matrilineal system of descent and inheritance began to be questioned.[51]

The *Ka Seng Iktiar Longbriew Manbriew* Khasi Organisation, founded in 1961, demands a change in inheritance and property rights. According to this organisation, the share of property including land and business equally should also be given to sons. Recently a new organisation known as *Ka Syngkhong Rympei Thymmai* was formed which also advocates a change over from matrilineal to the patriarchal system.[52]

According to Sobhlei Sngi Lyngdoh, long before the British conquest, the Khasi matrilineal system began to give way to a change. Earlier the boys used to get married from the same village. When the boys started getting married to girls from far villages or towns the situation changed. Because of the distance, it was not possible for maternal-uncles to go to their wives houses in the evening and then to return early in the morning to their sisters' houses. In this way the maternal-uncle began to disappear from his sister's house and from his nephews and nieces. The father began to stay with his wife and children, but only as a tolerated outsider, since he was not the member of the clan. Authority and discipline began to wane in the Khasi homes.[53]

The Meghalaya Government passed an Act known as the Meghalaya Succession Act 1984 to self-acquired property, which

---

[51] Philomath Pasah, "Changes in the Matrilineal System of Khasi Jaintia Family," *Matriliny in Meghalaya*, (New Delhi: Regency Publications, 1998), 76.

[52] *Ibid.*, 20.

[53] Sobhlei Sngi Lyngdoh, "The Khasi Matriliny: Its Past and its Future," *Matriliny in Meghalaya. op.cit.*, 39-40.

received the approval of the President of India in 1986. The Act enables the parents to give their self-acquired property by the will system to any of their sons or daughters.[54] Today many Christian and sophisticated orthodox Khasis make wills to distribute property among their children.[55] There has been continue complain against the Property Inheritance Act. United Khasi and Jaintia Hills appreciated the movement against the Property Inheritance Act. The Meghalaya Act 1984 does not apply to the ancestral properties. A provision was made to enable the parents to dispose of their self- acquired property by a will. Every family has now its own way of bestowing property. The will of the parents is respected.[56]

It seems that there is a little impact of the Ramakrishna Mission teachings and the teachings of the Christian missionaries on the law of property inheritance. As before, no one as such could claim it. Sons now could be given a fair deal and other daughters too are treated in a just manner.[57] At present, though legally men can inherit only the self-acquired property. This has received further back up with the passage of the Khasi Lineage Bill, 1997 by the Khasi Hills Autonomous District Council. This was due to the influence of the Christian missionaries and the Ramakrishna Mission.[58]

It was seen that a group of young Khasis has been against the inheritance system. It might be due to the influence of either the Ramakrishna Mission or Christian society whose root is found in patriarchy. Some young Khasis have started criticising matrilineal system where only daughters are empowered to own property and not sons. This is one of the defects of the system as male is marginalised within his own house.[59]

---

[54] M.P.R. Lyngdoh, "Inheritance, Property Rights and Entrepreneurship in the Khasi Society," *The Dynamics of Family System in a Matriliny of Meghalaya, op.cit.,* 20.

[55] Nalini Natarajan, The Missionary among the Khasis, New Delhi: Sterling Publishers Pvt. Ltd., 1977, 169

[56] Kamaleshwar Sinha, *Meghalaya Triumph of the Tribal Genius,* (Delhi: Publication Division, 1970), 139-140.

[57] Personal interview with Headman of Laitryngew Village on 24.4.2006 at Laitryngew.

[58] Velentina Pakyntein, "Gender Preference in Khasi Society," Wonder that is Culture, ed. by T.B. Subha, 179.

[59] Margaret B. Challam, "Introduction," *The Dynamics of Family System in a Matriliny of Meghalaya, op.cit.,* 33.

6.17 Showing opinion on: "A Change has taken place in the Property Inheritance."

N=280, AH= 156, NAH= 124

Sr. No.	Particulars	Selected Rural Households		Sample Average for both the groups
		Adopted Villages	Non-adopted	
1	Total No. of Households	156(100.00)	124(100.00)	280(100.00)
a.	Agree	60(38.46)	40(32.26)	100 (35.71)
b.	Disagree	87(55.77)	80(64.52)	167(59.65)
c.	Undecided	9(5.77)	4(03.23)	13(4.64)

Figures in parentheses indicates percentage.

The data in table 6.17 indicates that 38.46 percent households from adopted villages and 32.26 percent households from non-adopted villages opined that a change has taken place in the Khasi opinion on property inheritance through the Ramakrishna Mission. 55.77 percent households from adopted villages and 64.52 percent households from non-adopted villages agreed that no change has taken place in the Khasi opinion on the property inheritance. However, 5.77 percent households from adopted villages and 3.23 percent households from non-adopted villages remained undecided.

(f) Political Change

Until its annexation by the British (1833), the Khasi Hills had maintained a fair degree of isolation to condition its political system according to its needs and environment. The institution of *Syiemship* was considered as an ancient one. The ruler combined in himself the fiscal, legal, administrative and military powers. The system as such was, however, an aristocracy or limited monarchy as the *Syiems* were from special clans. The scope of election was also limited as the law of succession was clear and limited by the eldest of the uterine brothers of the deceased *Syiem* and failing this, by maternal cousin brother, or son of the sister. In course of time, the elements of feudalism and capitalism had infiltrated into the system as the *Syiems* had the privileges of controlling the vest crown lands and the command of the service of the people.⁶⁰

In 1874, the new province of Assam was created with Shillong as its capital. Around 1895, there was a spirit of nationalism among the Khasis. In 1904 with the merger of Assam with the United Province of East Bengal, Shillong became the headquarters. The year 1923 saw the formation of the Khasi National Durbar and in the years 1934-1935, the Khasi States Federation. The traditional pattern of polity went side by side with modern systems in which members of the Parliament, Legislative Assembly, District Council and Municipality were returned on modern universal adults' suffrage without any consideration to the hereditary basis. In fact, modern institutions contain more elite than the traditional state form of polity.⁶¹

Since independence, the political, economic and social forces at work in the country have brought about a large measure of integration of the Khasis with the rest of India. In 1953, in the wake of independence under Article 244 and the Sixth Schedule of the Constitution of India, District Councils were set up. The *syiemship* is continued subject to the provisions of the Sixth Schedule. All the powers and functions exercised by the Deputy Commissioner over the *Syiems* were transferred to the District Council and the State Government. The chiefs or *Syiems* have to carry all the orders issued to them by the Autonomous District Council. The Khasi Hills District Council framed a Law regulating succession of the *syiems* and headmen.

The United Khasi Jaintia Hills Autonomous District Act, 1959, made the provisions not only for its authority to appoint the chiefs and headmen, but even the removal and suspension of the offices by the Executive Committee of the District Council if in its opinion the chiefs and headmen violate the terms and conditions of their appointment. Further, the Khasi Hills Autonomous District Council in its amendment of the Principal

---

⁶⁰ Dr. Jatanta Bhushan B., "The Changing Khasis: An Historical Account," *The Tribes of North East India*, 338.

⁶¹ Nalini Natarajan, *The Missionary among the Khasis*, op.cit., 140.

Act on Appointment and Succession of *Syiems* and headmen, 1980, went even to the extent of passing an Act debarring the chiefs, deputy chiefs, acting chiefs, in taking any part in politics and elections either of the State or of the District Council. This is another way of control enforced by the District Council over the traditional chiefs.[62] Moreover, the District Council should confirm the appointment of the *Syiems*. This is the outside influence, which has led the Khasi society to adopt a new political system in the East Khasi Hills District.

Nowadays with the existence of the District Councils and the Judicial Courts in the State all disputes are referred to them for final decision. With the administration getting out of the hands of the traditional headmen, their authority has been undermined. This has led to the emergence of a new leadership of District Counsellors (MDCs) and elected representatives of the Meghalaya Legislative Assembly (MLAs).[63]

Today most of the political leaders in the rural areas are from advance villages. Even most of the Autonomous District Council members are from advance villages. A good number of them are the product of the Christian missionaries schools and some of them from the Ramakrishna Mission schools in the study areas. Due to illiteracy and lack of proper communication in the non-adopted villages, the rural Khasis have few members in the District Councils. They struggle for their survival. Until 2001 many Khasis in the district lived below the poverty line. Even in 2007, poverty was dominating in the non-adopted villages.

The Ramakrishna Mission and the church have been instrumental in fostering the spirit of nationalism. Ramakrishna Mission also has taught about the national democratic system of politics. Moreover, there were some weaknesses in the traditional political system that compelled the Khasis to find an alternate political system for themselves. Christianity did not oppose the traditional polity. The Ramakrishna Mission missionaries have brought about some changes in the Khasi political thinking due

---

[62] Dr. S.K. Chattopadhayay, *Tribal Institutions of Meghalaya*, 46.
[63] District Statistical Hand Book: East Khasi Hills District, *op.cit.*, 46-48

to education. The Ramakrishna Mission laid stress on the ideas of nationhood. The Mission has also helped the traditional Khasi leaders to be aware of their political rights. Women were deprived of political participation in decision-making bodies.

Due to education, even Khasi women were made aware of the importance of their political participation. Khasi women have also started demanding for their rights in decision-making bodies, which is the result of education. The leadership is enlightened and of a superior calibre, and highly respected by the public.[64]

Due to western education, local leadership of a high calibre emerged on a large scale. As the demand for political rights began to be pressed, misgivings arose in the minds of the Indian politicians all over India. The demand for political rights in the Khasi Hills was unique because it was peaceful. All Khasis spoke with one voice. The result of the one voice was that democracy came to have a new dimension in the East Khasi Hills, which was supported by the Ramakrishna Mission.[65]

When we look at the statistics we find that some respondents have witnessed the contribution of the Ramakrishna Mission to political awareness and change among the Khasis. Earlier Khasis were limited to their areas except business relationship with the outsiders. They were aware of their traditional political system. They were away from the central democratic system. Now they have had lot of contribution to the national politics.

6.18 Showing opinion on: "A Change has taken place in the Khasi Political Life in the study area."

N= 280, AH= 156, NAH= 124

Sr. No.	Particulars	Selected Rural Households		Sample Average for both the groups
		Adopted Villages	Non-adopted	
1.	Total No. Of Households	156(100.00)	124(100.00)	280(100.00)
a.	Agree	50(32.05)	30(24.19)	80(28.57)

---

[64] Mary Pristilla Rina Lyngdoh, *The Festivals in the History and Culture of the Khasis*, op.cit., 46.

[65] Ibid.

Contd., 6.18 Showing opinion on: "A Change has taken place in the Khasi Political Life in the study area."

N= 280, AH= 156, NAH= 124

Sr. No.	Particulars	Selected Rural Households		Sample Average for both the groups
		Adopted Villages	Non-adopted	
b.	Disagree	100 (64.10)	90(72.58)	190(67.86)
c.	Undecided	6(03.85)	4(03.23)	10(3.57)

Figures in parentheses indicates percentage

Table 6.18 showed that 32.05 percent households from adopted villages and 24.19 percent households from non-adopted villages opined that the Ramakrishna Mission has also been instrumental in fostering the spirit of nationalism among the Khasis in the study area. However, 64.10 percent respondents from adopted villages and 72.58 percent households from non-adopted villages were of the opinion that the Ramakrishna Mission alone has not fostered the spirit of nationalism among the Khasis. There were other factors which were responsible for it. They believed that this change has been brought about by modernisation, education and good communication.

(g) Economic Change

The study reveals that the Ramakrishna Mission has been able to bring about economic changes in the Khasi society. This section deals with economic change in the Khasi society through the Ramakrishna Mission.

(i) Total Asset Value

To get a better understanding of the income sources, the data collected on the various types of assets owned by the households are listed under two categories. The data collected on the various types of assets owned by the households' fewer than two categories are presented in Table 6.19. It is very clear that all these respondents were Khasis and belonged to selected sample villages in Shella-Bholaganj Block of the East Khasi Hills District. Unlike other parts of the country, we cannot see the same criteria for this region to fix up the property. Since land belongs to the whole clan and not to a particular family, the value of the land cannot be assigned to any particular family. Only a few families have their own private land. The asset value covers machinery, housing, furniture, vehicle, equipment, kitchen articles and animal husbandry.

Table 6.19 Asset Value Distribution of Rural Households

N= 280, AH= 156, NAH= 124

Sr. No.	Particulars	Selected Rural Households		Sample Average for both the groups
		Adopted Villages	Non-adopted	
1	Total No. of Samples	156(100.00)	124(100.00)	280(100.00)
2	Value Categories (in ₹)			
	a. 0-30000	(3) 28860 1.92	(6) 26540 4.84	(9) 27700 3.21
	b. 30000-60000	(5) 58620 3.20	(8) 50214 6.45	(13) 54387 4.64
	c. 60000-90000	(10) 87600 6.41	(12) 70240 9.68	(22) 78920 7.86
	d. 90000-120000	(15) 110600 9.67	(15) 100690 12.10	(30) 105645 10.71
	e. 120000-150000	(20) 143200 12.82	(18) 132700 14.52	(38) 137950 13.57
	f. 150000-180000	(25) 167542 16.02	(22) 160000 17.74	(47) 163771 16.79
	g. 180000-210000	(30) 200084 19.22	(25) 186800 20.15	(55) 195000 19.64
	h. 210000-300000	(25) 287600 16.03	(8) 210000 6.45	(33) 255000 11.79
	i. 300000-450000	(11) 423000 7.04	(7) 410000 5.65	(18) 226150 6.43
	j. 450000-600000	(7) 570000 4.47	(3) 523000 2.42	(10) 546500 3.57
	k. 600000-1000000	(5) 870900 3.20	Nil 0.00	(5) 870900 1.79

Figures in parentheses indicates percentage

Table 6.19 indicates that the asset value of 3 households was ₹ 28,860/- (1.92 percent) in the adopted villages and that of 6 households was ₹ 26,540 (4.84 percent) in the non-adopted villages. The asset value of 5 households from adopted villages was ₹ 58,620 (6.45 percent) and the asset value of 8 households from non-adopted villages was ₹ 50,214 (6.45 percent). The asset value of 10 households from adopted villages was ₹ 87,600 (6.41) and that of 12 households from non-adopted villages was ₹ 70,240, (9.68 percent). Likewise, the asset value of 15 households from adopted villages was ₹ 1,10,600 (9.63 percent) and the asset value of 15 households from non-adopted villages was ₹ 1,00,690 (12.10). The asset value of 20 households from adopted villages was ₹ 1,43,200 (12.82 percent) and in the non-adopted villages the asset value of 18 households was ₹ 1,32,700 (14.52 percent). In the same manner the asset value of 25 households from adopted villages was ₹ 1,67,542 (16.02 percent) and the asset value of 22 households from non-adopted villages was ₹ 1,60,000 (17.74 percent). The asset value of 30 households from adopted villages was ₹ 2,00084 (19.22 percent) and of the 25 households in the non-adopted villages was ₹ 1,86,800 (20.15). The asset value of 25 households from adopted villages was ₹ 2,87,600 (16.03 percent) and the asset value of 8 households in the non-adopted villages was ₹ 2,10,000 (6.45 percent). The asset value of 11 households from adopted villages was ₹ 4,23,000 (7.04 percent), and in the non-adopted villages the asset value of 7 households was ₹ 4,10,000 (5.65 percent). The asset value of 7 households in the adopted villages was ₹ 5,70,000 (4.47 percent) and in the non adopted villages the asset value of 3 households was ₹ 5,23,000 (2.42 percent). The asset value of 5 households in the adopted villages was ₹ 8,70,900.

(ii) Income with Reference to Occupation

Income can be defined as the flow of money or goods accruing to an individual or a group of individuals, a firm or the economy over sometime period. It may originate from the sale of productive services. The rural communities in general and in the East Khasi Hills District in particular have made considerable economic progress. The total selected households' gross income was obtained by summing the income from agriculture, animal husbandry, household industry/trade/mining and other resources like salaries and agricultural and manual labour. There are 8 livelihood activities in which the Khasis are engaged. Not all the families in the adopted and non-adopted villages engaged in all occupations. On the other hand, the occupations in the adopted villages have undergone rapid changes. There were increasing opportunities of secondary sources of income. Some benefits in the form of labour from the Government developmental works in the rural areas were also found. Many families have undertaken cultivation of commercial crops. Social factors too influence living habits and the pattern of expenditure.

The households were divided into four groups according to their occupations. The four occupations were: cultivation, live stock, household industry/mining & trade and others (salary holders, casual and agricultural labourers).

The primary occupation of the Khasis was agriculture. Agricultural occupation was supplemented by private and government jobs. There were families who depended on agriculture and the forest for their living, which belongs neither to the government nor to any particular family but to the whole village community or clan. Some families fully depended on livestock. Many families did not like to engage in cultivation since a huge part of the land is barren. In Mawmluh and Mawsmai villages only a small portion of land was good for cultivation. In the uplands, they cultivate the traditional crops like potatoes, rice, maize, pineapples, bananas, oranges, and so on. All the 50 families collect firewood from the community forest. They also collect timber for the construction of their houses from the forest. Some families depend on timber factories to earn their livelihood. There was no bonded labour in the East Khasi Hills District. Agricultural production did not show a rapid rise due to the low levels of technological development in this area. Therefore, it was important for them to learn the lessons of transition that mainland India has adopted. Agriculture, both terrace and shifting cultivation was the primary basis of the agrarian economy of the Khasis. In the East Khasi Hills District potato cultivation has become a part of life apart from paddy. The category wise frequency and distribution of the total income are given below in table 6.20.

Table 6.20 Level of Income Distribution in Adopted & Non-adopted Households

N= 280, AH= 156, NAH= 124

Sr. No.	Particulars	Selected Rural Households		Sample Average for both the groups
		Adopted Villages	Non-adopted	
1.	Total No. of Samples	156(100.00)	124(100.00)	280(100.00)
2.	Level of Annual Income by Adopted & Non-adopted Rural Households (in ₹)			
a.	0-30000	(15)28550 9.61	(20)25580 16.31	(35) 26853 12.50
b.	30000-60000	(15)42355 9.61	(26)41355 20.96	(41) 41721 14.64
c.	60000-90000	(21)62840 13.46	(25)62130 20.10	(46) 62454 16.43
d.	90000-120000	(25)95524 16.03	(21)91510 16.96	(46) 93691 16.43
e.	120000-150000	(28)132500 17.95	(15)121520 12.09	(43)128670 15.36
f.	150000-180000	(20)175267 12.82	(8) 160050 6.45	(28) 170919 10.00
g.	180000-210000	(17)192000 10.91	(7)182350 5.53	(24) 189185 8.57
h.	210000 & above	(15)232000 9.61	(2) 212300 1.60	(17) 229682 6.07

Figures in Parenthesis indicate the Households and their Percentage.

Table 6.20 indicated that 9.61 percent households from adopted villages had ₹ 28550 as their annual income per household, 16.31 percent households from non-adopted villages had ₹ 25580 annual income per household and the average income of 12.50 percent households from both the groups was ₹ 26,853 per household. 9.61 percent households from adopted villages had ₹ 42355 as their annual income per household, 20.96 percent households from non-adopted villages had ₹ 41355 as annual income per household and average income of 14.64 percent households from both the groups was ₹ 41721 per household. 13.46 percent households from adopted villages had ₹ 62840 as annual income per household, 20.10 percent households in the non-adopted villages had ₹ 62100 as annual income per household and the average income of 16.43 households from both the groups was ₹ 62454 per household. 16.03 percent households from adopted villages had ₹ 95524 as annual income per household, 16.96 percent households from non-adopted villages had ₹ 91510 as annual income per household and the average income of 16.43 percent households had annual income ₹ 93691 per household. 17.95 percent households from adopted villages had ₹ 132500 as annual income per household, 12.09 percent households from non-adopted villages had ₹ 121500 as annual income per household and the average income of 16.43 percent households was ₹ 128670 per household. 12.82 percent households from adopted villages had ₹ 175267 as annual income per household, 6.45 percent households from the non-adopted villages had ₹ 160050 as annual income per household and the average income of 10.00 households from both the groups was ₹ 170919. Likewise 10.91 percent households from adopted villages had ₹ 192000 as annual income per household, 5.53 percent households in the non-adopted villages had ₹ 182350 as annual income and the average income of 8.57 percent household had annual income of ₹ 189185 per household. However, 9.61 percent households from adopted villages had ₹ 232000 as annual income per household, 1.60 percent households from non-adopted villages had ₹ 212300 as annual income per household and the average income of 6.07 percent households from both the groups was ₹ 229682 per household.

Table 6.21 Distribution of Average Income of Rural Households in Adopted & Non-adopted Villages.

N=280, AH= 156, NAH= 124

Sr. No.	Particulars	Selected Rural Households		Sample Average for both the groups
		Adopted Villages	Non-adopted	
1.	Total No. of Samples	156 (100.00)	124 (100.00)	280 (100.00)
2.	Average Income of Rural Households in different Sources (in ₹)	1,01,972.00	79,565.00	92,048.90

Sr. No.	Particulars	Selected Rural Households		Sample Average for both the groups
		Adopted Villages	Non-adopted	
a.	Primary	38,749.36 (38.00)	47,739.00 (60.00)	42,730.48 (46.42)
b.	Secondary	21,414.32 (21.00)	11,934.75 (15.00)	17,216.12 (18.71)
c.	Tertiary	41,808.32 (41.00)	19,891.25 (25.00)	32,102.40 (34.87)

Figures in Parenthesis indicates percentage

Table 6.21 revealed the average income of rural households in adopted and non-adopted villages. The average income of rural households in adopted villages from primary source was ₹ 38749.36 (38.00 percent) and in the non-adopted villages ₹ 47739 (60 percent). The average income of rural households in adopted villages from secondary source was ₹ 21414.32 90 (21 percent) and in the non-adopted villages ₹ 11934.75 (15 percent). From the tertiary sources the average income of rural households in the adopted villages was ₹ 41808.32 (41 percent) and in the non-adopted villages ₹ 19891.25 (25 percent). It was found that in the adopted villages the average income of rural households from secondary and tertiary sources was higher than the income of the selected households in the non-adopted villages. Nevertheless, the average income of selected rural households in the adopted villages was less than the average income of the households in the non-adopted villages.

Table 6.22 Showing Opinion on: "Do you agree that you have sufficient income to run about the primary, secondary and tertiary occupation?"

N= 280, AH= 156, NAH= 124

Sr. No.	Particulars	Selected Rural Households		Sample Average for both the groups
		Adopted Villages	Non-adopted	
1.	Total No. of Sample	156(100.00)	124(100.00)	280(100.00)
a.	Agree	60 (38.46)	40(32.26)	100 (35.71)
b.	Disagree	90(57.69)	80(64.52.)	170(60.72)
c.	Undecided	6(3.85)	4(3.22)	10(3.57)

Figures in Parenthesis indicates percentage

Table 6.22 showed that 38.46 percent households from adopted villages and 32.26 percent households from non-adopted villages opined that they have sufficient income to run about their primary, secondary and tertiary occupation. Similarly, 57.69 percent households from adopted villages and 64.52 percent households from non-adopted villages opined that their income is not enough to run about their occupations. However, 3.85 percent households from adopted villages and 3.22 percent households from non-adopted villages did not express their opinion on the statement.

(iii) Increase in Employment through Education

The Ramakrishna Mission runs 4 technical institutions in the district where many young Khasi males and females have been trained for different trades like tailoring, weaving, painting, computer training, candle making, making clothes, etc. In Cherapunji there is a big centre where many young people are given special training. Every year many young Khasi males and females have been trained by the Ramakrishna Mission to earn their livelihood. In each unit the Mission trains 20-30 people every year. According to the Ramakrishna Mission Office Record, the Ramakrishna Mission trains around 70 people every year in all the four centres. In Shella-Bholaganj Block there are three centres for technical training.[66] Those Khasi males and females who have earned their diploma certificate from the Ramakrishna Mission have started their work with the assistance of the Mission and the state Government. Table 6.23 gives the account of the activities of the Ramakrishna Mission.

Table 6.23 Total number of Technical Institutions in East Khasi Hills District & Shella-Bholaganj Block.[67]

Sr. No.	Particulars	Total No. of Technical Technical Centres & People Trained					
		East Khasi Hills District			Shella-Bholaganj Block		
		2001	2005	2007	2001	2005	2007
1.	Total No. of Training Centres	3	4	4	2	3	3
2.	Total People Trained	50	60	70	40	40	50

---

[66] Quoted from Ramakrishna Mission Office Record, Cherrapunji.
[67] Quoted from Ramakrishna Mission Headquarters, Cherrapunji.

The data in table 6.23 indicated that the Ramakrishna Mission run 3 technical institutions in 2001, 4 technical institutions in 2005 and 4 technical institutions in 2007 in the East Khasi Hills District. In Shella-Bholaganj Block the Mission run 2 technical institutions in 2001, 3 technical institutions in 2005 and 3 technical institutions in 2007. Altogether 50 people in 2001, 60 people in 2005 and 70 people in 2007 were trained in the East Khasi Hills District. However, 40 people in 2001, 40 people in 2005 and 50 people in 2007 were trained in Shela-Bholaganj Block.

It is apparent that education affects occupation also. Nevertheless, changes in occupational structure have not brought about rapid changes in the earlier traditional occupational pattern of Khasi tribal society. Education has changed their sources of income. The effects of past discriminatory practices in both employment and the acquisition of human capital continue to reduce still the earning power of the older males in the labour force. Past discrimination in both employment and other areas retards their ability to promote earnings parity between black and white, rich and poor.

The majority of villagers in the adopted villages were educated and in the non-adopted villages they were educationally backward. They were not able to take advantage of employment opportunities, especially white-collar jobs. Among the Khasis, land belongs to the people. People are showing interest in livestock and poultry. The persons who were engaged in any traditional occupation need education as to adopt the new technology, which has been developed in every sphere of occupations. Education, therefore, has played an important role in shaping the attitudes of the Khasis right from the early age. Though many educated people have been engaged in private or government jobs, yet agriculture and allied activities remain the most important sector of the rural Khasis in the District.

Household industry is also coming up in the district since the Ramakrishna Mission and the church have trained many young men and women for various trades like tailoring, weaving, carpentry, motor mechanism, handicrafts, painting, agriculture and animal husbandry. Many women have engaged themselves in these kinds of trades. The main problem to develop household industry and small-scale industry was the non-availability of cheap electric power and labour charge. Most of the educated Khasis aim at Government or private jobs. The road communication facilities in the rural areas of the district were not up to the mark. The district has no railway facility. Economic development was not equitably reaching the poor. The economic development of the people living in the border areas is yet a dream.[68]

With the process of growth and development, there has been a structural change in the scrotal share of income. This is accompanied by a shift in employment from the primary sector to the other sectors as surplus labour moves to more productive avenues of employment. The following table shows the increase in the total number of employees during 2007 due to education imparted by the Ramakrishna Mission and the Christian Church.

Table 6.24 The Rate of Increase of Employment in Adopted & Non-adopted Villages

N=280, AH=156, NAH= 124

Sr. No.	Particulars	Selected Rural Households		Sample Average for both the groups
		Adopted Villages	Non-adopted	
1.	Total No. of Households	156(100.00)	124(100.00)	280(100.00)
2.	Total No. of Employees in 2001	40(25.64)	20(16.13)	60(21.43)
3.	Total No. of Employees in 2005	60(38.46)	25(20.16)	85(30.36)
4.	Total No. of Employees in 2007	90(57.69)	35(28.22)	125(44.64)

Figures in parentheses indicates percentage

The data in table 6.24 indicated that the rate of growth in employment in adopted and non-adopted villages of Shella-

---

[68] n.n., Tribal Economy of North Eastern Region, ed. by T Mathew, (Gauhati: Spectrum Publications, 1980), 30; see also James E. Long, "Earning Productivity and Changes in Employment Discrimination during 1960: Additional Evidence," *The American Economic Review*, Vol. 66, No.2, March 1977, 223-227.

Bholaganj Block in the East Khasi Hills District was not equal. The rate of increase in employment in adopted villages and non-adopted villages in 2001 & 2007 was 12.82 & 4.03 percent. Due to education, there was increase in employment in 2005 to 2007 also. 38.46 percent households in the adopted villages and 20.16 percent households in the non-adopted villages were employees. There was 19.23 percent increase in employment in the adopted villages and 8.06 percent increase in non-adopted villages in 2005. However, 57.69 percent people were employees in the adopted villages and 28.22 percent were employees in the non-adopted villages in 2007.

Table 6.25 Showing Opinion on: "Do you have sufficient employment in your family?"

N=280, AH=156, NAH= 124

Sr. No.	Particulars	Selected Rural Households		Sample Average for both the groups
		Adopted Villages	Non-adopted	
1	Total No. of Samples	156(100.00)	124(100.00)	280(100.00)
a	Agree	60(38.46)	40(32.26)	100(35.71)
b	Disagree	90(57.69)	80(64.52)	170(60.72)
c	Undecided	6(3.85)	4(3.23)	10(3.57)

Figures in parentheses indicates percentage

Table 6.25 showed that 38.46 percent households from adopted villages and 32.26 percent households from non-adopted villages opined that they have sufficient employment in their families. However, 57.69 percent households from adopted villages and 64.52 percent households from non-adopted villages opined that they do not have sufficient employment in their families. Only 3.85 percent households from adopted villages and 3.23 percent households from non-adopted villages did not express their opinions on the question. In this regards the Ramakrishna Mission is also working in the study area to guide people for more employment. The Mission sends the Khasis out of Meghalaya for training in agriculture and other technical traders.

(iv) Contribution of Women to Family Income

Women in the rural areas of the East Khasi Hills District are equal contributors to family income. Women are engaged in Government or private jobs, business, trade, household industry, livestock and agriculture. Their contribution to family income has been recognised by the Khasi society. Table 6.26 showed the contribution of Khasi women to family income.

Table 6.26 Showing opinion on: "Do you believe that women also have contributed to Khasi family income?"

N=280, AH= 156, NAH= 124

Sr. No.	Particulars	Selected Rural Households		Sample Average for both the groups
		Adopted Villages	Non-adopted	
1.	Total No. of Samples	156(100.00)	124(100.00)	280(100.00)
2.	Agree	52(33.33)	40(32.26)	92(32.86)
3.	Disagree	100(64.10)	82(66.13)	182(65.00)
4.	Undecided	4(2.56)	2(1.61)	6(2.14)

Table 6.26 showed that 33.33 percent respondents from adopted villages and 32.26 percent respondents from non-adopted villages opined that women have contributed to the family income due to education. However, 64.10 percent respondents from adopted villages and 66.13 percent respondents from non-adopted villages were of the opinion that women alone have not contributed to the family income. Both male and female have contributed to the family income though female contribution to the family income may be more than male. Only 2.56 percent respondents from adopted villages and 1.61 percent respondents from non-adopted villages did not express their opinions. The data clearly indicates that the contribution of the female members to family income was not less important than men in the Khasi Society. Ramakrishna Mission has been working for the upliftment of the women through education and technical training programmes, which have contributed to the family income.

(v) Expenditure

Total expenditure consists of on-farm expenditure (production expenditure) and off-farm expenditure (consumption expenditure). It is well-known fact that general expenditure on various items relating to the Khasi livelihood may be different from the non-tribal communities. The production expenditure consists of recurring expenditure in agriculture and other items. The word consumption has a special meaning. Here, the quality of a product to satisfy human wants is called utility or consumption. The consumption expenditure was the sum of recurring expenses incurred on the consumption items like food, shelter, clothing, education etc. Table 6.27 shows the disposal of income of the rural households.

Table No. 6.27 Disposal of Income by
Rural Households (Value in ₹)

N= 280, AH= 156, NAH= 124

Sr. No.	Particulars	Selected Rural Households		Sample Average for both the groups
		Adopted Villages	Non-adopted	
1.	Average Income of Rural Households in ₹	101972.00 (100.00)	79565.00 (100.00)	92048.90 (100.00)
i)	Family Consumption	76173.08 (74.70)	63811.13 (80.20)	70647.53 (76.75)
ii)	Investment on Production Resources	15346.90 (15.05)	9110.19 (11.45)	12380.58 (13.45)
iii)	Saving	10452.02 (10.25)	6643.68 (8.35)	9020.79 (9.80)

Figures in Parenthesis indicates percentage

Table 6.27 indicated that ₹ 76,173.08 (74.70 percent) from average income was spent on family consumption in the adopted rural households and ₹ 63811.13(80.20 percent) in the non-adopted rural households. The investment on production consumption resources was ₹ 15346.90 (15.05 percent) in the adopted villages and ₹ 9110.19 (11.45 percent) in the non-adopted villages. The family consumption in the adopted households was 74.70% and in the non-adopted villages 80.20% of their average annual income. The selected rural households in adopted and non-adopted villages did the saving. In the adopted villages, the saving was ₹ 10452.02 (10.25 percent) and in the non-adopted villages ₹ 6643.68 (8.35 percent). The data showed that the family consumption was more in the non-adopted villages.

Different households from adopted and non-adopted villages spend maximum share of their income on food, shelter and clothing. The amount differs from family to family. Those who have more income spent more. However, the poor households spent more on food and clothing. Table 6.28 indicates the amount the households spent on food, shelter, clothing and other needs of the family.

Table 6.28 Showing Opinion on: "How much income do you spend on food, shelter, clothing and others?"

N=280, AH= 156, NAH= 124

Sr. No.	Particulars	Selected Rural Households		Sample Average for both the groups
		Adopted Villages	Non-adopted	
1	Total No. of Samples	156 (100.00)	124 (100.00)	280 (100.00)
2	Income spends on Family consumption	76173.08 (100.00)	63811.13 (100.00)	70647.53 (100.00)
a	Food	46084.71 (60.5)	41477.23 (65.0)	44331.33 (62.75)
b	Shelter	11045.10 (14.50)	8933.56 (14.0)	10067.27 (14.25)
c	Clothing & Others	19043.27 (25.0)	13400.34 (21.0)	16248.93 (23.00)

Figures in Parenthesis indicates percentage

Table 6.28 indicated that the total income spent on food by the households from adopted villages was 46084.71 (60.5 percent) and in the non-adopted villages ₹ 41477.23(65.00). Income spent on shelter was ₹ 11045.10(14.50) in the adopted and in the non-adopted villages the amount spent on shelter was ₹ 8933.56 (14.00). The amount spent on clothing & other items in the adopted villages was ₹ 19043.27 (25.00) and in the non-adopted villages the amount spent on clothing & other items was ₹ 13400.34 (21.0).

(vi) Status of Standard of Living

From the income difference, it was understood that there was a difference in their standard of living too. The question was asked whether they had sufficient income to meet out the needs such as food, shelter, clothing etc. The answer was not the same.

Table 6.29 Showing Opinion on: "Do you agree that your standard of living has improved through the service of the Ramakrishna Mission?"

N=280, AH= 156, NAH= 124

Sr. No.	Particulars	Selected Rural Households		Sample Average for both the groups
		Adopted Villages	Non-adopted	
1.	Total No. of Samples	156(100.00)	124(100.00)	280(100.00)
2.	Agree	50(32.05)	20(16.13)	70(25.00)
3.	Disagree	100(64.10)	100(80.64)	200(71.43)
4.	Undecided	6(3.85)	4(03.23)	10(03.57)

Figures in Parenthesis indicates percentage

Table 6.29 indicated that a change has taken place in the standard of living of the households in the adopted and non-adopted villages. 32.05 percent households from adopted villages and 16.13 percent households from non-adopted villages opined that a change has taken place in the Khasi standard of living through the Ramakrishna Mission. But 64.10 percent households from adopted villages and 80.64 percent households from non-adopted villages opined that this change in the Khasi standard of living has not taken place through the Ramakrishna Mission alone. Even Christian church has also played a vital role in bringing about a change in the Khasi living standard in the study area. The Ramakrishna Mission has played a partial role in lifting up the living standard of the Khasis in the study area. However, 3.85 percent households from adopted villages and 3.23 percent households from non-adopted villages did not express their opinions.

Table 6.30 Showing an Opinion on: "Do you agree that you have sufficient income to meet your needs like food, shelter, clothing etc.?"

N=280, AH= 156, NAH= 124

Sr. No.	Particulars	Selected Rural Households		Sample Average for both the groups
		Adopted Villages	Non-adopted	
1.	Total No. of Samples	156(100.00)	124(100.00)	280(100.00)
a.	Agree	80(51.28)	40(32.26)	120(42.86)
b.	Disagree	70(44.87)	80(56.45)	150(53.57)
c.	Undecided	6(3.85)	4(3.23)	10(0.37)

Figures in Parenthesis indicates percentage

Table 6.30 indicated that 51.28 percent households from adopted villages and 32.26% households from non-adopted villages opined that their income was sufficient to meet their needs for food, clothing and shelter. But this does not mean that they have sufficient income to meet their need only through the Ramakrishna Mission. Even Christian missionaries and government have also played very important role in making them self-sufficient in meeting their needs. On the other hand, 44.87 percent households from adopted villages and 56.45 percent households from non-adopted villages opined that their income was not sufficient to meet their need for clothing, shelter and food. However, 3.85 percent households from adopted villages and 3.23 percent households from non-adopted villages did not express their opinions.

(vii) Saving

Saving indicates the surplus amount that they have after meeting their daily needs. Many families in the rural areas were not concerned for saving because their income was limited. There were only few families who could do saving. The average annual saving in the adopted villages was higher than the saving of the households in the non-adopted villages as it is found in table No.6.31.

Table 6.31 Showing Opinion on: "What is your status of saving over total Income?"

N=280, AH= 156, NAH= 124

Sr. No.	Particulars	Selected Rural Households		Sample Average for both the groups
		Adopted Villages	Non-adopted	
1.	Saving of Selected Rural households (in ₹)	156.00 (100.00)	124 (100.00)	280 (100.00)
a.	Satisfactory	60 (38.46)	55 (44.35)	115 (41.07)
b.	Unsatisfactory	30 (19.23)	30 (24.20)	60 (21.43)
c.	Undecided	66 (42.31)	39 (31.45)	105 (37.50)

Figures in Parenthesis indicates percentage

The table 6.31 revealed that 38.46 percent households from adopted villages and 44.35 percent households from non-adopted villages opined that their status of saving was satisfactory over the total income. 19.23 percent households from adopted villages and 24.20 percent households from non-adopted villages were of the opinion that their saving was unsatisfactory because their income was not sufficient to meet their needs. However, 42.31 percent households from adopted villages and 31.45 percent households from non-adopted villages remained undecided.

Poverty is one of the foremost social problems facing India and other countries. Poverty is a condition in which a person fails to maintain a living standard adequate for his physical and mental efficiency. According to Goodhard, "Poverty is insufficient supply of those things which are requisite for an individual to maintain himself and that dependant upon him in health and vigour". In other words, poverty is defined as a condition in which a person because of either inadequate income or other expenditure does not maintain a scale of living high enough to provide for his physical and mental efficiency. There may be different reasons for poverty like illiteracy, lack of developed technology, exploitation, lack of proper marketing and lack of proper communication.

Table 6.32 Showing an Opinion on: "You are living above poverty line?"

N= 280, AH= 156, NAH= 124

Sr. No.	Particulars	Selected Rural Households		Sample Average for both the groups
		Adopted Villages	Non-adopted	
1	Total No. of Samples	156(100.00)	124(100.00)	280(100.00)
2	Agree	90(57.69)	30(24.19)	120(42.86)
3	Disagree	60(38.46)	90(72.58)	150(53.57)
4	Undecided	6(3.85)	4(3.23)	10(3.57)

Figures in Parenthesis indicates percentage

Table 6.32 showed that 57.69 percent households from adopted villages and 24.19 percent households from non-adopted villages opined that Khasis in the rural areas were living above poverty line in the study area. However, 38.46 percent households from adopted villages and 72.58 percent households from non-adopted villages were of the opinion that Khasis were living below poverty line in the study area. Only a small number of households did not express their opinions.

(8) Cultural Change

The second hypothesis is that the Ramakrishna Mission in Khasi society has brought about a cultural change. Science, education, modernisation, inculturation and other forces have brought about changes at the periphery.[69] The change has made its impact on various spheres of cultural life of the Khasis. It is believed that Khasi culture has been influenced by different cultural and religious elements. The cultural change has also taken place due to the exposure of the Khasi society to contact from outside.[70] After the pre-colonial period, Christian missionaries have worked

---

[69] K.P. Bahadur, *Caste, Tribes and Culture of India*, Delhi, 1977, Preface.

[70] M.P.R. Lyngdoh, "Inheritance, Property and Entrepreneurship in the Khasi Society," *The Dynamics of Family System in a Matriliny of Meghalaya*, (Shillong: Directorate of Printing & Stationary, 1999), 20.

among the Khasis to bring about a change in their cultural life.[71] For instance, with the coming of the British Administration, iron smelting on which thousands of families gained their livelihood received a death-blow, and with it went the skills and many Khasi families out-turned in goods and implementation of various kinds. Weaving has diminished in many places. Gold washing, excavation of copper, silver and precious metals went to extinction. It was believed that the new contacts with outsiders did contribute to bring about changes when Shillong became the capital of Assam.[72]

Just as culture influences education, in the same way education also exerts its powerful influence upon the culture of a community. The function of education not only preserve and transmit the culture of society, but it also brings about the needed and desirable changes in the cultural ideals and values for the progress and continued development of society, without which social progress will stratify and come to naught.[73] This cultural awakening found expression through a literary movement initiated by U Babu Jeebon Roy who was influenced by Bramo Samaj and the Ramakrishna Mission. Both the Ramakrishna Mission and the Brahmo Samaj were against conversion to Christianity, and the deterioration of Khasi culture and religion. Through education, they made the Khasis aware of their cultural values.[74]

The Ramakrishna Mission has been active from the very beginning of its ministry in strengthening the traditional Khasi culture. It has been working to bring awakening among the traditional Khasis through the Seng Khasi Organisation since the traditional Khasi culture was influenced by the western cultural

---

[71] Mary Pristilla Rina Lyngdoh, *The Festivals in the History and Culture of the Khasi*, op.cit., 38.

[72] H.G. Joshi, *Meghalaya: Past and Present*, op.cit., 214-215; see also Lynne G. Duncan & Phillip H.K. Seymour, "Socio-Economic Differences in Foundation-Level Literacy," *British Journal of Psychology*, Vol. 91, Part I, February 2000, 145-165.

[73] Yogendra K. Sharma, *Sociological Philosophy of Education*, (New Delhi: Kanishka Publishers, 2003), 229.

[74] Personal interview with Khasi Youth Group at Sohbhar on 23.4.2005.

norms through the Christian missionaries. The Ramakrishna Mission has been successful to some extent in protecting the traditional Khasi culture from further deterioration through education. This may include change in cultural traits, habits, worldview and some values.[75] Through the awareness by the Ramakrishna Mission, the traditional Khasis have realised the importance of their old cultural values. The Government of Meghalaya has established a new department known as the Art and Culture Department at State level. It organises cultural programmes at State level to encourage the Khasis to learn the values of their traditional culture. The cultural functions were organised by the Ramakrishna Mission to preserve their artistic life and ancient culture. Music, dance, architecture, festivals and environmental issues were given importance by the Ramakrishna Mission.[76] Through the awareness given by the Ramakrishna Mission in the said district, the Seng Khasis have felt that their traditional religion, culture and social life would be in danger, if they are not protected from western influence. Education imparted by the Ramakrishna Mission to the Khasis has proved to be a veritable boon to them in many ways.[77] The following section deals with the changes through the Ramakrishna Mission in different Khasi cultural aspects.

(a) Change in Traditions, Customs and Festivals

According to Oxford Dictionary of Sociology (1994), "Customs are established by ways of thinking and acting in societies." It refers both to the routines of daily life and to the distinctive features which mark off one culture from another. Traditions and customs of a society control the whole life of the society. Each society has customs and traditions. Even celebrations of the traditional festivals were encouraged by the Ramakrishna Mission in the study area. The Ramakrishna Mission has been instrumental in encouraging the Seng Khasi Organisation to give importance to the celebration of the Khasi festivals and maintain their traditional customs and religious traditions. Today the Khasi

---

[75] Personal interview with a group of Traditional Khasis at Cherrapunji on 24.5.2006.
[76] Personal interview with J.D. Kynta at Mylliem on 20.4.2005.
[77] H.G. Joshi, *Meghalaya: Past and Present*, op.cit., 218.

festivals are celebrated all over the state. The Art and Culture Directorate has been established at state level. Table 6.33 shows the opinions of the households in the adopted and non-adopted villages.

Table 6.33 Showing Opinion on: "Impact of Ramakrishna Mission is seen on the observing of the Khasi festivals."

N=280, AH= 156, NAH= 124

Sr. No.	Particulars	Selected Rural Households		Sample Average for both the groups
		Adopted Villages	Non-adopted	
1.	Total No. of Samples	156(100.00)	124(100.00)	280(100.00)
2.	Yes	76(48.72)	30(24.19)	106(37.86)
3.	No	74(47.43)	90(72.58)	164(58.57)
4.	I do not know	6(3.85)	4(3.23)	10(3.57)

Table 6.33 indicates that 48.72 percent households from adopted villages and 24.19 percent households from non-adopted villages opined that there is an impact of the Ramakrishna Mission on the Khasi festival celebration and traditions. However, 47.43 percent households from adopted villages and 72.58 percent households from non-adopted villages were of the opinion that the impact of the Ramakrishna Mission is not found on the celebration of the traditional festivals and observing traditions. Only 3.85 percent households from adopted villages and 3.23 percent households from non-adopted villages did not express their opinions.

(b) Change in the use of Scientific Technology

The term technology is used to mean technical means and skills characteristic of a particular civilisation, community or period. Technology is a body of systematic knowledge through which man sets the facility of using machines and tools in industry. Through technology, man can acquire supremacy over nature. Technology and society are inter-linked. Social structure and its relationship also changes with the development in technology. Through technological use agriculture was commercialised and it affected farmers and labour relations making them market related. Technology is the basic input in the process of development. Resources are converted into useful and consumable products with the technologies. In the rural areas of the East Khasi Hills District old methods of cultivation are still used. However, some farmers used developed seeds and modern technologies. The Ramakrishna Mission does not have any impact on the use of technology.

Table 6.34 Showing attitude on: "Do you agree that Khasis use scientific technologies in Productive Sector?"

N=280, AH= 156, NAH= 124

Sr. No.	Particulars Villages	Selected Rural Households		Sample Average for both
		Adopted	Non-adopted the groups	
1.	Total No. of Samples	156(100.00)	124(100.00)	280(100.00)
a.	Agree	40(25.64)	20(16.13)	60(21.43)
b.	Disagree	110(70.51)	100(80.64)	210(75.00)
c.	Undecided	6(3.85)	4(3.23)	10(3.57)

Table 6.34 indicated that 25.64 percent households from adopted villages and 16.13 percent households from non-adopted villages opined that they have been using scientific technologies in productive sector. However, 70.51 percent households from adopted villages and 80.64 percent households from non-adopted villages were of the opinion that they did not use scientific technology in productive sector. 3.85 percent households from adopted villages and 3.23 percent households from non-adopted villages did not express their opinion.

(c) Change in the Food Habits and Traditional Ornaments

The Khasis through education, modernisation and mass communication have been brought to a world of modern civilisation. The process of modernisation may take various ways. Some traditions undergo change and some of them indeed may help in the process of modernisation to carry forward the past traditions and bring about a new pattern and a fresh combination.[78]

---

[78] M.P.R. Lyngdoh, *The Festivals in the History and Culture of the Khasi*, 181.

It was felt that education was the main tool to change their way of living and food habits. Modern dietary supplemented indigenous habits of eating. Change in dietary has become applicable in which besides relishing their traditional food, new methods of cooking, frying and preparations of meal in combination with other condiments have become perceptible. Food like eggs, chicken and milk that was previously rejected now has begun to be eaten. The missionaries were particularly concerned that the old taboos like drinking of milk should be removed in the interest of people's health. New healthful food items like cauliflower and tea have replaced beer. There are tea-stalls and restaurants where indigenous cakes and meals are catered.[79]

Moreover, interaction between the tribal and non-tribal society eventually leads to the borrowing and assimilation of each other's mode of living. Today many Khasis take different types of items prepared by non-tribals. There is a process of indigenisation and integration with the rest of the country. It seems that a change has taken place in the food habits of the Khasis through the non-Khasis and the Ramakrishna Mission coming from outside Meghalaya. Their presence in the study area seems to have some influence on the food habits of the Khasis.[80]

6.35 Showing opinions on: "A Change has taken place in Khasi Way of Living and Food Habits through the Ramakrishna Mission."

N=248,AH=156,NAH=124

Sr. No.	Particulars	Selected Rural Households		Sample Average for both the groups
		Adopted Villages	Non-adopted	
1	Total No. of Households	156(100.00)	124(100.00)	280(100.0)
a	Agree	50(32.05)	15(12.10)	65(23.21)
b	Disagree	100(64.10)	101(81.45)	201(71.79)
c	Undecided	06(3.85)	08 (6.45)	14(5.00)

Figures in parentheses indicates percentage

---

[79] H.G. Joshi, *Meghalaya: Past and Present, op.cit.,* 219.
[80] *Ibid.*

Table 6.35 revealed that 32.05 percent households from adopted villages and 12.10 percent households from non-adopted villages opined that a change has taken place in the Khasi way of living and food habits through the Ramakrishna Mission. However, 64.10 percent households from adopted villages and 81.45 percent households from non-adopted villages were of the opinion that no change has taken place in Khasi way of living and food habits through the Ramakrishna Mission. This change has not happened through the Ramakrishna Mission alone. Modernisation, westernisation and their contact with outsiders have also played an important role. 3.85 percent households from adopted villages and 6.45 percent households from non-adopted villages did not express their opinions. The data shows that the Ramakrishna Mission has also influenced the Khasi way of living and food habits to some extent.

(d) Change in House Models

A change in the house model has become noticeable in the towns and advance villages, which has largely resulted from the widespread use of new building incentives. The very concept of housing and living changed on account of the influence of Christian missionaries. The change in the economic status has also changed the Khasi house style. Earlier, the houses were oval-shaped, low and thatch-roofed, without ventilation and windows, which made the inside of the house dark. Houses with stilt, lime-washed walls and corrugated iron for roofs replaced the old houses built of wood, stone and plank and thatched with straw. Advancement in mechanical skill has caused abandonment of important traditional carpenter's tools and instruments connected with masonry, iron smelting and stone erecting. It has brought about the use of modern tools and equipments.[81] Thus, hundreds of modern types of houses had not only been constructed but the techniques were quickly spread into the nearby villages from Shillong. Some people combined traditional and modern models. The quality of house environment has an important bearing on their quality of life. But the house condition in the non-adopted villages is still poor.

---

[81] *Ibid.,* 215.

The change in communication and scientific education, economic condition, thinking, standard of living and occupations have changed the lot of the people. Similarly, the value of local ceramics, wood and bamboo arts, crafts and furniture has diminished with the coming of the cooking utensils, vessels, cups, mugs, jugs, bowls, trays as well as raincoats, curtains, carpets, dressing tables and many more household items.[82]

The very concept of housing changed because of the influence of income. Owing to the influence from outsiders like that of the Ramakrishna Mission and Christianity in the study area, many families have realised the importance of latrine and proper drainage. For the first time, not utility alone but beauty too became the criterion for a house. Windows made more light and air possible. Domestic animals are now kept in one corner of the compound.[83] An elementary system of sewage has been introduced to drain away the waste. The influence was also seen in the equipment that furnished the house. Some Khasis combined traditional and modern models. The British missionaries did not emphasise the concrete buildings and gave importance to the Assam type houses with modern facilities due to the earthquakes.

There are still thatched houses seen in the non-adopted villages due to poverty, lack of proper communication and illiteracy. Villages and houses facing the East are still considered lucky. In the non-adopted villages, 50 percent of families were without proper latrines. They attend the call of nature outside the village in the fields. It seems a good number of the prevalent diseases like diarrhoea; dysentery, worm, stomach problems, skin disorder and urinary tract infection among the Khasis of the non-adopted villages originate from unhygienic living conditions, poor environmental sanitation, lack of proper personal cleanliness and lack of a balanced diet. Moreover, due to illiteracy and poverty they do not care even for proper drainage and latrines.[84] Another reason for different diseases is the impure and contaminated

---

[82] *Ibid*, 214.
[83] Nalini Natarajan, The Missionary among the Khasis, 131.
[84] Personal interview with the village heads of the non-adopted villages at Umkhabaw on 26.4.2005.

drinking water, poor lightening in the houses, too much smoke in the crowded houses and poor ventilation.

The Ramakrishna Mission organised special programmes to make the rural Khasis aware about the importance of latrines, sewage and boiled water for drinking to avoid diseases. The impact of their work is seen on some families in the adopted villages and very less in the non-adopted villages. Church has brought more impact on the Khasi society. Moreover, household goods and furniture equipped in the houses of household respondents in the adopted families was much better than the furniture and other goods of households' respondents in the non-adopted villages. There were wooden or iron beds, cupboards, chairs, almirahs, sofas, TV, fan, refrigerator and dining tables in the houses of the respondents of the adopted villages. The kitchen had utensils, crockery, cutlery and other vessels and spoons commonly used by the households in the adopted villages. The quality of such goods was not found in the non-adopted villages.

Earlier ceremonies connected with house building were observed both by rural and urban Khasis. Now only traditional Khasis observe these ceremonies. Even divination is practiced by traditional Khasis to select the site for a house construction. The Ramakrishna Mission encouraged the traditional Khasis to follow their traditional religious practices to select a place for house construction. The effect of the Ramakrishna Mission concerning divination and religious ceremony was seen among the traditional Khasis in the adopted and non-adopted villages to some extent.[85] But majority of the Khasis do not follow the rites related to the construction of the house.

In 2001 the road facility was available to 38.33 percent of the villages. According to Government Office Record of 2007-08, a considerable increase was also seen in the number of *pucca* roads and *pucca* houses. The *pucca* road facility had reached to 85 percent of the village areas by 2007-08. *Pucca* roads were there, which were in bad condition due to heavy rainfall.[86] But where

---

[85] Nalini Natarajan, *The Missionary among the Khasis*, 130-132.
[86] Personal interview with the village heads of Umkhabaw village on 23.2.2005 at Shella.

the Ramakrishna Mission has reached the road condition has improved a great deal.

In 2001 only 38.65 percent of the houses had been electrified in the non-adopted villages. According to the Shella-Bholaganj Block Office Record, out of 137 villages 87 villages were electrified and 50 villages were without the supply of electricity. In 2007-08 about 5,548(78 percent) houses were electrified in Shella-Bholaganj Block. In the East Khasi Hills District in 2007-08, only 95 percent villages enjoyed the electricity facility.

Table 6.36 Showing opinion on: "A Change has taken place in Khasi House Style through the Ramakrishna Mission."

N= 280, AH= 156, NAH= 124

Sr. No.	Particulars	Selected Rural Households		Sample Average for both the groups
		Adopted Villages	Non-adopted	
1	Total No. of Households	156(100.00)	124(100.00)	280(100.00)
a	Agree	30(19.23)	20(16.13)	50(17.86)
b	Disagree	126(80.77)	100(80.65)	226(80.71)
c	Undecided	Nil	04(3.22)	4(1.43)

Figures in parentheses indicates percentage

Data in table 6.36 showed that a change has taken place in the Khasi house style in the adopted and non-adopted villages. The difference in their house style was due to their economic condition. The Ramakrishna Mission was also the contributor to their income through education and training programmes. From the field study, it was found that 19.23 percent households from adopted villages and 16.13 percent households from non-adopted villages opined that a change has taken place in Khasi house style. However, 80.77 percent households from adopted villages and 80.65 percent respondents from non-adopted villages did not agree to the change being brought about by the Mission in Khasi house style. As the income has increased so the house standard has also gone up. The low-income families in the non-adopted villages do not have a proper electricity facility, good furniture, proper bath-room and drainage system in their houses because they cannot afford them due to poverty. They do not even have a proper place for keeping the cattle. The pigs also pass stool nearby the houses, which causes many diseases. Moreover, the quality of the *kacha* houses in the adopted villages was far better than that of *kacha* houses in the non-adopted villages.

(e) Change in Khasi Music and Musical Instruments

It is generally believed that over the years traditional music has undergone change. Folk music with rural roots grew branches over urban areas.[87] The musical mind of the Khasis is also seen in their ingenuity to create musical instruments that are unique and original. The impact of Christian missionaries was seen on the Khasi music and musical instruments. The traditional music and original musical instruments used earlier in performing rites, rituals and dances were about to be out of use except in the deep interior villages. The Christian missionaries produced translation of western hymns in the Khasi language. Due to the western influence, the Khasi original songs and music started disappearing very fast.

With the influence of the outsiders like Ramakrishna Mission after 2001, the Khasis have started realising the importance of the traditional Khasi music, musical instruments and dances. There are some musical schools run by the Mission, which teach Khasi folk-songs and encourages them to use their traditional musical instruments. Some Khasis, under the influence of the Ramakrishna Mission, have already picked up the indigenous music and the importance of indigenous musical instruments and dance. The Catholic Church has also given importance to the indigenous music and musical instruments in the church. A new class of modern Khasi songs blending indigenous notes and the harmony of western music is getting popular in towns and advance villages. Devotional songs were sung at prayer meetings at Shella, Sohbhar, Ishamati, Cherrapunji and Laitryngew.[88]

---

[87] Dr. Hamlet Bareh, *The History and Culture of the Khasi People*, op.cit., 316-17
[88] Personal interview with H. Livingstone Marbaniang at Sorah on 26.4.2006.

Khasi folk songs and community singing are still heard in the rural areas. Many Khasis of the Shella-Bholaganj Block opined that the Ramakrishna Mission encourages the young Khasis to use their indigenous musical instruments and traditional music. Some outsiders who are related to the Ramakrishna Mission in Meghalaya have also encouraged the Khasis to use indigenous musical instruments like drums, duitara, and Khasi traditional music. Through encouragement by the Ramakrishna Mission and the church to some extent, the young Khasis have realised the importance of traditional musical instruments and traditional songs. This impact of indigenous instruments is seen not only on the traditional Khasis but on Khasi Christians also. Today many Khasi youth use Khasi musical instruments even in the churches. Earlier the traditional musical instruments were not encouraged in the Church.

Table 6.37 Showing opinion on: "A Change has taken place in Khasi Music & Musical Instruments"

N= 280, AH= 156, NAH= 124

Sr. No.	Particulars	Selected Rural Households		Sample Average for both the groups
		Adopted Villages	Non-adopted	
1	Total No. of Households	156(100.00)	124(100.00)	280(100.00)
a	Agree	50(32.05)	30(24.19)	80(28.57)
b	Disagree	100 (64.10)	90(72.58)	190(67.86)
c	Undecided	6(3.85)	4(3.23)	10(3.57)

Figures in parentheses indicates percentage

The data in table 6.37 indicated that the Ramakrishna Mission has brought about a little change in the Khasi indigenous music and musical instruments in the study area. 32.05 percent households from adopted villages and 24.19 percent households from non-adopted villages opined that a change has taken place in Khasi music and musical instruments through the Ramakrishna Mission. Likewise 64.10 percent households from adopted villages and 72.58 percent households from non-adopted villages opined that the Ramakrishna Mission has brought no change in the Khasi traditional music and musical instruments. The data showed that a good number of respondents from adopted and non-adopted villages did agree to the change being brought about by the Ramakrishna Mission.

(f) Change in Sports

Today both rural and urban Khasis play various indoor and outdoor games. Archery competition is still practiced. Archery still ranks as a community game. New games have been developed. Advancement in games is due to encouragement by the state and Central Government. The Ramakrishna Mission does encourage games in the schools run by it. The Ramakrishna Mission does contribute to the development of games in the district as table 6.38 indicates.

6.38 Sowing opinion on: "A Change has taken place in Khasi Sports."

N= 280, AH= 156, NAH= 124

Sr. No.	Particulars	Selected Rural Households		Sample Average for both the groups
		Adopted Villages	Non-adopted	
1	Total No. of Households	156(100.00)	124(100.00)	280(100.oo)
a	Agree	58(37.18)	35(28.23)	93(33.21)
b	Disagree	91(58.33)	84(67.74)	175(62.5)
c	Undecided	7(04.49)	5(04.03)	12(04.29)

Figures in parentheses indicates percentage

Table 6.38 shows that 37.18 percent households from the adopted villages and 28.23 percent households from the non-adopted villages opined that a change has taken place in Khasi sports through the Ramakrishna Mission. However, 58.33 percent households from adopted villages and 67.74 percent households from the non-adopted villages believed that no change has taken place in Khasi sports through the Ramakrishna Mission. The State Government spends a huge amount on sports to encourage the youth for sports in schools and colleges. Even Christian missionary schools have contributed to Khasi sports in the district. Sport is compulsory in all schools and colleges. The Ramakrishna Mission has also contributed to develop the Khasi sports in the

SOCIO-CULTURAL AND RELIGIOUS CHANGES 271

East Khasi Hills District as the data indicated. The Ramakrishna Mission like other schools emphasises games along with academic courses in 58 schools it has been running in the district.

(g) Change in the Habit of chewing Betel-nut

Kwai or betel-nut is still consumed largely not only as means of entertainment but as a socially cultivated habit. Both Christians and traditional Khasis chew it. They find it difficult to give up chewing betel-nut because it has become a part of their life except some Christians. No religious or social function was complete without it. Even labourers also expected betel-nut in addition to their wages. The traditional Khasis believe that women in the Khasi traditional religion put betel-nut in their husbands' mouths as a last rite. Moreover, the Khasi traditional religion teaches that betel-nut will be served even in the house of God (heaven). Betel-nut is used at social and cultural gatherings of the Khasis. Some young Khasis both Christians and non-Christians have given up chewing betel-nut.

6.39 Showing attitudes on "A change has taken place in Khasi Chewing Betel-nut through Ramakrishna Mission"

N= 280, AH= 156, NAH= 124

Sr. No.	Particulars	Selected Rural Households		Sample Average for both the groups
		Adopted Villages	Non-adopted	
1	Total No. Of Households	156(100.00)	124(100.00)	280(100.00)
a	Agree	25(16.02)	15(12.10)	40(14.29)
b	Disagree	123(78.85)	107(86.29)	230(82.14)
c	Undecided	8(5.13)	2(01.61)	10(03.57)

Figures in parentheses indicates percentage

Table 6.39 showed that those young people who have studied in the Ramakrishna Mission Schools have given up the habit of chewing betel-nut. However, this impact was on a small portion of the Khasi youth. The majority of the Khasis still chew betel-nut. The data indicated that 16.02 percent households from adopted villages and 12.10 percent households from non-adopted villages opined that a little change has taken place in Khasi habit of chewing betel-nut in the study area through the Ramakrishna Mission. However, 78.85 percent households from adopted villages and 86.29 percent households from non-adopted villages opined that no change has taken place in the habit of chewing betel-nut of the Khasi society through the Ramakrishna Mission. Only 5.13 percent households from adopted villages and 1.61 percent households from non-adopted villages did not express their opinions.

The study showed that only some Khasis who have their education from the Ramakrishna Mission schools were influenced by the teachings of the Mission. Even Christian church also does not encourage the use of betel-nut. But the majority of Khasi families in the district continue taking betel-nut. The Ramakrishna Mission and the church should be praised for the attempts they have been making to bring about a change in the usual habits of chewing betel-nut which is very expensive and at the same time dangerous for the individual and family health because lime and tobacco cause cancer.

(h) Change in the Habit of Alcohol Use

Alcohol is a powerful stimulant, and in some diluted form is used as an intoxicating beverage among all races and conditions of people. Alcohol represents such drinks as beer, wine, brandy, whisky, rum, country liquor, etc. Alcohol is proving to be a grave social problem in East Khasi Hills District as the use of wine is increasing. Alcohol addiction is harmful not only for the individuals but also for the families and the society. It is unlikely that this is entirely due to a feeling of frustration induced by poverty because many who are well-to-do are among the victims.[89]

The World Health Organisation Expert Committee defines, "Alcohol addiction as a state of periodic or chronic intoxication, detrimental to the individual and to society, produced by repeated consumption of a drug either natural or synthetic. Its characteristics include: i) an overpowering desire or need to continue taking wine and to obtain it by any means; ii) a tendency to increase the dose; and iii) a psychological and sometimes a physical dependence on the effects of the wine.[90]

---

[89] *Meghalaya District Gazetteers: Khasi Hills District*, ed. by I.M. Simon, 1991, 57.
[90] K.Mitra, "Drug Addiction in India," *Social Welfare in India*, 1960,149.

Wine is still served in some special social and religious gatherings of the traditional Khasis. The influence of culture is very great in the causation of use of wine and alcohol. It has been openly sold in the market. The State Government has not put any ban on it. Moreover, many young and old people also use the local made wine. Although crimes have been part of every civilisation yet its types, incidents, prevention and treatment varies from time to time. The use of wine among the Khasis is found among all age groups in general and in the age group of 16-35 in particular.

Though the Ramakrishna teaches against the use of wine yet no particular change is seen both in individual and society. Only some Khasis who have got their education from the Mission schools witnessed that they have given up wine. They were taught in the Ramakrishna Mission schools to refrain from wine.

Table 6.40 Showing attitude on: "A Change has taken place in the use of wine through the Ramakrishna Mission in the study area"

N= 280, AH= 156, NAH= 124

Sr. No.	Particulars	Selected Rural Households		Sample Average for both the groups
		Adopted Villages	Non-adopted	
1	Total No. of Households	156(100.00)	124(100.00)	280(100.00)
a	Agree	20 (12.82)	10(8.06)	30(10.71)
b	Disagree	130(83.33)	110(88.71)	240(85.72)
c	Undecided	6(3.85)	4(3.23)	10(3.57)

Figures in parentheses indicate percentage

Table 6.40 shows those 12.82 percent households from adopted villages and 8.06 percent households from non-adopted villages opined that the Ramakrishna Mission has brought about a little change in Khasi habit of drinking wine in the study area. The church has been working against the use of wine. However, 83.33 percent households from adopted villages and 88.71 percent households from non-adopted villages opined that the Ramakrishna Mission has brought about no change in the Khasi habit of drinking wine. Nevertheless, the young and small in the non-adopted villages were influenced by the use of wine. The use of local wine is still prevalent in the non-adopted villages due to the lack of education and traditional religious influence. From the field study, it was also found that youth that are more Christian were in the habit of taking wine than non-Christian youth. It showed that there was the impact of modernisation and media on the Khasi Christian and non-Christian youths.

(i) Change in hunting practice

To a certain extent, most of the primitive tribal groups of India often practiced hunting. In olden days, the Khasis used to understand the language of the animals and birds since they lived in the midst of nature and they felt one with their natural environment. The love and respect which the Khasis had for nature have made them look at everything as sacred.[91] The impact was also seen on the non-adopted villages though it was much less. The Khasis practiced hunting in the pre-Christian missionary era. It has been stopped in the towns and in the advanced villages but not in the interior villages of the district. Due to hunting, great varieties of birds and animals have also disappeared. Some Khasis in the non-adopted villages still practice hunting. The majority of the youth do not have the knowledge of old legends and folktales connected with nature. The young Khasi generation do not have the knowledge of the cultural heritage and their relationship with nature. Moreover, only a small area of forest land has been under the control of the State Government. Thus, people have the liberty to have free access to the forest. Some of the beautiful species of birds, found in the forest are: horn-bills, peacocks, fowls, quails, spot-bills, cotton teals, geese, ducks, and so on. Now due to education, many Khasis in the rural areas have also given up hunting. The Ramakrishna Mission conducts seminars and essay competitions in schools, colleges and university. Even the Christian Church has concern for the hunting practice. Even in the church, seminars on the ecological crisis are conducted to bring awareness among the Khasis. However, many educated young people who have studied in the Ramakrishna

---

[91] Barnes L. Mawrie, The Khasis and their Natural Environment, *op.cit.,* 142

Mission schools or are directly linked with it, do not practice hunting. It shows the impact of the Ramakrishna Mission on the hunting practices on some Khasi families.

Table 6.41 Showing opinion on: "A change has taken place in Khasi Hunting Practice through the Ramakrishna Mission in the study area."

N= 280, AH= 156, NAH= 124

Sr. No.	Particulars	Selected Rural Households		Sample Average for both the groups
		Adopted Villages	Non-adopted	
1	Total No. of Households	156(100.00)	124(100.00)	280(100.00)
a	Agree	20(12.82)	10 (8.07)	30 (10.71)
b	Disagree	130(83.33)	110(88.71)	240 (85.71)
c	Undecided	6(3.85)	4 (3.22)	10 (3.57)

Figures in parentheses indicates percentage

Table 6.41 clearly reveals that 12.82 percent households from adopted villages and 8.07 percent households from non-adopted villages opined that a change has taken place in the hunting practice of the Khasis through the Ramakrishna Mission in the study area. Likewise, 83.33 percent households from adopted villages and 88.71 percent households from non-adopted villages opined that no change has taken place in Khasi hunting practice through the Ramakrishna Mission. Many rural Khasis still practice hunting. 3.85 percent households from adopted villages and 3.22 percent households from non-adopted villages did not express their opinions. Those households who said that a change has taken place in Khasi hunting practice are those who have given up hunting practice after getting education from the Ramakrishna Mission schools. They said that they feel pity for the animals and birds. More Khasis are realising about the importance of birds and animals. It seems that the Ramakrishna Mission continue to influence the minds of the young Khasis in this regard. The impact of the Ramakrishna Mission on the hunting practice of the people in the study area is very minor. Christian Church also conducts seminars and educate its members.

(j) Change in Khasi Attitude towards Deforestation

The Forest is one of the valuable resources of the district as far as the life of the tribal people is concerned. The total area under forest in the district was 13270 Sq. Kms. On the other hand, the reserved forest area of the district was 155.40 Sq. Kms. Forests were considered the abode of gods and goddesses. They were protected and preserved through a religious taboo. The ethics of management of these forests lies upon self-restraint and fear and respect for gods. The people were scared of disturbing the sanctity of these forests in order to avoid any displeasing to gods and goddesses. However, today the sense of fear among the Khasis seems to be on decline. Only 8.5% of the total forest area is under direct control of the State Government. Even the clan forests have been destroyed since many so-called educated youth have started showing rebellion against the authority of the elders. There is a change in the attitude of the present generation due to their exposure and contact with the outer world.[92]

The institution of village forests has been in existence since time immemorial. The forests were left to be looked after and managed by the *village Durbar*. Today it is disappointing to note that excepting a few, many of such forests have been ruined beyond repair. With the opening of a network of roads and with the boom in the timber market it is sad to say that these forests have been over exploited often with the sanction and approval of the village headmen who wanted the money.[93]

Moreover, every two or three years a fresh plot is to be prepared for *jhum cultivation*. This is the most widely practised way of cultivation in the East Khasi Hills District. This method, although a traditional way of cultivation, is detrimental to ecology. Forest is a very important component of the environment. Deforestation is causing great social imbalance and ethnic problems in rural areas. From an ecological point of view deforestation increases environmental deterioration, recycling of nutrients, and increases surface run-off, nutrient leaching and

---

[92] Krishan Kumar Gaur, "Traditional Management System of Forests in Meghalaya: Some Reflections," *Environment Forest and Tribes*, ed. by Ramesh Chandra, (New Delhi: Himanshu Publications, 2000), 156-159.

[93] *Ibid.*, 130-31

soil erosion because tree roots and stems impede these processes. It causes a great soil loss from forest. It is a carbon-dioxide sink and an oxygen bank. The loss of green plants causes an imbalance in the Oxygen-Carbon Dioxide ratio that brings about health hazards to every form of life. It is the habitat of flora and fauna and protects genetic diversity.[94]

The Central Government has certain amounts reserved for the development of the tribal areas in India in general and in North East India in particular. The developmental programme aims at bringing about ecological balance in these areas by checking further desertification through a forestation water-harvesting measures, and agriculture, besides providing employment opportunities to the tribal areas in general and to the Khasis in particular.[95]

Most of the villagers in the adopted and non-adopted villages depend on forest for timber, bamboo, wooden poles and thatching leaves. The growth of the timber industry is also responsible for the indiscriminate felling of trees. It is estimated that between April 1994 and 1995 about 25,772 timber trucks passed the Byrnihat Check Gate.[96] Daily 100 trucks carry the timber from the forest of the East Khasi Hills District to other parts of the country. Due to the uncontrolled consumerist attitude of the Khasis and outsiders towards forest, thousands of trees are being cut down every day in the East Khasi Hills District.[97] Besides this, cutting of trees is done in the most unscientific manner sometimes even tender trees are not spared.

Another traditional occupation prevalent among the Khasis is the burning of wood for charcoal. In many of the interior villages of the East Khasi Hills District we can see the alarming depletion of forests. While the timber industry has been checked, the charcoal industry is still rampant. Only a few Khasi families

---

[94] R.K. Jha, *Deforestation and Village Life*, (New Delhi: Mittal Publications, 1999), 125.
[95] M.L. Kapur, "A Profile of Tribals in Himachal Pradesh," *The Tribal Development Administration in India*, ed. (New Delhi: Mittal Publications, 1994), 117.
[96] K.N. Kumar, *Youth and Environment* (An unpublished paper delivered at the Regional Consultation on Youth Ministry in North East India on 18-22 April, 1995), 10.
[97] Barnes L. Mawrie, The Khasis and their Natural Environment, *op.cit.*, 164.

are earning their livelihood by selling charcoal from the forest. They cut down many trees daily to make charcoal. In many of the non-adopted villages of the district, charcoal industry is still rampant. Fuel wood has been used for cooking, warming and lightening. The use of kerosene oil in the rural villages is common. Nevertheless, due to the non-availability of kerosene and electricity many Khasi families still use wood. Deforestation also isolates the rural Khasis from the natural environment and leads to the loss of important cultural, ethical and historical resources.

Table 6.42 Showing attitude on "A Change has taken place in Deforestation in East Khasi Hills District through Ramakrishna Mission in the study area."

N= 280, AH= 156, NAH= 124

Sr. No.	Particulars	Selected Rural Households		Sample Average for both the groups
		Adopted Villages	Non-adopted	
1.	Total No. of Households	156(100.00)	124(100.00)	280(100.00)
a.	Agree	40(25.64)	10(8.06)	50(17.86)
b.	Disagree	110(70.51)	110(88.71)	220(78.57)
c.	Undecided	6 (3.85)	4(3.23)	10 (3.57)

Figures in parentheses indicates percentage

Table 6.42 revealed that the Ramakrishna Mission in the Khasi attitude towards deforestation has brought about a change. 25.64 percent households from adopted villages and 8.06 percent households from non-adopted villages opined that the Ramakrishna Mission has brought about a change in the Khasi attitude towards deforestation in the study area. However, 70.51 percent households from adopted villages and 88.71 percent households from non-adopted villages believed that no change has taken place in the Khasi attitude towards deforestation through the Ramakrishna Mission. The data in the table clearly revealed that the Ramakrishna Mission has not been able to influence the minds of the Khasis in the study area regarding cutting down the trees. Moreover, due to poverty and way of depending on the forest their attitude towards cutting down of trees has not changed much.

9. Religious Change among the Khasis

The Ramakrishna Mission has helped to revive pride of the Khasis in the indigenous religion in the face of increasing Christianisation. As compared to Hinduism, Christianity in the early days appealed to the Khasi mind more as it was practical in approach and its mission better organised. It was also the religion of the rulers. The Khasis were converted to Christianity and as a result, their identity and culture were threatened. The traditional headmen found a threat in the morality that the Christian missionaries preached. Therefore, they opposed religious change. However, education helped the emergence of a new set of leaders. To some extent, Khasi traditional leaders could oppose the Khasi conversion to Christianity. The religion and culture of their neighbours in the East Khasi Hills have made an impact on Khasi religious life since the pre-colonial period and a process of assimilation had actually began in the bordering areas.

Actually, the concept of God, birth, death and rebirth, rites relating to harvest, disposal of dead, and dispelling the evil spirits, and so on, were similar to all aboriginal or indigenous cultures in the greater Indian sub-continent and the Khasis were not an exception. It was quite natural to borrow some religious elements when two different religious communities interact with one another. Due to various reasons, people changed their religion. What followed from this was that with the change of religion, customs, traditions, practices and so on, underwent change. Christian missionaries and other missionaries like that of the Ramakrishna Mission brought about changes at the core of religious life. The leaders of the Ramakrishna Mission like Ketaki Maharaj, cautioned the Khasis against losing their identity as a race. The Ramakrishna Mission wants them to be progressive, but not at the expense of their fine religious traditions and culture. Through the service and teachings of the Ramakrishna Mission, the Khasis have come to the knowledge of *Vedantic* culture and religion. Through education by the Ramakrishna Mission, there is awakening of the consciousness about the past folk tales, oral traditions and religious mythologies. Many young Khasis, both Christians and non-Christians, have begun to realise the importance of cultural values.

The Ramakrishna Mission along with other religious organisations has been trying to bring religious revival among the traditional Khasis of this district. Some religious meetings were held in the rural areas. This revival was to protect the traditional Khasis from embracing Christianity and realise the importance of their traditional religious elements.[98] Literature has played an important role in bringing revival among the traditional Khasi youth. Now it has been accepted that the Ramakrishna Mission has made impact on the Khasi traditional religious life. It has been able to unite the traditional Khasis by encouraging them to maintain their indigenous faith and their religious life.

Table 6.43 Showing opinions on: "Ramakrishna Mission is encouraging the Traditional Khasis in their Spiritual Life in the study area."

N=280, AH= 156, NAH= 124

Sr. No.	Particulars	Selected Rural Households		Sample Average for both the groups
		Adopted Villages	Non-adopted	
1	Total No. Of Households	156(100.00)	124(100.00)	280(100.00)
a	Agree	90(57.69)	50(40.32)	140(50.00)
b	Disagree	60(38.46)	70(56.45)	130(46.43)
c	Undecided	6 (03.85)	4(03.23)	10 (3.57)

Figures in parentheses indicates percentage

Table 6.43 indicated that 57.69 percent respondents from adopted villages and 40.32 percent respondents from non-adopted villages opined that Ramakrishna Mission has been encouraging the Khasis in their spiritual growth in the study area. However, 38.46 percent respondents from adopted villages and 56.45 percent respondents from non-adopted villages were of the opinion that Ramakrishna Mission has not given any encouragement to the traditional Khasis. The Ramakrishna Mission is rather trying to convert the traditional Khasis to Hindu faith. 3.85 percent households from adopted villages and 3.23

---

[98] Personal interview with a group of Khasis at Shella on 15.5.2007.

percent households from non-adopted villages did not give their opinion on the above statement.

(a) Change in Concept of God

Another phenomenon developed among the rural Khasis of the East Khasi Hills District was the adaptation of Hindu deities. This concept of having many deities under one God was rather an outside influence. Another polytheistic view says that the Khasi traditional religion is a sister religion of the Hindu religion rooted in Indian soil and having similarities in customs and beliefs.[99] Yet, another writer expressed his view that Khasis believe in knowing man, knowing God, but give thanks to God, the mother of God in the image of Kali and Shondi annually. This view tries to compromise and project Khasi religion with Hindu religion.[100]

The Ramakrishna Mission continues to encourage the Khasis to maintain their religious practices. *Ka Lukhmi* or *Ka Leikba* goddess of rice and agriculture, symbolises the wealth and prosperity of the Khasis, and may be identified as the goddess Lakshmi. Again, *u Biskorom* of the Pomblang Nongkrem has been identified as Vishwakarma. The influence of the Ramakrishna Mission is seen on Sobhar, Kalibari, Ishamati, Shella, Sohra, Mawmluh, and Laitryngrew villages.[101]

According to M.P.R. Lyngdoh, the religion and culture of the Hindu neighbours of the plains have made some impact in the pre-colonial period, and a process of assimilation started in the bordering areas.[102] It was noted that owing to the outside influence, Khasi traditional religion has become polytheistic and animistic. Originally, it was monotheistic. In some areas of Shella-Bholaganj Block, some Khasis influenced by Hinduism began to worship *Bishwakarma* and *Synshar*, which were not their deities

---

[99] Personal interview with Miss Bhakti Ksniang at Cherrapunji R.K. Mission School Office on 24.5.2006.
[100] *Khasi Heritage*, Shillong, 1978, 4.
[101] Nalini Natarajan, *The Missionary among the Khasis, op.cit.,* 144.
[102] J.B. Bhattacharjee, "Changing Khasis—A Historical Account," *The Tribes of India*, ed., *op.cit.,* 332.

originally. Some Khasi families have started worshipping Chandi and also have adopted other religious practices. However, they do not call themselves Hindu. The Orthodox Khasis have shown religious tolerance to the Ramakrishna Mission.[103]

Now it is believed that the Ramakrishna Mission has made an impact on the traditional Khasi religious life along with some Christian families in Shella Bholaganj Block. Some Christian Khasis are also interested in Vedantic teachings. The Ramakrishna Mission has influenced many traditional Khasis. However, they do not consider themselves to be Hindus or belonging to the Ramakrishna Mission. Those families influenced by the services and teachings of the Ramakrishna Mission believe that the religious teachings of Khasi traditional religion and that of the Ramakrishna Mission are the same. Moreover, many Khasi families who have received peace of mind through the teachings and service of the Ramakrishna Mission, have taken initiation in the Ramakrishna Mission as the Khasi Christians did by embracing Christianity. It is estimated that about 2000 Khasi families in the study area have been influenced by the Ramakrishna Mission. These families are very close to the Ramakrishna Mission. The Ramakrishna Mission can accommodate and appreciate Khasi traditional religious practices.

Table 6.44 Showing attitude on: "A Change has taken place in the Concept of God of the Traditional Khasis through the Ramakrishna Mission."

N= 280, AH= 156, NAH= 124

Sr. No.	Particulars	Selected Rural Households		Sample Average for both the groups
		Adopted Villages	Non-adopted	
1	Total No. Of Households	156(100.00)	124(100.00)	280(100.00)
a	Agree	58(37.18)	40(32.26)	98(35.00)
b	Disagree	92(58.97)	80(64.52)	172(61.43)
c	Undecided	6(3.85)	4(3.23)	10(3.57)

Figures in parentheses indicates percentage

---

[103] Nalini Natarajan, *The Missionary among the Khasis, op.cit.,* 182.

Table 6.44 showed that 37.18 percent respondents from adopted villages and 32.26 percent respondents from non-adopted villages were of the opinion that a change has been brought about in the concept of God of the traditional Khasis through the teachings of the Ramakrishna Mission. Moreover, 58.97 percent respondents from adopted villages and 64.52 percent respondents from non-adopted villages opined that no change has taken place in the concept of God of the traditional Khasis through the Ramakrishna Mission. The change in the concept of God has occurred in few families in the border areas. The data clearly indicates that a slight change has taken place in the concept of God of the Traditional Khasis and not among Khasi Christians. Khasi Christians still believe that Jesus Christ is the Messiah. They also believe that Father, Son and the Holy Spirit are one God. Khasi Christians do not offer animal sacrifices to God. They do not worship ancestors' spirits. However, 3.85 percent respondents from adopted villages and 3.23 percent respondents from non-adopted villages did not express their opinions.

(b) Funeral Rites and Sacrifices

Many Khasis do not observe funeral ceremonies. Some Khasis keep the bones of the members of their clan in the family cromlech. They believe that funeral ceremonies were very expensive and time consuming. Only rich families can now afford ceremonies like the bone-burial ceremonies or elaborate sacrifices. Some believe that it was the result of Christian influence.[104] Belief in divination had disappeared among almost all Christians and not among all the traditional Khasis. Nevertheless, in rural areas of Shella-Bholaganj Block and in areas around Cherrapunji, people still follow these funeral rites. Christian devotees of the Ramakrishna Mission said that among the traditional Khasis, funeral practices were changing partly due to Christian influence but partly this was due to paucity of funds and changing times. Some traditional Khasis still follow the funeral rites. The Ramakrishna Mission has been active in

---

[104] Personal interview with a group of Seng Khasis at Sohbhar on 26.4.2006.

encouraging the traditional Khasis to maintain their funeral rites, which was found to be successful to some extent among the traditional Khasi religious life. The Ramakrishna Mission has encouraged the traditional Khasis to remain faithful to their religious practices. Funeral ceremonies, ancestor-worship and other animistic celebrations are still practised by some of the traditional Khasis, which shows the impact of the Ramakrishna Mission to some extent

Table 6.45 Showing attitude on: "A Change has taken place in Funeral Rites of the Traditional Khasis through the Ramakrishna Mission."

N= 280, AH= 156, NAH= 124

Sr. No.	Particulars	Selected Rural Households		Sample Average for both the groups
		Adopted Villages	Non-adopted	
1	Total No. Of Households	156(100.00)	124(100.00)	280(100.00)
a	Agree	60(37.03)	40(32.20)	100(35.71)
b	Disagree	90(59.12)	80(64.58)	170(60.72)
c	Undecided	6(3.85)	4(3.22)	10(3.57)

Figures in parentheses indicate percentage

Table 6.45 clearly showed that 37.03 percent respondents from adopted villages and 32.20 percent respondents from non-adopted villages opined that a change has taken place in the religious funeral rites of the traditional Khasi society through the Ramakrishna Mission. However, 59.12 percent households/ respondents from adopted villages and 64.58 percent households/ respondents from non-adopted villages opined that no change in the funeral rites of the traditional Khasis has taken place through the Ramakrishna Mission. Actually, the influence of Christianity has been able to bring about a change in the funeral rites. Many traditional Khasis have given up funeral rites due to the influence of the Christian missionaries. Nevertheless, majority of the traditional Khasis still observe the funeral rites, which was the result of the influence of the teachings and social service of the Ramakrishna Mission to the traditional Khasis. The Ramakrishna Mission has united the traditional Khasis as a traditional religious community to observe the funeral rites practices.

(c) Change in the concept of Sacrifices

In the traditional Khasi religious life, sacrifices to appease the spirits and the Supreme Being have been offered. In the town, this was practised less. However, in the rural areas traditional Khasis still offer sacrifices of animals to appease the spirits. The sacrifices are no more practiced by Khasi Christians. However, in the traditional Khasi religion sacrifices are practiced even today.[105] In the East Khasi Hill District, the Ramakrishna Mission encourages the rural Khasis to maintain the sacrificial practices. The Ramakrishna Mission does not want the traditional Khasis to be converted into Christianity. Due to the encouragement given by the Ramakrishna Mission to the traditional Khasis, they are becoming strong in the traditional faith and continue to maintain sacrifices to the ancestral spirits and sacrifices on behalf of those spirits committed sins (sang).

Table 6.46 Showing attitude on: "A change has taken place in the Practice of Animal Sacrifices through the Ramakrishna Mission in the study area."

N= 280, AH= 156, NAH= 124

Sr. No.	Particulars	Selected Rural Households		Sample Average for both the groups
		Adopted Villages	Non-adopted	
1	Total No. of Households	156(100.00)	124(100.00)	280(100.00)
a	Agree	60(38.46)	45(36.29)	105(37.5)
b	Disagree	89(57.05)	79(63.71)	168(60.0)
c	Undecided	7(4.49)	0(0)	7(02.50)

Figures in parentheses indicate percentage

Table 6.46 shows that 38.46 percent households/respondents from adopted villages and 36.29 percent households/respondents from non-adopted villages were of the opinion that a change has taken place in the animal sacrifice of the traditional Khasis through the Ramakrishna Mission. However, 57.05 percent

---

[105] Personal interview with a group of Khasi Religious Leaders at Ishamati, Sohbhar and Laitryngew on 23.5.2005.

respondents from adopted villages and 63.71 percent respondents from non-adopted villages said that no change has been brought about by the Ramakrishna Mission in the practice of animal sacrifice of the traditional Khasis. They believe that this change is the result of the efforts made by the Seng Khasi Organisation. However, the Ramakrishna Mission encourages the traditional Khasis to continue their sacrificial practices. The data clearly shows that more than half of the respondents from adopted and non-adopted villages have witnessed a change in the practice of animal sacrifice among the traditional Khasis through the Ramakrishna Mission.

(d) Change in the practice of Divination and worship of *thlen*

Many early taboos being practised by the Khasis have died down. The belief in witchcraft and sorcery has not completely died down. The belief in the *Thlen* also vanished considerably among many Orthodox and educated Khasis. The Ramakrishna Mission does not encourage the traditional Khasis to practice magic. The Mission speaks against the magical practices, which harm the society.

It was believed that Khasis and Jaintias used to practice magic in the early days. However, after the arrival of the Gospel many Khasis have given up the magical or *tantric* practices. It is said that majority of the Khasi Christians have almost given up beliefs in superstitions, witchcrafts, taboo, black magic and sorcery. The taboo, against the use of iron delayed the laying down of pipelines for water supply in Orthodox villages, has not been observed anymore.[106] It has also been realised that strict observance of taboo against certain items of food will deprive their children, the sick and the old of nourishment. Some rural and urban traditional Khasis still believe in the power of magic, practice of divination and taboo. Modern systems of education no doubt have broken such traditional biased practices. Other factors have played equally their role in breaking down the old superstitious practices. Some rural Christians and the traditional Khasis still practice divination and believe in the power of magic.

---

[106] Nalini Natarajan, *The Missionary among the Khasis*, 182.

Table 6.47 Showing attitude on "Ramakrishna Mission has worked for the strengthening of the ritual practices."

N= 280, AH= 156, NAH= 124

Sr. No.	Particulars	Selected Rural Households		Sample Average for both the groups
		Adopted Villages	Non-adopted	
1	Total No. Of Households	156(100.00)	124(100.00)	280(100.00)
a	Agree	70(44.87)	40(32.26)	110(39.28)
b	Disagree	80(51.28)	80(64.51)	160(57.14)
c	Undecided	6 (3.85)	4(3.23)	10(3.57)

Figures in parentheses indicates percentage.

The table 6.47 showed that 44.87 percent respondents from adopted villages and 32.26 percent respondents from non-adopted villages opined that a change has taken place in the magical and divination practices of the Khasis through the Ramakrishna Mission. On the other hand, 51.28 percent respondents from adopted villages and 64.51 percent respondents from non-adopted villages opined that the Ramakrishna Mission has brought about no change in the practice of divination and magical practices of the Khasi society. They believed that the Ramakrishna Mission has rather been encouraging them to continue with the practice of divination and magic. The data clearly showed that a change in divination took place through the Christian missionaries. Most of the Christian Khasis and some educated traditional Khasis gave up the practice of divination and magic. But traditional Khasis still practice magic and divination. Nevertheless, the Ramakrishna Mission encouraged them to maintain the old practices. So, the traditional Khasis in the adopted villages and non-adopted villages still practice divination and rituals.

(e) Changes in Khasi Christian Society

It was believed that the impact of the Ramakrishna Mission was also found on the Khasi Christian society in education, health, living standard, and so on. It was because many Khasi Christians of this district were the products of the Ramakrishna Mission schools. Not only that even in the field of health care and employment many Khasi Christians of the East Khasi Hills District have been benefited through the service of the Ramakrishna Mission. Many Khasi Christians have been found being influenced by the teachings of the Ramakrishna Mission.

Table 6.48 Showing attitude on: "A Change has taken place among Khasi Christians."

N= 280, AH= 156, NAH= 124

Sr. No.	Particulars	Selected Rural Households		Sample Average for both the groups
		Adopted Villages	Non-adopted	
1	Total No. Of Households	156(100.00)	124(100.00)	280(100.00)
a	Agree	90(57.69)	80(64.52)	170(60.71)
b	Disagree	60(38.46)	40(32.26)	100(35.72)
c	Undecided	6(03.85)	4(03.22)	10(03.57)

Figures in parentheses indicates percentage

Table 6.48 showed that 57.69 percent households from adopted villages and 64.52 percent households from the non-adopted villages opined that a change has taken place in different areas of Khasi Christian life like living standard, education, health, indigenous music, income, employment, birth and death rate and so on, through the Ramakrishna Mission. On the other hand, 38.46 percent households from adopted villages and 32.26 percent households from non-adopted villages opined that the Ramakrishna Mission has brought about no change among the Christians. The data clearly indicated that the Ramakrishna Mission's social service and teachings have made impact on the Christian and non-Christian community in the East Khasi Hils District. But the maximum impact was seen on the socio-economic, cultural and religious life of the traditional Khasis of the district.

Modern system of education has no doubt broken such traditional biased instructions. Other factors have played equally their role in breaking down the old isolationist tendency. Christian missionaries and western education played a vital role in eradicating ill-fated practices and customs such as sorcery, human sacrifice, and superstitious beliefs in tribal areas like East Khasi

Hills District. Ramakrishna Mission has also done good works in the Khasi Hills by preaching a secular outlook and inculcating a sense of nationhood even though the Christian Church structures also developed new more democratic forms of leadership. Ramakrishna Mission has succeeded in uniting the traditional Khasis and not embracing Christianity. The impact of the Ramakrishna Mission is also found on the physical health, birth and death rate, cultural practices like festivals, music and musical instrument, concept of God, animal sacrifices, divination etc. The field survey shows that about 2000 families mainly in Shella, Cherra, Sohbarpunji and other surrounding areas, have become interested in the teachings of the Ramakrishna Mission though they do not say that they are Hindus. Some Khasi families have taken initiation in the Ramakrishna Mission since the teachings of the Mission have influenced them.

Conclusion: Khasi society has greatly been transformed by many changes. With the advent of Christianity and western education, transformation in the social, cultural and religious life of the Khasi society took place. Christianity has played a major role in the field of education and health. Integration of the area in the colonial dominion of the British resulted in a change by exposing the traditional society to modern forces. Adaptation to the western life was quickly made although the matrilineal laws of inheritance and succession and the other cultural traits were retained. The converts abandoned their former religious rites, beliefs and ritual, and accepted the Christian teachings.

Another most successful among the Indian mission to bring about changes in the East Khasi Hills District of Meghalaya, however was Ramakrishna Mission. The Ramakrishna Mission has been working in the district since 1920. It runs 58 schools, 3 dispensaries, mobile clinics and other vocational training centres. Khasi music and songs are still heard in the rural areas and dancing festivals are still maintained by the traditional Khasis. The Ramakrishna Mission has been working to strengthen the traditional Khasi culture and religion. It has been successful to some extent. Through education and medical care of the Ramakrishna Mission some changes have taken place in the study area. It has brought about religious and cultural change in the society. It has been working to develop the education and health of the Khasis. Even birth and death rate has been affected. The living standard of the Khasis has changed to some extent through the Ramakrishna Mission in the adopted villages. The Mission has also brought changes in the religious life of the traditional Khasis. It has been working to strengthen the traditional Khasi religious and cultural life, It has been successful in strengthening the traditional Khasis, their religious practices and uniting them through the Seng Khasi Organisation. It has also been successful in spreading the *vedantic* teachings among the Khasis.

B A a b

Chapter 7

Conclusion

The study aims to find out the changes brought about by the Ramakrishna Mission in the socio-cultural and religious life of the Khasis in the East Khasi Hill District of Meghalaya. It is true that no society can successfully resist change, although some societies are more resistant to change than others. The relatively static social patterns include status and roles, social stratification and the various social institutions. Khasi society in the East Khasi Hills District has also been transformed by many changes which have been brought about by Christianity and the Ramakrishna Mission. This chapter is an attempt to show that the Ramakrishna has helped Khasi society through education, medical care and other developmental projects, which has brought changes to some extent in the Khasi socio-cultural and religious life of the Khasis.

It was also true that the Khasi society by and large have cherished great pride in their traditional milieu. Respect for the paternal and maternal relations is always kept alive; love for clearing themselves of all taboos (sang) especially in times of marriage, pride in cherishing traditional precepts and other values imbedded in the traditional society are always kept alive in the East Khasi Hills District.

In Khasi culture, the clan is one of the basic structures. One cannot understand the Khasi culture without taking seriously the nature of the formation and the relationship of the clans. Fertility rites, worship of mountains and rivers, spirits, and glorification of the ancestors have been the most popular practices among the Traditional Khasis. It was found that the matrilineal system of inheritance, which is along the female line, has its impact on the economic growth and development of the state. The youngest daughter is the custodian of the family or clan properties except in some parts, which are to be managed and controlled by her uncle and after their death by her brothers. The study showed that the women in Khasi society definitely enjoy a number of privileges as the clan lineages is taken from the mother and the last daughter of *Ka Khadduh* becoming the custodian of the ancestral property.

This research also indicated that matriliny indeed places the male in a position of great disadvantage. After marriage the Khasi male leaves his father's house and starts a new life in his in-laws' house. He experiences adjustment problems and undergoes the same difficulties that a new bride in a Hindu society does. In Khasi society, whatever a man earns before marriage belongs to his clan. He does not inherit any land property from his parents except in few places. It is said that the son is not allowed to take a decision even about his career. He leaves even decision-making to his mother before marriage and to his wife after it. There is the other extreme of course where parents somehow sideline their sons and prefer to consult their daughters on all-important matters because daughters will always remain with them whereas sons are mere temporary residents.

The study indicated that there is a tendency in the new Khasi generation to trivialize the heritage of the past. During the nineteenth century the Khasi Hills were brought under British administration. The advent of British Rule and Western Missions, followed by introduction of Christianity and modern education, brought about social changes in the traditional Khasi way of living. A transition took place from past to present–it is a transition from primitivism to modernity. After 1947, the political system started changing. Modernization and technological revolution have been thrust upon the Khasis, which has shaken the foundation of their traditional structures.

The study indicated that the prominent role played by the maternal uncle, who was burdened by his own family have dwindled, while that of the father has increased. Economic constraints make it impossible for him to give any kind of financial help to his nieces and nephews unless he is very well off. The role of the father has assumed more importance. But a question raised by the Khasi male is-"If I am a father of many children, why do they not carry my clan name? If I am the head of the family why do my in-laws interfere with the decisions that I want to make in the family?" Through this study it is found that the young Khasis are demanding patriarchy due to their interaction with Bible culture and the culture of the Hindus that are patriarchal in nature. Because of cross-cultural marriages and living with Hindus especially in the urban areas, some young Khasi children use their father's clan name or both their father and mother's clan name. Moreover, in recent years there have been a number of defenses raised in favour of the unchallenged authority of the mother especially in the light of the ancestral property.

The present scenario is dictated by economic imperatives and as land is the only wealth that a Khasi has, it becomes crucial that ownership of land should also be vested with the male. It means parents should give some share of the assets to the sons as it is practiced in some areas of this district. Parents can give some share of their property to their sons by will. This kind of practice will give him a sense of security. It will give freedom to utilize that land for business and commercial purposes and multiply his earning. Khasi Customary Law should allow males to have shares in parents' property which is given only by will.

The study showed that a Khasi woman is a born leader but in the context of a matrilineal set up, she is deprived of leadership rights in all indigenous institutions. Though lineage is traced through a mother, she is not permitted to act as leader or be a member of a clan *Durbar*. Provision to the post of rulers from the level of a clan, village, *raid* and up to the state level was reserved for men. In spite of the development of the Khasi women on different fronts, one may wonder why there are only a negligible number of women representatives to Meghalaya Legislative Assembly. Even in the Khasi Autonomous District Council there are hardly women representatives. There is also an insignificant representation of women in the various decision-making bodies. They are excluded even from priestly powers. However, there is no restriction on their joining politics. All the political parties in

Meghalaya have their women wing led by dynamic party workers.

The study showed that the reason why the Khasi women are not coming forward to contest election from time immemorial is because a woman is regarded as only one device and power. On the other hand man is regarded as a man of twelve devices and powers. It is a wrong notion to think that just because the Khasi people follow matrilineal system, that makes it easy for women to enter politics and win elections. In today's context when women are advanced in every sphere of life, is it not ripe time to encourage women to participate in decision-making bodies? Is it not discrimination done against women in the East Khasi Hills District of Meghalaya? Even the Ramakrishna Mission supports the equal participation of women in politics in the state. But the impact of its teachings on the Khasis is very less.

Through this study it is found that the age-old tradition of intimacy with nature was there, but today, there is a growing dissociation of the Khasis from their natural environment. The pristine relationship that existed once upon a time has almost disappeared due to man's consumerist attitude, which results in a sort of enmity between man and nature. Knowledge of nature and respect for the environment is diminishing which has led to ecological crisis. This is seen in the growing percentage of their ignorance about the elements of nature and the cultural heritage related to nature handed down to them from their ancestors.

The study also reflected that the traditional religion of the Khasis, which has all the basic features of religious beliefs, practices and moral teachings based on oral traditions and customs was challenged by the Christian faith. The main agency of change beginning in the 19th century was the British Government, which provided political power to effect change in the Khasi society. It was found that in the highly resilient Khasi society, resistance grew to conversions to Christianity and latent forces of pride in the ancient Khasi culture and tradition were provoked and unleashed. The resultant Seng Khasi Movement which revived all cherished values retarded the growth of Christianity and in some respect, mellowed the missionary endeavors.

Traditional Khasis are both polytheists and animistic. They believe that their religion is given by God. They also worship spirits of their forefathers apart from God. God is known as *U Blei, Ka Blei* and *Ki Blei*. One of the fundamental beliefs of the Khasi religion is that human beings have come into the world to learn truth and earn righteousness. They also believe in life after death. They consider earth as a temporary place.

The study showed that the ancestor worship is an important feature of the Traditional Khasi Religion. The concept of God and other world is also found in Traditional Khasi Religion. Through this study we learned that in Traditional Khasi Religion, trees, mountains and rivers were worshipped and treated with due respect and reverence, which shows their close relationship with nature. Fertility rites, worship of spirits, and glorification of the ancestors have been the most popular practices among the Traditional Khasis.

The Khasi society in the East Khasi Hills District has to some extent undergone changes due to their contact with the socio-cultural and religious influences coming from outside. The study reflects that the Khasi cultural, social and religious lives were influenced by Christian missionaries. It was also found that the religion and culture of the Hindu neighbours of the plains like Ramakrishna Mission has made some impact on the socio-economic, cultural and religious life of the Khasis in the East Khasi Hills District of Meghalaya.

It was found that the Ramakrishna Mission has been working to protect and strengthen the Khasi traditional culture and Traditional Religion through education and social service. The study showed that the aim of the Ramakrishna Mission is to make the poor tribal and backward people to stand on their feet, to expose them to the main stream of Indian culture and to raise them to a status of equality. The service of the Ramakrishna Mission to the weaker sections of the society should be praised.

The Ramakrishna missionaries work has also brought beneficial changes in the Khasi society of the East Khasi Hills District. By providing education, medical care and relief, the Ramakrishna Mission pays special attention to those who are poor. Through its service an impact on the different areas of the Khasi life was seen. It chose education primarily and medicine secondarily as a tool to spread its work. This Mission is respected alike by all sections of the Khasi society. It was because its primary goal was to serve the people as it is mentioned in the aim of the Ramakrishna Mission. All these social services are rendered not in the spirit of pity but in the spirit of worship.

Education lays impetus to social transformation. The study showed that a good number of households from adopted and non-adopted villages were illiterate. It was found that there is impact of the Ramakrishna Mission on educational life of the Khasis. The illiteracy percentage was very high in the non-adopted villages due to lack of educational facilities. It was also found that many households from adopted villages have become literate through the educational facility provided by the Ramakrishna Mission in the study area. However, those who have no access to the educational facilities of the Ramakrishna Mission are still illiterate. Less impact of the educational facilities is seen in the non-adopted villages. In spite of the educational change being brought about by the Ramakrishna Mission in the educational life of the Khasis, there are a good number of respondents who opined that even the Christian Mission schools have been working in educating the Khasis to eradicate illiteracy in the study area since 19th century. It is believed that Christian church has contributed more than the Ramakrishna Mission to the educational change in the study area.

The Ramakrishna Mission's social service to Khasi society in the district is commendable. Even the Christian community in the study area has been affected by the service the Ramakrishna Mission has rendered to the society. The study showed that the Ramakrishna Mission has brought about a change in the educational life and living standard of the Traditional Khasis and Khasi Christian community in the study area. Through education the Ramakrishna Mission has been able to win the hearts of the Khasis due to free quality education. Where the number of students in the Christian mission schools and government schools in certain villages was 45-50, the number of students in the Ramakrishna Mission schools was 400-500. According to 1991 Census, the literacy rate in this block was just 39 percent. While the literacy rate, according to the 2001 Census, was 69.4 percent. Many Khasis have got their secular education both in rural and urban areas from the Ramakrishna Mission schools. The Ramakrishna Mission gives free education to all strata of society which the church also needs to give to win the hearts of the Khasis. Many Khasi parents find it difficult to afford the expenditure in the Christian schools. The church needs to learn a lesson from the Ramakrishna Mission.

The study also revealed that a change has taken place in the status of Khasi women through the Ramakrishna Mission in the East Khasi Hills Diatrict. After the arrival of the Ramakrishna missionaries in the rural areas of the East Khasi Hills District, the status of Khasi women has also changed to some extent. However, majority of the respondents from adopted and non-adopted villages did not agree to the change in the status of Khasi women through the Ramakrishna Mission alone. They believed that Christian Church has contributed more than the Ramakrishna Mission to the upliftment of Khasi women through education, which has lifted up their living standard.

The study showed that Khasi males' attitude towards Khasi female has changed. Some households from both adopted and non-adopted villages opined that a change has taken place in Khasi males' attitude toward Khasi female through the Ramakrishna Mission. However, majority of households from both adopted and non-adopted villages did not agree to the change. They believe that education, modernization and westernization are the main sources to bring about change in the Khasi male's attitude towards Khasi females.

Through this study it was learned that there is a positive impact of the Ramakrishna Mission on the Khasi society. Earlier the Khasis were not tolerant to the non-Khasis. But now through the Ramakrishna Mission, they have become more tolerant and receptive to the outsiders. The Khasis now have identified themselves as Indians. Through the service of the Ramakrishna Mission, the Khasis have become more open and tolerant to other cultures, ideologies and social norms. The study indicated that more than half respondents from adopted and non-adopted villages opined that a change has taken place in Khasi attitudes towards non-Khasis through the Ramakrishna Mission. However, a good number of households from adopted and non-adopted villages did not agree to the change. They believe that this change has taken place due to education, communication and modernization. Christianity has been instrumental in bringing about change in Khasi attitude towards non-Khasis in the study area.

The study showed that a change has taken place in Khasi physical health in the study area of the district through the medical service rendered by the Ramakrishna Mission. However, many people did not agree to the above statement. The non-beneficiaries of the medical service have denied the change in Khasi physical health and not the beneficiaries. The study showed that a majority of the rural Khasis appreciated the medical service rendered by the Ramakrishna Mission to them. Approximately, 66,433 patients in the district and 22,436 patients in the Shella-Bholaganj Block got free treatment from the Ramakrishna Mission in 2007. The study also showed that the medical service of the Ramakrishna Mission has even brought down the birth and death rate in the adopted villages. Every year over 1,50,000 people get free medical service from the Ramakrishna Mission, which has solved health problems of the rural masses.

It was found that the Ramakrishna Mission did not pay much attention to the property inheritance. They are not in favour of change in the Law of Property Inheritance. They believe that present Law of Property Inheritance should continue without any change. Ramakrishna Mission has not been able to win the hearts of the majority of the Khasis in this regard.

The study showed that a change has taken place in the indigenous political institutions through the Ramakrishna Mission. Ramakrishna Mission is in favour of the decentralization of power. It also suggests that people should engage in decision making bodies at grass root level for the formulation of schemes for development. The present politicians may not like the

CONCLUSION

involvement, strengthening and decentralization of power with the indigenous traditional institutions, as they think that these institutions are hindrance to their liking. But the only way to work for true development of the Khasis in the rural areas is the involvement of these traditional institutional heads in decision making bodies and developing schemes. In order to take the developmental schemes to the rural masses in the East Khasi Hills District there is a need of community participation in developmental programs.

The study indicated that a change has taken place in the Khasi political system through the Ramakrishna Mission in the study area. It is supported by the respondents' opinions. However, a good numbers of households from adopted and non-adopted villages opined that this change has not been brought about by the Ramakrishna Mission alone. They believe that the Christian missionaries have played an important role in this regard.

The study revealed that the average income of the rural households in the adopted villages was ₹ 101,972.00 and in the non-adopted villages ₹ 79565.00. The households engaged in tertiary occupation have 41 percent of the total average income. The households engaged in primary occupation have 38 percent of the total average annual income. 21 percent households engaged in the secondary occupation having 38 percent income. The data clearly indicates the difference in the average income of the rural households in the adopted villages and the average income of the rural households in the non-adopted villages. Majority of respondents from adopted villages and a few respondents from non-adopted villages were of the opinion that their income has increased through the help of the Ramakrishna Mission, which has provided jobs to many peoples and given them vocational training in the study areas. Due to technical training provided by the Ramakrishna Mission, many Khasis have been encouraged to start small scale industries, which have raised their income.

The study indicated that a change has taken place in their income. 74.70 percent of the total annual income was spent on family needs by the households from adopted villages and 80.02 percent of the total income was spent on family consumption by the households from non-adopted villages. 15.05 percent income of the households from adopted villages and 11.45 percent income of the households from the non-adopted villages was invested on production resources. Only 10.25 percent income of the households from adopted villages and 8.35 percent income of the households from non-adopted villages saved their income. 38.46 percent households from adopted villages and 44.35 percent households from non-adopted villages opined that their saving over their total income was satisfactory. Nevertheless, 19.23 percent households from adopted villages and 24.20 percent households from non-adopted villages said that their income was not enough to meet the family needs.

This study showed that majority of the Khasis in the study area have sufficient income to meet them their needs like food, shelter and clothing. However, it was not accepted by all the Khasis. A good number of people opined that their income was not sufficient to meet their needs. Those who said that their income is not sufficient to meet their needs are the non-beneficiaries of the service rendered by the Ramakrishna Mission in the district.

The study showed that a change has taken place in their employment problem. Through this study it was found that the Ramakrishna Mission has been able to train many Khasis to start their own work. They need not depend on Government jobs. They have sufficient employment in their families. However, a good number of households from adopted and non-adopted villages opined that they do not have sufficient employment in their families. Those who have been benefited through the service of the Ramakrishna Mission claimed to have sufficient employment in their families.

The study also revealed that a change has taken place in the Khasi standard of living. A good number of households from adopted and non-adopted villages were of the opinions that a change has taken place in the rural Khasi standard of living through the Ramakrishna Mission. However, it was also found that this change has not taken place through the Ramakrishna Mission alone. Even other factors like Christian missionaries have also contributed more than Ramakrishna Mission towards the education, communication, and industrial revolution of the Khasis that have uplifted their standard of living. Urbanization together with modern communications and transport systems also helped in breaking down the barriers that had earlier isolated the area from the main facilities. Wherever there was better communication and better transportation facilities, the standard of living was developed. The Ramakrishna Mission has been working for the upliftment of the living standard of the Khasis that was witnessed by many Khasis in the study area.

Through this study it was found that a change has taken place in the food habits of the Khasis. The Traditional Khasi throw some morsels of food on the ground in honour of mother earth, which is very similar with the habit of the Hindus. Even some Hindu Bengalis, who are living in Meghalaya, practice this. It may be the influence of outsiders like Ramakrishna Mission followers on the Khasis. The study showed that a change in food habits and way of living of the Khasis has taken place through the Ramakrishna Mission. However, a good number of households from adopted and non-adopted villages believed that behind the change in Khasi food habits and way of living even Christian missionaries have played an important role. They denied the change through the Ramakrishna Mission alone.

The study indicated that a change has been noticeable in the Khasi house models in the towns, township and advanced villages which has largely resulted from good income and modern technology. It is the opinions of many respondents who believe that the Ramakrishna has been instrumental to some extent in the change of Khasi house model. Today hundreds of modern types of houses had not only been constructed but the techniques were quickly spread into the nearby and far villages from Shillong. The people have learnt to construct better buildings. But in the deep interior villages we still come across with indigenous houses which still exhibit old traits and in which present transformation seems to have very little impact. The change in the house models has been witnessed by a good number of respondents from adopted and non-adopted villages. The difference in the house style in adopted and non-adopted villages showed the difference in their socio-economic and educational standard. Ramakrishna Mission has also contributed a lot to the change in the house models of the Khasis in the study area. However, a majority of the Khasis did not agree fully to the statement. They believe that the change in the house style has been brought about by even the church which has been instrumental for communication, education, modernization and scientific development.

The study showed that there has been a spurt in the Khasi economy since there has been increasing opportunities of secondary sources of income like carpentry, tailoring, bakery, weaving, poultry farms, and small-scale industry etc. The Ramakrishna Mission has been providing training to the Khasi men and women in the rural areas in order to have secondary source of income. The impact of the Ramakrishna Mission is seen on the individual and family economic life of this district. Almost 100% respondents believe that a change has taken place in the economic life of the Khasis in the said district through the education and social service that the Ramakrishna Mission has rendered apart from other social organizations like church. Many families have got government and private jobs which has raised their economic standard.

The study of the traditional music and musical instruments revealed that a change has taken place in Khasi traditional music and in the use of traditional musical instruments through the Ramakrishna Mission and through some church leaders. When majority of the Khasis were adopting the western music and giving up their traditional music and musical instruments, the Ramakrishna Mission came to the study area and taught the Khasis Indian music. The traditional Khasis changed their mind and started turning to the traditional music and musical instruments. In this way, through the Ramakrishna Mission's teachings a change took place in the Khasi attitude towards their traditional music and musical instruments. However, majority of households from adopted and non-adopted villages did not agree to the above statement.

CONCLUSION

Ramakrishna Mission encourages the Khasi traditional festivals. It celebrates Khasi traditional festivals in their compounds to encourage the Khasi youths and parents to maintain their festivals. Now the Khasi young generation has started realizing the importance of the traditional Khasi festivals. Many people who were interviewed said that the Ramakrishna Mission has been a backbone in strengthening the Khasi festivals through Ka Seng Khasi. The Christian youths have felt the need of knowing their cultural values. Even the Government of Meghalaya has set up a full-fledged directorate known as Directorate of Art and Culture. It is believed to be the result of the attempts made by the Ramakrishna Mission and the Seng Khasi Organisation. The Khasi festivals, however, have lost religious significance of their traditional festivals because the government has secularized them. There is a need to emphasize the religious spirituality of the traditional festivals, which is diminishing. Even Christian Church should theologize the Traditional Khasi festivals in order to have unity with them. It will also attract the traditional Khasis to the love of Christ.

The study showed that the influence of the Ramakrishna Mission is seen on the hunting practices of the Khasis. The study indicated that the Mission has been trying to awaken the Khasi parents and children about the importance of wild life. But it is education that has changed the minds of the Khasis not to kill the wild life. The forest department is also working hard to protect the wild life in Meghalaya. Even the Church has been trying to educate the people regarding the importance of the forest and wild life. This change has not taken place through the Ramakrishna Mission alone but the church and the State Government have also contributed to this change.

The Traditional Khasis believe that betel- nut will be enjoyed even in the house of God after this life. Therefore it has become a religious norm. It may be difficult to give up this bad habit of chewing-pan, which causes throat cancer. Many Khasis use tobacco in the pan, which causes stomach cancer. There is a need to think about the chewing of pan from physical health point of view. Today betel-nut is not the only source of welcoming the guests in the house. There are so many other sources better than this to welcome the guests. The fable (u Kwai, u Tympew bad u Dumasala meaning Betel-nut, betel leaf and tobacco) is no more relevant in today's context. We rather need to understand things from health point of view. Therefore it should not become a religious norm. Ramakrishna Mission has been working to bring awareness among the Khasis about the bad affect of chewing-pan on the health of the people through education.

The study showed that a change has taken place in the deforestation through the Ramakrishna Mission. The study showed that the Ramakrishna Mission educate the Khasis through seminars to protect then forests. Even the mission conducts special programs among the school children to know the value of the trees. However, majority of the people from adopted and non-adopted villages that this change has not been brought about by the Ramakrishna Mission alone but even the church has brought awareness among the Khasis regarding deforestation.

The Ramakrishna Mission suggested education as the principal agent in concretising people about the need to respect and preserve the ecological system. Environmental education must be given to the people in various forms through lectures, exhibitions, essay writings, seminars/workshops, discussions and documentary films as the Ramakrishna Mission is doing in the East Khasi Hills District, but it is not sufficient. But so far very limited influence of the Ramakrishna Mission teachings is seen on the Khasis in terms of deforestation.

The Khasi worship today may be called neither a natural worship nor animism nor ancestral nor divine worship. It seems that today the Khasi traditional religion has many deities to be worshipped. Instead of fearing God the Creator, they fear the evil deadly spirits and worship them. Ramakrishna Mission worked through different programs on the preservation of environment to bring awareness among the parents, youth and children. The Mission also encouraged the Traditional Khasis to maintain their Traditional Religion and religious practices. The Traditional Khasis have been united and strengthened in their religious practices by the Ramakrishna Mission which was witnessed by many respondents in the study area.

The study indicated that the Ramakrishna Mission has been working to uplift the spiritual life of the Traditional Khasis. It has been able to have some impact on the spiritual life of the traditional Khasis. The Ramakrishna Mission along with other religious organizations has been trying to bring religious revival among the Khasis. This revival was to protect the Khasis from embracing Christianity. Khasi literature produced by the Ramakrishna Mission has played an important role in bringing about religious revival among the traditional Khasis. It seems that the Ramakrishna Mission has been trying to revive the traditional Khasi religion and its practices. It is also trying to spread the *Vedantic* philosophy among the Khasis as it is the motto of the Ramakrishna Mission. The Mission should pay attention to the traditional Khasi religious spirituality and work for religious harmony among Khasi Christians and traditional Khasis in Meghalaya.

The study revealed that a change has been brought about by the Ramakrishna Mission in the Khasi concept of God in the study area. It was witnessed by a majority of respondents both from adopted and non-adopted villages. However, 38.46 percent households from adopted villages and 56.45 percent households from non-adopted villages opined that this change is not brought about by the Ramakrishna Mission alone. Even other neighbouring Hindus have also made impact on the Khasis in the bordering areas regarding adoption of Hindu deities. Some traditional Khasis worship Hindu deities which show the Hindu influence on them. Some Khasis even said that the God of the Khasis and the God of the Ramakrishna Mission is the same.

Through this study it was found that a change has taken place in the Khasi funeral rites through the Ramakrishna Mission. The Mission continues to encourage the Traditional Khasis to maintain the funeral rites. However, a good number of households did not agree to the change. They rather believe that a change in funeral rites of the traditional Khasis has been brought about by the church. It is clear that a good number of respondents were of the opinion that the Ramakrishna Mission has been working to educate the Traditional Khasis through the Seng Khasi Organization to maintain their funeral rites which were almost out-dated. It has been successful to some extent.

The study also indicated that a change has taken place in Khasi animal sacrifices to the spirits. However, a good number of respondents did not accept it. They are of the opinion that no change has taken place in Khasi animal sacrifice through the Ramakrishna Mission. Somehow, it is very clear that the Ramakrishna Mission have been encouraging the Traditional Khasis to maintain their traditional religious practices where animal sacrifices play very important role.

The study revealed that a change has taken place in the magical practices of the Traditional Khasis. About a good number of respondents both from adopted and non-adopted villages opined that a change has been brought about by the Ramakrishna Mission in the magical practice of the traditional Khasis. However, this opinion is not accepted by a majority of the Khasis. They rather believed that the Ramakrishna Mission did not bring any change in the magical practices of the Khasis. It is the Seng Khasi Organization that has influenced the minds of the Traditional Khasis to maintain the religious practices like *tantric* practice of their forefathers.

The study reflected that the Ramakrishna Mission's Philosophy of Universal tolerance and harmony of all religions, which gives equal regards to all religions, all sects, and creeds and all faiths in the world, is ultimately based on the Universal Principle of oneness of truth. It not only proves universal brotherhood but also emphatically points out to the root of our oneness that we all have our being in God. On the one hand the Mission teaches that all religions are capable of leading to God but it is obvious that the Ramakrishna Mission believed that all other religions are at a lower level compared to *Advaita Vedanta*. They allow only the lower stages of an ascent towards the highest stage of *Advaita*. In fact, the Ramakrishna Mission stated that *Advaita*

CONCLUSION

Vedanta philosophy provides the only path to lead humanity to liberation and social harmony.

The Ramakrishna Mission not only taught universal brotherhood but also emphatically pointed out the root of our oneness in God. The Mission taught the harmony of all religions and true brotherhood of all human beings. Through this study we also learned that the Ramakrishna Mission invites the people of all faiths to be harmonized. Can harmony of all religions be possible in Meghalaya where majority of Khasis are Christians and the Ramakrishna Mission preaches against Christianity? Moreover, Ramakrishna Mission, on the one hand, preaches that all religions are same, on the other hand, is active in Meghalaya to bring them to the *Vedantic* teachings and culture. Are Khasi traditional religion and Christianity in Meghalaya not God given religions?

The study showed that the Khasi society of Meghalaya who have experienced significant socio-cultural and religious transformation in their lives and worldviews have experienced so because of the influence of other outside agencies of change like Ramakrishna Mission and Christian missionaries that have taken place in the 19th and 20th centuries.

This study is neither an end itself nor is it absolute; it rather opens up for comments that will contribute to any further serious research on the subject.

B A a b

Bibliography

Primary Sources

n.n., *Adi Kathamrta, Vol. 3*, ed. by Shyamal Basu, Calcutta: College Street,1983.

n.n., *Annual Report of Ramakrishna Mission, (From 1999-2000)*, New Delhi: Ramakrishna Mission Ashrama, 2002.

n.n., *Annual Report of Ramakrishna Mission School, Along (2000)*, Vivekanangar: Ramakrishna Mission School, n.d.

n.n., Annual Report of Ramakrishna Mission, (From 1999 to 2000), New Delhi: Ramakrishna Mission, 2000.

n.n., *Annual Report of Ramakrishna Mission (2000-2001)*, Palimangal: Ramakrishna Math and Ramakrishna Mission, n.d.

n.n., *Annual Report and Account of the Ramakrishna Mission*, Shillong: Ramakrishna Mission Ashrama, 2002.

n.n., *Annual Report and Account for the Years 2003-2004*, Cherrapunji: Ramakrishna Mission Ashrama, 2004.

n.n., *Annual Report and Account*, Shillong: The Ramakrishna Mission, n.d.

n.n., *A Report on Ramakrishna Math and Ramakrishna Mission Youth Convention 1985*, Hawrah: Belur Math, n.d.

n.n., *A General Report on the Ramakrishna Math and Mission for 1956*, Calcutta: Ramakrishna Math & Mission, 1957.

n.n., *A Brief History*, Cherrapunji: Ramakrishna Mission Ashrama, 2005.

n.n., *The Bulletin of the Ramakrishna Mission Institute of Culture, Vol. LI, No. 7*, July 2001, Back Cover Page.

n.n., *Bulletin of the Ramakrishna Mission Institute of Culture, Vol. LVI, No. 11*, November 2005, cover page.

n.n., *Census of India 2001, Series 18: Meghalaya*, Shillong: Directorate of Census Operations, 2003.

n.n., *The Complete Works of Swami Vivekananda, Vol. 1*, Advaita Asharama, Calcutta, 1999.

n.n., *The Complete Works of Swami Vivekananda, Vol 2*, Calcutta: Advaita Asharama, 1999.

n.n., *The Complete Works of Swami Vivekananda, Vol. 3*, Calcutta: Advaita Ashrama, 1999.

n.n., *The Complete Works of Swami Vivekananda, Vol. 4*, (Calcutta: Advaita Ashrama), 1999.

n.n., *The Complete Works of Swami Vivekananda, Vol 5*, Calcutta: Advaita Ashrama, 1999.

n.n., *The Complete Works of Swami Vivekananda, Vol. 6*, Calcutta: Advaita Ashrama, 1999.

n.n., *The Complete Works of Swami Vivekananda, Vol. 7*, (Calcutta: Advaita Ashrama), 1999.

n.n., *The Complete Works of Swami Vivekananda, Vol. 8*, Calcutta: Advaita Ashrama, 1999.

n.n., *The Complete Works of Swami Vivekananda, Vol. 9*, Calcutta: Advaita Ashrama, 1999.

n.n., *The Condensed Gospel of Sri Ramakrishna*, Mylapore: Sri Ramakrishna Math, 1998.

n.n., *Diamond Jubilee Souvenir (1937-1997)*, Shillong: Ramakrishna Mission, front page.

n.n., *A Dictionary of Advaita Vedanta*, compiled by Nirod Baran Chakraborty, Kolkata: The Ramakrishna Mission Institute of Culture, 2003.

n.n., *District Statistical Handbook: East Khasi Hills District 2002*, Shillong: Directorate of Economics & Statistics, 2002.

n.n., *The Forty Seventh General Report of Ramakrishna Math and Ramakrishna Mission*, Mumbai: Ramakrishna Mission, 2002.

n.n., *Golden Jubilee souvenir*, Shillong: Ramakrishna Mission, n.d.

n.n., *Golden Jubilee Souvenir*, Sobharpunji: Ramakrishna Mission Ashrama, 1979.

n.n., *Golden Jubilee Souvenir*, Shillong: Ramakrishna Mission, 1987.

n.n., Encyclopedia of North-East India: Meghalaya, Vol. IV, ed. by H.M.Bareh, New Delhi: Mittal Publications, 2001.

n.n., *Festivals and Ceremonies in Meghalaya*, ed. by K.R.Marak & R.Wankhar, Shillong: Department of Arts & Culture, 1994.

n.n., *Khasi Heritage*, Shillong: Ri-Khasi Press, 1978.

n.n., *Gazetteer of India: Meghalaya District Gazetteers*, ed. by I.M. Simon, Shillong: Government of Meghalaya, 1991.

n.n., *The Gospel of Sri Ramakrishna*, Vol. I, translated by Swami Nikhilananda, Mumbai/Madras: Sri Ramakrishna Math, 1964.

n.n., *Heritage of Meghalaya*, Shillong: Directorate of Arts and Culture, Government of Meghalaya, 2001.

n.n., *Meditation and Its Methods: According to Swami Vivekananda*, ed. by Swami Chetananda, Calcutta: Advaita Ashrama, 1998.

n.n., *Meghalaya, Basic Facts*, Shillong: DIPR, 1975.

n.n., *Meghalaya: Flora and Fauna*, Shillong: Directorate of Information and Public Relations, Government of Meghalaya, 1975.

n.n., *Pocket Statistical Handbook Meghalaya*, Shillong: Directorate of Economics & Statistic, Government of Meghalaya, 2003.

n.n., *Annual Report and Account of the Ramakrishna Mission*, Shillong: Ramakrishna Mission, 2002.

n.n., *Ramakrishna Math and Ramakrishna Mission*, Howrah: Ramakrishna Math and Ramakrishna Mission, n.d.

n.n., *The Ramakrishna Mission's Annual Report (2002-2004)*, Shillong: Ramakrishna Mission, 2005.

n.n., *Ramarishna Mission, 95th Annual General Meeting Report*, Calcutta: Ramakrishna Mission, 2004

n.n., *Ramakrishna Math and Ramakrishna Mission*, Howrah: Ramakrishna Math and Ramakrishna Mission, n.d.

n.n., *Ramakrishna Mission New Delhi: Annual Report for 1999 to 2000*, New Delhi: Ramakrishna Mission, 2000.

n.n., *Ramakrishna Mission: Report of the Governing Body on the Working of the Association in 2003- 2004*, 95th Annual General Meeting, Calcutta: Ramakrishna Math, December 2004.

n.n., *The Ramakrishna Movement*, Calcutta: The Ramakrishna Mission Institute of Culture, 2000.

n.n., *The Ramakrishna Movement*, Calcutta: The Ramakrishna Mission Institute of Culture, 2005.

n.n., *Reflections on Swami Vivekananda*, ed. by M. Sivaramakrishna & Sumita Roy, New Delhi: Sterling Publishers Private Limited, 1993.

n.n., *Report of Activities of Ramakrishna Mission Seva Samiti from April 1999 to March 2000*, Karimganj: Ramakrishna Mission, 2000.

n.n., *Sayings of Sri Ramakrishna*, Madras: Sri Ramakrishna Math, 1975.

n.n., *Selection from the Complete Works of Swami Vivekananda*, Calcutta: Advaita Ashrama, 1993.

n.n., *Souvenir of the Ramakrishna Math and Ramakrishna Mission Convention 1980*, Howrah: Belur Math, 1980.

n.n., *Studies on Sri Ramakrishna*, The Ramakrishna Mission Institute of Culture, Calcutta: Ramakrishna Mission, 1988.

n.n., *Sri Ramakrishna and the Women: An In-depth Study*, Shillong: Ramakrishna Mission, n.d.

n.n., *Teachings of Sri Ramakrishna*, Calcutta: Advaita Ashrama, 1985.

n.n., *Vedanta: Concept and Application*, Calcutta: The Ramakrishna Mission Institute of Culture, 2000.

n.n., *Vivekananda: His Call to the Nation*, Compiled, Kolkata: Advaita Ashrama, 2001.

n.n., *Vivekananda writes to you*, Mylapore: Sri Ramakrishna Math, n.d.

n.n., *What Religion is in the Words of Swami Vivekananda?* ed. by Swami Vidyatmananda, Kolkata: Advaita Ashrama, 2004.

Abhedananda, Swami, *Attitude of Vedanta towards Religion*, Calcutta: Ramakrishna Vedanta Math, 1947.

Abhedananda, Swami, *Doctrine of Karma*, Calcutta: Ramakrishna Vedanta Math, 2000.

Abhedananda Swami, *Our Relation to the Absolute*, Calcutta: Ramakrishna Vedanta Math, 1946.

Abhedananda, Swami, *The Philosophy of Progress and Perfection*, Calcutta: Ramakrishna Vedanta Math, 1994, Second Edition.

Abhedananda, Swami, *Religion of the Twentieth Century*, Calcutta: Ramakrishna Vedanta Math, 1968.

Abhedananda, Swami, *The Steps towards Perfection*, Calcutta: Ramakrishna Vedanta Math, 1984.

Abhedananda, Swami, *Thoughts on Philosophy and Religion*, Calcutta: Ramakrishna Vedanta Math, 1989.

Ashokananda, Swami, *When the Many Become One*, Calcutta: Advaita Ashramas, n.d.

Abhedananda, Swami, *Women's Place in Hindu Religion*, Calcutta: Ramakrishna Vedanta Math, 2001.

Abhedananda, Swami, *Yoga it's Theory and Practice*, Calcutta: Ramakrishna Vedanta Math, 1987.

Bareh, H., *A Short History of Khasi Literature*, Shillong: Ramakrishna Mission, 1969.

Bareh, Hamlet Dr., *The History and Culture of the Khasi People*, Guwahati/Delhi: Spectrum Publications, 1997.

Bareh, Hamlet, *The History and Culture of the Khasi People*, Calcutta: Naba Mudran Private Ltd.,1967.

Bareh, H.M., *Encyclopedia of North-East India, Vol., IV*, New Delhi: Mittal Publications, 2001.

Berry, Radhon Singh, *Ka Jingsneng Tymmen (The Teachings of Elders, Part I)*, Translated by Bijoya Sawian, Shillong: Ri Khasi Press, n.d.

Berry, R.S., *Ka Jing Sneng Tymmen, Part II*, Shillong: Ri Khasi Press), 1960.

Budhananda, Swami, *The Ramakrishna Movement*, Calcutta: Advaita Ashrama, 1994.

Budhananda, Swami, *The Ramakrishna Movement: It's Meaning for Mankind*, Calcutta, Advaita Ashrama, 1994.

Costa, G., *Ka Riti Ka Ri Ki Laiphew Syiem, Vol. II*, Shillong: St. Antony's College, 1937.

Devamayananda, Swami, *A Brief History*, Cherrapunji: Ramakrishna Mission Ashrama, n.d.

Gahanananda, Swami, *Ramakrishna Movement for All*, Mylapore: Sri Ramakrishna Math,n.d.

Gambhirananda, Swami, *The Apostles of Ramakrishna*, Calcutta: Advaita Ashrama, 1995.

Gambhirananda, Swami, *History of Ramakrishna Math and Ramakrishna Mission*, Third Revised Edition, Calcutta: Advaita Ashrama,1983.

Gambhirananda, Swami, *History of the Ramakrishna Math and Ramakrishna Mission*, Calcutta: Advaita Ashrama, 1957.

Gassah, L.S.Dr., *Traditional Institutions of Meghalaya: A Study of Doloi and his Administration*, New Delhi: Regency Publications, 1998.

General Opinion of the Presbyterian Churches in Manipur, Meghalaya, Mizoram, and Cachar Hill.

Gokulananda, Swami, *Some Guidelines to Inner Life*, Mylapore: Sri Ramakrishna Math, n.d.

Harshananda, Swami, *Hinduism through Questions amd Answers*, Mylapore: Sri Ramakrishna Math, n.d.

Harshananda, Swami, *Modern Problems and Ancient Solutions*, Bangalore: Ramakrishna Math, 1999.

Harshananda, Swami, *Philosophy of Sri Ramakrishna*, Bangalore: Ramakrishna Math, 2000.

Harshananda, Swami, *Relevance of Ramakrishna to Modern Life*, Bangalore: Ramakrishna Math, 2000.

Harshananda, Swami, *The Three Systems of Vedanta: An Introduction*, Mylapore: Sri Ramakrishna Math, 2002.

Harshananda, Swami, *Uniqueness of the Ramakrishna Monasticism*, Bangalore: Ramakrishna Math, 1998.

Hitananda, Swami, *Worship of Sri Ramakrishna*, Calcutta: Sri Ramakrishna Math, n.d.

Hossianur, Rahman, *Sri Ramakrishna: The Symbol of Harmony of Religions*, Calcutta: The Ramakrishna Mission Institute of Culture, 2000.

Jagadatmananda, Swami, *Gospel of the Life Sublime, Vol I*, Singapore: Ramakrishna Mission, 1998.

Julius Richter, *History of Mission in India*, London, 1908.

Jitamananda, Swami, *Immortal India: Short Plays on India's Spiritual Heritage*, Rajkot: Sri Ramakrishna Ashrama, 2002.

Jyrwa, Fortis J. Rev., *The Wondrous Works of God*, Shillong: Mrs. M.B. Jyrwa, 1980.

Kharmawphlang, I, *A Study of the Contribution of Non-Christian Missionaries to the Development of Education in Khasi Society,* M.A. Thesis, Submitted to the North Eastern Hills University, 1988.

Kharkongor, Felix H., *The Revealed Christ of the Khasi Religion,* Worthing Lorwood Press, 1994.

Kharkonggor, Iarington. Rev., *The Preparation for the Gospel in Traditional Khasi Belief,* Shillong: Ri Khasi Press, 1973.

Kharkongngor, Iarington Rev., *The Tribal People,* Jaiaw: Shandora Press, 1994.

Kharshiing, U Hipshon Roy, Ed., *The Land where Women are Women and Men are Men,* Shillong, n.d.

Kymboi, T.R., *Report of the Land Reform Commission for Khasi Hills,* Shillong, n.d.

Kyndiah, P.R., *Meghalaya: Yesterday and Today,* New Delhi: Vikas Publishing House Pvt. Ltd., 1990.

Lamare, O., *Ka Lukhmi,* Shillong: Ri Khasi Press, 1974.

Lokeswarananda, Swami, *Religion and Culture,* Calcutta: Ramakrishna Mission Institute of Culture, 1995.

Lokeshwarananda, Swami, *Religion Theory and Practice,* Calcutta: The Ramakrishna Mission Institute of Culture, 2000.

Lokeshwarananda, Swami, *Science and Religion,* Calcutta: The Ramakrishna Mission Institute of Culture, 2000.

Lokeshwarananda, Swami, *Vedanta in Practice,* Calcutta: The Ramakrishna Mission Institute of Culture, 2001.

Laloo, D.T., Ka Sajer, Ka Raid Nonglyngdoh, Vol. I, Shillong: Ri-Khasi Press, 1982.

Lyngdoh, H., *Ka Niam Khasi,* Ri-Khasi Press, Shillong, 1937.

Lyngdoh, Mary Pristilla Rina, *The Festivals in the History and Culture of the Khasi,* Vikas Publishing House, New Delhi, 1991.

Majaw, S.S., *Ki Syrwet Jingshai,* Shillong: Scorpio Printers, 1982.

Malngiang, Pascal, Aspects of Khasi Philosophy, Shillong: Seven Huts Enterprise, 1991.

Mann, K., Tribal Women in a Changing Society, Delhi: Mittal Publications, 1987.

Marwein, P.T., *Meghalaya Handbook*, Shillong: Government of Meghalaya, 1981.

Morris, J.H., *William Lewis Pioneer in Khasi*, Liverpool, 1939.

Mawlong, Aldila M, *Aspects of Change in the Family System among the Khasis*, M.Phil. Dissertation, North Eastern Hill University, Shillong, 1996.

Mawrie, H..O., *The Essence of the Khasi Religion*, Shillong, 1980.

Mawrie, H.O., *The Khasi Milieu*, New Delhi: Concept Publishing Company, 1981.

Mawrie, H.O., *Ka Pyarkhat U Khasi*, Shillong: Ri Khasi Press, 1974.

Mawrie, Barnes L.SDB, *The Khasis and their Natural Environment*, Shillong: Vendrame Institute Pvt. Ltd., 2001.

Mawrie, Barnes L. Dr. SDB, *Introduction to Khasi Ethics*, Shillong: DBCIC Publications, 2005.

Nakane, Chie, Khasi *and Garo: A Comparative Study in Matrilineal Systems*, Paris, 1967.

Nirvedananda, Swami, *Sri Ramakrishna and Spiritual Renaissance*, Calcutta: The Ramakrishna Mission Institute of Culture, 1940.

Nityaswarupananda, Swami, *Education for Human Unity and World Civilization*, Kolkata: Ramakrishna Mission Institute of Culture, 2003.

Nongsiej, T., *Khasi Cultural Theology*, Delhi: ISPCK, 2002.

Nongkhlaw, Aniema, Miss, *Modernization of the Khasi Society: A Sociological Study*, Unpublished M.Phil. Thesis Submitted to the North East Hill University, Shillong, 1990.

Paramananda, Swami, *Concentration and Meditation*, Mylapore: Sri Ramakrishna Math, 2002.

Paramananda, Swami, *The Problem of Life and Death*, (Mylapore: Ramakrishna Math, n.d).

Paramananda, Swami, *Reincarnation and Immortality*, Madras: Sri Ramakrishna Math, 1974.

Paramananda, Swami, *Vedanta in Practice*, Madras: Sri Ramakrishna Math, 1987.

Pohlong, Basil, *Culture and Religion: A Conceptual Study*, New Delhi: Mittal Publications, 2004.

Prabhananda, Swami, *Swami Vivekananda's Vision of Rural Development*, Kolkata: Ramakrishna Mission Lokashiksha Parishad, 2003.

Prabhananda, Swami, *The Early History of the Ramakrishna Movement*, Chennai: Sri Ramakrishna Math, 2005.

Prabhavananda, Swami, *Spiritual Heritage of India*, Madras/Mylapore: Sri Ramakrishna Math, 2000.

Prajananda, Swami, *The Philosophy of Progress and Perfection*, Calcutta: Ramakrishna Vedanta Math, 1994.

Quoted from Cherrapunji Ramakrishna Mission Office Record.

Quoted from the Deputy Commissioner of East Khasi Hills District's Office record.

Quoted from Headmaster's Office at Nartiang and Ummulong on 15.5.2005.

Ramakrishnananda, Swami, *God and Divine Incarnations*, Mylapore/Madras: Sri Ramakrishna Math, n.d.

Ranganathananda, Swami, *The Approach to Truth in Vedanta*, Kolkata: Advaita Ashrama, 2004.

Ranganathananda, Swami, *Children: Humanity's Greatest Assets*, Mumbai: Bhartiya Vidya Bhavan, 2004.

Ranganathananda, Swami, *Democratic Administration in the Light of Practical Vedanta*, Madras: Sri Ramakrishna Math, 1996.

Ranganathananda, Swami, *The Essence of Indian Culture*, Calcutta: Advaita Ashrama, 1996.

Ranganathananda, Swami, *Eternal Values for A Changing Society: Philosophy & Spirituality*, Vol. 1, Bombay: Bhartiya Vidya Bhavan, 1994.

Ranganathananda, Swami, *National Integration through Love and Service*, Bombay: Bhartiya Vidya Bhavan, 1996.

Ranganathananda, Swami, *The Philosophy of Democratic Administration*, Kolkata: Advaita Ashrama, 2003.

Ranganathananda, Swami, *Proceedings of the Question Answer Session in Chicago*, Kolkata: Advaita Ashrama, 2002.

Ranganathananda, Swami, *The Ramakrishna Mission: Its Ideals and Activities*, 7th Edition, Calcutta: The Ramakrishna Mission Institute of Culture, 1966.

Ranganathananda, Swami, *Role & Responsibility of Teachers in Building up Modern India*, Mumbai: Bhartiya Vidya Bhavan, 2004.

Ranganathananda, Swami, *Social Responsibilities of Public Administration*, Mumbai: Bhartiya Vidya Bhavan, 2000.

Ranganathananda, Swami, *Spiritual Life of the Householder*, Kolkata: Advaita Ashrama, 2005.

Ranganathananda, Swami, *Swami Vivekananda and Human Excellence*, Calcutta: Advaita Ashrama, 2004.

Ranganathananda, Swami, *Swami Vivekananda on Universal Ethics and Moral Conduct*, Bombay: Bhartiya Vidya Bhavan, 1995.

Ranganathananda, Swami, *The Universal Symphony of Swami Vivekananda*, Kolkata: Advaita Ashrama, 2003.

Ranganathananda, Swami, *What Life has taught me*, Mumbai: Bhartiya Vidya Bhavan, 2004.

Ranganathananda, Swami, *Women in the Modern Age*, Mumbai: Bhartiya Vidya Bhavan, 2004.

Ramakrishnananda, Swami, *God and Divine Incarnations*, Madras/Mylapore: Sri Ramakrishna Math, n.d.

Ranganathananda, Swami, *Practical Vedanta and the Science of Values*, Calcutta: Advaita Ashrama, 1996.

Rodborne, T., *U Khasi*, Shillong: n.p., 1973.

Roy, Jeebon, *The Book About One God*, Shillong: Ri-Khasi Enterprise, 2005.

Roy, Jeebon, *Ka Kitab Batai Pynshyrma Shapnang U Wei U Blei*, Shillong: Ri-khasi Press, 1900.

Roy, Sib Charan, *Ka Niam Ki Khasi*, 4th Edition, Shillong: Ri-Khasi Press, 1979.

Roy, Sib Charan Jait Dkhar, *Ka Niam Khasi Ka Niam Tip Blei Tip Briew*, Shillong: Ri Khasi Press, 1959.

Roy, Sib Charan Roy, Jait Dkhar, *Ka Niam Ki Khasi*, Shillong: Ri Khasi Press, 1979.

Rymbai, R.T., *The Origin and Settlement of the Khasi-Pnar*, Seminar on the History of Meghalaya, 1979, 7.

Rynjah, Sweetymon, *Tyngkai Ia Ki Symbai (Preserve one's own Culture)*, Shillong: Scorpio Printers, 1995.

Sangma, Milton S., *History and Culture of the Garos*, (New Delhi: Mittal Publications, 1981).

Satprakashananda, Swami, *The Goal and The Way*, Mylapore: Sri Ramakrishna Math, n.d.

Satprakashananda, Swami, *How is a Man Reborn?*, Calcutta: Advaita Ashrama, 2000.

Simon, I.M., *Gazetter of India: Meghalaya District Gazetters*, ed, Shillong: Government of Meghalaya, 1991.

Singh, Berry Radhon, *Ka Jingsneng Tymmen* (The Teachings Of Elders), Translated by Bijoya Sawian, Shillong: n.d.

Singh, Rabon, *Ka Niam Khasi*, Shillong: Ri-Khasi Press, 1960.

Singh, Rabon, *Ka Kitab Niam Khoin Ki Khasi*, Shillong: Ri Khasi Press, 1950.

Snaitang, O.L. Dr., *Christianity and Social Change in North East India*, Calcutta: Vendrame Institute Pvt. Ltd., 1993.

Sohliya, Hopewell Elias, *Na Mihngi Sepngi*, Shillong: St. Antony College, 1973.

Srikantananda, Swami, *The Intelligent Way to Yoga*, Mylapore: Sri Ramakrishna Math, 2001.

Srikantananda, Swami, *Youth! Arise, Awake and Know Your Strength*, 3rd edition, Domalguda: Vivekananda Institute of Human Excellence, 2005.

Streamnet Dhkar, *Ka Jinglong Ornnai U Briew Kat Kum Ki Khasi Drama*, Shillong: Streamlet Dhkar, 1986.

Syiemlieh, David R., *British Administration in Meghalaya*, New Delhi: Heritage Publishers, 1989.

Syiemlieh, Joseph, *The Funeral Rites and Practices in the Khasi Mainland: An Anthropological Study*, Ph.D. Unpublished Thesis Submitted to the North-Eastern Hills University, Shillong, 1995.

Synrem, H.K., *Revivalism in Khasi Society*, New Delhi: Sterling Publishers, 1992.

Swahananda, Swami, *Service and Spirituality*, Mylapore: Sri Ramakrishna Math, 1979.

Tapasyananda, Swami, *For Inquirers about Ramakrishna Math and Ramakrishna Mission*, Madras: Sri Ramakrishna Math, 1995.

Tapasyananda, Swami, *The Nationalistic and Religious Lectures of Swami Vivekananda*, Calcutta: Advaita Ashrama, 1990.

Tapasyananda, Swami, *Ramakrishna Math and Ramakrishna Mission*, Mylapore: Sri Ramakrishna Math, n.d.

Tapasyananda, Swami, *Sri Ramakrishna: Life and Teachings*, Calcutta: Sri Ramakrishna Math, n.d.

Tejasananda, Swami, *A Short Life of Sri Ramakrishna*, Calcutta: Advaita Ashrama, 1999.

Tejasananda, Swami, *The Ramakrishna Movement: Its Ideal and Activities*, Belur: Ramakrishna Mission Shardapith, 1954.

Vireswarananda, Swami, *Religion and Spiritual Life*, New Delhi: Ramakrishna Mission, 1982.

Vireswarananda, Swami, *Spiritual Ideals for the Modern Age*, Calcutta: Advaita Ashrama, 1999.

Vivekananda, Swami, *Bhakti or Devotion*, Calcutta: Advaita Ashrama, 1989.

Vivekananda, Swami, *Caste, Culture and Socialism*, Kolkata: Advaita Ashrama, 2001.

Vivekananda, Swami, *Is Vedanta the Future Religion?* Calcutta: Advaita Ashrama, 1993.

Vivekananda, Swami, *Life after Death*, Kolkata: Advaita Ashrama, 2002.

Vivekananda, Swami, *Practical Vedanta*, Kolkata: Advaita Ashrama, 2002.

Vivekananda, Swami, *Ramakrishna and His Message*, Hawrah: Sri Ramakrishna Math, 1971.

Vivekananda, Swami, *Salvation and Service*, Calcutta: Advaita Ashrama, 1998.

Vivekananda, Swami, *State, Society and Socialism*, Calcutta: Advaita Ashrama, 1998.

Vivekananda, Swami, *To the Youth of India*, Kolkata: Advaita Ashrama, 2003.

Wolflang, Coralton, *Khasi Drama: A Study of Social Awareness*, Ph.D unpublished thesis submitted to the North Eastern Hills University, Shillong, 1992.

Yogeshananda, Swami, *The Visions of Sri Ramakrishna*, Mylapore: Sri Ramakrishna Math, n.d.

Secondary Sources

n.n., *A Dictionary of Advaita Vedanta*, compiled by Nirod Baran Chakraborty, Kolkata: The Ramakrishna Mission Institute of Culture, 2003.

n.n., *Gazetteer of India: Meghalaya District Gazetteers*, Edited by I.M. Simon, Shillong: Government of Meghalaya, 1991.

n.n., *Matriliny in Meghalaya: Tradition and Change*, ed. by Pariyaram M. Chacko, New Delhi: Regency Publications, 1998.

n.n., *Mega Peoples of India, Part III*, Hyderabad: India Missions Association, 2006.

n.n., *The Oxford English Dictionary, Vol. III*, Oxford: Clarendon Press, 1933.

n.n., *Oxford Dictionary, Vol. IV,* Oxford: Oxford Press, 2000.

n.n., *People of India: Meghalaya*, ed. by K.S. Singh, et.el., Calcutta: Seagull Books, 1994.

n.n., *Reflections on Swami Vivekananda*, ed. by M. Sivaramakrishna & Sumita Roy, New Delhi: Sterling Publishers Private Limited, 1993.

Aggarwal, J.C., *Census of India (2001)*, Delhi: Doaba House, 2001.

Aier, K.I. Rev., *The Growth of Baptist Churches in Meghalaya*, Gauhati: Christian Literature Centre, 1978.

Allen, B.C., et.al, *Gazetteer of Bengal and North-East India*, New Delhi: Mittal Publications, 2001.

Allen, W.J., *Report on the Administration of the Cossyah and Jynteah Hill Territory 1858,* Reprinted, Shillong, 1903.

Aniema, Nongkhlaw, *Modernization of the Khasi Society: A Sociological Study*, Unpublished M.Phil. Thesis Submitted to the North East Hill University, 1990.

Assam tribune, May 20, 1999, p.2.

Baccheallo, J., *Diengjat U Longshwa,* Shillong: n.p., 1977.

Balslev, Anindita Niyogi Dr., *Religious Tolerance or Acceptance*, Calcutta: The Ramakrishna Mission Institute of Culture, 1987.

Barkataki, S., *Tribes of Assam*, New Delhi: National Book Trust, 1969.

Barkataki, S.N., *Tribal Folk-Tales of Assam* (Hills), Gauhati: Publication Board, Assam, 1970.

Bhowmik, K.L., *Tribal India*, Calcutta: The World Press Pvt. Ltd., 1971.

Cantlie, K., *Notes on Khasi Laws*, Shillong: Ri Khasi Press, 1971.

Chandra, Bipan, *Communalism in Modern India*, New Delhi: Vikas Publishing House, 1989.

Chattopadhayaya, S.K., *The Jaintias*, New Delhi: Cosmo Publications, 1988.

Chattopadhyaya, S.K., *Tribal Institute of Meghalaya*, ed., Guwahati: Spectrum Publications, 1985.

Chowdhuri, J.N., *The Khasi Canvas*, Shillong: Chapala Book Sellers and Publishers, 1970.

Choudhury, Kamal Narayan, *Folklore in North-Eastern India*, Calcutta: Punthi Pustak, 2001.

Choudhury, P.C., *History of the Civilization of the People of Assam to the 12th Century AD*, Ist Edition, Delhi, 1959.

Christopher, Isherwood, *Ramakrishna and his disciples*, Calcutta: Advaita Ashrama, 1969.

Costa,G., *Ka Riti Jong Ka Ri Laiphew Syiem*, St. Antony's College, Shillong, 1936.

Dasgupta, R.K., *Revolutionary Ideas of Swami Vivekananda*, Calcutta: The Ramakrishna Mission Institute of Culture, 2000.

Dasgupta, R.K., *Swami Vivekananda's Neo-Vedanta*, Calcutta: The Asiatic Society, 1999.

Dasgupta, R.K., *Swami Vivekananda's Vedantic Socialism*, Calcutta: Ramakrishna Mission Institute of Culture, 1995.

Dasgupta, Santwana, *Social Philosophy of Swami Vivekananda*, Calcutta: Ramakrishna Mission Institute of Culture, 2005.

Devdas, Nalini, *Sri Ramakrishna*, Bangalore: CISRS, 1966.

Down, Fredrick S., *Essays on Christianity in North-East India*, New Delhi: Indus Publishing Company, 1994.

Datta, P.S., India's North-East: A Study in Transition, New Delhi: Manas Publications, 1991.

Dutta, Sujit Kumar, *Functioning of Autonomous District Councils in Meghalaya*, New Delhi: Akansha Publishing House, 2002.

Eliade, Mircea, *Myth and Reality*, New York: Harper & Row Publishers, 1963.

Farquhar, J.N., *Modern Religious Movements in India*, Delhi: Munshiram Manohar Lal, 1967.

Gait, E.A., *History of Assam*, Calcutta: Thacker Spink & Co., 1963.

Ghose, G.K., *Tribals and their Culture: Assam, Meghalaya and Mizoram, Vol 1*, New Delhi: Manas Publications, 1992.

Ghosh, Sukla G.K., *Fables and Folk Tales of Meghalaya*, (Calcutta: Firma KLM Private Limited, 1998).

Giri, Helen, *The Khasis under British Rule (1824-1947)*, New Delhi: Regency Publications, 1998.

Gosh, Santikumar, *Universal Values*, Kolkata: The Ramakrishna Mission Institute of Culture, 2004.

Gopalakrishnan, R., *Meghalaya: Land and People*, New Delhi: Omsons Publications, 1995.

Gupta, Pranab Das K., *Life and Culture of Matrilineal Tribe of Meghalaya*, New Delhi: Inter-India Publications, 1982.

Gurdon, P.R.T., *The Khasis*, New Delhi: Cosmo Publications, 1975. http://eastkhasihills.gov.in/district profile.htm,1 http:/www.rkmathnagpur.org/ramkrishna movement/activity rm.htm.2

Isherwood, Christpher, *Ramakrishna and His disciples*, Calcutta: Advaita Ashrama, 1969.

Joshi, H.G., *Meghalaya: Past and Present*, New Delhi: Mittal Publications, 2004.

Julius, Richer, *History of Mission in India*, London, 1908.

Laloo, D.T., *Ka Sajer, Ka Raid Nonglyngdoh, Vol. I*, Shillong: Bynta I, 1982.

Lamin, Henry, *Economy and Society in Meghalaya*, Shillong: Har-Anand Publications, 1995.

Mackenzie, A., *History of the Relations of the Government with the Hill Tribes of the North East Frontier of Bengal*, Delhi, 1979.

Madan, S.N., *Dictionary of Anthropology*, New Delhi: Anmol Publications, 1989.

Majumdar, R.C., *Swami Vivekananda Centenary Memorial Volume*, ed., Calcutta: Advaita Ashrama 1963.

Mathur, P.R.G., *The Khasis of Meghalaya: A Study in Transition and Religion*, New Delhi: Cosmo Publications, 1979.

Mills, A.J.M., *Report on the Khasi, Jaintia Hills (1853)*, Reprinted, Shillong: North Eastern Hill University, 1985.

Morris, John Huges, *The History of the Welsh Calvinistic Methodists' Foreign Mission*, Carnavon: C.M. Book Room, 1910.

Morris, John Hughes, *The Story of our Foreign Mission*, Aizawl: Synod Publication Board, 1930.

Morris, J.H., *William Lewis Pioneer in Khasi*, Liverpool, 1939.

Natarajan, Nalini, *The Missionary Among The Khasis*, New Delhi: Sterling Publications, 1977.

Nalini Devdas, *Ramakrishna*, Bangalore: CISRS, 1966.

Padmashri,. Shashi S.S., *The Tribal World in Transition*, New Delhi: Anmol Publications Pvt. Ltd., 1995.

Pillai, Narayana P.K., *The Spiritual Sea*, Trivandrum: St. Joseph Press, 1990.

Presler, Henry H., *Primitive Religions in India*, Madras: C.L.S., 1971.

Rafy, Mrs., *Khasi Folk Tales*, Guwahati: Spectrum Publications, 1985, Reprinted.

Rahman, Hossianur, *Sri Ramakrishna: The Symbol of Harmony of Religions*, Calcutta: The Ramakrishna Mission Institute of Culture, 2000.

Rajagopalachari, C., *Ramakrishna Upanisad*, Madras: Sri Ramakrishna Math, 1981.

Rana, B.S., *The People of Meghalaya*, Calcutta: Punthi Pustak, 1989.

Rao Sankar C.N., *Sociology*, New Delhi: S. Chand & Company, 1997.

Rao, Venkata V., *A Century of Tribal Politics, In North East India*, New Delhi: S.Chand & Company Ltd, 1975.

Richter, Julius, *History of Mission in India*, London, 1908.

Rolland, Romain, *The Life of Vivekananda and the Universal Gospel*, Calcutta: Advaita Ashrama, 1988.

Roy, S.C., *Ka Niam Ki-Khasi*, Shillong, 1919.

Roy, S.C., *Ka Niam–Ki Khasi Ka Niam Tip-Blei Tip-Briew*, Shillong, 1959.

Schiffman, Richard, *Sri Ramakrishna: A Prophet for the New Age*, Calcutta: The Ramakrishna Mission Institute of Culture, 1994.

Sen, N.C.S., *The Origin and Early History of the Khasi Synteng People*, Calcutta, 1981.

Sen, Shadap & Namita Cathrine, *The Origin and Early History of the Khasi-Synteng People*, Calcutta: FIRMA KLM Private Limited, 1981.

Simon, I.M., *Gazetter of India: Meghalaya District Gazetters*, Ed., Government of Meghalaya, Shillong, 1991.

Simon, I.M., *Meghalaya*, Directorate of Economics and Statistics, Government of Meghalaya, Shillong, 2002.

Sinha, Kamaleshwar, *Meghalaya Triumph of the Tribal Genius*, Publications Division (I.S.S.D.), Delhi, 1970.

Singh, B.P., *A Dictionary of Modern Politics and Political Sociology*, Mittal Publications, Delhi, 1987.

Sten, H.W., *Khasi Poetry: Origin & Development*, Mittal Publications, New Delhi, 1990.

Sten, H.W., *Meghalaya Year Book 1980*, Scorpio Printers, Shillong, 1980.

Stephen, Abraham, *The Social Philosophy of Swami Vivekananda: Its Relevance to Modern India*, I.S.P.C.K., Delhi, 2005.

Verma, C.D., *Sterling General Studies and General Knowledge*, New Delhi: Sterling Publishers, 1987.

Articles

n.n., "Classical Approaches to the Study of Religion", *Cited in J. Wardenburg*, Mouton & Co., Paris, 1973.

n.n., "The Ramakrishna Math and Ramakrishna Mission Seva Samiti, Karimganj", *Temple Dedication Souvenir*, Ramakrishna Math & Ramakrishna Mission, Karimganj, 1992, 19.

n.n., "Sri Ramakrishna – Ardent Demonstrator of the Inter-Religious as well as Inter-Religious Harmony", *Bulletin of the*

Ramakrishna Mission Institute of Culture, Vol. XVII, No. 1, March 2003, 19-29.

n.n., *The Journal of the North East India Council for Social Science Research,* Vol II, No. I, April 1978, Shillong, 5.

n.n., *Report of Activities of Ramakrishna Mission Seva Samiti from April 1999 to March 2000,* Karimganj, 2-4.

n.n., "Spirituality Yours", *Panorama News Magazine of North East,* Vol X, No. 10, August 2002, 34-35.

n.n., "Swami Vivekananda on the Hell and Heaven in Man", *Prabuddha Bharata,* Vol 109, July 2001, cover page.

Aldila Mawlong, "Some Aspects of Change in the Family System of the Khasis", *Matriliny in Meghalaya,* ed. by Pariyaram M. Chacko, Regency Publications, New Delhi, 1998, 80-93.

A.M.Shaljan, "Population, Gender and Development in Maldives", *Economic and Political Weekly,* Vol xxxix, No. 18, May 1, 2004.

Anant Sadashiv Altekar, "Ideal and Position of Indian Women in Social Life," *Great Women of India,* Advaita Ashrama, Calcutta, 1953, 47.

A.K.Nongkynrih, "The Khasi Folk Dances", *Heritage of Meghalaya,* Directorate of Arts and Culture, Govt. of Meghalaya, Shillong, 1998, 32-33.

Arabinda Basu, "Garo", *People of India: Meghalaya,* Vol. XXXII, n.d., 90.

Alpana Kateja, "Role of Females Literacy in Maternal and Infant Mortality Decline", *Social Change,* Vol 37, No. 2, June 2007, 29-39.

B. Jatanta Bhusan, "The Changing Khasis: An Historical Account", *The Tribes of North East India,* (Ed) 332-341.

B.Pakem," Maintenance of Ethnic Identity and Administrative Framework: The Jaintia Sequence", *Nationality, Ethnicity and Cultural Identity in North East India,* (ed.) Omsons Publications, New Delhi, 1990, 292.

B.Pakem, "The Socio-Political System of the Jaintia Tribe of Assam: An Analysis of Continuity and Change", *in Tribal Situation in India,* edited by K.Suresh Singh, Simla, 1972, 353-357.

B.Pakem, "The Jaintia Concept of the Supreme Being", *J.G.C.U.*, 1976-1977, 5-7.

B.Pakem, "The Changing Power Structure of the Political Institution of Jaintia Chieftainship", *The Journal of the North East India Council for Social Science Research*, Vol. 1, No. 1, 1977, 1.

B. Margarete Challam., "Introduction", *The Dynamic of Family System in a Matriliny of Meghalaya*, (Shillong: Directorate of Printing and Stationary 1999), 1-33.

Burke, Marie Louise, "Swami Vivekananda's Message of Vedanta", *Bulletin of the Ramakrishna Mission Institute of Culture*, Vol. XXV, No. 6, June 1974, 137-146.

CFR Mawrie & H. Onderson, "God and Man", Khasi Heritage, (Ed). U Hipshon Roy, Shillong 1979, 10-55.

David Chander, "A Dialogue on Politics", *Vedanta*, No. 325, Sept.-October 2005, 238.

Dr. Asit Sarkar, "National Integration in the Light of Swami Vivekananda's Ideas", *Vivek Jivan*, Vol XXXIV, No. 7, January 2003, 21.

Dr. C.Wolflang, "Property Rights and Entrepreneurship in a Matriliny", *The Dynamics of Family System in a Matriliny of Meghalaya*, ed. by Margarret B. Challam, Directorate of Printing and Stationary, Shillong, 1999, 16.

Dr. Dominic Jala, "The Khasi-Christian Concepts of Death and after Life", *Impact of Christianity on North East India*, ed. by J. Puthenpurakal, Vendrame Institute Publications, Shillong, 1996, 176-185.

Dr. Jayanta Bhusan Bhattacharjee, "The Messenger of Khasi Heritage", *Khasi Heritage*, Revised and Enlarged Edition, Ri Khasi Press, Shillong, 1996, 1.

D.R. Syiemlieh, "Colonialism and Syiemship Succession: A Study of Cherra State (1901-1902)", *Proceedings of the North East India History Association*, ed. by Jayanta Bhushan Bhattacharjee, Shillong, 1983,147-157.

David Roy, "Khasi Religion", *in Seng Kut Snem 1990*, Shillong, 1990, 36.

David Roy, "Principles of Khasi Culture", *Folklore*, Vol. XLVII, December 1936 collection, 3.

Dr. Helen Giri, "The Dynamics of Being U KPA (Father) and U KNI (Maternal Uncle) in Khasi Society", *The Dynamics of Family System in a Matriliny of Meghalaya*, ed. by Margret B Challam, Directorate of Art and Culture, Tribal Research Institute, Shillong, 1999, 52.

Dr. Helen Giri, "Social Institutions among the Khasis with special reference to Kinship, Marriage, Family Life and Divorce", *Tribal Institutions of India*, ed. by S.K. Chattopadhyaya, Spectrum Publications, Guwahati, 1985, 166.

Faisal Al-Matalka, "Juvenile Delinquency in Jordan", *Dimensions of Human Society and Culture*, ed., New Delhi: Gyan Publishing House, 1996.

Fr. G. Costa, "The Garo Code of Law", *Anthropos, Vol. 49*, 1954, 1056-1057.

F.Max Muller, "Sri Ramakrishna", *World Thinkers on Ramakrishna-Vivekananda*, ed. By Swami Lokeswara-nanda, Ramakrishna Mission Institute of Culture, Calcutta, 1983, 1-15; see also Swami Tapasyananda, *Sri Ramakrishna: Life and Teachings*, Sri Ramakrishna Math, Mylapore, n.d., 136; see also Swami Paramananda, *Concentration and Meditation*, Sri Ramakrishna Math, Mylapore, 2002, 17.

Gankhu Sumnyan, "Upliftment of Tribal Women", *Narottam*, Ramakrishna Mission, Narottam, 2004, 10.

Ganguly, Tapas "Arise, Awake! The Call has been given out for 100 years now", *The Week*, Ramakrishna Mission, Calcutta, 5.

Gemini Paul, "The Place of Khadduh-the youngest daughter in Khasi and Synteng Society", in *Vanyajati, Vol. IV*, 2001, 151.

George M. Willium, "The Ramakrishna Movement: A Study in Religious Change", *Religion in Modern India*, (Ed.) by Robert D. Baired, Third Revised Edition, Manohar Publications, New Delhi, 1998, 76-77.

Gurudas Das, "Social Change and Traditional Tribal Political Systems in Meghalaya", *Power To People in Meghalaya*, ed. by M.N. Karna, LS Gassah & CJ Thomas, Regency Publications, New Delhi, 1998, 32-49.

G.W. Kharkongor, "Life, Religion and Culture of the People of Meghalaya," *Heritage of Meghalaya*, Directorate of Arts and Culture, Shillong, n.d., 14-20.

Hipson Roy, "My Faith", *Khasi Heritage*, Ri Khasi Press, Shillong, 1979, 119.

H.O., Mawrie "A Short View of the Khasi Religion", *Where Lies the Soul of our Race*, Edited by Hipshon, Shillong, 1982, 66-67.

H.O. Mawrie, "God and Man", *Khasi Heritage*, Ri Khasi Press, Shillong, 1979, 87.

Hugh R. Page Jr., "Khasi", *Encyclopedia of World Culture: South Asia, Vol. III*, ed. by Paul Kockings, G.K. Hall & Co. Boston, 1992, 122-124.

I.M. Syiem, "Khasi Matriliny in Transition", *The Dynamics of Family System in a Matriliny of Maghalaya*, ed. by Margaret B. Challam, 1999, Tribal research Institute, Shillong, 31.

J.B. Bhattacharjee, "Changing Khasis-A Historical Account", in S. Karotemprel, *The Tribes of North East India*, Shillong, Vendrame Institute, 1990, 332.

Jayanta Chandra," Towards Fulfillment of a Dream", *Souvenir*, Ramakrishna Mission, Cherapunji, 1996, 50-51.

Jayanta Bhusan Bhattacharjee, "The Messenger of Khasi Heritage", *Khasi Heritage*, Revised and Enlarged Edition, Ri Khasi Press, Shillong, 1996, 1.

J.N. Chowdhuri, "The Khasi: Conjectures about their Origin", *The Tribes of North-East India*, ed. by Sebastian Karotemprel, 68-70.

John B. Chethimattam, "Vedanta as a Method for Inter-Religious Theology", *Vedanta: Concepts and Application*, The Ramakrishna Mission Institute of Culture, Calcutta, 2000, 200.

Jonathan H.Thumra, "The Primal Religious Tradition", *Religious Traditions of India*, (ed), I.S.P.C.K., Delhi, 2001, 65.

Joseph Dalton Hooker," Notes on Khasi Hills and People", *Journal of the Asiatic Society of Bengal*, Vol. XIII, 1844, 485.

Joseph Puthenpurakal, "Christianity and Mass Movement among the Khasis: A Catholic Perspective", *Christianity in India*, ISPCK, New Delhi, 1998, 198.

The Journal of the North East India Council for Social Science Research, Vol II, No. I, April 1978, Shillong, 5.

Juanita War, "Family Structures, Customary Laws and Christianity: The Khasi Context", *Impact of Christianity on North East*, ed. by J. Puthenpurakal, SDB, Vendrame Institute Publications, Shillong, 1996, 229.

Juantia War, "The Khasi Concept of Family: Changes in Structure and Function", *Matriliny in Meghalaya: Tradition and Change*, ed. by Pariyaram M. Chacko, Regency Publications, New Delhi, 1998, 18.

Juantia War, "Panchayati Raj and Traditional Khasi Institutions: A Comparison", *Power to People in Meghalaya*, ed, by M.N. Karna, L.S. Gasah & C.J. Thomas, Regency Publications, New Delhi, 1998, 74.

Julius L.R.Karak, "Traditional Institutions of the People of Meghalaya", *Heritage of Meghalaya*, Directorate of Art and Culture, Govt. of Meghalaya, Shillong, n.d., 9.

Krishan Kumar Gaur, "Traditional Management System of Forests in Meghalaya: Some Reflections", *Environment Forest and Tribes: Anthropological Concomitance*, New Delhi: Himanshu Publications, 2000, 157.

Ksaniang, Bhakti, "Contributions of the Ramakrishna-Vivekananda Movement to Khasi Society", *Golden Jubilee Souvenir*, Ramakrishna Mission Higher Secondary School, Cherrapunji, 2001, 17.

Kapila Chatterji, "Christianity in Meghalaya- Trends and Reactions", *Vivekananda Kendra Patrika*, Vol. 8, No. 2, August, 1979, 217.

Kapila Chatterji, "Ramakrishna Mission in the South Khasi Hills", *Golden Jubilee Souvenir*, Ramakrishna Mission, Shella, 1982, 10.

Kedarnath Labh., "Swami Vivekananda's Visit to the West: The Impact on the Indian Mind", *Souvenir*, Ramakrishna Mission Ashrama, Calcutta, 1997, 38.

Kees W. Bolle, "Myth", in *Encyclopedia of Religion, Vol. 9*, ed. by Mircea Eliade, Macmillan Publishing Company, New York, 1987, 261.

Kynpham Singh, "The Khasis-their Houses and Housewarming Customs", *Khasi Heritage*, Ri Khasi Press, Shillong, 1996, 173.

Kynpham Singh, "Khasi and Jaintia Religion", in Roy Hipshon (ed.), *Khasi heritage*, Ri Khasi Press, Shillong, 1979, 100.

Kynpham Singh, "Khasi Religion and Khasi Society", *Religion and Society of North East India*, ed. by Sujata Miri, Vikas Publishing House, Pvt. Ltd., New Delhi, 1980, 42-55.

Kynpham Singh, "The Monoliths of the Khasi-Jaintia Hills", *Khasi Heritage*, U Hipshon Roy, Shillong, 1996, 167.

Leut. H. Yule, "Notes on the Khasi Hills and People ", *Journal of the Asiatic Society of Bengal, Vol. XII, Part II*, July-December 1894, Nos., 151-156, New Series, Bishop's College Press, Calcutta, 1894, 612.

L.S. Gassah, "Jaintia", *People of India: Meghalaya, Vol XXXII*, Seagull Books, Culcutta, 1994, 69-73.

L.S.Gassah, "The War Jaintias", *Heritage of Meghalaya, Vol. II*, Departmental Journal 1998-1999, Directorate of Arts & Culture, Shillong, n.d., 9-16.

Maham, Singh, "Nongkrem Dance" in Roy, U Hipshon, Edited, *Khasi Heritage*, Shillong, 1979, 148.

Minimon Laloo, "Meghalaya.... The Matrilineal Society ", *Heritage of Meghalaya*, Directorate of Art & Culture, Shillong, 1998, 21.

M.P.R, Lyngdoh, "Inheritance, Property Rights and Entrepreneurship in the Khasi Society", *The Dynamics of Family System in a Matriliny of Meghalaya*, Directorate of Printing & Stationary, Meghalaya, Shillong, 1999, 19-24.

M.S.Sangma, "The Concept of Pantheon", *Heritage of Meghalaya, Vol. V*, Directorate of Arts & Culture, Shillong, 2002-2003, 1.

Niraj Hatekar, "Malnutrition, Policy & Action", *Economic and Political Weekly, Vol. XXXIX, No. 44*, October 30-November 5, 2004, 4890-4891.

N.N. Acharya, "A Cursory Glance on the History of the Garo Hills from the Original Historical Records", *Garo Hills Land and the People*, ed. by L.S.Gassah, Gauhati/New Delhi: Omsons Publications, 1984, 114-115.

O.L. Snaitang, "Christianity and Matrilineal Women of Meghalaya", *N.C.C. Review, Vol. CXVIII, No. 6*, June-July 1998, 370.

P.C. Choudhury, *History of the Civilization of the People of Assam to the 12th Century AD,* Ist Edition, 1959, 62-65.

Patricia Mukhim, "Crisis of Authority in the Matrilineal Society", *The Dynamics of Family System in A Matriliny Of Meghalaya,* (ed) by Margaret B. Challam, Shillong, 1999, 35-38.

Paresh Paria, "A Forgotten Chapter ", *Narottam,* Sri Ramakrishna Mission School, Narottam Nagar, 2003, 14-15.

Patricia Mukhim," Swami Vivekananda's Concept Of Education", *Diamond Jubilee (1937-1997) Souvenir,* Ramakrishna Mission, Shillong, 1997, 27-28.

P.S.Nianglang," Evolution Of Riangsih Sirdarship", *Heritage Of Meghalaya,* Directorate of Art and Culture, Shillong, n.d., 15.

Paul Panachikkal, "Impact of Christianity on the Garos", *Impact of Christianity on North East India,* ed. by J. Puthenpurakal, Vendrame Institute Publications, Shillong,, 252-254.

Prof. S.C. Dube, "The Tribal Situation in India", *Annual Magazine of Ramakrishna Mission,* Narainpur, 1989, 151-155.

Pranab Kumar Das Gupta, "Land Tenure and Seng Among the War Khasis", *The Tribes of North East India,* ed. Shillong: Centres for Indigenous Cultures, 1998.

P.R.Kyndiah, "A Peep Into Khasi and Jaintia Music," in *Khasi Heritage,* Shillong, 1979, 132

P.S.Nianglang, "Evolution of Riangsih Sirdarship", *Heritage of Meghalaya,* Directorate of Art and Culture, Govt. of Meghalaya, Shillong, n.d., 15.

Radhon Singh Berry, *Ka Jingsneng Tymmen (The Teachings of Elders),* n.p., n.d., viii-ix.

Ramesh Chandra Majumdar, "Ideal and Position of Indian Women in Domestic Life," *Great Women of India,* Advaita Ashrama, Calcutta, 1953, 16.

Ranajit Nag, "One Man's Dream Come True", *Golden Jubilee Souvenir (1928-1978),* Ramakrishna Mission Ashrama, Sobharpunji, 1979, 9.

R.K. Dasgupta., "Sri Ramakrishna's Religion (III)", *Bulletin of Ramakrishna Mission and Institute of Culture,* Vol XLIX, No. 1, January 1998, 21.

R.T. Rymbai , "Some Aspect of the Religion of the Khasi Pnars", *Religion and Society of North-East India*, ed. by Sujata Miri, Vikas Publications, New Delhi, 1980, 51-52.

R.T.Rymbai, "The Khasi Concept of God", *Golden Jubilee Commemoration Souvenir (1937-1987)*, Ramakrishna Mission, Shillong, 47.

R.T.Rymbai," Some Aspects of Khasi Culture and Religion", *Ki Symboh Na Ka Seng Kut Snem*, Shillong, 1988, 32.

R.T.Rymbai, "U Hynniewtrep Bad U Blei," in Sawian S.S., (Ed.), *Seng Kut Snem*, 1989, Shillong, 1998, 37.

Sabastian Karotemprel, "The Impact of Christianity on the Tribes of North East India", *Impact of Christianity on North East India*, ed. by J. Puthenpurakal, Vendrame Institute Publications, Shillong, 1996, 16-17.

Santana Mukherjee, "Swami Vivekananda's Sociological Ideas of Integration", *Swami Vivekananda: His Global Vision*, ed. by Santi Nath Chattopadhayaya, Punthi-Pustak, Calcutta, 2001, 329 – 340

Shashadhar Bhattacharjee, "Reminiscences of Sri Ramakrishna Mission, Shillong", *Diamond Jubilee Souvenir (1937-1991)*, Ramakrishna Mission, Shillong, 1997, 15-17.

Sibani Roy & S.H.M. Rizvi, "Tribal Festivals of Meghalaya", *Festivals and Ceremonies in Meghalaya*, ed. by K.R.Marak & Wankhar, Historical and Antiquarian Studies, Department of Arts and Culture, Shillong, 1994, 8.

Shibshankar Chakraborty, "Role of Youth in Rural Construction", *Report On Ramakrishna Math & Ramakrishna Mission Youth Convention 1980*, Belur Math, Howrah, 1985, 84.

Silbi Passah, "Sawdong Ka Iyngwiar Dpel" *Heritage of meghalaya*, Directorate of Art and Culture, Shillong, n.d., 26.

Sngi Lyngdoh, "The Khasi Matriliny: Its Past and Its Future", *Matriliny in Meghalaya: Tradition and Change*, ed. by Pariyaram M. Chacko, Regency Publications, New Delhi, 1998, 39-40.

Sri Harsha Dutta, "Swami Vivekananda's Concept of Oneness", *Souvenir- 1997*, Ramakrishna Mission Ashrama, Patna, 1998, 7.

Sujata Miri, "Holism in the Khasi Religion", *The Tribes of North East India*, ed. Centre for Indigenous Cultures, Shillong, 1998, 359.

Sumen Sen, "Seng Khasi and Idealization of Khasi Religion", *Proceedings of North East India History Association*, Seventh Session, Pasighat, 1986, 239.

Sumit Mukherjee, "Geomedical Aspects of Acute Respiratory Infection Diseases in Meghalaya" *in Tribal Studies in North East India*, ed. by Sarthak Sengupta, Mittal Publications, New Delhi, 2002, 161-175.

S.Rynjah, "The Khasi Family: Dynamic Role of Father and Maternal Uncle", *The Dynamics of Family System in a Matriliny of Meghalaya*, Tribal Research Institute, Shillong, 1999, 46-51.

S.Rynjah, The Khasi Family: Dynamic Role of Father and Maternal Uncle", *The Dynamics of Family System in a Matriliny of Meghalaya*, Tribal Research Institute, Shillong, 1999, 46-51.

Swami Aparananda, "A Few Years at Cherrapunji", *Golden Jubilee Souvenir*, Ramakrishna Mission Ashrama, Cherrapunji, 1982, 22.

Swami Bhaktirupananda, "Sentinels of the Frontier", *Narottam*, Ramakrishna Mission School, Narottam Nagar, 1997, 38-41.

Swami Baneshananda, "Ramakrishna Mission Shillong: A Glimpse of Its Growth", *Golden Jubilee (1937-1987)*, Shillong: Ramakrishna Mission, 1987, 22.

Swami Bhajanananda, "Rural Development Work in the Perspective of Swami Vivekananda's Social Philosophy", *Souvenir 2002*, Ramakrishna Mission High School, Asansol, 2002, 14.

Swami Bhajanananda, "Global Ethics and Vivekananda", *Swami Vivekananda: His Global Vision*, ed. by Santi Nath Chattopadhyaya, Punthi Pustak, Calcutta, 2001, 167- 204.

Swami Baneshananda, "Ramakrishna Mission Shillong: A Glimpse of Its Growth," *Golden Jubilee Souvenir*, Shillong, 2000, 23.

Swami Bhaskarananda, "My Reminiscences of Shillong Ashrama", in *Diamond Jubilee Souvenir (1937-1997)*, Ramakrishna Mission, Shillong, 1997, 15-18.

Swami Bhoomananda, "A Challenge To Householders", *The Vision*, Vol. 73, No. 2, November 2005, 49.

Swami Brahmeshananda, "Holy Mother and Women Empowerment", *Bulletin of the Ramakrishna Mission Institute of Culture*, Vol. LVI No. 1, January 2005, 5-12.

Swami Chetanananda, "To Love All is the Basis of the Ramakrishna Mission", *Bulletin of Ramakrishna Mission Institute of Culture*, Vol. XLIX, No. 1, January 1998, 9.

Swami Gahanananda, "Message from Revered Gahananandaji Maharaj", *Diamond Jubilee Souvenir (1937-1997)*, Ramakrishna Mission, Shillong, n.p., 13.

Swami Lokeshwarananda, "Benoy Sarkar and the Ramakrishna-Vivekananda Movement", *Bulletin of the Ramakrishna Mission Institute of Culture*, Vol. LI, No. 2, February 2000, 64.

Swami Lokeswarananda, "The Ramakrishna Movement", *Studies on Sri Ramakrishna*, The Ramakrishna Mission Institute of Culture, Calcutta, 1988,190-191.

Swami Lokeswarananda, "Swami Prabhananda: His Pioneering Work in the Khasi Hills", *Golden Jubilee Souvenir*, Ramakrishna Mission Ashrama, Charrapunji, 15 September, 1982, 10-19.

Swami Prabhananda, "A Fresh Look At Swami Vivekananda", *Souvenir*, 27 May, 1996, Ramakrishna Mission, Education Complex Vivekanagar, 34-35.

Swami Prabhananda, "Vivekananda's Approach to the Uplift of the Masses", *Report on Ramakrishna Math and Ramakrishna Mission Youth Convention 1985*, Belur Math, Howrah, n.d., 53.

Swami Purnatmananda, "Swami Vivekananda's Gift to the West", *Swami Vivekananda: His Global Vision*, ed. by Santi Nath Chattopadhyay, Punthi Pustak, Calcutta, 2001, 141-145.

Swami Ranganathananda, "Message from Revered Ranganathananda Maharaj, Vice-President, Ramakrishna Math and Ramakrishna Mission, " *Diamond Jubilee Souvenir*, 1997, cover page.

Swami Ranganathananda, "Swami Vivekananda and Today's Youth", *Report on Ramakrishna Math and Ramakrishna Mission Youth Convention 1985*, Belur Math, Howrah, n.d., 206.

Swami Ranganathananda, *The Essence of Indian Culture*, Advaita Ashrama, Calcutta, 1996, 134.

Swami Shantarupananda, "Fifty Years of the Ramakrishna Mission Ashrama at Cherrapunji- A Flesh Back (1931-1981)", *Golden Jubilee Souvenir*, Ramakrishna Mission, Sohbar, 1979, 5-9.

Swami Someswarananda, "The Ramakrishna Math and Ramakrishna Mission among Common Men", *Souvenir*, 1980, 109-111.

Swami Sumedhananda, "Preface", *Souvenir*, Ramakrishna Mission Educational Complex, Vivekanagar, May 1996, 1-2.

Sumit Mukherjee, "Geomedical Aspects of Acute Respiratory Infection Diseases in Meghalaya" *Tribal Studies in North East India*, ed. by Sarthak Sengupta, New Delhi: Mittal Publications, 2002, 161-175.

Tapas Ganguly, "Arise, Awake! The Call has been given out for 100 years now." *The Week*, Ramakrishna Mission Ashrama, Calcutta, 5.

T.T. Awojemi, T.O.Amao & O.O.Fatogum, "Household Expenditure Pattern on Food in Ibadan, OYO State Nigeria", *Journal of Rural Development, Vol 26, No. 3*, July-September 2007, 336-338.

U Hipshon Roy, "My Faith" *Khasi Heritage*, ed. by U Hipshon Roy, Shillong :Ri Khasi Press, 1979, 119.

U.R. Ehrengfels, "Khasi Kinship Terminology in Four Dialects "*Anthropos, Vol. 48,* 1953, 396-412.

V.Pakyntein, " The Khasi Clan: Changing Religion and its Effect", *Kinship and Family in North East India, ed.* by J.S. Bhandari, Cosmo Publications, New Delhi, 1996, 36.

Viswanath, Chatterji, "Vivekananda's Vedanta As Universal Religion", *Swami Vivekananda: His Global Vision*, Punthi-Pustak, Calcutta, 2001, 323-328.

W.R.Laitflang, "Glimpses of the Festivals and Music of the Khasis", *Festivals and Ceremonies in Meghalaya*, ed. by K.R. Mark & R. Wankhar, Department of Art and Culture, Shillong, n.d., 1.

www.ingramcontent.com/pod-product-compliance
Lightning Source LLC
Chambersburg PA
CBHW081838230426
43669CB00018B/2750